Managing Big Data Integration in the Public Sector

Anil Aggarwal
University of Baltimore, USA

A volume in the Advances in Public Policy and
Administration (APPA) Book Series

Information Science
REFERENCE
An Imprint of IGI Global

Published in the United States of America by
Information Science Reference (an imprint of IGI Global)
701 E. Chocolate Avenue
Hershey PA, USA 17033
Tel: 717-533-8845
Fax: 717-533-8661
E-mail: cust@igi-global.com
Web site: http://www.igi-global.com

Library of Congress Cataloging-in-Publication Data

Names: Aggarwal, Anil, 1949- editor of compilation.
Title: Managing big data integration in the public sector / Anil Aggarwal,
    editor.
Description: Hershey, PA : Information Science Reference, [2016] | Includes
    bibliographical references and index.
Identifiers: LCCN 2015037580| ISBN 9781466696495 (hardcover) | ISBN
    9781466696501 (ebook)
Subjects: LCSH: Public administration--United States--Data processing. | Big
    data--United States.
Classification: LCC JK468.A8 M28 2016 | DDC 352.3/8028557--dc23 LC record available at http://lccn.loc.
gov/2015037580

This book is published in the IGI Global book series Advances in Public Policy and Administration (APPA) (ISSN: Pending; eISSN: Pending)

British Cataloguing in Publication Data
A Cataloguing in Publication record for this book is available from the British Library.

All work contributed to this book is new, previously-unpublished material. The views expressed in this book are those of the authors, but not necessarily of the publisher.

For electronic access to this publication, please contact: eresources@igi-global.com.

Advances in Public Policy and Administration (APPA) Book Series

ISSN: Pending
EISSN: Pending

MISSION

Proper management of the public sphere is necessary in order to maintain order in modern society. Research developments in the field of public policy and administration can assist in uncovering the latest tools, practices, and methodologies for governing societies around the world.

The **Advances in Public Policy and Administration (APPA) Book Series** aims to publish scholarly publications focused on topics pertaining to the governance of the public domain. APPA's focus on timely topics relating to government, public funding, politics, public safety, policy, and law enforcement is particularly relevant to academicians, government officials, and upper-level students seeking the most up-to-date research in their field.

COVERAGE

- Government
- Law Enforcement
- Political Economy
- Politics
- Public Administration
- Public Funding
- Public Policy
- Resource Allocation
- Urban Planning

IGI Global is currently accepting manuscripts for publication within this series. To submit a proposal for a volume in this series, please contact our Acquisition Editors at Acquisitions@igi-global.com or visit: http://www.igi-global.com/publish/.

The Advances in Public Policy and Administration (APPA) Book Series (ISSN Pending) is published by IGI Global, 701 E. Chocolate Avenue, Hershey, PA 17033-1240, USA, www.igi-global.com. This series is composed of titles available for purchase individually; each title is edited to be contextually exclusive from any other title within the series. For pricing and ordering information please visit http://www.igi-global.com/book-series/advances-public-policy-administration/97862. Postmaster: Send all address changes to above address. Copyright © 2016 IGI Global. All rights, including translation in other languages reserved by the publisher. No part of this series may be reproduced or used in any form or by any means – graphics, electronic, or mechanical, including photocopying, recording, taping, or information and retrieval systems – without written permission from the publisher, except for non commercial, educational use, including classroom teaching purposes. The views expressed in this series are those of the authors, but not necessarily of IGI Global.

Titles in this Series

For a list of additional titles in this series, please visit: www.igi-global.com

Management and Participation in the Public Sphere
Mika Markus Merviö (Kibi International University, Japan)
Information Science Reference • copyright 2015 • 400pp • H/C (ISBN: 9781466685536) • US $200.00 (our price)

Teaching Research Methods in Public Administration
Richard W. Schwester (City University of New York, USA)
Information Science Reference • copyright 2015 • 313pp • H/C (ISBN: 9781466681163) • US $185.00 (our price)

Emergency Management and Disaster Response Utilizing Public-Private Partnerships
Marvine Paula Hamner (LeaTech, LLC, USA) S. Shane Stovall (True North Emergency Management, USA) Doaa
M. Taha (GMI, Ltd, USA) and Salah C. Brahimi (GMI, Ltd, USA)
Information Science Reference • copyright 2015 • 345pp • H/C (ISBN: 9781466681590) • US $200.00 (our price)

ICT Adoption and Application in the Malaysian Public Sector
Abdul Raufu Ambali (Universiti Teknologi MARA, Malaysia & Kwara State University Malete, Nigeria) and
Ahmad Naqiyuddin Bakar (Universiti Teknologi MARA, Malaysia)
Information Science Reference • copyright 2015 • 316pp • H/C (ISBN: 9781466665798) • US $195.00 (our price)

Human Rights and the Impact of ICT in the Public Sphere Participation, Democracy, and Political Autonomy
Christina M. Akrivopoulou (Hellenic Open University, Greece) and N. Garipidis (Aristotle University of Thessaloniki, Greece)
Information Science Reference • copyright 2014 • 371pp • H/C (ISBN: 9781466662483) • US $185.00 (our price)

Chaos and Complexity Theory in World Politics
Şefika Şule Erçetin (Hacettepe University, Turkey) and Santo Banerjee (University Putra Malaysia, Malaysia)
Information Science Reference • copyright 2014 • 374pp • H/C (ISBN: 9781466660700) • US $210.00 (our price)

Transforming Politics and Policy in the Digital Age
Jonathan Bishop (Centre for Research into Online Communities and E-Learning Systems, Belgium)
Information Science Reference • copyright 2014 • 312pp • H/C (ISBN: 9781466660380) • US $200.00 (our price)

www.igi-global.com

701 E. Chocolate Ave., Hershey, PA 17033
Order online at www.igi-global.com or call 717-533-8845 x100
To place a standing order for titles released in this series, contact: cust@igi-global.com
Mon-Fri 8:00 am - 5:00 pm (est) or fax 24 hours a day 717-533-8661

This book is dedicated to my grandchildren, Arnab and Sanaaya, my mother, my uncles, and Nick, without whose sacrifice, love, and guidance this book would never have been completed.

Table of Contents

Section 5
Big Data: Emerging Issues

Detailed Table of Contents

Section 1
Big Data: Issues and Models

Chapter 1

    Anne L. Washington, George Mason University, USA

Interoperability sets standards for consistency when integrating information from multiple sources. Trends in e-government have encouraged the production of digital information yet it is not clear if the data produced are interoperable. The objective of the project was to evaluate interoperability by building a retrieval tool that could track United States public policy from the legislative to the executive branch using only machine-readable government information. A case study of policy created during the 2008 financial crisis serves as an illustration to investigate the organizational, technical, syntactic, and operational interoperability of digital sources. The methods of citing law varied widely enough between legislation and regulation to impede consistent automated tracking. The flow of federal policy authorization exemplifies remaining socio-technical challenges in achieving the interoperability of machine-readable government data.

Chapter 2

    Anil Aggarwal, University of Baltimore, USA

Data has always played a critical part in business decision making. The digital economy is generating Tsunami of data which must be analyzed and used by both the public and private sector. Survival and citizen satisfaction may depend on how governments use big data to develop citizen-centric services. Big data analysis can lead to better transparency, less corruption and citizen satisfaction. Big data is an emerging area where models and applications are still emerging. Currently there are few, if any, models that provide guidance in developing applications. This chapter proposes a hybrid approach which can be used as a starting point for future development.

Pertinence of big data is necessary especially in the field of corporate governance where large amount of data is collected, stored, retrieved and manages. The major challenge arises for the government organizations therefore are how to use the breadth and depth of the large amount of available data in an appropriate manner. The purpose of the study was to find out the relevance of Big Data in corporate governance and investigates about the role and reasons behind adopting this technique in various government schemes. The data was collected from the 393 respondents of IT companies through a pre-tested and a structured questionnaire. Thematic analysis, descriptive statistics and factor analysis were used to explain the factors needed to identify transparency and enhanced efficiency & accountability by big data adoption. It was found there were an explosion of big data in the corporate governance and various activities of the government which could be highly relevant.

Cloud computing provides access to the high volume of data to individuals and enterprises. Immense data analytics and mobile technologies contain useful knowledge. Data storage, security, and privacy, on the other hand, are the main issues for any organization or enterprises in the business world. Big data processing is within reach due to easy access to cloud architectures and open-source software. Now, interoperability of big data and cloud has become a necessity in this era of data-intensive world.

Section 2
Big Data: Management Issues

The industry experts' claim that big data will be the next frontier for innovation, competition, and productivity, has turned from an unfounded omen to an obvious reality. In the looming data-driven business era, data will pervade organizations and will thus affect their nature and functioning. The central role played by data is about to impact the main mechanism that fuels the life of organizations, decision making, which will then gradually redefine the job and function of managers. In May 2014, a French top-ten business school launched a 2-week big data initiative aiming at immersing future managers into a big data simulation and also sensitizing them to the overall cultural shift that big data is about to engender within organizations. Using semi-real data about a French newspaper, 100 graduating students were engaged into a big data serious game which main objective was to use data visualization techniques on a large dataset hosted on a Hadoop cluster in order to derive business recommendations to higher management. By conducting observations, taking field notes, and interviewing participants, important insights could be derived for educational institutions that are contemplating the importance of including big data into their curricula but also for organizations that strive to engrain a big data mindset within their managers.

Chapter 6

Alireza Bolhari, Islamic Azad University, Science and Research Branch, Iran

Competency matters. Social media, customer transactions, mobile sensors, and feedback contents are all piled up with data. This might be unstructured and complex data in voluminous quantity, often called Big Data. However, if this Big Data is managed, it might bring competency for organizations. This chapter introduces the must-know concepts and materials for organizational managers who face Big Data. Through the chapter, Big Data is defined and its emergence over the time is reviewed. The four Vs model in Big Data literature and its link to a banking system is analyzed. The chapter concludes by making a managerial awareness concerning ethical issues in Big Data. This is of high priority in public sectors as data relies for every individual in the society.

Chapter 7

Jurgen Janssens, TETRADE Consulting, Belgium

To make the deeply rooted layers of catalyzing technology and optimized modelling gain their true value for education, healthcare or other public services, it is necessary to prepare well the Big Data environment in which the Big Data will be developed, and integrate elements of it into the project approach. It is by integrating and managing these non-technical aspects of project reality that analytics will be accepted. This will enable data power to infuse the organizational processes and offer ultimately real added value. This chapter will shed light on complementary actions required on different levels. It will be analyzed how this layered effort starts by a good understanding of the different elements that contribute to the definition of an organization's Big Data ecosystem. It will be explained how this interacts with the management of expectations, needs, goals and change. Lastly, a closer look will be given at the importance of portfolio based big picture thinking.

Chapter 8

George Avirappattu, Kean University, USA

Big data is characterized in many circles in terms of the three V's – volume, velocity and variety. Although most of us can sense palpable opportunities presented by big data there are overwhelming challenges, at many levels, turning such data into actionable information or building entities that efficiently work together based on it. This chapter discusses ways to potentially reduce the volume and velocity aspects of certain kinds of data (with sparsity and structure), while acquiring itself. Such reduction can alleviate the challenges to some extent at all levels, especially during the storage, retrieval, communication, and analysis phases. In this chapter we will conduct a non-technical survey, bringing together ideas from some recent and current developments. We focus primarily on Compressive Sensing and sparse Fast Fourier Transform or Sparse Fourier Transform. Almost all natural signals or data streams are known to have some level of sparsity and structure that are key for these efficiencies to take place.

Section 3
Big Data: Health Care Issues and Applications

Chapter 9

Md Rakibul Hoque, University of Dhaka, Bangladesh
Yukun Bao, Huazhong University of Science and Technology, China

This chapter investigates the application, opportunities, challenges and techniques of Big Data in healthcare. The healthcare industry is one of the most important, largest, and fastest growing industries in the world. It has historically generated large amounts of data, "Big Data", related to patient healthcare and well-being. Big Data can transform the healthcare industry by improving operational efficiencies, improve the quality of clinical trials, and optimize healthcare spending from patients to hospital systems. However, the health care sector lags far behind compared to other industries in leveraging their data assets to improve efficiencies and make more informed decisions. Big Data entails many new challenges regarding security, privacy, legal concerns, authenticity, complexity, accuracy, and consistency. While these challenges are complex, they are also addressable. The predominant 'Big Data' Management technologies such as MapReduce, Hadoop, STORM, and others with similar combinations or extensions should be used for effective data management in healthcare industry.

Chapter 10

Jyotsna Talreja Wassan, University of Delhi, India

The digitization of world in various areas including health care domain has brought up remarkable changes. Electronic Health Records (EHRs) have emerged for maintaining and analyzing health care real data online unlike traditional paper based system to accelerate clinical environment for providing better healthcare. These digitized health care records are form of Big Data, not because of the fact they are voluminous but also they are real time, dynamic, sporadic and heterogeneous in nature. It is desirable to extract relevant information from EHRs to facilitate various stakeholders of the clinical environment. The role, scope and impact of Big Data paradigm on health care is discussed in this chapter.

Chapter 11

Rajendra Akerkar, Western Norway Research Institute (Vestlandsforsking), Norway

Nowadays, making use of big data is becoming mainstream in different enterprises and industry sectors. The medical sector is no exception. Specifically, medical services, which generate and process enormous volumes of medical information and medical device data, have been quickening big data utilization. In this chapter, we present a concept of an intelligent integrated system for direct support of decision making of physicians. This is a work in progress and the focus is on decision support for pharmacogenomics, which is the study of the relationship between a specific person's genetic makeup and his or her response to drug treatment. Further, we discuss a research direction considering the current shortcomings of clinical decision support systems.

Section 4
Big Data: Other Application

Chapter 12

Yuko Murayama, Iwate Prefectural University, Japan
Dai Nishioka, Iwate Prefectural University, Japan
Nor Athiyah Binti Abdullah, Iwate Prefectural University, Japan

This chapter presents the issues on disaster communications. The Great East Japan Earthquake on March 11th, 2011 caused severe damage to the northern coast of the main island in Japan. We report our support activities in Iwate prefecture as well as our findings and experiences. We call disaster communications in this chapter. disaster communications. Following the requests from many organizations and groups of people, we started our support for the disaster area with a few of us in the department of Software and Information Science, Iwate Prefectural University ten days after the disaster. Through our support activities we came across an interesting issue concerning collaboration with people from heterogeneous backgrounds. Disagreements and distrust happened quite easily. We found that trust plays an important role in such communications. In our chapter, we introduce disaster communications as an area for research and practice as well as our trials on the recovery phase after the emergency response.

Chapter 13

A. G. Rekha, Indian Institute of Management Kozhikode, India

With the availability of large volumes of data and with the introduction of new tools and techniques for analysis, the security analytics landscape has changed drastically. To face the challenges posed by cyber-terrorism, espionage, cyber frauds etc. Government and law enforcing agencies need to enhance the security and intelligence analysis systems with big data technologies. Intelligence and security insight can be improved considerably by analyzing the under-leveraged data like the data from social media, emails, web logs etc. This Chapter provides an overview of the opportunities presented by Big Data to provide timely and reliable intelligence in properly addressing terrorism, crime and other threats to public security. This chapter also discusses the threats posed by Big Data to public safety and the challenges faced in implementing Big Data security solutions. Finally some of the existing initiatives by national governments using Big Data technologies to address major national challenges has been discussed.

Chapter 14

N. Nawin Sona, Government of India, India

This chapter aims to give an overview of the wide range of Big Data approaches and technologies today. The data features of Volume, Velocity, and Variety are examined against new database technologies. It explores the complexity of data types, methodologies of storage, access and computation, current and emerging trends of data analysis, and methods of extracting value from data. It aims to address the need for clarity regarding the future of RDBMS and the newer systems. And it highlights the methods in which Actionable Insights can be built into public sector domains, such as Machine Learning, Data Mining, Predictive Analytics and others.

Section 5
Big Data: Emerging Issues

Chapter 15

Amir Manzoor, Bahria University, Pakistan

Technological advancements have made it easier to collect and store data. We are generating and storing data on a nearly pervasive basis and across multiple environments including work and home. Big data, a general term for the massive amount of digital data being collected from all sorts of sources, is too large, raw, or unstructured for analysis through conventional relational database techniques. For public managers, big data represents an opportunity to infuse information and technology into the design and management of organizations, personnel, and resources. Although the business sector is leading big-data-application development, the public sector has begun to derive insight to help support decision making in real time from fast-growing in-motion data from multiple sources. This chapter explores the big-data applications associated with the public sector and provide suggestions for follower governments.

Chapter 16

Anil Aggarwal, University of Baltimore, USA

Data has always been the backbone of modern society. It is generated by individuals, businesses and governments. It is used in many citizen-centric applications, including weather forecasts, controlling diseases, monitoring undesirables etc. What is changing is the source of data. Advances in technology are allowing data to be generated from any devise at any place in any form. The challenge is to "understand", "manage" and make use of this data. It is well known that government generates unprecedented amount of data (ex: US census), the question remains: can this data be combined with technology generated data to make it useful for societal benefit. Governments and non-profits, however, work across borders making data access and integration challenging. Rules, customs and politics must be followed while sharing data across borders. Despite these challenges, big data application in public sector are beginning to emerge. This chapter discusses areas of government applications and also discusses challenges of developing such systems.

Foreword

The topic and issues associated with managing big data integration in the public sector are on the minds of numerous stakeholders. A variety of perspectives and needs exist based on the roles that individuals and organizations as well as governments embody in pursuit of dealing with this complex situation.

Big data opens the way for new ways of thinking but, without integration, can easily not have the envisioned impact. Far too often, data exists in silos without appreciation of the benefits of integration. Public sector agencies are particularly susceptible given their varied history and differences in use of big data. Integration, when done effectively, opens the door to sustainable solutions that here-to-fore have not been recognized. Unfortunately, relatively few examples exist that can provide meaningful insight.

The sections and associated papers bring a variety of issues to the fore that warrants recognition and serious consideration. The papers are well chosen to cover a wide gamut of perspectives. The projects and studies described in the papers help underscore issue importance and additionally suggest solution strategies. The reality is there is no "one size fits all" prescription but experiences can help assist in intelligent approaches. This book is a solid step in that direction.

The sections and associated papers go significantly beyond issue description and offer sound managerial advice in bringing technology and people together in a culturally sensitive fashion. This is especially important in arriving at robust and sustainable solutions through behavioral change. Sustained behavior change is difficult and warrants special attention to continuously react, adapt and avoid relapse. Management attention is paramount to success.

Healthcare provides special challenges as well as opportunities in the integrated application and management of big data as a salient example. Particularly sensitive issues related to privacy and security must be addressed while, at the same time, recognizing the benefits and potential of insight that can be gained by citizens as well as healthcare professionals and their respective organizations. Simply put, no country in the world can continue to pursue healthcare as it is currently being implemented given the dramatic change in population dynamics.

In conclusion, *Managing Big Data Integration in the Public Sector* is a particularly useful book with appeal to a wide range of stakeholders interested in the topic area. Although numerous challenges remain, this book provides a step forward that is insightful and useful as stakeholders struggle to achieve sustainable solutions. Emerging issues are introduced that encourage thinking beyond the current state that can lead to an even brighter future and genuine societal benefit.

Douglas R. Vogel
Harbin Institute of Technology, China

Preface

Big data is an emerging area which has only recently caught the attention of practitioners, academicians and researchers. Unprecedented amount of data is generated from social networking sites, cameras, "smart" devices, sensors etc. which to some extent is still untapped. With the proliferation of social networks, data is generated in non-traditional places like Twitter, Facebook, and Flickr to name a few. Government and businesses are aggressively monitoring and trying to make sense out of the data which is generated from these sites. Big data is the term used for such data maybe due to its volume, variety, velocity and/or veracity. Advances in technologies are making it feasible to mine and make sense of this data. Like any emerging technology concept, big data is not free from problems, controversies and challenges. Many universities are starting programs in big data, data analytics and business intelligence and training students for upcoming challenges. Like any emerging technology big data is going through its own phases. The first phase is focusing on "what" of big data and the next phase will focus on "how" of big data.

WHY THE BOOK?

This book identifies and provides opportunities related to the emerging field of big data and data analytics. As more and more data is generated there is urgency of being the "first" to make sense out of this data. The field is evolving very fast. There have been many 'isolated' application of big data both in public and private sectors and literature typically has focused on social networks and data mining in isolation but has not merged the areas to provide meaningful insights. This book proposes to go beyond and identify big data open platforms, big data technology and big data management, especially in non-profit applications. It will also address how big data can be combined with cloud platforms and how business analytics can be used to provide opportunities for decision makers. The book will identify strategies for public sectors like the government agencies, hospitals, cities, states etc. to be more responsive to stake-holders, namely the citizen, needs. In addition, this book will also address ad-hoc situations like disasters (missing planes, earthquakes, fires etc.) that create swift team that use big data to solve these problems.

The main objective of this book is to assist the reader in better understanding the early adopters and to address issues such as trends, opportunities, and problems facing public sector in effectively utilizing data to address citizen's concerns. The chapters of this book are a compilation of the experiences, knowledge, and research findings of early adopters of big data.

BOOK AUDIENCE

This book is intended for anyone interested in developing and diffusing big data issues in the public sector. The book provides a theoretical and conceptual background related to big data. Greatly beneficial are the author's descriptions of their experiences, presented with the 'what' of big data with extensions to the next phase "how" of big data. The book is also meant for academician and universities interested in developing, offering, and managing big data programs. This book is also meant for researchers, already conducting, or looking for new research topics in big data. In several chapters, recommendation for future research in specific area are presented.

BOOK STRUCTURE

As in any emerging idea must be defined, the issues must be addressed, and the theories must be presented and tested. I used the same concept in dicing the book in four sections. In the first section, section questions around "what" of big data are centered, where we are and what can be expected are discussed. In the second section management issues related to big data are addressed. In the third section health care and other ad-hoc applications are discussed and the final section discusses opportunities and challenges of big data applications in public sector.

- Big Data: Issues and Models
- Big Data: Management Issues
- Big Data: Health Care Issues and Applications
- Big Data: Other Issues and Applications
- Big Data: Emerging Issues

These sections are created for the reader's convenience only. The issues discussed are not isolated, and there are overlapping ideas and concepts across each of these sections.

The first section consists of four chapters and focuses on issues, models and techniques that can be used for big data systems. Washington evaluates the government interoperability by building a retrieval tool that could track United States public policy from the legislative to the executive branch using only machine-readable government information. She uses a case study of policy created during the 2008 financial crisis serves as an illustration to investigate the organizational, technical, syntactic, and operational interoperability of digital sources. She discusses socio-technical challenges in achieving the interoperability of machine-readable government data. Aggarwal proposes a novel hybrid approach to developing big data applications, as it combines both structure and unstructured data in its model. Aggarwal uses the ethical lens theory proposed by William May in developing the hybrid model, and also describes several current applications of big data. Jain and Sharma discuss the relevance of Big Data in corporate governance and investigate the role and reasons behind adopting various technique in various government schemes. They conduct an experiment by collecting data from 393 respondents of IT companies through a pre-tested and a structured questionnaire. Thematic analysis, descriptive statistics and factor analysis were used to explain the factors needed to identify transparency and enhanced efficiency & accountability by big data adoption. They found there were an explosion of big data in the corporate governance and various activities of the government which could be highly relevant for future studies. Ahmad Yusairi Bani Hashim argues data storage, security, and privacy, on the other hand, are the main issues for any organization or enterprises in the business world. He argues that big data processing is within reach due to easy access to cloud architectures and open-source software and further argues that interoperability of big data and cloud has become a necessity in this era of data-intensive world.

The second section consists of four papers and focuses on management issues related to big data. Carillo argues the central role played by data is about to impact the main mechanism that fuels the life of organizations, decision making, and will then gradually redefine the job and function of managers. He describes an experiment of a French top-ten business school that launched a 2-week big data initiative aiming at immersing future managers into a big data simulation and also sensitizing them to the overall cultural shift that big data is about to engender within organizations. He discusses the insights that could be derived for educational institutions that are contemplating the importance of including big data into their curricula but also for organizations that strive to engrain a big data mindset within their managers.

Bolhari discusses the must-know concepts and materials for organizational managers who face Big Data. He reviews the emergence of big data over time and uses a bank link to illustrate the concepts. He also discussed managerial awareness concerning ethical issues in big data as it relates to privacy of individuals. Janssen argues that it is necessary to prepare the big data environment well in which the big data will be developed, and integrate elements of it into the project approach. He argues that by integrating and managing these non-technical aspects of project reality that analytics will be accepted. His discussion shed lights on complementary actions required on different levels. He discusses how this layered effort starts by a good understanding of the different elements that contribute to the definition of an organization's big data ecosystem. He further explains how this interacts with the management of expectations, needs, goals and change. He gives a closer look to the importance of portfolio based big picture thinking. Avirappattu discusses ways to potentially reduce the volume and velocity aspects of certain kinds of data (with sparsity and structure), while acquiring itself. They conduct a non-technical survey, bringing together ideas from some recent and current developments and primarily focus on Compressive Sensing and sparse Fast Fourier Transform or Sparse Fourier Transform since almost all natural signals or data streams are known to have some level of sparsity and structure that are key for these efficiencies to take place.

The third section consists of three papers that focuses on health care issues and applications. Health care is leading in big data application due to emergence of deadly diseases and the efforts to contain them. Hoque and Bao argue that big data can transform the healthcare industry by improving operational efficiencies, by improving the quality of clinical trials, and by optimizing healthcare spending from patients to hospital systems. They also argue that the health care sector lags far behind compared to other industries in leveraging their data assets to improve efficiencies and make more informed decisions. They discuss challenges faced by big data but also argue that these challenges are addressable with 'Big Data' Management technologies such as MapReduce, Hadoop, STORM, and others with similar combinations or extensions. Wassan discusses Electronic Health Records (EHRs) and argues that digitized health care records are form of Big Data, not because of the fact they are voluminous but also they are real time, dynamic, sporadic and heterogeneous in nature. It is desirable to extract relevant information from EHRs to facilitate various stakeholders of the clinical environment. She also discusses role, scope and impact of Big Data paradigm on health care. Akerkar presents a concept of an intelligent integrated system for direct support of decision making of physicians. He focuses on decision support for pharmacogenomics, which is the study of the relationship between a specific person's genetic makeup and his or her response to drug treatment. Further, he discusses a research direction considering the current shortcomings of clinical decision support systems.

The fourth section consists of two chapters and discusses other issues related to big data and application of big data. Murayama, Nishioka and Abdullah present the issues on disaster communications. They discuss the example of The Great East Japan Earthquake on March 11th, 2011 which caused severe damage to the northern coast of the main island in Japan. They report their experiences and findings from this disaster. Rekha discusses challenges of cyber security and argues that government and law enforcing agencies need to enhance the security and intelligence analysis systems with big data technologies. Intelligence and security insight can be improved considerably by analyzing the under-leveraged data like the data from social media, emails, web logs etc. Rekha provides an overview of the opportunities presented by Big Data to provide timely and reliable intelligence in properly addressing terrorism, crime and other threats to public security and also discusses the threats posed by Big Data to public safety and the challenges faced in implementing Big Data security solutions. In addition, she discusses existing initiatives by national governments using Big Data technologies to address major national challenges. Sona explores the complexity of data types, methodologies of storage, access and computation, current and emerging trends of data analysis, and methods of extracting value from data. She highlights the methods in which actionable insights can be built into public sector domains, such as Machine Learning, Data Mining, Predictive Analytics and others.

The fifth section consists of two chapters focusing on opportunities and challenges of moving forward. Manzoor argues that big data represents an opportunity to infuse information and technology into the design and management of organizations, personnel, and resources. He discusses the role of public sector as it begins to derive insight to help support decision making in real time from fast-growing in-motion data from multiple sources. He further explores the big-data applications associated with the public sector and provide suggestions for follower governments. Aggarwal discusses opportunities and challenge of big data. He argues that government generates unprecedented amount of data (ex: US census), the question remains: can this data be combined with technology generated data to make it useful for societal benefit. He discusses challenges of governments and non-profits who work across borders making data access and integration challenging. Rules, customs and politics must be followed while sharing data across borders. He argues despite challenges, big data application in public sector are beginning to emerge.

Acknowledgment

A book of this nature requires assistance from many individuals. The chapters went through several screenings. The initial proposal and then the first draft were reviewed by at least two experts in the area. Conditionally accepted papers were revised and re-reviewed by the original reviewers. I would like to acknowledge all of the reviewers who gave their time and effort to help make this a quality publication.

I would like to thank Professor Doug Vogel, Harbin Institute of Technology, who agreed to forward this book and provided suggestions for improving the content. A book like this cannot be completed without sacrifice and dedication of other individuals. My sincere thanks go to Mr. Nicholas St. Angelo for helping with editing, logistics, and streamlining of the content, many times with little notice. This book could not have been finished in time without his help and support. In addition, I would also like to thank Ms Tashi Jelani for helping with drawings and correspondence. I appreciate all the support and guidance provided by Idea Group Publishing. My special thanks to Ms. Rachel Ginder and Ms. Jan Travers, Director of Intellectual Property and Contracts at Idea Group Publishing for their understanding and patience. I would also like to thank the staff at Idea Group Publishing for their hard work in editing and making this book a reality. Last but not least, I would like to thank Professor Mehdi Khosrow-Pour for giving me this wonderful opportunity to edit this timely book.

Anil K. Aggarwal
University of Baltimore, USA

Section 1
Big Data:
Issues and Models

Chapter 1

The Interoperability of US Federal Government Information:
Interoperability

Anne L. Washington
George Mason University, USA

ABSTRACT

Interoperability sets standards for consistency when integrating information from multiple sources. Trends in e-government have encouraged the production of digital information yet it is not clear if the data produced are interoperable. The objective of the project was to evaluate interoperability by building a retrieval tool that could track United States public policy from the legislative to the executive branch using only machine-readable government information. A case study of policy created during the 2008 financial crisis serves as an illustration to investigate the organizational, technical, syntactic, and operational interoperability of digital sources. The methods of citing law varied widely enough between legislation and regulation to impede consistent automated tracking. The flow of federal policy authorization exemplifies remaining socio-technical challenges in achieving the interoperability of machine-readable government data.

INTRODUCTION

Legislatures pass laws that authorize executive agencies to enact public policy. Is it possible, using only digital government documents, to track the flow of policy authorization? The answer is an investigation into interoperability and the potential of building "big data" to describe government activity. Big data connects machine-readable sources in order to identify patterns through computational analysis. Interoperability sets consistency standards for the integration of both technology and information structures. Aside from promoting transparency, digital public sector information (PSI) contains valuable descriptions of how governments do business. Breaking barriers to institutional data silos could have a

DOI: 10.4018/978-1-4666-9649-5.ch001

broader impact on promoting transparency objectives. Computational methods could enhance internal and external understandings of governance patterns.

Management scholars have embraced the study of big data as a continuation of existing information systems research (Agarwal & Dhar, 2014; Dhar, 2013; Sundararajan, Provost, Oestreicher-Singer, & Aral 2013). Big data brings the potential of using methods such as business analytics (Chen, Chiang & Storey, 2012), predictive analytics (Shmueli & Koppius, 2011), machine learning (Domingos, 2012), and data mining (Hand, Mannila & Smyth 2001). Business analytics is a driving force behind many private sector innovations (Goes, 2014; Quaadgras, Ross, & Beath 2013). The public sector has equal potential (Kim, Trimi, & Chung, 2014; Washington, 2014). In response to eGovernment directives, transparency initiatives, and open data advocacy, public sector managers have published increasing amounts of digital material. The proliferation of government information has opened up the potential for linking multiple sources into large-scale big data collections.

This chapter investigates interoperability as part of a larger investigation into the research potential of open government data. In a multi-year funded effort our research group, PI-Net, is using "big data" computational methods to ask questions about policy, politics, and governance (Wilkerson & Washington, 2012). New data collections give researchers new ways to ask questions, and large government collections present many opportunities. The unique features of government information may give rise to computational research challenges not seen in other data. Interoperability was a starting place to identify the challenges and potential of current data sources. We approached the problem by building a collection of data and documents from multiple government organizations.

The connection between the legislative and executive branches exemplifies a critical aspect of governance as well as the coordination of multiple organizations. Legislation instructs other government organizations to implement policy described in laws. Laws must be widely distributed to those who are impacted and to those who must implement public policy. Regulations, also known as secondary legislation or administrative law, are the specific rules set by agencies for implementing policy. Law is already conceptually interoperable with standardized systems of references and citations. Legal citations reference specific blocks of text, although each reference might be to a portion or to the entirety of the text. Previous research has recognized the potential of digital legal documents and investigated law as a digital library (Arnold-Moore, Anderson & Sacks-Davis 1997), as hypertext (Wilson, 1988), and as artificial intelligence (Liebwald, 2013; Matthijssen, 1998). This chapter builds on previous research on digital legislation.

The research design was to build and evaluate a system that tracks the policy authorization process using only United States federal open government data. The United States has a long history of federal information policy that promotes the release of material. The commitment to print publications has been expanded to a commitment to publish digital information. The project tracked policy released in electronic formats from Congress to federal agencies. Although conceptual systems for tracking legislative proposals to administrative activity have existed, it is only recently that the requisite standards, mandates, and requirements are in place to attempt machine-readable tracking.

The objective of the project was to evaluate interoperability by building a retrieval tool. First, we designed a logical model of information shared across organizations. The logical model is refined to specific documents and activities in a model we call Authority-Tracker. Next, we built a proof-of-concept retrieval tool based on that model called AUTHORITY-TRIEVE. The retrieval tool consolidated digital sources from the executive and legislative branches. Finally, we used the tool to trace United States public policy and evaluate the interoperability of the data. This paper presents a case study of tracking a single legislative provision into administrative law. The Troubled Asset Relief Program (TARP) was the first Congressional policy response to the 2008 global financial crisis. TARP is used as a snapshot to evaluate the interoperability of US open government data and the potential of building government "big data" collections. While the technical standards and data were widely available, we found that different levels of operational compliance hampered complete automated tracking.

INTEROPERABILITY

Public sector information, a rich description of networks, invites connections and combinations. The ability to share information has been a consistent aspect of eGovernment scholarship (Dawes, 1996; De-Nardis, 2010; Pardo, Nam & Burke, 2012). Interoperability supports compatibility and interdependence in eGovernment projects (Janssen, Chun & Gil-Garcia, 2009). Charalabidis, Lampathaki and Psarras (2009) highlight the range of worldwide interoperable efforts from Germany, Denmark, Hong Kong, and the European Union.

Interoperability is the ability to exchange between two or more separate ways of doing things. It can be the exchange between independent technology systems, information sources, organization infrastructures, data models, syntax standards, semantic definitions, or administrative processes. Interoperability standards make it possible to share machine-readable data between applications. Transparency disclosure mandates and eGovernment infrastructure projects have encouraged public sector organizations to steadily release data and documents in interoperable formats.

Technical interoperability is the compatibility of hardware components, software functions, file formats, or data models. Wegner (1996) identified two approaches to technical interoperability, which he defined as the ability to cooperate despite differences. First, interoperability can be designed directly through the use of a common standard. For instance, battery sizes are standardized so they can fit in many types of devices. Second, interoperability can be dynamic, where the exchange is negotiated in real-time based on an exchange protocol. For instance, any Internet browser on any device can display a web file using the exchange protocols established for the World Wide Web. Kubicek, Cimander, and Scholl (2011) offer specific types of technical interoperability: semantic and syntactic. Syntactic interoperability is an exchange that uses similar syntax, citations, or formal structure of a shared language (Van der Aalst & Kumar, 2003). Semantic interoperability is an exchange of shared meaning based on established definitions or interpretations (Charalabidis & Askounis, 2008). A syntactic interoperability example might clarify that dates are in month-day order instead of day-month order. Semantic interoperability would be able to match the name "Upper Chamber" to the "Senate" in one jurisdiction and "Lords" in another.

Although interoperability is often considered to be only technical by information systems managers, there are multiple other aspects. Dawes (1996) identified three barriers to information sharing: technical, organizational, and political. The European Interoperability Framework for pan-European e-Government Services defined three types of interoperability: organizational, semantic, and technical (European Commission, 2009). Pardo, Nam, and Burke (2012) argue that information sharing in eGovernment is based on policy, management, and technology interoperability. Organizational or management interoperability is defined by shared business practices and administrative processes. Policy and political definitions of interoperability include the concerns of leadership and stakeholders. DeNardis (2010) considers the interoperability life cycle. The life cycle begins with an open standards process for all stakeholders. The next stage in the life cycle is implementation, when standards are designed into project requirements.

Table 1. Interoperability types

Organizational Interoperability	Shared business practices and administrative processes
Technical Interoperability	Shared file formats or data models
Syntactic Interoperability	Shared syntax or language structure
Operational Interoperability	Compliance with shared standards in data production

Four types of interoperability were the basis for evaluation.

Finally, the standards must meet operational compliance when they are in active use in the production of data. Interoperability, especially for the public sector, extends beyond technical compatibility.

The forms of interoperability evaluated in this study are organizational, technical, syntactic, and operational, as shown in Table 1. The exchange of information will be evaluated to see if it matches administrative processes, file formats, citation standards, and production compliance.

INFORMATION POLICY

The interoperability of digital material emerges from earlier information policy. In the public sector and particularly in legislatures, information policy consists of choices made to manage documents. Information policy is considered to include the laws, regulations, policies, technologies, and practices that impact the interoperability of public sector sources. Information policy has been defined as guidelines for creating, collecting, exchanging, presenting or deleting objects that contain recorded knowledge (Braman, 2011; Relyea 1989). Often associated with governments only, information policy can apply to any institution that manages knowledge.

Tracking the flow of government business between organizations has historically been a challenge because of competing policy, conceptual and technical systems. Before the advent of reliable and regular production of digital information, government agencies had little incentive to share (Relyea, 1989). Data often languished in individual repositories or were isolated in incompatible information systems. Moreover, individual agencies rarely are mandated to create systems that extend beyond their internal needs. Buckley Owen, Cook and Matthews (2012) considered how a single policy did not uniformly apply across multiple United Kingdom departments. To avoid policy fragmentation, the UNESCO National Informatin Systems (NATIS) suggests that nations have a single coordinating body (UNESCO, 1975). The worldwide push for modernization created the technology infrastructure for producing open government data. Legislatures from the late 1990s through the 2000s were very active in developing systems that could be shared with constituents on the Internet (Washington & Griffith, 2007).

An important development in the United States was the digital government research program sponsored by the National Science Foundation (NSF) from 1998-2004. Partnerships between agencies and universities improved the technology available to government and opened up many research opportunities for understanding the public sector (Marchionini, Haas, Plaisant & Shneiderman, 2006). The United States government continued to emphasize the interoperability of information infrastructure through funding opportunities and mandates. If US digital government information is widely available, what is the level of interoperability between information from the legislative and executive branches?

AUTHORITY-TRACKER MODEL

The goal of the Authority-Tracker model was to create an abstract representation of the movement of documents and information between different branches of government. The model had to make logical sense as well as represent actual documents that were available as electronic files. Because we were interested in the movement of documents, we chose to map the full path from end to end. We start with the creation of a policy in the legislature and end with its refinement and enforcement. This is not a technical model. The model captures the flow of information exchanged between agencies. The model is also intended to identify points of interoperability between documents that contain shared information.

The simplest description of coordinated activity is similar to what is taught in most civics classes. A legislative proposal with a successful vote is codified into law and becomes a regulation implemented by an agency. Each stage of activity produces documents. All documents are systematically numbered and regularly printed. A series of related Congressional documents is called a legislative history. If a bill is proposed, considered in committee hearings, and debated on the floor, the legislative history includes hearing transcripts, a committee version of the bill, committee reports, and debate transcripts. Executive agencies assign numbers to proposed and final regulations and file them with associated documents, such as public comments. Conceptually, we can divide this into three logical sections: legislation, law, and regulation. While these steps are generally true, there are many exceptions to this basic description.

The first step in the research design was to build a logical model describing how US federal organizations coordinate activity by sharing information. The model, called Authority-Tracker, established the organizational interoperability between the US legislative and executive branches. The Authority-Tracker model began with a description of the documents and naming models that make up Congressional legislative history. The open government data produced from the legislative history is mapped in the first stage of the model, as shown in Figure 1.

The US Congress is really two organizations: the House of Representatives and the Senate. Each chamber of Congress operates differently in accordance with its constitutional role (Krehbiel, 1991; Oleszek, 2001; Polsby, 1968). The House and the Senate must agree to a legislative proposal, or bill, for it to become law. As Congress proposes, amends, and votes on legislation, each step is recorded in a transactional database, and often a document is created. Legislative documents are numbered sequentially, with additional acronyms to indicate the document type and originating chamber. For instance, S.1 is the first bill introduced in the Senate for a Congressional term.

Legislation may be closely related to other legislation. Most policy ideas are represented by multiple proposals that compete for legislative attention. Consider the simplest example of opposing perspectives on an issue.

A very complicated example of legislation is how two bills with different numbers may be the continuation of the same idea. In other words, the same bill number throughout the process is not the equivalent of following the same policy idea. S.1 may contain environmental policy when introduced, but by the final vote it may contain education policy. This complication was a strong factor in understanding the financial crisis policy discussed below. For organizational convenience and to meet procedural rules, the contents of one proposal are often replaced with the text of another unrelated proposal. This detail was difficult for our model to consider but is an important component of tracing a new legislative proposal through to its regulatory implementation. Conversely, this creates problems for tracing a final bill to

Figure 1. Model for legislation
The first stage of the conceptual model for organizational interoperability considered the legislative branch.

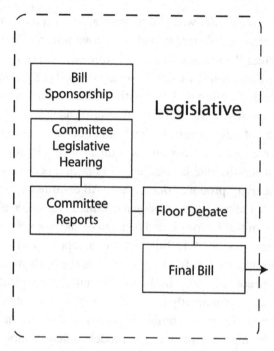

early legislative proposals. The practice of substituting the entire text means that bill numbers are stable but bill topics might radically shift between stages in the process.

If legislation passes, it becomes law and generates several document types that are widely promulgated, as shown in Figure 2. Enacted legislation, or law, first becomes a statute. While Statute numbers are often unique, it is possible to have multiple laws with the same citation if they are less than one page long. In the current era, where the legislative documents are long, the first page of the Statute number is usually a unique identifier.

Since 1926, when the United States Code (USC) started, general and permanent laws receive two numbers: the Statute-At-Large number and the USC number. All laws are published in date order in the Statutes-At-Large, while the United States Code is organized in subject order. The United States Code is an essential part of the interoperability between the legislative and executive branches.

The key to interoperability between the two branches is a table that converts citations. The first connection point is Table III of the United States Code. When a bill becomes a law, it is entered into this table. Table III shows how each law is distributed by topic across subject titles in the United States Code. For instance, a law might have provisions relating to taxes in Title 26 and others relating to commerce in Title 15. Table III serves as an important organizing point for moving from legislation to regulation.

Once a law is placed in the United States Code, it is used by the executive branch to set administrative law, which establishes regulations through a process known as rule-making. Proposed regulations are described and then codified in a way similar to legislation, as shown in Figure 3.

The Federal Register, published daily, contains all administrative notices that have the force of law. A citation such as 74 FR 28405 indicates volume 74 of the Federal Register, page 28,405, and it is usually followed by a specific date such as (July 19, 1999). The Federal Register is similar to the Statutes-At-

Figure 2. Model for laws
The second stage is the transition from a legislative proposal to an enacted law. This stage stands between the legislative and regulatory organizations.

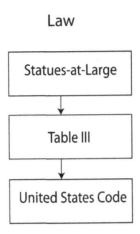

Large because it is a date-ordered list. The Code of Federal Regulations (CFR) is similar to the United States Code in that it is a subject-ordered list. The Code of Federal Regulations citations follow a structure similar to the United States Code: 12 CFR 112, which may include a part number.

The second connection point between the two branches is a table that converts administrative law back to authorizing law. The Parallel Table of Authorities (PTOA) converts Code of Federal Regulations citations into United States Code citations. Like Table III of the United States Code, it is an appendix to the main codification document. The PTOA appears as an index to the Code of Federal Regulations.

Figure 3. Model for regulation
The third stage is the executive branch authorization of regulation, also referred to as secondary legislation.

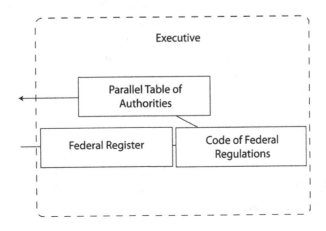

Figure 4. Authority-Tracker model

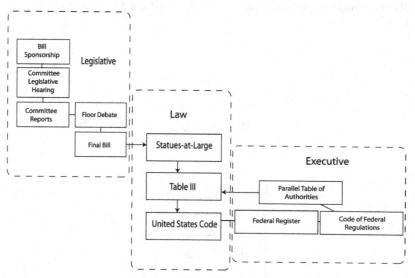

References to the law are key to both the executive and legislative branches. The indexes attached to the two codification publications are vital for moving dynamically between legislation and regulation.

Authority-Tracker is a conceptual model of how documents are shared between the two branches of the US government. The model captures the organizational interoperability between Congress and the federal executive agencies.

The complete Authority-Tracker model, as shown in Figure 4, indicates the documents and citations that span between legislative and executive organizations. The consistency of the numbering systems masks a complex system of usage. All documents referenced throughout the legislative process use the bill number, but as indicated the bill number might not reference the same policy ideas. Laws do not have a consistent naming structure. A law may be referenced by public law number, statute number, or United States Code number. In addition, a law may be referenced in executive documents by its act name, such as the Social Security Act.

The Authority-Tracker model captures the basic flow of information from legislation to regulation. There are several limitations to the Authority-Tracker model. Administrative law is restrained to two documents, the Code of Federal Regulations and the Federal Register. The model does not include other documents that are part of the rule-making process, such as the Unified Agenda, which tracks agency actions. Interoperability with the third branch of government, the judiciary, was not considered. These omissions could be useful in future research. The interoperability of case law with the other branches would be an avenue for an expanded model.

DATA SOURCES

The second step in the research design was to identify digital sources produced by organizations in the Authority-Tracker model. A digital source is a machine-readable file with an equivalent paper publication. Any digital source described here was openly available through the Internet from a government website. All documents were available for download from the Government Publishing Office, and many were available directly from agencies.

While all the materials were available in some digital form, there were significant variations in the formats available. All file formats require some preprocessing, but PDF files, or Portable Document Format, are very difficult to parse into meaningful structures. We used the text files, which are flat files that contain only simple text encoding characters and no structure. Indexes that coordinate between the two branches were unfortunately not in easy-to-parse file formats. These indexes, which are regularly produced tables, serve as crosswalks between legislation and regulation. Although available in digital formats, the files were not in any structured form and had to be parsed as simple text. The tables, Table III and the Parallel Table of Authorities, explicitly connect documents from legislative and executive organizations. The text file had to be carefully parsed to turn text tables into rows and columns. After parsing both tables for standard citation formats, it was possible to build a structured table of connections. Table III connected public law numbers to their United States Code citations. The Parallel Table of Authorities connected CFR citations to their equivalent USC citations.

Documents from both branches reference laws using act names and unique identifiers. Act names, such as the Social Security Act, refer to specific laws by the names of provisions. The granularity of a citation may fluctuate. Granularity is defined here as the level of specificity of a document. Is it referenced by a name, a citation to the whole document, or a citation to a part of the document? A citation could refer to a specific provision or to the beginning of the entire act name.

There were sufficient digital sources, as shown in Figure 4, to build a data collection based on the model. The data sources for the Authority-Tracker model included the Parallel Table of Authorities, the Code of Federal Regulations, the Federal Register, the United States Code, and the Statutes-At-Large, as shown in Table 2. Some specific digital sources were not available in file formats that were easy to parse. In particular, key index tables were not available in structured formats.

METHODS

The intent of the retrieval tool was to track the flow of policy authorization through related agencies and organizations. After determining that all files were digitally available, the next stage was to build a collection and a retrieval tool. The tool, called AUTHORITY-TRIEVE, retrieved the chain of authority from legislation through regulation using the Authority-Tracker model. AUTHORITY-TRIEVE was a

Table 2. Sources used to track legislation to regulation

Document	Year	Source	Rows	Digital Size
Statutes at Large	1951	GPO	37,409	251 MB
Table III	---	Congress	288,871	44 MB
United States Code	1994	GPO & Congress	815,060	16 MB
Parallel Table of Authorities	---	GPO	80,620	11 MB
Code of Federal Regulation	1996	GPO	9,105	45 MB
Federal Register	2000	GPO	86,381	886 MB

Digital files that are available based on the legislation to regulation model.

proof-of-concept tool to evaluate the feasibility of connecting digital sources. It retrieved the text of a law and the text of its related regulations simultaneously. Specifically, given any United States Code citation AUTHORITY-TRIEVE would provide the related public law, Statutes-At-Large, Code of Federal Regulations, and Federal Register citation and associated texts.

All available historic information was downloaded and parsed. Although semi-structured formats such as XML (Extended Markup Language) are widely available for some document types, historic data are often only available in text. To increase the breadth of the tool's function, all sources were reduced to plain text file formats.

This tool is designed so that a United States Code citation retrieves administrative law. In other words, it moves from legislation to regulation but not in the opposite direction. Future improvements to the tool will enable a searcher to start with any citation and find its related documents. This would involve parsing the entire Code of Federal Regulations to include notices not related to United States Code citations.

This experience emphasized the need to combine both technical skills and policy knowledge. The tool itself, a MySQL database, required basic technical skills and was built by a law student as a summer project. This was seen as a promising step because the goal is to make these data available to social scientists. The team behind the tool design had experience in computer science, political science, and law. All sources were combined into a series of relational tables in a MySQL database. The tables contained citations and complete texts. In addition, two tables were created for the codification of citation formats. One key was for the United States Code and the other was for the Code of Federal Regulations. The key tables clarified citations by parsing them into all possible subdivisions. The range of citations were approximated since they occurred irregularly.

The retrieval tool served as an illustration of the interoperability of public laws, the United States Code, the Federal Register, and the Code of Federal Regulations. It proved that open government data had enough conceptual interoperability to surpass institutional data silos. However, reducing rich data sources to text to gather longitudinal data highlighted a weakness in existing sources. While it was possible to track legislation to regulation using only digital files, it was based on the simplest file formats.

AN EXAMPLE: FINANCIAL CRISIS POLICY

The collapse of prominent financial services firms in 2008 initiated the Congressional response to the worldwide financial crisis. On September 29, 2008, the House of Representatives failed to pass a legislative proposal and the stock market dropped—its worst single-day descent—within 30 minutes of the vote. The policy eventually passed a few days later and was implemented by several federal agencies. What aspects of this story are visible in the available open data?

The simplest tracking would indicate that The Troubled Assets Relief Program (TARP) was voted into law as H.R. 1424 of the 110th Congress on October 3, 2008. The program was established through the authority of the "Emergency Economic Stabilization Act of 2008," Public Law 110-343, also known as 122 Stat. 3765. Authority to implement the policy was given, in part, to the Security and Exchange Commission and to the Department of the Treasury. It was established in many federal register listings, including at least two parts of the Code of Federal Regulations: 17 CRF 240, Part 240 – General Rules and Regulations, Securities Exchange Act of 1934 and 31 CRF 30, Part 30 – TARP Standards for Compensation and Corporate Governance. The Troubled Assets Relief Program was in effect from October 3, 2008 through October 3, 2010; however, some regulation and enforcement provisions, such as executive compensation rules, were still in effect in 2012. The retrieval tool was able to depict a broad understanding of events and connect legislative documents to executive ones, but it did not fully capture the story described above.

The legislative history was relatively short but included complex Congressional procedure. First, the most important historic event was not visible through our model and required extensive knowledge of Congressional procedure to uncover. The vote that sent shock waves through financial markets on September 29, 2008 was a procedural resolution to H.R. 3997, a different bill than the one that passed. Resolutions are often used for procedural votes, which determine how more substantive issues are handled. The text of this important legislation was buried as a conference report to a resolution connected to another bill number. When this three-page proposal became several hundred pages in the final bill, there were few who could trace its origins.

Second, in order to bring the proposal to a vote quickly in response to the crisis, bills that already existed were used. The contents of existing bills were substituted in their entirety with the text of the TARP policy. As discussed earlier, replacing the contents of a bill in its entirety is common practice. H.R.1424, the bill that eventually became the law, was introduced in March 2007 with the title "Paul Wellstone Mental Health and Addiction Equity Act of 2007." Because legislators have to vote to change titles, titles often do not change when the contents of bills are completely substituted with other text. While the bill is referred to as the "Emergency Economic Stabilization Act of 2008," that name is the title of Division A of H.R. 1424. The title of H.R. 1424 was never officially changed.

Third, the practice of using act names can vary. The act name can refer to a subsection, a supersection, or the entire law. The granularity of a name can change depending on which title is used. In this example, the authority could be given under the act name, "Emergency Economic Stabilization Act of 2008," or under the program name, "The Troubled Assets Relief Program." Without structured information, automatically determining name references requires complex processing although popular name tables do exist.

Finally, granularity is an issue both for act names and for unique identifiers. The most puzzling finding was that unique identifiers could be used in different ways. The public law for TARP contains three different legislative acts. TARP is one program in one of the acts. Because a Statues-At-Large citation is a page number, it can refer to a specific provision or to the beginning of a set of provisions. 122 Stat. 3765 is the beginning of Public Law 110-343. 122 Stat. 3767 is the beginning of the "Emergency Economic Stabilization Act of 2008." 122 Stat. 3776 is the policy on executive compensation. A fully automated system would need to determine whether a reference is to the beginning of a public law or a specific act or program.

In summary, this case study showed that the retrieval tool can be used to identify general movements of documents between the executive and legislative branches. The current data do not interconnect failed legislative proposals, which may be important in interpreting current law. Because of the varieties of use in titles and referencing, it was difficult to confirm that the right items were found without further inspection of the actual text or knowledge of procedure. Given distinctions in use, tracking policy authorization through sets of organizational documents can be very difficult to interpret without knowledge of Congressional procedure.

Table 3. Evaluation US executive and legislative branch interoperability

Organizational Interoperability	Shared business practices and administrative processes exist throughout all organizations across both branches. STABLE
Technical Interoperability	All share .txt and .pdf file formats in addition legislative organizations share an XML exchange standard. STABLE
Syntactic Interoperability	While syntax formats for citations are standard, the granularity of the citation could vary from specifying the entire law to a single provision. INCONSISTENT
Operational Interoperability	Operational compliance varied making it challenging to computationally anticipate patterns of use. Documents could reference the same law using either statute, public law or United States Code citations. INCONSISTENT

Stable organizational and technical interoperability made it possible to logically track legislation to regulation yet inconsistent syntactic and operational interoperability are still challenges for computational tracking.

EVALUATION

Our research found that legislation and regulation documents share similar conceptual and technical standards. The building of the retrieval tool made it possible to evaluate the interoperability of digital material that traces legislation to regulation. Four types of interoperability are considered in this evaluation: organizational, technical, syntactic, and operational, as shown in Table 3.

Organizational interoperability was confirmed in the Authority-Tracker model. Both the legislative and executive branches interact by exchanging documents. A law, which is a final Congressional document agreed upon by the House and Senate, is shared with the executive branch. The United States Code and Code of Federal Regulations are key transition points between the two branches.

Technical interoperability was confirmed across all organizations. The House and Senate share a data model that is used in the legislative XML exchange standard. The Government Publishing Office (GPO) publishes important documents shared across organizations in XML file formats, easy-to-read PDFs that perfectly represent print documents, and text files that can be processed by any computer.

Syntactic interoperability was not consistent. Although there are many structured languages and syntax structures for law, there is no consistency in use. Sometimes a law is referred to by its name or by the many documents in which it appears. For instance, the Emergency Economic Stabilization Act of 2008 is also Public Law 110-343 or 122 Stat. 3765. However, the more worrisome inconsistency is the difference in granularity of the reference. A syntactic reference can be to an overall bill or a specific provision. There is no automated way to identify when these shifts in granularity occur. Current citation use is adequate for a person with some knowledge of the system but not precise enough for automatic parsing. Granularity (Blair & Kimbrough, 2002) is a concern for both the names of laws and for parsing citations.

The final type of interoperability was operational compliance. The Code of Federal Regulations uses a mix of act names, United States Code citations, and public law numbers, making it difficult to consistently track back to the legislative branch. It is not clear that conventions for citing laws have been mandated across organizations as a standard. One exception is the legislative XML exchange standard (xml.house.gov), which describes a canonical set of references. However, legislative proposals can reference existing law as either an act name or a law citation. Multiple conventions for referencing law make sense to knowledgeable human readers but impede automated computational analysis.

In summary, organizational processes and technical standards are well coordinated. However, things begin to fall apart with the syntax used to reference laws. Even if a specific syntax is used, the level of granularity may cause misinterpretations in automatic processing. Overall the case study found stable organizational and technical interoperability but inconsistent syntactic and operational interoperability.

RESULTS

The evidence suggests that open government data does not yet contain enough information in and of itself to completely track governance patterns. The translation from legislation to regulation includes two crosswalk tables that are available in digital form. However, they require additional work to process into machine-readable structure. What was available for the case study is only accessible to sophisticated data customers proficient in computational skills and government procedure. However, that leaves open many possible future directions for computational research using open government data.

Policy collections may prove interesting for combining research in natural language processing, human-computer interaction, and information retrieval. The unique features of policy documents challenge assumptions about the uniformity of texts. For instance, titles used in legislation may not be associated with the meaning of the text, and titles of policy documents may contain completely unrelated information due to procedural complexities. What innovative interface designs could support this complexity? How can topic maps (Blei, 2012) help to identify and differentiate policy ideas across time?

Government information is an abundant resource of spoken, written, and visual material that can advance computational science. The ability to connect unstructured information using "big data" computational methods enables longitudinal studies on extensive natural language sources. Machine learning scholars also may be interested in these data because they are tied to defined outcomes that may be used for predictive analytics. Those interested in natural language can compare the differences between video and audio of fully transcribed meetings without licensing restrictions.

These opportunities have in many ways been met by commercial legal publishers. With the expectations of profits, commercial vendors have added value by building tools that interpret government data. Open government data efforts have primarily emphasized releasing increasing amounts of information. Perhaps future transparency efforts could focus on how information is combined and not just what information is produced.

This paper reports on the first stage of Poli-Informatics, an interdisciplinary funded effort to investigate the research potential of open government data. These collections require some expert knowledge to interpret. Only through interdisciplinary collaborations can we find the best balance for learning from these documents.

Connecting between US legislation and regulation has the appearance of interoperability, but the operational differences are still a hindrance. Future researchers could continue to explore the challenge of building models for interoperability between two branches of government. Large-scale technical infrastructure is essential especially within organizations like the European Union (Charalabidis & Askounis, 2008; Charalabidis, Lampathaki & Psarras, 2009; European Commission, 2009), however, work on the logical interconnections is still needed. Legislative open data efforts currently take place at a distance from executive efforts (Janssen, Chun & Gil-Garcia 2009; Lewis, 1995). Ideally, we need approaches that consider both how laws are made and how they are used by lawyers, incorporating scholarship on artificial intelligence, law and legal information systems. We need to understand how these two distinct ecosystems fit together to gain a holistic perspective on how government, overall, is doing.

The transition from eGovernment interoperability to big data will have to confront the legacy of existing documents. Government documents are carefully constructed artifacts representing detailed public sector work. The historic format and use of these documents is not built to withstand the level of granularity expected for fully reliable machine-readable processing.

The documents that were critical to build connections between legislation and regulation are remnants of the print era. Both Table III of the United States Code and the Parallel Table of Authorities of the Code of Federal Regulations are indexes. An index was the primary form of interoperability between print documents. Often considered as an alphabetical list, an index is a table that matches a location with a concept (Anderson, 1985). Conceptual analysis is the result of the often overlooked intellectual work of information infrastructure (Bowker, 1996; Star, 1999). An index can organize the content within a collection of any size. Some collections are so complex that they require multiple indexes to provide sufficient access to different conceptual arrangements. For instance, the United States Code is a subject-ordered index, while the Statutes-At-Large is date-ordered index. An index can be a critical crosswalk between different systems of thinking (Star & Griesemer, 1989). Different systems of thinking are more pronounced at scale and across competing modes of organizing (Baker & Bowker, 2007). This is particularly true for government indexes that connect the output of multiple organizations.

What can a simple index do in comparison to advanced computational tools such as algorithmic analytics, personalized retrieval, and precision Internet search engines? The current indexes were developed when page space was limited. They are more like a compass than exact directions. The 2013 Parallel Table of Authorities connects 1 USC 112 to 1 CFR Part 2. The United States Code citation is about 200 words long, while the Code of Federal Regulations citation is closer to 1000 words. Perhaps a specific Code of Federal Regulations paragraph could be connected to the smallest unit in the United States Code. While there are limits to human-generated indexes, the connections between the print indexes have been highly stable over decades. They will be a crucial step towards either generating or checking the accuracy of advanced computational techniques (Bookstein & Swanson, 1976; Salminen, Tague-Sutcliffe & McClellan, 1995; Willis & Losee, 2013). In an advanced indexing system, granularity (Blair & Kimbrough, 2002; Hearst, 2009) will be an additional point of access.

DISCUSSION

Future research may consider how to use advanced search interface designs to retrieve specific targets and related adjacencies within a large document.

Some big data analysts will abandon all retrieval tools in favor of text mining tools. The debate about searching or browsing is a classic concern (Bates, 1989; Speier & Morris, 2003; Van Noortwijk, Visser & Mulder, 2006). Search tools locate a specific known item. Browse tools locate related groups of items. Brown and Duguid (2002) consider that direct search can sometimes lead to tunnel vision, where possibilities are overly restricted. Consider the conundrum of searching within the document called the "Federal Register" for the organization that creates it. Because organizations are listed without designations, the "Office of the Federal Register" is listed as the "Federal Register." Only through a dedicated index, not search, is it possible to locate recent rule-making activity from the Office of the Federal Register in the Federal Register. In this example, a browse had more successful results that a search.

Assuming that an algorithm always brings clarity and simplicity can mask hidden nuance and subtlety (Diakopoulos, 2014). An index holds layers of intellectual work that are still useful as machine-readable retrieval systems are perfected.

Government information is driven by processes. The identifiers, documents, and other structures are unique to internal processes within the organizations that produce them. What tools are available to support operational compliance? Internal mechanisms could identify and standardize consistent use within an organization. As e-science initiatives establish elaborate communication schemes (Borgman, Bowker, Finholt & Wallis, 2009), eGovernment could develop mechanisms for cross-organization use. Without internal consistency or explicit translation tools, the interpretative complexity increases with machine-generated connections between organizations.

The intent of any index is to build stable connections. Big data collections rely on stable information for interpretation. Government indexes provide potential sources for understanding the design, procedures, and intent behind document collections. While adding convenience for human readers, an index also builds connections for machine-readable interoperability. Despite the limits to both human-generated and algorithmic methods, index publications will serve as pivotal guides to the next generation of tools for interoperable government data.

CONCLUSION

The promise of eGovernment interoperability has been partially reached with the necessary first step of releasing digital files to the public. Meanwhile, there are many opportunities for scholars who are interested in using "big data" computational methods on unstructured data. This case study of tracking policy authority from legislation to regulation contributed an understanding of the current state of interoperability for US federal open government data. Data can cross boundaries, but operational compliance between organizations needs to be resolved through new standards or dynamic translation tools. Complete interoperability will be possible when files in presentation formats are available in machine-readable formats. The interoperability of information between two US federal branches exemplifies remaining socio-technical challenges in achieving the integration of machine-readable government data.

ACKNOWLEDGMENT

This project was supported by the U.S. National Science Foundation Grant No. #1243917.

REFERENCES

Agarwal, R., & Dhar, V. (2014). Editorial—Big Data, Data Science, and Analytics: The Opportunity and Challenge for IS Research. *Information Systems Research*, 25(3), 443–448. doi:10.1287/isre.2014.0546

Anderson, J. D. (1985). Indexing systems: Extensions of the mind's organizing power. In B. D. Ruben (Ed.), *Information and behavior* (pp. 287–323). New Brunswick, NJ: Transaction Books.

Arnold-Moore, T. J., Anderson, P., & Sacks-Davis, R. (1997). Managing a digital library of legislation. In *ACM/IEEE-CS Joint Conference on Digital Libraries* (pp. 175–183). ACM/IEEE.

Baker, K. S., & Bowker, G. C. (2007). Information ecology: Open system environment for data, memories, and knowing. *JIIS Journal of Intelligent Information Systems*, *29*(1), 127–144. doi:10.1007/s10844-006-0035-7

Bates, M. J. (1989). The design of browsing and berrypicking techniques for the online search interface. *Online Review*, *13*(5), 407–424. doi:10.1108/eb024320

Blair, D. C., & Kimbrough, S. O. (2002). Exemplary documents: A foundation for information retrieval design. *Information Processing & Management*, *38*(3), 363–379. doi:10.1016/S0306-4573(01)00027-9

Blei, D. M. (2012). Probabilistic Topic Models. *Communications of the ACM*, *55*(4), 77–84. doi:10.1145/2133806.2133826

Bookstein, A., & Swanson, D. R. (1976). Probalistic models for automatic indexing. JASIS. *Journal of the American Society for Information Science*, *25*(5), 312–318. doi:10.1002/asi.4630250505

Borgman, C. L., Bowker, G. C., Finholt, T. A., & Wallis, J. C. (2009). Towards a virtual organization for data cyberinfrastructure. In *Proceedings of the 9th ACM/IEEE-CS Joint Conference on Digital Libraries* (pp. 353–356). New York: ACM Press. doi:10.1145/1555400.1555459

Bowker, G. C. (1996). The history of information infrastructures: The case of the international classification of diseases. *Information Processing & Management*, *32*(1), 49–61. doi:10.1016/0306-4573(95)00049-M

Braman, S. (2011). Defining information policy. *Journal of Information Policy, 1*.

Brown, J. S., & Duguid, P. (2002). *The social life of information*. Boston: Harvard Business School Press.

Buckley Owen, B., Cooke, L., & Matthews, G. (2012). Information Policymaking in the United Kingdom: The Role of the Information Professional. *Journal of Information Policy*, *2*(0).

Charalabidis, Y., & Askounis, D. (2008). Interoperability registries in eGovernment. In *Hawaii International Conference on System Sciences, Proceedings of the 41st Annual* (pp. 195–195). IEEE.

Charalabidis, Y., Lampathaki, F., & Psarras, J. (2009). Combination of interoperability registries with process and data management tools for governmental services transformation. In *System Sciences, 2009. HICSS'09. 42nd Hawaii International Conference on* (pp. 1–10). IEEE.

Chelimsky, E. (1991). On the Social Science Contribution to Governmental Decision-Making. *Science*, *254*(5029), 226–231. doi:10.1126/science.254.5029.226 PMID:17787972

Chen, H., Chiang, R., & Storey, V. (2012). Business Intelligence and Analytics: From Big Data to Big Impact. *Management Information Systems Quarterly*, *36*(4), 1165–1188.

Dawes, S. S. (1996). Interagency Information Sharing: Expected Benefits, Manageable Risks. *Journal of Policy Analysis and Management*, *15*(3), 377–394. doi:10.1002/(SICI)1520-6688(199622)15:3<377::AID-PAM3>3.0.CO;2-F

DeNardis, L. (2010). E-Governance Policies for Interoperability and Open Standards. *Policy & Internet*, 2(3), 129–164. doi:10.2202/1944-2866.1060

Dhar, V. (2013). Data Science and Prediction. *Communications of the ACM*, 56(12), 64–73. doi:10.1145/2500499

Diakopoulos, N. (2014). Algorithmic Accountability. *Digital Journalism*, 0(0), 1–18.

Domingos, P. (2012). A Few Useful Things to Know About Machine Learning. *Communications of the ACM*, 55(10), 78–87. doi:10.1145/2347736.2347755

European Commission. (2009). *European Interoperability Framework (EIF) for pan-European eGovernment Services*. Interoperable Delivery of European eGovernment Services to public Administrations. Retrieved from http://ec.europa.eu/idabc/en/document/2319/5644.html

Goes, P. (2014). Editor's Comments: Big Data and IS Research. *Management Information Systems Quarterly*, 38(3), iii–viii.

Halevy, A., Norvig, P., & Pereira, F. (2009). The Unreasonable Effectiveness of Data. *IEEE Intelligent Systems*, 24(2), 8–12. doi:10.1109/MIS.2009.36

Hand, D. J., Mannila, H., & Smyth, P. (2001). *Principles of data mining*. Cambridge, MA. MIT Press.

Hearst, M. A. (2009). *Search user interfaces*. New York: Cambridge University Press. doi:10.1017/CBO9781139644082

Janssen, M., Chun, S. A., & Gil-Garcia, J. R. (2009). Building the next generation of digital government infrastructures. *Government Information Quarterly*, 26(2), 233–237. doi:10.1016/j.giq.2008.12.006

Kim, G.-H., Trimi, S., & Chung, J.-H. (2014). Big-data Applications in the Government Sector. *Communications of the ACM*, 57(3), 78–85. doi:10.1145/2500873

Krehbiel, K. (1991). *Information and legislative organization*. Ann Arbor, MI: University of Michigan Press.

Kubicek, H., Cimander, R., & Scholl, H. J. (2011). *Organizational Interoperability in E-Government: Lessons from 77 European Good-Practice Cases*. Springer. doi:10.1007/978-3-642-22502-4

Lewis, J. R. T. (1995). Reinventing (open) government: State and federal trends. *Government Information Quarterly*, 12(4), 427–455. doi:10.1016/0740-624X(95)90078-0

Liebwald, D. (2013). Vagueness in law: a stimulus for'artificial intelligence & law'. In *Proceedings of the Fourteenth International Conference on Artificial Intelligence and Law* (pp. 207–211). doi:10.1145/2514601.2514628

Marchionini, G., Haas, S., Plaisant, C., & Shneiderman, B. (2006). Integrating data and interfaces to enhance understanding of government statistics: Toward the national statistical knowledge network project briefing. In *International Conference on Digital Government Research Dg.o* (pp. 334–335). Academic Press.

Matthijssen, L. (1998). A task-based interface to legal databases. *Artificial Intelligence and Law*, 6(1), 81–103. doi:10.1023/A:1008291611892

Oleszek, W. J. (2001). *Congressional procedures and the policy process (vol. 5)*. CQ Press.

Pardo, T. A., Nam, T., & Burke, G. B. (2012). E-Government Interoperability Interaction of Policy, Management, and Technology Dimensions. *Social Science Computer Review*, 30(1), 7–23. doi:10.1177/0894439310392184

Polsby, N. W. (1968). The Institutionalization of the U.S. House of Representatives. *The American Political Science Review*, 62(1), 144–168. doi:10.2307/1953331

Quaadgras, A., Ross, J. W., & Beath, C. M. (2013). You May Not Need Big Data After All. *Harvard Business Review*.

Relyea, H. C. (1989). Historical Development of Federal Information Policy. In C. R. Mcclure & P. Hernon (Eds.), *United States Government Information Policies* (pp. 25–48). ABLEX publishing.

Salminen, A., Tague-Sutcliffe, J., & McClellan, C. (1995). From text to hypertext by indexing. *ACM Transactions on Information Systems*, 13(1), 69–99. doi:10.1145/195705.195717

Shmueli, G., & Koppius, O. R. (2011). Predictive Analytics in Information Systems Research. *Management Information Systems Quarterly*, 35(3), 553–572.

Speier, C., & Morris, M. G. (2003). The influence of query interface design on decision-making performance. *Management Information Systems Quarterly*, 27(3), 397.

Star, S. L. (1999). The Ethnography of Infrastructure. *The American Behavioral Scientist*, 43(3), 377–391. doi:10.1177/00027649921955326

Star, S. L., & Griesemer, J. R. (1989). Institutional Ecology, "Translations" and Boundary Objects. *Social Studies of Science*, 19(3), 387–420. doi:10.1177/030631289019003001

Sundararajan, A., Provost, F., Oestreicher-Singer, G., & Aral, S. (2013). Information in Digital, Economic, and Social Networks. *Information Systems Research*, 24(4), 883–905. doi:10.1287/isre.1120.0472

UNESCO. (1975). *Intergovernmental Conference on the Planning of National Documentation, NATIS, national information systems: COM- 74/NATIS/3 Rev*. Paris: UNESCO.

United States Emergency Economic Stabilization Act of 2008, 122 Stat. 3765. 110 HR 1424. (2008). Retrieved from https://www.congress.gov/bill/110th-congress/house-bill/1424

United States. (2014). *United States Code Classification Tables*. Retrieved July 2, 2014, from http://uscode.house.gov/classification/tbl110pl_2nd.htm

Van der Aalst, W. M. P., & Kumar, A. (2003). XML-Based Schema Definition for Support of Interorganizational Workflow. *Information Systems Research*, 14(1), 23–46. doi:10.1287/isre.14.1.23.14768

Van Noortwijk, K., Visser, J., & Mulder, R. V. D. (2006). Ranking and Classifying Legal Documents using Conceptual Information. *The Journal of Information Law and Technology*, 2006(1).

Washington, A. L. (2014). Government Information Policy in the Era of Big Data. *Review of Policy Research*, *31*(4), 319–325. doi:10.1111/ropr.12081

Washington, A. L., & Griffith, J. C. (2007). Legislative Information Websites: Designing Beyond Transparency. In A. R. Lodder & L. Mommers (Eds.), *Legal Knowledge and Information Systems JURIX 2007 The Twentieth Annual Conference* (p. 192). JURIX.

Wegner, P. (1996). Interoperability. *ACM Computing Surveys*, *28*(1), 285–287. doi:10.1145/234313.234424

Wilkerson, J. D., & Washington, A. L. (2012). *PI-Net Poli-Informatics NSF 1243917*. Retrieved from http://poliinformatics.org

Willis, C., & Losee, R. M. (2013). A random walk on an ontology: Using thesaurus structure for automatic subject indexing. *Journal of the American Society for Information Science and Technology*, *64*(7), 1330–1344. doi:10.1002/asi.22853

Wilson, E. (1988). Integrated information retrieval for law in a hypertext environment. In *Annual International ACM SIGIR Conference On Research And Development In Information Retrieval* (pp. 663–677). doi:10.1145/62437.62505

Chapter 2
A Hybrid Approach to Big Data Systems Development

Anil Aggarwal
University of Baltimore, USA

ABSTRACT

Data has always played a critical part in business decision making. The digital economy is generating Tsunami of data which must be analyzed and used by both the public and private sector. Survival and citizen satisfaction may depend on how governments use big data to develop citizen-centric services. Big data analysis can lead to better transparency, less corruption and citizen satisfaction. Big data is an emerging area where models and applications are still emerging. Currently there are few, if any, models that provide guidance in developing applications. This chapter proposes a hybrid approach which can be used as a starting point for future development.

INTRODUCTION

Big data is an emerging area which has only recently caught the attention of researchers. Data has always played a critical role in decision making, and these analyses typically use structured (or well-behaved) data. In the digital age, however, there is an abundance of untapped unstructured data that needs to be mined and analyzed for useful information. This data is generated via social networking, sensors, mobiles, apps and many smart devices. Much of this data contains important information that is still unexplored. The volume, speed and variety with which this data is generated is prompting both the public and private sectors to think about new ways of managing and analyzing data--big data analytics is an outgrowth of this thinking. Literature has typically focused on social networks and data mining but has not merged the areas to provide meaningful insights. Big data combines many disciplines such as analytics, statistics, database, sociology, etc., in order to provide useful information. Many isolated big data applications have been reported in literature but there is no model that provides guidance in developing these applications. This chapter proposes a hybrid approach to developing big data applications, as it combines both structure and unstructured data in its model. This chapter uses the ethical lens theory proposed by William May in developing the hybrid model, and also describes several current applications of big data.

DOI: 10.4018/978-1-4666-9649-5.ch002

What is "Big" Data?

Big data, by definition, is "big" and that's where the definition ends, but what is big is still being debated. Big is a moving target that changes with time as more and more data is being generated at lightning speed. By some estimates (Gartner group), big data will grow at a 45% rate to 35 zettabytes annually by 2020. According to estimates from emarsysglobal.com, 21 billion Short Message Services (SMS) are sent and 1 billion users visit YouTube every day, while 80% of online content is user generated. There are 1 billion Facebook members and almost 700 million Twitter users, which generates almost 600,000 tweets every second. Figure 1(a) and 1(b) shows big data and HADOOP searches from 2005-2015 and beyond from both the general and government perspectives. It is clear from Figures 1(a) and 1(b) that interest in these two concepts started to rise in 2011, with the trends continuing a steep upward for both big data and HADOOP.

The Google search engine processes almost 12 billion searches and has 75% of the search market, generating a big volume of data. Processing this level of data requires new thinking and new technologies. Big data definitions are many (Chen et al, 2012; Dutcher, J, 2014; Garnet, 2015; NIST publication, 2015),

Figure 1

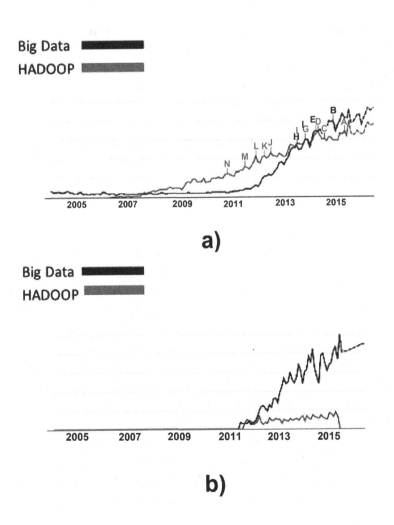

a)

b)

but for many researchers, it follows 4 Vs; volume, variety, velocity and veracity. The first three Vs refer to data whereas the fourth V, veracity, refers to the source or truthfulness of data. According to Gartner, "Big data is high-volume, high-velocity and high-variety information assets that demand cost-effective, innovative forms of information processing for enhanced insight and decision making". According to the National Institute of Standards and Technology (NIST), "Big Data refers to the inability of traditional data architectures to efficiently handle the new datasets." In addition, "Big Data consists of extensive datasets—primarily in the characteristics of volume, variety, velocity, and/or variability—that require a scalable architecture for efficient storage, manipulation, and analysis". The common denominators are the three Vs characteristics of big data. In addition, they argue that current data storage and management techniques are not sufficient to handle this data. They suggest a new way of storing, managing, manipulating and analysis is needed that can provide scalability and massive parallel processing capabilities. As we move from smart TVs, to smart appliances, to smart watches, to smart homes, to smart cities, to smart government and smart societies, big data and its applications are becoming the new norm.

Isolated big data applications are numerous in both the public and private sectors. The private sector has mined social media data to learn about customer sentiments about a company, its products and its image. This has helped them to rebrand their product, improve customer service and retain customer goodwill. Public sector applications are also emerging with public-private partnership, government leadership and support (Kim et al, 2014; Lu, Y. Q, 2014). The Obama Administration (2012) is encouraging big data research by starting "the Big Data Research and Development Initiative", which states, "By improving our ability to extract knowledge and insights from large and complex collections of digital data, the initiative promises to help accelerate the pace of discovery in science and engineering, strengthen our national security, and transform teaching and learning." Big data applications are spreading throughout the public sector. NIST (2015) identifies some of the big data applications, which includes:

- How can a potential pandemic reliably be detected early enough to intervene?
- Can new materials with advanced properties be predicted before these materials have ever been synthesized?
- How can the current advantage of the attacker over the defender in guarding against cyber-security threats be reversed?

In addition, big data has been used for urban planning (Awaluddin, 2014; Batty, M., 2013; Batty, M. et al, 2012; Clarke, R.Y., 2013) to develop smart cities (Batty, M., 2013; Bettencourt, L. M., 2013), track and contain diseases like the Ebola virus (Booker, E., 2014; Polwart, N., 2015), track terrorists, study and understand airplane tragedies (Storageeserver.com, 2014), develop citizen-centric services (Sharma et al, 2014) and enhance public safety, among other things. Healthcare is not far behind. One health care application that has used big data successfully is the public-private partnership case of IBM's data baby. IBM Canada, in partnership with the University of Ontario, Institute of Technology (UOIT) in Oshawa, Ontario developed a system called "Artemis". According to Dr. McGregor, the lead researcher, "Data is coming out of those machines at a rate of a thousand readings per second, and we're taking that down to make a note of a single reading every 30 or 60 minutes. There's an enormous amount of data loss". Dr. McGregor looked to integrate, "the range of physiological readings that are captured from hospital monitoring equipment – at birth, during transport, and in the intensive care unit – to give neonatologists the tools and intelligent support systems they need to analyze a tsunami of data almost immediately." As a result of deep analytics,"... the system is proving to be the key to early detection of conditions

Table 1. Examples of public application of big data

The Vs of Big data	Typical Examples	Vs intensity	Examples of data
Volume/Variety	Tracking terrorists, urban planning, Patient quality care	Average volume, Average variety	Individual/group postings in text, pictures, movies, animation
Velocity/Volume	Disruptive events, like Missing Malaysian Flight, Baltimore riots, Earthquakes and Tsunami in Japan	High volume High velocity	Flight tracker, authorities, interviews (pilot, relatives) sensors
Variety	Solving Crime, Tracking diseases	High Variety	Lab results, suspect profiles, speed cameras

like sepsis – and the insights provided to physicians may ultimately be the difference between life and death…". There are many similar public-private and public-university partnerships applications in the health and human sectors of the government.

Given the accessibility, applicability and potential of big data, it is not surprising that it is being touted as the next major disruptive force, likely to transform the public and private sectors forever (Court, 2015). Big data analytics is not good or suited for all applications. It is most useful when an application requires discovery, exploration, detection, or deep analytics of a large volume of data. Table 1 provides some examples of big data applications.

Examples in Table 1 are not necessarily mutually exclusive in terms of the three V's (volume, variety and velocity), but based rather on those factors that may be dominant. Some tragic events are also example of big data, such as Malaysian Airlines Flight 370, which was flying from Kuala Lumpur International Airport to Beijing Capital International Airport when it suddenly disappeared. A variety of data was available, including satellite communication information with Inmarsat's satellite, engine and radar data, and passenger and captain data. The data was analyzed by a team of government and private experts to explore the possible location and causes of the airline tragedy. Storagerservers (2014) described the variety of data and analytics that were used in attempts to locate the lost Malaysian flight. Data from the satellites was transmitted into big data storage banks and big data analytics were used to analyze data archived from more than 4.5 billion square kilometers of global coverage. High powered data/photo analytics engines identified about 421,338 photos taken from the Indian Ocean. Though the plane is still missing, this demonstrates how a variety of data can be analyzed by swift teams to explore tragic events.

Big data has been used and mined extensively in the public health sector. The next section describes some applications of big data in the public health sector.

Examples of Public Healthcare applications:

A significant big data application is in public health, with pandemics of Ebola, HIV, Cholera, etc (Booker, e., 2014; Shaman et al, 2014). In tracking the spread of the Ebola virus, Booker (2014), reported, HealthMap's Ebola page, "takes data from a variety of places: formal sources like health ministries and the WHO, as well as informal ones like social media and news reports. HealthMap's objective is to organize, filter, tag, and make real-time surveillance of emerging public health threats available to clinicians, policy makers, and citizens. Among other uses, the Ebola map can help clinicians make a diagnosis faster. "If a patient has a travel history, this can help inform a diagnosis," In the tracking of the disease, Chowell et al, (2014) analyzed epidemic growth patterns. Specifically, the analysis used a variety of data at three different spatial scales (regional, national, and sub national) of the Ebola Virus Disease (EVD) epidemic in Guinea, Sierra Leone and Liberia by compiling publicly available weekly time series of reported EVD case numbers from the patient database obtainable from the World Health Organization website for the period 05-Jan to 17-Dec 2014. They concluded, "The slower than expected growth pattern of local EVD outbreaks could result from a variety of factors, including behavior changes, success of control interventions, or intrinsic features of the disease such as a high level of clustering". They concluded that, "Quantifying the contribution of each of these factors could help refine estimates of final epidemic size and the relative impact of different mitigation efforts in current and future EVD outbreaks".

Another example is patient generated data. "Millions of people are tracking their levels of activity daily and healthcare providers are increasingly examining ways to leverage this data to improve levels of care and efficiency," says ABI Research principal analyst Jonathan Collins. Wearable device sales according to the Gartner group are projected to rise to $5 billion by 2016. Fitbit is a popular wearable device that records many different types of data by the minute, hour or day. This creates a tremendous amount of data that can be used by physicians to monitor health risk patients or to infer health conditions. For example, Hernandez (2014) noted, "...Dr. Eric Topol, a cardiologist at the Scripps Clinic in San Diego, knows when his patients' hearts are racing or their blood pressure is on the rise, even if they're sitting at home. With high-risk patients hooked up to "personal data trackers" -- a portable EKG electrocardiogram built into a smartphone case, for instance -- he and his researchers can track the ups and downs of patients' conditions as they go about their lives. "It's the real deal of what's going on in their world from a medical standpoint," says Topol, whose work is part of a clinical trial. Author concluded that the integration of Fitbit data with the classical medical record (structured data) is vital for diagnostic and treatment purposes.

Another use of big data in the health industry was reported by the Wall Street Journal (2014), which stated that, "...David Cook, an anesthesiologist at the Mayo Clinic College of Medicine, who, along with colleagues, used Fitbit, Inc.'s namesake gadget to track activity levels of cardiac-surgery patients." The researchers found that patients who moved about more the day following surgery were more likely to be discharged sooner. The findings prompted the hospital to dispatch physical therapists to study patients who weren't moving as much, according to Dr. Cook. There are many other examples showing the breadth and depth of big data applicability.

All the data, however, is useless unless it can be processed efficiently and used effectively. In order to be useful, big data needs to be extracted, stored, managed, analyzed and applied. While this itself is not an easy task, this chapter describes the attempts to begin the process. The next section explains data types and the section following that describes the model.

Structured vs. Unstructured Data

Traditionally, data that has been used by both the public and private sectors is structured in nature. It can be stored, queried and analyzed using traditional methodologies like structured query language (SQL). Structured data is linear and transactional in nature. However, big data by its very nature consists of a variety of information (like videos, images, graphs, text, voice, etc.) that requires a different frame and approach. Table 2 gives some examples of different data types.

Table 2 is not an exhaustive list but a sample of data types that are emerging. Though business transactional (operational) data is still dominant, user and smart-device generated data is emerging rapidly. The McKinsey group (2011) reported that there will be 40% more global data generated per year and 15 out of 17 sectors in the United States have more data stored than the Library of Congress (235 terabytes of data). Crawford (2014) quoted an International Development Corporation (IDC) report:"...

Table 2.

Data Type	Structured	Unstructured
Transactions	X	
Documents	X	
E-mail	X	X
Sensors (ex: traffic)		X
Weblogs		X
Social media (Facebook, Twitter, etc.)	X	X
Videos (YouTube etc.)		X
Pictures (Instagram)		X
Smart devices (mobile phones, watch, digital camera etc.)		X
Equipment-generated (planes, Fitbits, etc.)	X	X
Service –generated (ex: electronic medical records)	X	X
Satellites		X
Apps	X	X

the sheer amount of data generated doubles every two years. By the year 2020, the total amount of data will equate to 40,000 *exabytes* or 40 *trillion gigabytes*. To put this in perspective, that's more than 5,200 gigabytes for every man, woman and child in 2020." IDC (2015) reported that "...Big Data technology and services market will grow at a 26.4% compound annual growth rate to $41.5 billion through 2018, or about six times the growth rate of the overall information technology market. Additionally, by 2020, IDC believes that a line of business buyers will help drive analytics beyond its historical sweet spot of relational performance management to the double-digit growth rates of real-time intelligence and exploration/discovery of the unstructured worlds."

Before we describe our model, we summarize the salient differences between current, mostly structured data types and new data types that are typically unstructured. Table 3 summarizes the differences. It should be noted that big data consists of both structured and unstructured data, but Table 3 comparisons are only for the unstructured part of the big data and traditional structured part of operational data.

Table 3 comparisons are based on the premise that structured data is modeled as relational and unstructured data follows the NOSQL environment and modeled in HADOOP.

Relational systems are typically transactional data driven and have (ACID) properties - Atomicity, Consistency, Isolation and Durability, whereas unstructured systems are more model/data driven and do not have ACID properties. Initially, relational systems were built for one CPU but have evolved to include distributed processing. However, unstructured data use massive parallel distributed systems that may only achieve two of the three desirable properties of consistency, availability, and partition tolerance - The CAP theorem [26, 9] possibility resulting in loss of currency of data. Structured data follows Chen's Entity-Relationship Diagram (ERD) model, where entities, attributes and relationships and degree of associations can be specified. Extract Transform Load (ETL) operations are performed to clean the data before it is aggregated in the data warehouse. Relational systems can be processed real-time (ad-hoc) or batch and use a well-developed structured query language (SQL) for manipulating and accessing data. These systems are mature and supported by big vendors.

Table 3. Characteristics of structured/unstructured data

Features/Data Type	Structured (Traditional)	Unstructured (Big Data)
Driver(s)	operational Data	Data/Model/Analytic
Processing	Real time	Typically batch/some real time
Efficiency/effectiveness	Optimization emphasis (more on efficiency)	Less optimization emphasis(more on effectiveness)
Data representation	Integrated relations modeled in ERD (entity relationship diagram)	Typically, file system e.g. HADOOP (node-based system), HDFS, MapReduce etc.
Query Language	SQL	NOSQL, NEWSQL, BIGSQL
Databases	Relationalobject	Key-ValueColumn Family, Graph, etc.
Analysis unit	Sample	Population
Typical outcome	Various reports/decision support	Detection/classification/exploration
Data Modeling	ERD, Normalization	Data redundancy, duplication
Modeling	Model first	Model later
Flexibility	Downtime for updates	Nodes can be added anytime
Data characteristics *	More entity driven data	User-generated
Data characteristics *	Domain-based data	hyperlinks to "other" data

* These are besides the three Vs

Big data analysis requires massive storage and processing capabilities that are provided by the NOSQL environment. The NOSQL movement started as the volume of user generated data started to swell. Both public and private sectors saw the potential of user-generated data. New systems started to emerge such as HADOOP, which is a system distributed file system consisting of thousands of computers stacked in clusters and scalable from one node to thousands of nodes. HADOOP can store a large amount of data for processing. A task is divided into small "tasks" and each node in HADOOP can process the task independently. A file/task is repeated on several nodes to account for failures. HADOOP draws its power from parallel processing (Brewer, 2000; Gilbert et al, 2012) and utilizes MapReduce (one of the techniques) to process data. Tasks are mapped (divided), processed and then reduced (combined), which allows for a large volume of information to be processed at the same time. If a node fails, duplicate nodes take over. This permits massive data in any format to be stored and processed (Dean, J. and Ghemawat, S., 2008; Chang F. et al, 2008).

NOSQL is an alternative (or a supplement) to SQL for big data processing. With NOSQL, data can be distributed as sharding (different data on different nodes) or replication (data is replicated on multiple nodes to account for node failures). Distribution allows for massive parallel processing, a necessity for big data processing. Some of the NOSQL databases are classified as Kroenke and Auer, 2015):

- **Key-Value:** Dynamo and MemcacheDB
- **Document:** Couchbase and MongoDB
- **Column Family:** Apache Cassandra and HBase
- **Graph:** Neo4J and AllegroGraph

These databases do not require structure (ERD) or normalization. They are basically flat and are adaptable to changes without extensive maintenance time. More information about these and other NOSQL databases is available at http://nosql-database.org/.

Structured data is useful for generating reports, ad-hoc queries and domain specific intelligence. Big data analytics are used by governments to explore population and economy trends, to track fraud and terrorist cells, and to manage public health and similar citizen-centric applications. Big data analytics can be applied to the whole population, instead of just a sample, giving a "better" picture of the environment. The next section describes the Hybrid model which can be used for big data modeling and processing.

The Hybrid Model

Data is both document and user generated and consists of both structured and unstructured formats. It is the user generated data which is creating "new" or "big" data. Both the public and private sectors have been manipulating structured data using conventional techniques by creating schemas, models, and structured query language to provide decision making support via various management models (DSS: Decision Support Systems; ES: Expert Systems, etc.). Typically, unstructured data was untapped until now. In many cases it was thrown away. According to the McKinsey report (2011), hospitals were throwing away 90 percent of the data they generated (almost all real time data video feeds created during surgery). A lot of big data was wasted. Advances in parallel processing are creating environments where this discarded data can be processed and analyzed to provide insights in case of hospital related accidents or malpractice suits.

Though we have discussed "new data" in detail, "transactional data" is equally as important. In fact, they are the two sides of the same coin. According to SAS thought leader Anne Buff, "the addition of Big Data does not negate the need, purpose, or existence of traditional business data. In many situations Big Data adds to the value (and headaches) of existing data." We follow the integrated approach in developing the model. The model is a hybrid in the sense that it combines both traditional and big data to create value for both the public and private sectors. Big data does not replace but supplements traditional analysis, which forms the basis of our hybrid model.

Big data is characterized in terms of the following Vs:

- **Volume:** Amount of data generated, like Twitter, Facebook and other social media websites generating zenta, penta, and exabytes of data per minute.
- **Velocity:** Speed with which data is generated, Twitter, Facebook and other sites, where data goes viral in seconds
- **Variety:** Different forms of data, text, video, pictures, voice, etc.
- **Veracity:** Trust factor of data: is data from a trusted source, and consistent and complete?
- **Validity:** Usability of data: is the data useful?
- **Value:** What value can be generated from data?

We argue, that all Vs are not equal. Some are basic and others are derived. We propose three-tier Vs:

- **Level 1:** Selection of raw data that relates to three Vs (volume, velocity and variety) characteristics
- **Level 2:** Relate to usability of data (veracity, validity), derived after filtering data from level 1
- **Level 3:** Relate to refined data used for output (value), derived from filtered data from level 2

Figure 2.

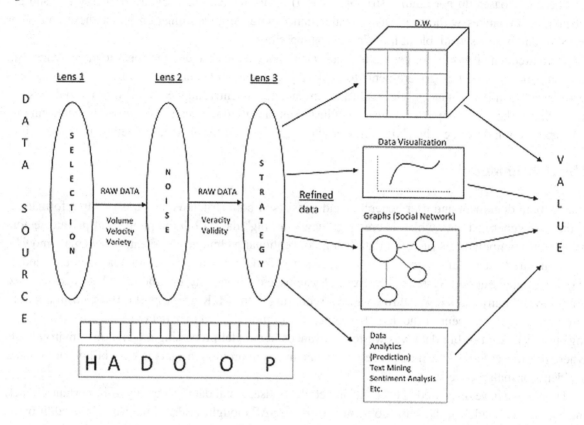

Though researchers have argued against filtering big data, we argue for an initial source selection filter that will make data more meaningful and application oriented. In addition, it will remove "noise" from the data. Using this argument, we propose the hybrid model. In developing the hybrid model, we use the corrective lens theory advocated by William May (1983), a medical ethicist who described ethics as supplying "a type of CORRECTIVE lens". Though not directly related to big data, it provides a basis for developing the proposed hybrid model. We present a three lens model that "corrects/filters" data, summarized in Figure 2.

Filter Lens 1 (3 Vs: Selection)

There is an abundance of data generated by users, smart devices, documents, social networks, apps, blogs and appliances, in addition to others. The first step is to select appropriate sources of data. This requires planning and understanding the scope and purpose of the study. If the purpose is to discover, find opinions, and find connectivity, then broader data sources are needed since it is like looking for a needle in a haystack. On the other hand, if the purpose is to study citizen sentiment, track diseases, urban planning or similar narrow domain tasks, then limited (domain specific) sources may be useful since it is comparable to looking for a gold mine. In other words, we know gold is in the mine and it is not useful to look for gold in other places. Researchers need to decide on degrees of freedom for data collection. For example, if police are studying a citizen's complaint about their department, comments from one or one and a half degree of egocentric network (Fisher, D., 2005) contacts may be sufficient, i.e., what are citizens saying to their immediate contacts and what are those contacts saying to their contacts? In such cases, comments from social networking, police websites and similar sites will be crucial. On the other hand if police are investigating a crime, data collected from sensors, crime scenes, labs, computers, videos and social sites would be important. Commenting on the heterogeneity of data on climate change, Faghmous et al (2014) noted it is important to identify and select data sources as disparate sources (satellite, in situ, paleoclimate etc.) provide redundant data. They implied that it is for the data scientist to select data sources and data which may be complementary or redundant.

These examples are for discussion purposes only. In reality, data sources may be much more comprehensive. The purpose of the first step is to select appropriate data sources.

Filter/Lens 2 (Validation and Veracity)

The first lens generates "raw" data which is the data collected from various selected sources (Level 1) and has first level V (volume, velocity and variety) properties. We only include the first three properties at level 1, which reflect raw data, while other properties are based on "filtered" or "processed" data. Level 1 data should be filtered (Lens 2) for validation and veracity.

An important factor to maintain veracity is the "trust" factor of data sources. There are many sites that are generally reliable. Data from government sites is generally trustworthy because the way it is produced and maintained (USNC commission, 1982). Governments produce large amounts of data in a variety of formats. For example, the U.S. Census Bureau, Centers for Disease Control and Prevention, Department of Labor, etc., provide massive amounts of information that can be trusted. Most government data is structured in what researchers and organizations [(Chen H. et al, 2012; Mckinsey Report, 2011; NIST Pulication, 2015) call data-at-rest. In addition, there are global organizations, like the United Nations, World Bank, European Union etc. that can be trusted due to their charter and global support. Then there are trustworthy private organizations like Gartner, McKinsey etc. that can be trusted due to their reputation and long existence. The other type of data, data-in-motion, comes from social networking sites that are user generated. Most of this data is semi or unstructured. There are some well-established social networks (Facebook, Twitter, LinkedIn, Instagram, etc.) which can be trusted. However, there are other networks that should be evaluated (by checking the Better Business Bureau) before using them further in applications. Once trusted sites are filtered, next step is to ensure data validity.

Another important factor is validity or usability of data. Raw data from level 1 contains lots of information and some of it may be noise (not directly or indirectly connected to the task at hand). For example, if a government is tracking Ebola and they collect Twitter comments or Facebook postings, they may want to check that the postings are from legitimate participants. This could be done by checking the CDC list of patients diagnosed with Ebola, or Facebook pages for the professions of participants (making sure they are doctors, nurses, social workers, or other legitimate members), thus ensuring validity of the data. Another example is the Internal Revenue Service (IRS) studying a citizen's perception of their operations and they are scanning social media for this purpose. People may not have any comments about the IRS, but may have ill feelings about another agency, such as the Department of Commerce. They may confuse IRS with Commerce by posting unflattering comments about the Department of Commerce. Such entries may be useful if researchers were interested in an overall government perception, but it may not be particularly useful to the IRS. Such entries may be eliminated to improve data validity. Another example is shown in Figure 3, which are tweets for the doomed Malaysian Flight 340.

Figure 3.

Though most tweets are topic related, one tweet relates to self promotion. This and similar tweets may be filtered to give validity to the data. HADOOP and Mapreduce could be useful in removing noise based on text analytics or key word searches.

It is recommended that user generated data be filtered for spam and other irregularities. It has been noted that many times, participants tweet/blog about an event or a product that they have never used, seen or experienced. This may be due to the need for inclusion, deception or financial gain. There is lots of information but there is also a lot of spam on social networks. As Agichtein et al. (2008) noted, "The quality of user-generated content varies drastically from excellent to abuse and spam. As the availability of such content increases, the task of identifying high-quality content sites based on user contributions -- social media sites -- becomes increasingly important. Social media in general exhibit a rich variety of information sources: in addition to the content itself, there is a wide array of non-content information available, such as links between items and explicit quality ratings from members of the community."

Commenting on data validity, Tan et al. (2014) also noted that "The largest publicly available knowledge repositories, such as Wikipedia and Freebase, owe their existence and growth to volunteer contributors around the globe. While the majority of contributions are correct, errors can still creep in, due to editors' carelessness, misunderstanding of the schema, malice, or even lack of accepted ground truth. If left undetected, inaccuracies often degrade the experience of users and the performance of applications that rely on these knowledge repositories"

Several researchers are developing filters to extract credible data from social sites. For example, Castillo et al. (2011) analyzed microblog postings related to "trending" topics and classified the postings as credible or not credible, based on features extracted from them. They used features from user posting and re-posting ("*re-tweeting*") behavior, from the text of the posts, and from citations to external sources. Also commenting on noise filtration, Caroleo et al. (2015) suggested using a data-driven approach to measure the community engagement around some topics of interest. Their approach can also assist in selecting "valid" data of interest.

It is important to filter data for spam and unrelated data to ensure data validity. The purpose of the second step is to filter the data for noise and make it ready for the third stage.

Filter/Lens 3: (Creating Value)

Once data is verified and validated, the next step is to analyze it to create value. This can take many forms. Numerous analytical techniques are available for data analysis. Data can be used for exploration, detection, opinions, hidden relations, tracking, new discoveries, etc. There are infinite possibilities for creating "value" from the data. Sentiment analysis can be used to study a citizen's reaction to a "new" tax reform. Visualization may be used to discover complex relationships. Network analytics can help the Department of Homeland Security to track/trace suspects and their accomplices.

We discuss several options to create "value" once data is refined (these are not mutually exclusive applications). We do not discuss data analytics since all methods described below can use data analytics to create value.

Data Warehouse

Big data may be structured and merged with a data warehouse for further analysis. Since new data is digital in nature, it would be possible to couple it with structured data and use it in data warehouses. Key-value NOSQL databases can be helpful here. These databases are similar to relational databases except for the number of attributes for a given key that can be of different types. For example, one key may have {name, telephone, number} and another may have {Facebook account, e-mail, date of birth, picture, and spouse name}. These can be queried using low level languages. New attributes can be added without changing the initial key-value structure. Another example is data from Facebook. If a picture is posted on Facebook, it could be linked to the accounts of each of the persons in the picture. Pictures are in jpeg or similar format, and they could be appended to citizen records in relational databases (modern databases support object attribute) and data warehouses. This data warehouse could be used for traditional analytics to derive value.

There are also examples where researchers have integrated structured/unstructured data to create value. For example, Aslam, et. al. (2012) discuss how real time data combined with historic data can be used for urban planning. In a case study, they collected data from a real-time roving sensor network of taxi probes, which log their locations and speeds at regular intervals and are used to analyze traffic patterns. The authors argue that their techniques provide a powerful new approach for traffic visualization, analysis, and urban planning.

Also, old systems need to be able to talk to new systems. Since most legacy data is structured, it needs to be combined with unstructured data to create value. For example, Chin-Ho et. al. (2014) describe an experiment using data from Taiwan's National Health Insurance Research Database (NHIRD) that combines "legacy" data from relational databases and "new" data from MongoDB (a NOSQL platform). They combined cloud computing with query-Mapreduce-shared approach to enhance the search performance of data mining. Another example is the rioting in Baltimore, as the Baltimore Sun reported (May 2, 2015), where police combined structured data from court records, photos from sensors that were circulated online, and social media to apprehend the suspect. The suspect was photographed on videotape puncturing the fire hose and was traced to prison records by a fire marshal.

Above examples illustrate that traditional data can be integrated with new data to create value. Next, we describe value creation via visualization.

Data Visualization

Visualization is a process of understanding patterns, relationships and trends (Kaidi, 2000). It is well known that "A picture is worth a thousand words". Visualization, however, goes beyond simple graphs. According to the Intel Corporation, new visualization tools using interactive bubble charts, 3-D data landscapes, treemaps, boxplots, heat maps, word clouds, and many other types of graphics, can be used by government to view, interpret, and interact with complex data from a multitude of sources. 4-D applications are emerging making visualization even more useful in applications like tracking diseases, managing public health and ensuring citizen's welfare.

Visualization is useful to study clusters, make an association among data and/or to study emerging trends. Using visualization as one of the tools, Molesworth et. al. (2003) studied a meningitis epidemic in Africa. Using maps and graphs, they showed a relationship between the environment and location of the disease and were able to identify regions at risk for meningitis outbreaks. Varshney et. al., (2015), focused on the social good by discussing development activities aimed at uplifting rural populations out of "poverty traps". They noted that "Effective planning in poor rural areas benefits from information that is not available and is difficult to obtain at any appreciable scale by any means other than algorithms for estimation and inference from remotely sensed images." Due to the unavailability of data in poor countries, the authors used data visualization and models to discuss common problems of selecting sites and planning for rural development activities, as informed by remote sensing and satellite image analysis.

Ranganathan et al (2015) used data from the World Bank, United Nations and Freedom House to study democracy and development traps for four countries. They developed a non-linear dynamic system model and used heatmaps and scatter diagrams for their study. By using big data and visualization, they showed that many key developing countries, including India and Egypt, lay near the border of these development traps. They also investigated the time taken for these nations to transition toward higher democracy and socioeconomic well-being, which is a very important finding for governments trying to bring democracy to these countries.

Above examples demonstrate how visualization can help in creating value for big data.

New visualization tools are integrated with business analytics tools. As the trend continues and software continues to improve, visualization will become a major big data analytical tool.

The next section describes value created via social network graphs.

Social Networks (Graphs)

One of the greatest advantages of social media is connectivity. It creates communities of people who want to share, interact and keep themselves informed. Values can be generated using social networks. Governments can find citizen sentiments, groups/sub groups, influential person(s) in the network by analyzing graphs obtained from social media sites like Facebook, Twitter, Instagram, Snapchat, etc. For example, we have analyzed the popular TV sitcom "The Big Bang Theory", using an episode to access major characters. Figure 4 illustrates a network that shows the "Sheldon" character as the influential

Figure 4.

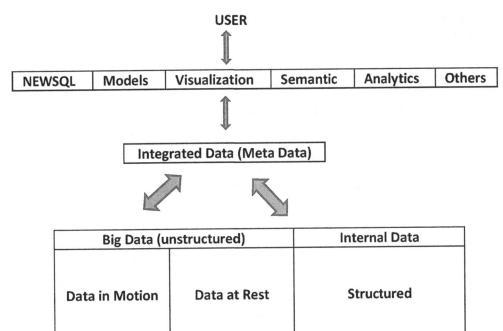

node with any changes having to go via Sheldon. If these were citizens, it would imply that postings by Sheldon are important and any policy changes should be channeled via the main node.

Graphics can be used to study both "normal" and "abnormal" relations from a complete set of data. Normal relations may reveal consensus or agreement or harmony, whereas abnormal relations may reveal dissension or exclusivity of outliers. Many times, outlier data provides more information than the normal data. For example, in the fight against terrorism, it may be useful to study social networks and track/follow nodes that have fewer connections (implying leadership) that may be transmitting their hate messages through more popular nodes. This could alert authorities to track not only outliers, but also people not on the social networking sites related to those outliers.

Human right groups have also used social media to monitor human right violations. Chen F. et al (2015) developed a non-parametric heterogeneous graph scan (NPHGS) model that "was able to accurately detect relevant clusters of human rights–related tweets prior to international news sources, and in some cases, prior to local news reports." Analysis of social media using NPHGS can enhance the information-gathering missions of human rights organizations by pinpointing specific abuses, revealing events and details that may be blocked from traditional media sources, and providing evidence of emerging patterns of human rights violations. This could lead to more timely, targeted, and effective advocacy, as well as other potential interventions. By utilizing social media like Twitter in some cases, they were able to forecast human rights abuses before they could occur. This could be very useful for governments in monitoring terrorist attacks on and tracking diseases affecting their citizens.

The three approaches described above are used to create value. However, these are not exhaustive or mutually exclusive. In fact, many times they are used in conjunction with each other to create value. The hybrid model described above is the first step in providing a systematic process of handing big data.

This is a work in progress. The challenge is to select right "source", right "filter" and right "analytics" to provide meaningful results. The next section describes an application that implicitly uses the hybrid model in its application.

A Hybrid Model Application

An example of big data that analyzes tweets to discuss trends in the Ebola virus spread (using the implicit hybrid model), is discussed by Odlum et. al. (2015). They selected Twitter (Level 1) as the primary source of data for their experiment and collected 42,236 tweets to monitor information spread, capture early epidemic detection, and examine the content of public knowledge and attitudes towards EVD. Twitter is a reputable site and considered valid for research and data analysis purposes. Authors then "cleaned symbols and Web addresses and transformed text to a vector form (level 2) and N-gram and reduced the dimensionality of the volume using Notepad++ and Weka software". Authors then used "descriptive statistics", including the volume of posted (unique and retweet) and disseminated tweets, which were traced according to geographic location. The posters' locations were indicated using an interactive, data visualization, and business intelligent software. A time series analysis, which used an exponential smoothing algorithm, was conducted to identify trends of how fast the tweets mentioning Ebola were disseminated. The trend model of the dissemination speed of tweets mentioning EVD was visualized. Authors concluded, "Twitter allows for government and health agencies to engage and guide the public during outbreak surveillance efforts. For effective data information messaging, Twitter can inform content for desired outcomes. Access to such data allows for greater accuracy and sensitivity in the assessment of behavioral response." Applying graphical and statistical methods, the authors created value (Level 3) by providing a means for effective surveillance during disease outbreaks. There are many such applications (Barrachina et. al, 2014; Chin-Ho, 2014, etc.) that can be mapped into a hybrid model.

CONCLUSION

Government applications of big data are numerous, from cutting waste, maintaining national security and cyber security, tracking terrorists, and providing transparency to its citizens. The government is collecting data from such sources as traffic cameras, sensors, social media, firewalls, law enforcement, and national park visitor centers and so on. In fact, personal data is collected as soon as citizens walk out of their residences, offices, etc. This data assists the federal government in keeping the country and its assets safe from intruders, and to listen and be transparent to its citizens. Big data is providing opportunities and every government should take advantage of it. Currently, however, there are no models that provide a systematic approach for managing such data. This chapter discusses a hybrid model which combines structured with unstructured data to generate value for its users. We do not discuss the technical details as they are beyond the scope of this chapter. However, we have outlined the first step in big data modeling, and hopefully a standardized approach/model like relational database (RDBMS) will eventually emerge from future discussions and research.

Dr. McGregor of the IBM data baby application stated it best when she said that "the babies give this data to us freely, so we should use it to make their lives better". There is plenty of data for everybody. The challenge is to analyze it and use it.

REFERENCES

Agichtein, E., Castillo, C., Donato, D., Gionis, A., & Mishne, G. (2008). Finding high-quality content in social media. In *Proceedings of the 2008 International Conference on Web Search and Data Mining* (pp. 183-194). ACM.

Aslam, J., Lim, S., Pan, X., & Rus, D. (2012). City-scale traffic estimation from a roving sensor network. In *Proceedings of the 10th ACM Conference on Embedded Network Sensor Systems* (pp. 141-154). ACM. doi:10.1145/2426656.2426671

Awaluddin, M. (2014). The Partnership Between Business and Government towards Sustainable City Development. In ICT For Smart Society (ICISS), (pp. 131-138). IEEE. doi:10.1109/ICTSS.2014.7013162

Baltimore Sun. (2015). Man Charged with Damaging hoses at CVS fire. *Baltimore Sun.*

Batty, M. (2013). Big data, smart cities and city planning. *Dialogues in Human Geography, 3*(3), 274–279. doi:10.1177/2043820613513390

Wachowicz, G. O., & Portugali, Y. (2012). Smart cities of the future. *The European Physical Journal. Special Topics, 214*(1), 481–518. doi:10.1140/epjst/e2012-01703-3

Bettencourt, L. M. (2013). *The Uses of Big Data in Cities.* Santa Fe Institute Working Paper.

Casas, J., Ferrer, J. L., & Garcia, D. (2010). Traffic simulation with aimsun. *Fundamentals of Traffic Simulation, 1*, 173–232.

Booker, E. (2014). Ebola Fight Hampered By Poor Analytics. *Information Week.* Available at: http://www.informationweek.com/government/big-data-analytics/ebola-fight-hampered-by-poor-analytics/d/d-id/1306998

Brewer, E. (2000). *Towards robust distributed systems.* Paper presented at Principles of Distributed Computing, Portland, OR. Available at: https://www.youtube.com/watch?v=H_nz936whfE

Caroleo, B., Tosatto, A., & Osella, M. (2015). Making Sense of Governmental Activities Over Social Media: A Data-Driven Approach. In Decision Support Systems V–Big Data Analytics for Decision Making (pp. 34-45). Springer International Publishing. doi:10.1007/978-3-319-18533-0_4

Castillo, C., Mendoza, M., & Poblete, B. (2011, March). Information credibility on twitter. In *Proceedings of the 20th International Conference on World Wide Web* (pp. 675-684). ACM. doi:10.1145/1963405.1963500

Chang, F., Dean, J., Ghemawat, S., Hsieh, W. C., Wallach, D. A., Burrows, M., & Gruber, R. E. et al. (2008). Bigtable: A Distributed Storage System for Structured Data. *ACM Transactions on Computer Systems, 26*(2), 1–26. doi:10.1145/1365815.1365816

Chen, H., Chiang, R. H. L., & Storey, V. C. (2012). Business intelligence and analytics: From big data to big impact. *Management Information Systems Quarterly, 36*(4), 1165–1188.

Chen, F., & Neill, D. B. (2015). Human Rights Event Detection from Heterogeneous Social Media Graphs. *Big Data, 3*(1), 34–40. doi:10.1089/big.2014.0072

Lin, H., & Chou, L. Cheng, & Chiang. (2014). Temporal Event Tracing on Big Healthcare Data Analytics. In *Proceedings of Big Data (BigData Congress), 2014 IEEE International Congress on.* IEEE.

Chowell, G., Viboud, C., Hyman, J. M., & Simonsen, L. (2014). *The Western Africa Ebola virus disease epidemic exhibits both global exponential and local polynomial growth rates.* arXiv preprint arXiv:1411.7364

Clarke, R. Y. (2013). *Smart Cities and the Internet of Everything: The Foundation for Delivering Next-Generation Citizen Services.* Alexandria, VA: Tech. Rep.

Court, D. (2015). Getting big impact from big data. *The McKinsey Quarterly.*

Crawford, T. (2014). *Are Enterprises Prepared for the Data Tsunami?* Available at: http://avoa.com/2014/01/20/are-enterprises-prepared-for-the-data-tsunami/

Dean, J., & Sanjay Ghemawat, S. (2008). MapReduce: Simplified data processing on large clusters. *Communications of the ACM, 51*(1), 107–113. doi:10.1145/1327452.1327492

Dutcher, J. (2014, September 3). What is Big Data. *Data Science at Berkeley Blog.* Retrieved from http://datascience.berkeley.edu/what-is-big-data/

Faghmous, J. H., & Kumar, V. (2014). A Big Data Guide to Understanding Climate Change: The Case for Theory-Guided Data Science. *Big Data, 2*(3), 155-163.

Fisher, D. (2005). Using egocentric networks to understand communication. *IEEE Internet Computing, 9*(5), 20–28. doi:10.1109/MIC.2005.114

Gartner.com. (n.d.). *Answering Big Data's 10 Biggest Vision and Strategy Questions.* Retrieved from http://www.gartner.com

Gilbert, S., & Lynch, N. (2012). Brewer's conjecture and the feasibility of consistent, available, partition-tolerant web services. *ACM SIGACT News, 33*(2).

Hernandez, D. (2014). *Activity trackers like Fitbit bring big data to US healthcare.* Available at: http://www.wired.co.uk/news/archive/2014-03/07/internet-things-health

ibm.com. (n.d.). *Achieving Small Miracles from Big Data.* Available at: https://www.ibm.com/smarter-planet/global/files/ca__en_us__healthcare__smarter_healthcare_data_baby.pdf

IDC. (2015). *Report.* Available at: https://www.idc.com/prodserv/4Pillars/bigdata

Intel. (2015). *Big Data Visualization: Turning Big Data Into Big Insights.* Retrieved from http://www.intel.com/content/dam/www/public/us/en/documents/white-papers/big-data-visualization-turning-big-data-into-big-insights.pdf

Kaidi, Z. (2000). *Data visualization.* National University of Singapore.

Kim, G. H., Trimi, S., & Chung, J. H. (2014). Big-Data Applications in the Government Sector. *Communications of the ACM, 57*(3), 78–85. doi:10.1145/2500873

Kroenke and Auer. (2015). Database Concepts (7th ed.). Pren_hall Pub.

Lu, Y. Q. (2014). Research on E-Government Model Based on Big Data. In *Advanced. Materials Research, 989*(994), 4905–4908. doi:10.4028/www.scientific.net/AMR.989-994.4905

May, W. F. (1983). *The Physician's Covenant*. Philadelphia: Westminster Press.

McKinsey Report. (2011). *Big data: The next frontier for innovation, competition, and productivity*. McKinsey Global Institute Report. Available at: http://www.mckinsey.com/insights/business_technology/big_data_the_next_frontier_for_innovation

Molesworth, A. M., Cuevas, L. E., Connor, S. J., Morse, A. P., & Thomson, M. C. (2003). Environmental risk and meningitis epidemics in Africa. *Emerging Infectious Diseases, 9*(10), 1287–1293. doi:10.3201/eid0910.030182 PMID:14609465

NIST Special Publication 1500-1. (2015). *DRAFT NIST Big Data Interoperability Framework: Volume 1, Definitions*. Author.

Odlum, M., & Yoon, S. (2015). What can we learn about the Ebola outbreak from tweets? *American Journal of Infection Control, 43*(1), 563–571. doi:10.1016/j.ajic.2015.02.023 PMID:26042846

Ranganathan, S., Nicolis, S. C., Spaiser, V., & Sumpter, D. J. (2015). Understanding Democracy and Development Traps Using a Data-Driven Approach. *Big Data, 3*(1), 22–33. doi:10.1089/big.2014.0066

Sharma, V., Guttoo, D., & Ogra, A. (2014, May). Next generation citizen centric e-services. In *IST-Africa Conference Proceedings, 2014* (pp. 1-15). IEEE. doi:10.1109/ISTAFRICA.2014.6880672

Shaman, J., Yang, W., & Kandula, S. (2014). Inference and forecast of the current West African Ebola outbreak in Guinea, Sierra Leone and Liberia. *PLoS Currents, 6*. PMID:25642378

Storageserver.com. (2014). *How Big Data analytics is helping in searching for missing Malaysian Airlines Flight MH370*. Author.

Tan, C. H., Agichtein, E., Ipeirotis, P., & Gabrilovich, E. (2014, February). Trust, but verify: Predicting contribution quality for knowledge base construction and curation. In *Proceedings of the 7th ACM international conference on Web search and data mining* (pp. 553-562). ACM.

The White House Office of Science and Technology Policy. (n.d.). Big Data is a Big Deal. *OSTP Blog*. Accessed February 21, 2014, http://www.whitehouse.gov/blog/2012/03/29/big-data-big-deal

United States National Commission on Libraries and Information Science. (1982). *Public sector/private sector interaction in providing information services: Report to the NCLIS from the Public Sector/Private Sector Task Force*. Washington, DC: US National Commission on Libraries and Information Science, Government Printing Office.

Varshney, K. R., Chen, G. H., Abelson, B., Nowocin, K., Sakhrani, V., Xu, L., & Spatocco, B. L. (2015). *Targeting Villages for Rural Development Using Satellite Image Analysis*. Big Data.

Wall Street Journal. (2014, June 3). Can Data From Your Fitbit Transform Medicine?. *Wall Street Journal*.

Chapter 3
Transparency and Enhanced Efficiency and Accountability Due to Big Data Adoption in Government Agencies and Other Enterprises

Dhiraj Jain
Symbiosis Centre for Management Studies- Symbiosis International University, India

Yuvraj Sharma
Cognus Technology Ltd., India

ABSTRACT

Pertinence of big data is necessary especially in the field of corporate governance where large amount of data is collected, stored, retrieved and manages. The major challenge arises for the government organizations therefore are how to use the breadth and depth of the large amount of available data in an appropriate manner. The purpose of the study was to find out the relevance of Big Data in corporate governance and investigates about the role and reasons behind adopting this technique in various government schemes. The data was collected from the 393 respondents of IT companies through a pre-tested and a structured questionnaire. Thematic analysis, descriptive statistics and factor analysis were used to explain the factors needed to identify transparency and enhanced efficiency & accountability by big data adoption. It was found there were an explosion of big data in the corporate governance and various activities of the government which could be highly relevant.

INTRODUCTION

According to IBM, Big data is a broad term for data sets which contains data from everywhere such as posts to social media sites, digital pictures, sensors used to gather climate information and videos and purchase transaction records etc. While Big Data Analytics s the process of examining and analyzing

DOI: 10.4018/978-1-4666-9649-5.ch003

the large amount of data and getting useful information that can be used to make better decisions. In order to carry out the research, particular IT industry and employees of various IT companies have been targeted because they were aware about the role and benefits of Big Data so that they can provide better information regarding to implementation of this technology in various functions of government and companies as well. The present study tries to find out the relevancy of Big Data technology in day to day operations of government agencies and companies (Johnstone, 2004). In order to better understand the concept and roles of this technology various examples have been taken. The rationale behind to selecting these two topics was to understand the benefits of Big Data in overcome various issues faced by government and other enterprises due to inadequate and absence of centralize system. In addition, present research emphasizes on the various tangible benefits such as enhanced corporate reporting, centralize storage of people data, improved governance procedure and their limitations, increasing transparency in their functioning and disclosure of information in an appropriate manner etc. Besides that, report tries to establish relation between Big Data technologies and corporate governance and role of this technology in performing various functions of government agencies in a quick manner.

Concept of Corporate Governance and Big Data

Corporate governance is considered a joint effort of all the concern parties including stakeholders, government, general public, professional, service providers and corporate bodies. Often organizations tend to globalize their business while at the same time intends survive and better compete with their competitor (Robinson, 2005). After the Big corporate scandals, engulfing the corporate world, corporate governance has become central to most of the companies. So that the investors and concerned people have started demanding organizations to implement rigorous corporate governance practices in order to achieve better return on their investment with increasing transparency and reduces cost. (IDC's, 2010) Suggested Big Data technologies as a new generation of technologies and architectures designed to economically extract value from large volumes of a wide variety of data by enabling high-velocity capture, discovery, and/or analysis. A series of Vs described the dimensions of big data and their linked with corporate governance activities (Desouza, 2014) like

- **Volume:** According to survey report of IBM, each day, 2.5 quintillion bytes of data are created and it can be said that size is indeed one important dimension that affects processing techniques and working of enterprises. Government agencies and corporate enterprises like, telecom providers can use Big Data technology for different purposes such as billing, monthly processing cycle and performing audit or legal action within stipulated time (Tallon, 2013).
- **Variety:** In digital era, varieties of information are present in many forms such as usage of text, video, images, tweets, apps, online collaboration, and social media etc. With help of Big Data technology, firms can access behaviour, preferences, and interests related information about their customers to derive new insights.
- **Velocity:** Due to rate of generated and consumed information and processing of information flowing at a rapid rate features of Big Data, enterprises could be able to automating the collection and analysis of customers and employees data in order to reduce fraud and inadequacy (Usha,2013). While on the other side, Volatility and Viscosity characteristics of Big Data would be beneficial for companies in terms of overcome resistance to flow of data and data storage in a safe and secure manner.

Background of the Study

The study emphasizes on the main reasons which motivates government and corporate agencies to implement Big Data technology in their business functions. According to Rijmenam government services or the public sector are facing various social frauds, managing large of data and many more. According to the UK free market think thank Policy Exchange, by using public Big Data more effectively, UK government could save up to £33 billion a year. Big Data could be helpful to control frauds, financial scandals, business inefficiencies and process inadequacy occurring in issues such as frauds, financial scandals, business inefficiencies and process inadequacy occurring in business (Rijmenam, n.d.). According to Helms, the major role of Big Data in Fraud Detection and Financial Market Analysis can be understood with help of example. Federal agencies and non-federal organizations of UK are emphasizing on developing and applying big data strategies in order to analyze massive amounts of unstructured data in the form of disability claims. In addition, after implemented this technique, the Social Security Administration (SSA) is now able to better identifying suspected fraudulent claims and recreate the decision making process effectively (Saran, 2014). The present study intends to understand the enhanced transparency and efficiency & accountability due to Big Data adoption in CG activities and role of Big Data in the various government ambitious schemes.

Aim and Objective of the Study

The main aim of the study is to evaluate the impact of Big Data in various corporate governance activities. The following were the objective framed for the study

- To understand the concept of Big Data and corporate governance
- To investigate roles and benefits of Big Data in government activities
- To identify the factors related to transparency disclosure that would be improve through uses of Big Data in Corporate governance.
- To identify the factors related to efficiency & accountability through the adoption of Big Data in Corporate governance.

LITERATURE REVIEW

This section has been conducted to understand the concept of Big Data, corporate governance and roles of this technique in increasing transparency and accountability of various business functions of companies.

Corporate Governance and Big Data

Council (2008) describes corporate governance refers as the processes and structures in which the business and affairs of the company are directed and managed. Good corporate governance enhances the company's long-term sustainable performance, long-term value creation and enhanced contribution in economic growth. Corporate governance included a much more sophisticated structure for improving decision-making and creating avenues for shareholder engagement. These good corporate governance techniques includes improvements in boards and compensated, how management is chosen and compensated, how much information is available to the investors and the community at large, how companies identify and analyze risks including the disclosure of these risks, providing for shareholder voting on board election and management compensation issues. (Gartner, 2010) explored that Big Data had the potential to add value; companies were using business intelligence and data mining tools to improve efficiency, spot new opportunities, provide the corporate world with better services, and predict future patterns of behavior. Big data was an evolving concept that referred to the growth of data and how it could be used to optimize business processes, create customer value, and mitigate risks. By using big data analytics solutions, businesses and governments could analyze huge amounts of data within few seconds and minutes to reveal previously unseen patterns, sentiments, timely disclosure reports and customer intelligence etc.

Cause and Facts of Implementing Big Data Technologies in Corporate Governance Activities

According to e-skill UK (2013), in order to solve business problems, most of the leading enterprises and government agencies turn to various Big Data technologies such as Hadoop, NoSQL, and stream computing etc. Although Hadoop is a powerful analytics platform and it is used to provide meaning to key business terms. According to Adoption and Employment Trends, 2012-2017, around one in seven (14 per cent) organisations in the UK with 100 or more staff (larger firms) have implemented big data analytics to analyse huge amounts of data in seconds and minutes and make better and faster decisions within stipulated time. As per Saran (2014), in order to analyse corporate tax, HM Revenue & Customs (HMRC) is focusing towards use of open source technologies including Hadoop ans NoSQL big data engine. According to Konrad (2013), Hadoop, SAP HANA and Business Intelligence are the three main pillars of Big Data. BI solution is beneficial for the traditional enterprises where business applications like ERP or CRM systems have used. By using SAP Business Objects (SAP BO) or an MS SQL server, business enterprises can access information and improve corporate reporting. In addition, these tools would be helpful for the companies in terms of improving communication and coordination of enterprise with their shareholders and employees as well (Konrad, 2013). SAP HANA tool would be beneficial for the government and stakeholders of the companies in the context of analyzing structured big data in real time, framing better accounting policies and timely disclosure of information to the people in an appropriate manner. While on the other side, to process extremely high volumes of structured and unstructured data, enterprises can use can use Hadoop and not only SQL technologies (NoSQL). By using these technologies, government can collect data first and later analyze it on the basis of targeted queries. However, enterprises should take care of some points during selection of Big Data tools such as cost (license, implementation and on-going), ease of use, support Data Policies, Standards, and Processes and data governance metrics etc. In such kind of situation, Big Data technology could play a crucial role because it provides facility of store huge amount of data in one central location with reducing errors and inefficiencies. Big Data technologies will enable stakeholders and other officials of companies to have access to the most up-to-date information from a centralized location such as company current position, profits & sales figure and challenges faced by enterprise at the workplace etc. By accessing massive big data sets and verifying information available, corporate companies would be able to monitor and control over financial frauds and scams kinds of activities (IBM Redbook, 2014). Big Data technology would be able to contribute to the transparency, accountability and build trust among people through stimulating the free-flowing of information. Big Data provided solutions would be helpful in the development of various corporate governance strategies like, transparent disclosure of report, improve communication & coordination, better decision making, control over unethical activities, accountability, information dissemination & performance management, enhance productivity and profitability of government etc. Big data could provide a game changing opportunity for corporate governance. Big Data technology had increase the demand for consumption and agility in business decisions - all indicating that the existing management functions were not sufficient and improvement was needed. It accelerated the business process by providing risk assessment & management, transparency, accountability, data management, effective business process management and quick decision making services which was an important aspect of corporate governance. Big data could be utilized in ways that have the potential to transform government service effectively, secure delivery of personalized and streamlined services that accurately and specifically meet individual's needs in a better way(Slugpost, 2014). Big Data in corporate governance could work as a quality control discipline for assessing, managing, using, improving, monitoring, maintaining, and protecting organizational information.

Major Reasons of Adopting Big Data in Government Functions

The main reasons which are motivating government authorities and corporate world to implement Big Data technology in their day to day business functions can be defined as follow. A lot of government tax agencies and many enterprise store personal data of people in different locations. If any change arises in the any policy or regulations then over and over again, people have to complete new forms with information which agencies already have. It is very hectic task for the people and enterprises also because it enhances chance of raise ambiguity and error also. In developing country like India and many more have no centralize system for managing data of their citizens and due to absence of this kind of system, personal data of people are stored in different locations (Lu and Han, n.d.). Even, for government also it is difficult to manage massive amount of data. In cases of launching any scheme or changing existing policies, over and over again, people have to complete new forms with information which agencies already have. At the present time around 42% of the population of the India is out of banking system and they depend on the moneylenders for the loans. Slow down the process of roll-out in the distant part of the country, lack of accountability in cash transfers, high magnitude of corruption in distribution of pension & direct cash scheme, raise funds for the insurance, high logistical & distribution cost and Gender gap in banking (by 2012, 1000 bank accounts were open with the name of the men while 394 were open in the women name), lengthier claim processing process, handle problem related to manage multiple bank account of an individual person, logistic and financial implication to setting up ATM machines in the wide geographical area of the country, successful implementation of KYC scheme, technology related issues (prefer offline transaction and scalability of campaign) and database maintenance (Insurance transaction linked with transaction history of the accountholders) would be creating hurdle in the successful implementation of the mega scheme (Slugpost, 2014).

Recently Indian PM had introduced PMJDY, Pension scheme, Pradhan Mantri Jeevan Jyoti Yojana (life insurance) Pradhan Mantri Suraksha Bima Yojana (accident insurance), and Atal Pension Yojana relating to insurance and pension. However, the major issues behind implementing these ambitious schemes are managing records of citizens and targeting the poor and unorganised sector who are neither covered by any form of insurance or get pension from any other sources. In order to provide benefits of these schemes to needed people, it is essential for the Indian government to check the complete background of the people such as, occupation, financial condition, family structure, income level and identify people who are already beneficiaries of any other schemes etc. In the context of implementing these strategies various issues including lack of integration between different departments, corruption, highly dependability on traditional system and absence of centralize database system can create hurdle (Sunil, 2012). The Dutch and Swedish governments pre-fills the annual tax forms with information of their citizens such as personal data and bank account information to reduce processing time. However, this technique provides temporary solutions regarding storage and usage of data.

The US federal government collects data and tries to get sufficient value out of it in order o accomplish their missions efficiently and effectively. Big Data technology helps them to overcome budgetary issues, support the collection and storage of large amounts of data through effective optimization of resources (SAS White paper, 2013). For example, In order to support open data and increase transparency, Obama administration has created a data-driven decision-making policy. Open-source initiatives like Hadoop and MapReduce provide opportunity to government agencies to combine, cleanse and transform huge quantities of data, robust reporting and flexible information sharing via Web and mobile devices in a safe and secure manner. US government agency uses this technology in different areas such as retirement, life insurance, long term care and health insurance etc. By effective use of data analysis technique, government of US was able to audit on more than 400 health insurance companies and 9 million federal employees and their families. It provides better opportunity to their citizens in order to analyze and share claims information with speed it never had before (SAS White paper, 2013). Securities Exchange Commission is using various types of Big Data analysis techniques such as natural language processors and network analytics in order to monitor financial market activities and identify nefarious trading activity in a proper manner (Rijmenam, n.d.). Apart from this, the need for big data strategies in the public sector can be determined with help of the example of U.S. Department of Homeland Security (DHS) because this department uses Big Data strategy for the purpose of increasing interoperability and integration of data across numerous government agencies in a safe and secure manner. However, along with the collection of huge amount of data, it is essential for government and other enterprise to maintain privacy and information of people must be protected.

Challenges arise in implementation of Big Data in government schemes and provide solutions to overcome those challenges

In such kind of circumstances, proper implementation of Big Data technologies including Hadoop and No–SQL could play an important role (NESSI, 2012). According to Open Government Data (OGD) Platform India, by using Big Data tool and OGD platform, government would be able to increase transparency in their functioning, online publish datasets, documents, services, tools and applications and to interact and share their zeal and views with citizens of the country.

Major Roles of Big Data Technologies in Corporate Governance and Successful Implementation of Various Government Schemes

In modern era, companies can improve their performance relative to competitors, on the basis of the real time collection of data from various sources and analyzing them in order to know radically more about their businesses so that better decision could be taken with stipulated time. Apart from this, organizations and government agencies can minimize tax fraud and or social security fraud through effective use of this technique. Big Data use pattern detection algorithm to identify suspicious transactions occurring in real-time which provides additional insights in the taxpaying behaviour of enterprise and citizens also. Besides that, firms and agencies can use demographic or social data and statistical parameters to see whether or not those outlier cases really perform fraudulent actions so that financial scandals, business inefficiencies and process inadequacy can then be monitored more closely. For example, the Las Vegas police use algorithm in order to access historical data sets and a broad range of other data sets to understand when and where violent crime is happening or is about to happen (SAS White paper,2013). For implementing various kinds of ambitious schemes, government would be required adequate amount of funds and for that firm will take helps of banks, public and private limited companies of same country and other countries. In addition, to support and implement government schemes, financial enterprises and stakeholders will contribute from their side according to their capabilities. In such situation, it is very essential for the government to provide better disclosure of information about usage of funds, provide return on investment and timely communicate with their investors and other persons who associated with the schemes and invested money. In such kind of circumstance, Big Data could play a crucial role in order to increase transparency in the functioning, overcome business inefficiencies and process inadequacy through monitoring these activities more closely. E.g. Jan lakshmi financial service has been taken Big Data initiative and done agreement with IBM (for 6 year and 400 crore rs.) to smooth functioning of core banking services as well as spread and monitor micro-finance services across the India in an appropriate manner(Tewari, 2014). By adopting Big Data technology, government would be able to successful implementation of mega scheme and will able to take and provide several advantages of these schemes to their citizens such as reduce corruption on the part of the bank employees, increase invest rate, improve financial literacy, encouraging people to invest, free insurance facility, employment opportunities, economic growth, facility to receive their subsidies from the same account, improving national figures (penetration of banking and insurance services), augment national saving, focus on the BPL families and ambitious target.

Impact of the Big Data in Corporate Governance Activities

Moore (2014) describe the impact of big data on present IT technology and the data center, restructuring of the data center, including the move to more converged IT infrastructures, alterations in data center traffic patterns and changes in the basic economics of storage. Vladimirov (2014) in his study showed how big data analysis could pushing the IT sector in the right direction. The results of this study could help create the framework for big data's future, making it easier for companies to better utilize the data. Big data has far-reaching capabilities, and as more organizations explore these possibilities, the need for safety and security could only likely only increase. Infosys (2013) in one of their reports concluded that speed and outcomes were the two biggest priorities for realizing the desired value from Big Data adoption. Federal, state and local government agencies agree that Big Data could save 10% or more from their annual budgets. Ang-Hoon Kim (2013) focused how Big Data could be helpful for government to provide services to their citizens and overcome national challenges (such as rising health care costs, job creation, natural disasters, and terrorism), describing the uses of Big Data efficiently into data management, extracting, transform, and loading data in a secure manner, identifying processes in which new technologies were used (such as Hadoop) for cleansing and organizing unstructured data in which big-data applications could be used. Panicker (2013) explored the various possibilities that Big Data could deliver with prospect to improve decision-making in critical development areas such as health care, employment, economic productivity, crime and security, natural disaster and resource management. Usha (2013) studied incorporates several guiding principles for data governance, specifically in a Big Data environment and discussed about length, a framework and an approach to data governance with

Big Data. With Big Data, governance functions would encompass data science and compliance as well. Sanal Nair (2014) studied the relationship between the firm performance and characteristics of corporate governance for selected Indian firms. It was found that the proportion of Board size and Independent Directors were positively correlated with financial performance indicating that more the number of independent directors in the board, better were the financial performance of the firm and better the firm management. Johnstone (2004) provide evidence that auditors assessed situations involving both aggressive management and inadequate corporate governance, and found that there were a relationship between assessments and auditors' planning and pricing decisions. Xiaoyue (2003) found that firms under the control of the government shareholder had lower value, poorer firm performance and weaker governance than the comparable firms under the control of a non-government shareholder; the change of the controlling shareholders was propitious to the improvement of governance effectiveness, scale economics and more professional management. The results suggested that the decreasing of state shares and the increasing controlled markets are playing an important role in improving firm reforms. Farber (2005) examined the association between the credibility of the financial reporting system and the quality of governance mechanisms. They showed that analyst followings and institutional holdings did not increase in fraud firms, suggesting that credibility was still a problem for these firms. However, the results also indicate that firms that took actions to improve governance had superior stock price performance, even after controlling for earnings performance. This suggested that investors appeared to value governance improvements. (Udi Hoitash, 2009) examined the association between corporate governance and disclosures of material weaknesses (MW) in internal control over financial reporting. The results showed that material Weakness disclosure was associated with designating a financial expert without accounting experience, or designating multiple financial experts. It was concluded that board and audit committee characteristics were associated with internal control quality. (AustralianGovernment, 2013) in one of their studies used to the opportunities provided by Big Data in government sector which included improved service delivery that could cover areas as diverse as remote medical diagnostics, major infrastructure management, personalized social security benefits delivery, improved first responder and emergency services and reduction of fraudulent or criminal activity across. The study also focused on challenges faced by Big Data in the government sector like data management and sharing, privacy, security & trust, skills and technology advancement. (EricSweden, 2013) explored that adoption of Big data carried many, big implications – for better and for worse. State government should be preparing for the potential of big data and ensure current investment in technology allows for future leverage of big data capabilities. They suggested that by build the capability to exploit Big Data, as well as other data resources, state governments must mature its data management discipline within its enterprise architecture program to prepare for governance, management and harvesting of big data information assets. (Tallon, 2013) discussed how data governance practices that maintained a balance between value creation and risk exposure is the new organizational imperative for unlocking competitive advantage and maximizing value from the application of big data. (Parmar, 2013) focused on some of the application of the Big Data in the field of Government, Public sector and the society . The result showed that Big Data could be really helpful if the data or record share were analyzed carefully and if the statistics could be used in a right way, it can really help developing countries like India and china. (Mountain, 2012) faced several unique market challenges and many of the same market challenges as other information management vendors servicing the government faced like Big Data marketplace, including Demonstrating leadership in the transition from information management to Big Data, offering competitive, differentiated solutions portfolios and security issues (Sunil Soares, 2012) framed a sample set of questions to assess the maturity of the big data in governances. He defined eleven categories included Business outcomes, Organizational structures and awareness, stewardship, data risk management, policy data quality management, information lifecycle management, information security and privacy, data architecture, classification and metadata, audit information logging and reporting to assess the maturity of big data in governance. (Soares, 2012) studied the Big data governance programs and issues that were faced by information governance initiatives and showed the expanded framework for information governance into various fields including Metadata governance, Master data governance, Reference data governance and Big Data governance. (Wim Van Grembergen, 2007) studied that the pervasive use of technology had created a critical dependency on IT that calls for a specific focus on IT governance. Implementing information technology governance: models, practices and cases presented an insight gained through literature reviews and case studies and provided practical guidance for organizations that want to start implementing IT governance or improve the existing governance models, and provided a detailed set of IT governance structures, processes, and relational mechanisms that can be leveraged to implement IT governance in practice. (Robinson, 2005) described the role of IT in governance of functions such as value creation (distilling company's mission and strategic direction into business needs for IT applications), value delivery (formal project management methodology and system development life cycle), value preservation (integrated control and risk management program), resource management, performance management (capability maturity model, balanced scorecard, Six Sigma), and oversight. Result showed that positive impact of IT on governance.

Performance Measurement of Big Data in Corporate Governance Activities

Commercial Hadoop big data-styled analysis systems are now being tested and used within the enterprises. These kinds of tools will be helpful for the companies and government agencies to measure performance of Big Data technologies in terms of directly compare the price performance across different offerings. Using the benchmark, overall performance and price-performance of systems can be measured (Lu & Han, n.d.). Transaction Processing Performance Council (TPC) developed rule to measure performance of Big Data system and the energy efficiency of the system. In addition, it also provides opportunity to shareholders of company to test the performance of transaction processing and database systems. Apart from this, performance of Big Data technologies can be measured in terms of velocity, volume, variety and veracity. Through generating benchmarking tests from operations and patterns, organizations would be able to conduct the investigations on big benchmarks.

Research Gap

From the above review it could be found that through their existed an extensive literature on corporate governance issues and importance of Big Data but various gaps exists in the relationship between big data adoption and corporate governance principles. No study has been conducted earlier that tried to understand the transparency and enhance efficiency due to Big Data adoption and hence the following study tries to explain the factor that are important to understand the enhanced than transparency and efficiency and accountability due to Big Data adoption. It also focused on the importance and requirement of the Big Data technology in new emerging government schemes.

RESEARCH METHODOLOGY

A survey of respondents from IT companies with different educational qualifications, designations and experience related to IT was conducted. Primary data were collected using a structured questionnaire and Secondary data was collected from different published sources. In the survey, researcher was asked question from the respondents of IT companies regarding to benefits of implementation of Big Data and related techniques in various schemes. By asking this question from respondents, investigator would be able to better insight into data management problems and solutions provided by Big Data to overcome those kinds of issues in an effective manner. The data was collected from the employees from IT companies, through a structured questionnaire. A total of 750 questionnaires were administered of which only 457 respondent. After filtration we ended with 393 questionnaires completely filled in all respect and hence only those 393 responses were used for the study. Purposive sampling technique was employed in the study because sample size has been chose by considering specific population in order to attain aim and objectives of the study in an appropriate manner. As per the given case scenario, survey method was used for collecting large amount of data from respondents in order to understand their views and opinions about benefits of Big Data. The other reason for selecting this technique was that investigator administered data remotely via online, email and telephone.

KMO statistic test is applied to measure sampling adequacy and it shows partial correlation for each pair of variables in the factor analysis. Cronbach alpha is a coefficient of reliability and it is a measure of internal consistency (Hartas, 2015). The validity of the data was listed using the KMO Bark cett test for study and the values were focused to be greater than 0.5 indicated the questions to be valid for the study. The cronbach alpha values were calculated for the responses and % was found they all lied between .71-.91 and hence the data was considered highly reliable for the study. The study was divided into different sections .The first section tried to understand the demographic profile of the respondents .The second section tried to study variables related to transparency and enhanced those variable needed to determine transparency. The third section tried to understand that enhanced efficiency and accountability in IT firms due to Big Data adoption exploration factor. Analysis was conducted in order to explore the factors needed to see enhanced transparency and efficiency & accountability .Descriptive like mean and standard deviation were calculated to understand the pattern of the responses. Respondents were requested to submit assessments based on a Five -point Likert scale (Helms,n.d.). All items were measured by responses in agreement to the relevance with statements, ranging from 1= strongly Disagree to 5= Strongly Agree. Descriptive statistics and Factor analysis were used to extract the factors needed to identify the potential of big data in corporate governance and to understand the influence of various demographic on the variables selected for the study.

DATA ANALYSIS AND FINDIGS

Theme 1: Demographic Profile of the respondents

Findings: In order to carry out the research, particular IT industry and employees of various IT companies have been targeted because they were aware about the role and benefits of Big Data. Particular industry and IT company employees were selected in order to get better information regarding to implementation of this technology in various functions of government and companies as well. Most of the respondents were male (56.7%), within the age group of 31-50 years (44.8%). Respondent's educational qualification were Graduate (49.1%) and PG & above were (47.1%), majority of the respondents were having the designation of IT executive (48.6%) and most of them were having an experience of 4-7 years (50.6%) in their profession.

Theme 2: Tangible benefits achieved through Big Data initiatives

Findings: Respondents across different demographics had different perceptions towards the tangibility of the benefits achieved through the adoption of various Big Data technology at the workplace. Most of the respondents were replied that after adopting Big Data technologies like Hadoop and No-SQL, enterprises would be able to take various tangible benefits such as enhanced corporate reporting, improved governance disclosures and their limitations, better defined accounting policies, enhanced credibility of disclosure better information discrimination and coordination etc. Big Data would enhance transparency in the entire business procedures and increased accountability of employees so that they will follow strictly guidelines of government and companies policies in order to produce best result at the workplace. The result of cross-tabulation and view of authors regarding to use of Big Data technologies in various corporate governance activities were similar. Managers of companies were agreed with the fact that Big Data technique would be beneficial for the organizations in terms of improving governance disclosures and corporate reporting. While finance executives of companies were stated that Hadoop and No SQL techniques would be beneficial for the enterprise were satisfied with the fact that by using Big Data, firms and their manager would be able better implement accounting policies and enhancing credibility of disclosures. Hence, it can be said that by using these tools, companies would be able to improve communication and coordination of them with their shareholders and employees in an appropriate manner.

Theme 3: Role of Big Data in various corporate governance and government activities

Findings: Most of the IT respondents who having 4-7 years of IT experience and done their graduation were agreed with the fact that Big Data would play a vital role in improvement the performance of the various government schemes such as PMJDY, Pension scheme, Pradhan Mantri Jeevan Jyoti Yojana (life insurance) Pradhan Mantri Suraksha Bima Yojana (accident insurance), and Atal Pension Yojana etc. Companies can improve their performance relative to competitors, on the basis of the real time collection of data from various sources and analyzing them in order to know radically more about their businesses so that better decision could be taken with stipulated time. They replied that Hadoop and SAP HANA techniques of Big Data would be more beneficial for the government in terms of managing CASA account and maintaining centralize database and transaction history of the accountholders with solving multiple bank account opening problems. Along with that respondents had positive perception towards the role of Big Data in the Better execution of KYC scheme & solve multiple bank account problems and Establish cost effective platform for execution of banking operations in an appropriate manner. It will also help in enhance accountability and transparency in transactions so that magnitude of corruption in distribution of pension & direct cash scheme would be reduced. Apart from these benefits, most of the IT employees agreed with the fact that by using Big Data tool, Indian government would be able to increase transparency in their functioning, online publish datasets, documents, services and to interact and share their zeal and views with the citizens of the country in a proper manner. Big Data would enable stakeholders and other authorize person of companies to have access to the most up-to-date information from a centralized location such as company current position, profits & sales figure and challenges faced by enterprise at the workplace etc. By accessing massive big data sets and verifying information available, corporate companies would be able to monitor and control over financial frauds and scams kinds of activities in an appropriate manner.

Factor Analysis: This test was applied to identify the factors that would be beneficial for the companies and government agencies in order to increase transparency and accountability in their day to day operations through adopting Big Data technologies.

Transparency Related to Big Data Adoption

Findings: Factor analysis was run in order to condense the variables selected. All these variables along with their description are shown in Table 1. The reliability test was conducted and the cronbach's alpha lied between 0.71 to 0.91 indicating that the responses to be considered reliable for the study. Further to test the sampling, KMO measure of sampling adequacy was computed which is found to be 0.795 indicating the sample to be good enough for the study. Moreover the overall significance of correlation matrices was tested with Bartlett Test (approx. Chi-square = 2167.936 and significant at 0.000) at 78 df which provided a good support for the validity of data for factor analysis. The results of factor analysis over the 13 factors showed that there were 2 key factors, which were determined by clubbing the similar variables & ignoring the rest, which were considered being the most important factors for determining transparency related to Big Data adoption in Corporate Governance. Table 2 shows the respective percentage of variance of all these factors derived from factor analysis.

Table 1. Variable relating to transparency

T1	Big data would be helpful to provide accurate and clear information to all concerned stakeholders
T2	Big data would helps in improving business environment and transparency
T3	Big data would delivers information to right persons at the right time in a proper manner
T4	Applying Big data in corporate governance would better result in disclosure of executives pay and control over fraudulent activities
T5	Big data would provides facility of high quality of disclosure including segment reporting
T6	Big data would be helpful to control over business inefficiencies and process inadequacies
T7	Big Data would be beneficial for the government to achieve excellence at all levels.
T8	Effective monitoring possible only by using Big Data in Corporate governance
T9	Substantive disclosure of all significant aspects of remuneration policies would be accurate with help of Big Data
T10	Big Data would cast a light on preventing financial crime activities causing a change in behavior
T11	Big data would help control unethical conduct involving financial corruptions crisis, fraud and misappropriations
T12	Big data would be helpful in fair and equitable sharing of gains of productivity improvements
T13	Big Data would encourage the release of public sector information (PSI) consistent with all privacy and security legislative instruments and guidance

Table 2. Descriptive table

	Mean	Std. Deviation
T1	3.77	1.106
T2	3.65	1.134
T3	3.62	1.128
T4	3.61	1.169
T5	3.70	1.091
T6	3.56	1.016
T7	3.82	1.111
T8	3.74	1.065
T9	3.80	.930
T10	3.91	.892
T11	3.63	1.127
T12	3.76	1.014
T13	3.78	.921

Findings: The mean of responses was highest with respect to Big Data casting a light on preventing financial crime activities causing a change in behavior and Big Data being beneficial for the government to achieve excellence at all levels. The standard deviation was highest in case of applying Big Data in corporate governance better disclosure of executives pay and control over fraud activities and it would be helpful in improving business environment and transparency.

Findings: It was observed from Table 3 that only 2 factors had Eigen value more than one and accordingly we proceeded with these factors. The total variance explained by these factors (1 and 2) independently were 30.441% and 21.072% of variance, whereas the cumulative variance explained by all these factors is 51.513 percent and rest of the variance was due to the factors which were beyond the scope of the study.

Findings: Table 4 shows the highlighted factor loading which are correlated with the factors corresponding to that factor loading. Higher the factor loading, stronger is the correlation between the factors and the statement. On the basis of the rotated component matrix the factor extraction table was prepared which is as under.

Findings: Table 5's stated factors are in the order of degree of importance i.e. factor 1 is more important than factor 2. The Factor 1 has the highest variance 30.441 as compared to factor 2 whose variance was 21.072. Hence it is found that BDIP and EMCS are the factors needed to understand enhanced the transparency of Big Data in Corporate governance.

Efficiency and Accountability Related to Big Data Adoption

Findings: Factor analysis was run in order to condense the variables selected. All these variables along with their description are shown in Table 6. The reliability test was conducted and the cronbach alpha was found to lie between 0.71 to 0.91 indicating that the responses to be considered reliable for the study. Further to test the sampling, KMO measure of sampling adequacy was computed

Table 3. Shows the total variance explained by various factors

Component	Initial Eigen values			Extraction Sums of Squared Loadings			Rotation Sums of Squared Loadings		
	Total	% of Variance	Cumulative %	Total	% of Variance	Cumulative %	Total	% of Variance	Cumulative %
1	5.365	41.270	41.270	5.365	41.270	41.270	3.957	30.441	30.441
2	1.332	10.243	51.513	1.332	10.243	51.513	2.739	21.072	51.513
3	.956	7.350	58.863						
4	.895	6.886	65.750						
5	.812	6.246	71.995						
6	.797	6.132	78.127						
7	.678	5.212	83.339						
8	.552	4.243	87.582						
9	.509	3.914	91.496						
10	.409	3.146	94.641						
11	.265	2.037	96.678						
12	.253	1.949	98.627						
13	.178	1.373	100.000						

Table 4. Rotated component matrix

Variables	1	2
T1	**0.628**	0.132
T2	**0.763**	0.298
T3	**0.684**	0.217
T4	**0.750**	0.182
T5	**0.616**	0.304
T6	**0.621**	0.165
T7	**0.722**	0.092
T8	0.467	**0.470**
T9	**0.485**	0.474
T10	0.117	**0.767**
T11	0. 266	**0.800**
T12	0.084	**0.738**
T13	0.346	**0.455**

Table 5. Factor extraction table shows variables in each factor with the corresponding loading and percentage of variance

Factors	Variance	Loading
F1(Better disclosure improves performance) (BDIP)		
T1	30.441	0.628
T2		0.763
T3		0.684
T4		0.750
T5		0.616
T6		0.621
T7		0.722
T9		0.485
F2 (Effective monitoring & controls system) (EMCS)		
T8	21.072	0.470
T10		0.767
T11		0.800
T12		0.738
T13		0.455

Table 6. Variable relating to efficiency and accountability

EA1	Better market framework could be encouraging freedom of competitions
EA2	Big data will improve public faith and confidence in organizations by providing information on time
EA3	To identify and assess the relevant requirements of all stakeholders with proper communication
EA4	Big data minimizing or eliminating ambiguity work and improve in government performance
EA5	Establish process performance baselines to enable improvement efforts
EA6	Big Data brings with it the ability to predict results and model scenarios based on the data
EA7	Big Data helps to measure and routinely disclose audited, quantitative data concerning the financial position and performance of publicly held firms in well planned manner
EA8	Big data provide detailed and error free faster financial reporting facility
EA9	Big data monitor over management performance or corporate control in better way
EA10	Big data create a balance between the economic and social goals of government in efficient way
EA11	By proper maintaining of large amount of data, government frame effective policies that are beneficial for citizens

which is found to be 0.730 indicating the sample to be good enough for the study. Moreover the overall significance of correlation matrices was tested with Bartlett Test (approx. Chi-square 1498.715 and significant at 0.000) at 55 df which provided a good support for the validity of data for factor analysis. The results of factor analysis over the 11 factors showed that there were 3 key factors, which were determined by clubbing the similar variables & ignoring the rest, which were considered being most important factors for determining efficiency & accountability related to Big Data adoption in Corporate Governance. Table 7 shows the respective percentage of variance of all these factors derived from factor analysis.

Findings: The mean of responses was highest (EA4=3.87) with respect to Big Data bringing with it the ability to predict results and model scenarios based on data. The standard deviation was highest

Table 7. Descriptive table

	Mean	Std. Deviation
EA1	3.81	.978
EA2	3.53	1.085
EA3	3.84	.897
EA4	3.68	1.038
EA5	3.76	1.081
EA6	3.87	.968
EA7	3.78	1.158
EA8	3.81	.985
EA9	3.64	1.274
EA10	3.59	.965
EA11	3.84	1.061

Table 8. Total variance explained by various factors

Component	Initial Eigen values			Extraction Sums of Squared Loadings			Rotation Sums of Squared Loadings		
	Total	% of Variance	Cumulative %	Total	% of Variance	Cumulative %	Total	% of Variance	Cumulative %
1	4.220	38.362	38.362	4.220	38.362	38.362	2.652	24.107	**24.107**
2	1.381	12.552	50.915	1.381	12.552	50.915	2.188	19.895	**44.001**
3	1.078	9.798	60.713	1.078	9.798	60.713	1.838	16.712	**60.713**
4	.917	8.335	69.048						
5	.740	6.725	75.773						
6	.717	6.521	82.294						
7	.543	4.936	87.230						
8	.464	4.217	91.447						
9	.410	3.728	95.175						
10	.330	3.000	98.175						
11	.201	1.825	100.000						

(EA7=1.158) in case that Big Data monitor over management performance or corporate control in better way and disclose routinely audited, quantitative data and improve performance of publicly held firms in well planned manner.

Findings: It was observed from Table 8 that only 3 factors had Eigen value more than one and so accordingly we proceeded with these factors. The total variance explained by these factors (1,2 and 3) independently were 24.107%, 19.895 and 16.712% of variance, whereas the cumulative variance explained by all these factors is 60.713% and rest of the variance was due to the factors which were beyond the scope of the study.

Findings: Table 9 shows the highlighted factor loading which are correlated with the factors corresponding to that factor loading. Higher the factor loading, stronger is the correlation between the factors and the statement. On the basis of the rotated component matrix the factor extraction table was prepared, presented in Table 10.

Findings: Table 10's stated factors are in the order of degree of importance i.e. Factor 1 is more important than factor 2 and factor 2 is more important than factor 3. Factor 1 has the highest variance was 24.107 as compare to factor 2 whose variance was 19.895 and factor 3 whose variance was 16.712. Hence it is found that EC, PTI and EDM are the factors needed to understand enhanced the efficiency & accountability of Big Data in Corporate governance. Hence, from the primary and secondary data collection methods, it is cleared that Big Data would be advantageous for the companies and government in order to carry out of various government ambitious schemes in an appropriate manner.

Table 9. Rotated component matrix

	1	2	3
EA1	**0.649**	0.256	-0.1027
EA2	0.181	**0.764**	0.182
EA3	**0.711**	0.222	0.082
EA4	**0.706**	-0.260	0.362
EA5	**0.739**	0.197	0.303
EA6	-0.037	0.402	**0.554**
EA7	0.139	**0.744**	0.273
EA8	**0.564**	0.488	0.038
EA9	0.470	**0.580**	0.190
EA10	0.289	0.042	**0.729**
EA11	0.065	0.303	**0.785**

Table 10. Factor extraction table shows the variables in each factor with the corresponding loading and percentage of variance

Factors	Variance	Loading
F1 Enhance communication (EC)		
EA1	24.107	0.649
EA3		0.711
EA4		0.706
EA5		0.739
EA8		0.564
F2 Provide timely information(PTI)		
EA2	19.895	0.764
EA7		0.744
EA9		0.580
F3 Efficient data management (EDM)		
EA6	16.712	0.554
EA10		0.729
EA11		0.785

CONCLUSION AND MANAGEMENT IMPLICATIONS

The study concluded various factors including IT experience, designation, tangible benefits achieved through Big Data initiatives, transparency related disclosures and the constraints that affect the acceptance of Big Data in the corporate world. Tangible benefits did accrue through Big Data adoption in the corporate governance activities. Hence it could be concluded that better disclosures improved performance and an effective monitoring & control system were important factors needed to identify the transparency related to Big Data in Corporate governance. In respect to the efficiency & accountability related to Big Data in Corporate governance factors needed were enhanced communication, provision of timely information and efficient data management. It was found that Big Data had a pivotal role to play in improving corporate governance practices, because critical business processes were usually automated and directors relied on the Information provided by IT systems for their decision making.

The following study tried to identify the factors related to transparency and efficiency & accountability that would be improved through the use of Big Data. It is considered that there is an explosion of big data in the corporate governance which could be highly relevant. The important factors that contributed towards the transparency were better disclosures that improved performance and effective monitoring & controls system. The factors that determined that determined the efficiency & accountability were enhanced communication, provision of timely information and efficient data management. From the result of the statistical test, it was found that better disclosure and effective monitoring and control systems were the factors that were needed to increase the transparency and accountability in various schemes of the government. Big Data technologies performance can be measured in terms of velocity, volume, variety and veracity. Through generating benchmarking tests from operations and patterns, organizations would be able to conduct the investigations on big benchmarks.

This study could be helpful to identify the impact of Big Data in corporate governance. Big Data has the capacity to enable corporate institutions to establish an effective risk assessment & management system; delivers scalable, flexible & responsive infrastructure to the organization; improve public faith and confidence in organizations by providing information on time and enhances organization productivity & profitability. Big Data could be helpful to control frauds, financial scandals, business inefficiencies and process inadequacy occurring in business. Big Data provides facility related to proper maintaining of large amount of data, improving business environment & transparency and providing accurate and clear information to all concerned stakeholders at the right time in a proper manner that would be beneficial. Federal agencies and non-federal organizations of UK are emphasizing on developing and applying big data strategies in order to analyze massive amounts of unstructured data in the form of disability claims. In addition, it enables stakeholders and other officials of companies to have access to the most up-to-date information from a centralized location such as company current position, profits & sales figure and challenges faced by enterprise at the workplace etc. By accessing massive big data sets and verifying information available, corporate companies would be able to monitor and control over financial frauds and scams kinds of activities.

FUTURE RESEARCH DIRECTIONS

This study would be helpful for all types of people such as entrepreneurs, research scholars and students etc. to understand the importance of the Big Data in corporate government sector to increase the transparency and accountability in their operations. Majority of the data were collected from employees in the IT companies in functional areas or business units but not in a whole enterprise. Impact of privacy policies, security concerns, and request for consent to use personal data, Business process management and decision making could play an important role but could not be considered into the samples size. Future research could also consider the impact of other demographic variable on economic, legal, moral, ethical and social & psychological issues related to Big Data also. In addition, time and money taken in order to carry out the study were the major constraints for the investigator.

REFERENCES

Ang-Hoon Kim, S. T.-H. (2013). Big-Data Applications in the Government Sector. *Communications of the ACM, 57*, 78–85.

Australian Government. (2013, March). *Big Data Strategy*. Author.

Desouza, K. C. (2014). Realizing the Promise of Big Data: Implementing Big Data Projects. IBM center for The Business of Government. India.

e-skill, UK. (2013). *Big Data Analytics: Adoption and Employment Trends*. Retrieved from http://www.sas.com/offices/europe/uk/downloads/bigdata/eskills/eskills.pdf

Gartner. (2010). *Big data and its impact*. Garner Report.

Hartas, D. (2015). *Educational research and inquiry: Qualitative and quantitative approaches*. Bloomsbury Publishing.

Helms, J. (n.d.). *Five Examples of How Federal Agencies Use Big Data*. Retrieved from http://www.businessofgovernment.org/BigData3Blog.html

IBM. (n.d.). *Analytics: The real-world use of big data in financial services*. IBM Institute for Business.

IDC. (2010). *Big Data technologies*. IDC Report.

James Manyika, M. C. (2011). *Big data:nThe next frontier for innovation,competition and productivity*. India: McKinsey & Company.

Johnstone, J. C. (2004). Earnings Manipulation Risk, Corporate Governance Risk, and Auditors'. *Planning and Pricing Decisions, 79*, 277–304.

Konrad, R. (2013). *The three big data pillars: Hadoop, SAP HANA and business intelligence*. Retrieved from http://www.t-systems.com/news-media/the-three-big-data-pillars-hadoop-sap-hana-and-business-intelligence-bi-/1149004

Letouzé, E. (2012, May). Big Data for Development:Challenges & Opportunities. *UN Global Pulse*.

Lu, X. & Han, R. (n.d.). *On Big Data Benchmarking*. Ohio State University.

Mountain, I. (2012, October). The Impact of Big Data on Government. *IDC Government Insights*.

NESSI. (2012, December). *Big Data A New World of Opportunities*. NESSI White Paper.

Open Government Data Platform India. (2015). *Information about Open Government Data (OGD) Platform India*. Retrieved from https://data.gov.in/about-us

Panicker, R. (2013). Adoption of Big Data Technology for the Development of Developing Countries. In *Proceedings of National Conference on New Horizons in IT*.

IBM Redbook. (2014). Information *Governance Principles and Practices for a Big Data Landscape*. Retrieved from http://www.redbooks.ibm.com/redbooks/pdfs/sg248165.pdf

Rijmenam, V. (n.d.). *4 Benefits for the Public Sector When Governments Start Using Big Data*. Retrieved from https://datafloq.com/read/4-benefits-public-sector-governments-start-big-dat/171

Robinson, N. (2005). IT excellence starts with governance. *Journal of Investment Compliance*, *6*(3), 45–49. doi:10.1108/15285810510659310

Sanal Nair, D. J. (2014). Corporate governance and firm performances -An empirical evidence from the leading Indian Corporates. India.

Saran, C. (2014). *HMRC uses Hadoop to tackle corporate tax avoidance*. Retrieved from http://www.computerweekly.com/news/2240217592/HMRC-uses-Hadoop-to-tackle-corporate-tax-avoidance>

SAS White Paper. (2013). *How Governments are Using the Power of High-Performance Analytics*. Retrieved from http://www.sas.com/resources/whitepaper/wp_61955.pdf

SlugPost. (2014). *Jan Dhan Yojna –Problems and Flaws in implementation*. Retrieved on October 24, 2014 from http://indianexpress.com/article/india/india-others/jan-dhan-yojana-concern-over-scope-for-misuse-slow-roll-out-of-debit-cards/

Soares, S. (2012, April 2). Big Data: A Boon For Governance Professionals. *IBM Data Magazine*.

Sunil Soares, T. D. (2012, April 7). Big Data Governance: A Framework to Assess Maturity. *IBM Data Magazine*.

Tallon, P. (2013). Corporate Governance of Big Data: Perspectives on Value, Risk, and Cost. *IEEE Computer Society*, *46*(6), 32–38. doi:10.1109/MC.2013.155

Tewari, R. (2014). *Jan Dhan Yojna: Concern over scope for misuse, slow roll-out of debit cards*. Retrieved on October 23, 2014 Retrieved from http://slugpost.com/2014/09/04/jan-dhan-yojana-problems-flaws-implementation/

Tyagi, P. K. (2015). *Using Cross-Lagged Correlation Analysis to Derive Causal Inferences in Quasi-Experimental Marketing Research*. Springer International Publishing. doi:10.1007/978-3-319-10966-4_71

Udi Hoitash, R. H. (2009). *Corporate Governance and Internal Control over Financial Reporting: A Comparison of Regulatory Regimes*. Academic Press.

Usha. (2013). *Data Governance for Big Data Systems*. L&T Infotech.

KEY TERMS AND DEFINITIONS

Big Data: It is the IT technology that provides facility to storage large amount of the data in an effective and efficient manner.

Corporate Governance: Corporate governance is considered a joint effort of all the concern parties including stakeholders, government, general public, professional, service providers and corporate bodies.

PMJDY: Pradhan Mantri Jan Dhan Yojana

Chapter 4
Big Data and Cloud Interoperability

Ahmad Yusairi Bani Hashim
Universiti Teknikal Malaysia Melaka, Malaysia

ABSTRACT

Cloud computing provides access to the high volume of data to individuals and enterprises. Immense data analytics and mobile technologies contain useful knowledge. Data storage, security, and privacy, on the other hand, are the main issues for any organization or enterprises in the business world. Big data processing is within reach due to easy access to cloud architectures and open-source software. Now, interoperability of big data and cloud has become a necessity in this era of data-intensive world.

INTRODUCTION

Cloud Computing (CC) implements a shared computer resource with an Internet connection. In CC, the resources must be accessible on demand, and it must adhere to the concept of the delivery of computing as a service. Cloud computing provides access to the high volume of data to individuals and enterprises. Immense data analytics and mobile technologies contain useful knowledge. One of the advantages of cloud computing infrastructure is that it provides large-scale data storage, processing, and distribution. Also, the importance of CC technology is its potential to save charges of investment and infrastructure. The central issues for any organization or businesses in the business world are the data storage, security, and privacy. Companies utilize online file access that CC is now becoming an industry trend. Moreover, the companies need to obtain the necessary knowledge as a basis for intelligent services and decision-making systems. The intelligent services and decision-making systems are the unique features of the Big Data science. Big data processing is within reach due to easy access to cloud architectures and open-source software. Now, interoperability of big data and cloud has become a necessity in this era of the data-intensive world.

DOI: 10.4018/978-1-4666-9649-5.ch004

Important Aspects of Big Data and Cloud Interoperability

The are four important aspects of the big data and cloud interoperability.

1. Structural Models
2. Data and Semantics
3. Interconnection, Network, and Interoperability
4. Security, Performance, and Privacy

Structural Models

Based on the characteristics of the cloud environment, the client will be able to identify the requirement for the infrastructure and framework, the storage resource, and the associated technologies.

1. **Infrastructure Requirement and Framework:** Cloud computing infrastructure provides large-scale data storage, processing, and distribution. The infrastructure allows enterprises worldwide to use the same resources without setting up a similar resource locally, therefore, reduces the energy emission. Mobile CC infrastructure could be one of the options because it provides unlimited storage with power dissipation prevention capabilities. The global carbon dioxide emissions of the information and communication technology account for four percents (Aminzadeh, Sanaei, & Ab Hamid, 2014). The global-scale allocation of computing resource could improve efficient energy usage. It also assures high performance (Ebejer, Fulle, Morris, & Finn, 2013), (Addis, Ardagna, Capone, & Carello, 2014) and (Sultan, 2013).

2. **Storage Resource:** The variability in data volumes such as that due to parallel memory bottlenecks, deadlocks, and inefficiency occur in processing big graph data could cause inconsistent computing and storage requirements. The types and the speed of CC applications are examples of the runtime resource configurations (RRC). One needs to evaluate the RRC when the phenomenon of data volume variability occurs (Li, Xu, Kang, Yow, & Xu, 2014). Computationally intensive applications when running on-demand may be resolved by optimizing the computing power of CPU, and GPU-based cloud resources.

3. **Big Data and Cloud Technologies:** Apache Hadoop offers a platform for distributed and parallel data processing. A Big Geo-Data Analytics is the future big data technology where it applies Hadoop clusters in connecting GIS to cloud computing environment. Map-reduce and NoSQL, on the other hand, are the examples of data architectures technology used in connecting global information system to CC environment (Gao, Li, Li, Janowicz, & Zhang, 2014).

Data and Semantics

Devices with heterogeneous hardware and software features may not able to interact with one another (Castiglione et al., 2014). In selecting an approach to data stream processing for devices with different hardware and software, one needs to consider the characteristics of interoperability, data models, programming languages and security. To realize the Big Data and cloud interoperability, the transfer of data must take place. The manner that the data is being transferred will depend on the methods semantics and programming languages applied, the way that the data stream is being processed, and the approach that the is data managed.

1. **Semantics:** Semantic models may be used to solve some of the issues of big data and cloud interoperability. The models should ease the integration and monitoring of knowledge-based systems. Also, the models should also allow for modeling for logical restrictions on data while publishing the new data and information.
2. **Datastream Processing:** There are features for selecting a technique of data stream processing are the data models, programming languages, interoperability, and security.
3. **Semantic Technologies:** The Linked Data provides new ways of data visualization. The RDF Data Cube Vocabulary allows the publication of statistical information (Kourtesis, Alvarez-Rodríguez, & Paraskakis, 2014).

Interconnection, Network, and Interoperability

A cloud-based worldwide collaboration in projects and remote processing of data require service-oriented architecture. The collaboration has the features of the virtual collaborative environment, Analytics-as-a-Service, and digital ecosystem.

1. **Collaborative Virtual Environment:** A virtual environment that enables worldwide collaboration and remote data processing. In a virtual collaborative environment, there is one remote shared display for all clients. Extensive collaboration in projects and remote processing of data requires a service-oriented architecture. The DIS/HLA IEEE standard is often used by the military (Belaud, Negny, Dupros, Michéa, & Vautrin, 2014).
2. **Analytics:** The attributes of Big Data Analytics include turning hardware and software into a commodity, increasing data volumes and increasing variation in types of data assets for analysis. The methods of data delivery and expectations for real-time integration of analytical results are some other attributes. These attributes impact the data analytics.
3. **Digital Ecosystem:** In a digital ecosystem, crowds and clouds support the analysis of Big Data to answer to the challenge of current computing infrastructure.

Communication over the Internet requires a cloud relay server where at least a client must present when the communication takes place. (Brand, 2010), (Brand, 2011), and (Brand, 2013) explains the steps to set up cloud-enabled devices.

Also, Cloud architectures, Remote Brain, Big Data and Shared Knowledge-base, Collective Learning, and Intelligence and Behavior are the concepts in the cloud environment. The concepts could be used to assess the performance of cloud robotics (Qureshi & Koubâa, 2014).

There are three layers in cloud-enable robotics: Cloud service layer, communication and collaborative layer, and the robot control layer (Mateo, 2013). Using the layers realizes the interoperability of robots, software service providers, computers, and sensor devices in the cloud environment.

1. **Cloud Service Layer:** The application services offer interfaces to the robots. The service components execute the task coordination and information sharing in the framework.

2. **Communication and Collaboration Layer:** Services in the cloud service layer realizes the robot interfaces. A middleware allows the communication between cloud services and the robots using the cloud collaboration framework. The framework is a message-based mechanism that manages the communication between the devices and the cloud environment.
3. **Robot Control Layer:** Controls strategies that utilize the functions and hardware capability of the robots. A node in a computer program represents a robot agent that is an actual robot on the floor. The robots function within the robot control layer with a reasoning capability.

Security, Performance, and Privacy

Information leakage on uploading to the servers and stolen of sensitive data are the concerns in CC infrastructure, in terms of, security. Some of the new classes of big data applications are health care, age care, and education. Information leakage on uploading to management domains and stolen sensitive data from the areas are some of the issues in cloud computing infrastructure. A new generation of the network-centric application is increasingly intelligent and autonomous. At times, it collects data rampantly and affect human privacy. When dealing with a robot, it is the operator's responsibility to manage the personal interaction with it. It is important that the operators train, treat, or manage their robot-in-the-cloud so that the robots would not harm animals, children, or employees. Also, care should be taken when deciding the types of information that are appropriate to share, exchange, or reveal, in a given cloud environment (Pagallo, 2013).

1. **Secure Data Management:** One should encrypt the sensitive data before uploads the data to the cloud servers. A storage system based on MySQL and together with CryptDB may be used to protect and secure the data (Castiglione et al., 2014).
2. **Security Assurance:** The design of an architecture that permits devices with dissimilar and heterogeneous hardware and software characteristics to interact with one another is one important aspect. The users should be aware of the dissimilarity of equipment and software so that it guarantees to security privileges and access controls.
3. **Performance Evaluation:** Criteria for evaluation of big data platform, including feasibility, reasonability, value, integrability, and sustainability.

Cloud-Enabled Devices

One example of the cloud-enabled devices is the cloud-enabled robotics (CER). An industrial robot may be cloud-enabled manipulator activates through a cloud environment. Cloud-enabled robotic operates within the manufacturing as a service (MaaS) infrastructure. CER allows the individual plant to be interfaced to one source that is the MaaS, where the information is being shared for use in a virtual collaborative environment. The robot as a Service may help to improve robot interactions and decision making, through mining of big data.

Privacy

There is an issue of a new generation of network-centric applications that collects data rampantly since they are increasingly intelligent and autonomous. As a result, personal interaction with machines and

Figure 1. A general representation of MaaS infrastructure and how this infrastructure is linked to individual plants within which a robot may become enabled through cloud environment (figure redrawn based on source (Qureshi & Koubâa, 2014))

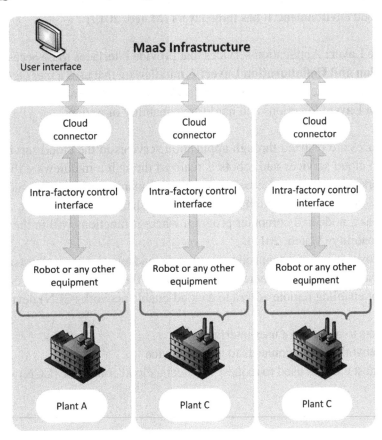

robots will affect privacy. It is the user's responsibility for the behavior of robots to the liability for harm provoked by animals, children, or employees. In fact, care should be taken on the different ways in which humans will treat, train, or manage their robots-in-the-cloud. The forms of information that are appropriate to reveal, share, or transfer, in a given context, may be changed by the ways human and robot interacts (Pagallo, 2013).

Manufacturing as a Service Infrastructure

Cloud-enabled robotic works within the manufacturing as a service (MaaS) infrastructure. A generalized MaaS infrastructure is shown in Figure 1. This infrastructure permits individual plants to be interfaced to one source that is MaaS where the information is being shared. An industrial robot may be cloud-enabled through a cloud environment.

Mining big data from the cloud environment may help to improve robot interactions and decision making, hence Robot as a Service (RaaS). The concepts in cloud environment that would improve the performance of cloud robotics are Remote Brain, Big Data and Shared Knowledge-base, Collective Learning, Intelligence and Behavior, and Cloud architectures (Qureshi & Koubâa, 2014).

Techniques

A cloud-enabled robotic is the interactions of software service providers, computers, sensor devices, and robots in the cloud environment. It has three layers (Mateo, 2013):

1. **Cloud Service Layer:** Application services that provide interfaces to be accessed by the robots
2. **Communication and Collaboration Layer:** A middleware that uses a message-based mechanism to manage the communication between cloud services and robots, and
3. **Robot Control Layer:** Functions and hardware capability of a robot

The robot interfaces are realized through application services in the cloud service layer. The communication between cloud services and robots is realized through a middleware that is the cloud collaboration framework where a message-based mechanism manages the communication. The service components execute the task coordination and information sharing in the context. A robot agent is an actual robot shown as a node in a computer program where it functions within the robot control layer with a reasoning capability (Mateo, 2013).

Communication over an internet connection requires a cloud relay server. At least one client must present when communication takes place where Figure 2 explains the clients access the cloud system. Figure 3 shows the steps for enabling remote access to a cloud-enable network (CEN) device (Brand, 2013):

1. A client requests to access to a user interface
2. A local area network (LAN) connects to a CEN device
3. A designated host name is used to request to detect a cloud connector (CCN)

Figure 2. A remote access for cloud-enabled network devices (figure redrawn based on source (Mateo, 2013))

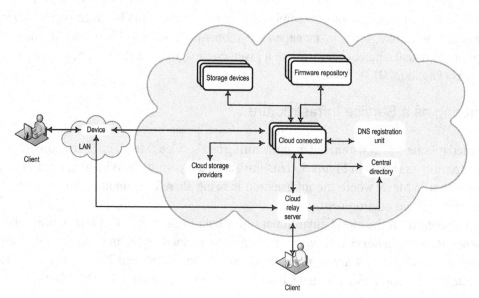

Figure 3. The process for enabling remote access to a network attached storage device that provides cloud services (figure redrawn based on source (Brand, 2013))

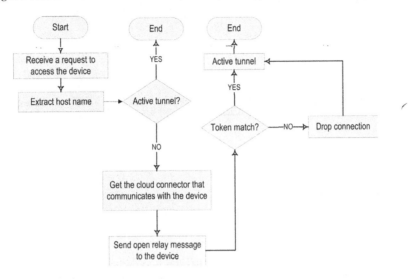

4. The CCN communicates with a CEN device by sending an open relay message over a management link
5. A secure tunnel between the CR serve and the CEN device is established
6. A safe connection between the client and the CEN device over the internet is enabled

A network attached storage (NAS) performs network attached storage operations with cloud storage services where Figure 4 depicts its block the interconnection of relevant modules while Figure 5 describes how the clients access the network storage. An NAS device has the following components and functionality (Brand, 2010):

1. There should be at least one network controller
2. The network controller assists in communication with a group of clients over an LAN. Also, it supports in communication with a cloud storage service (CSS) over a wide area network (WAN)

Figure 4. The block diagram of network attached storage (figure redrawn based on source (Brand, 2010))

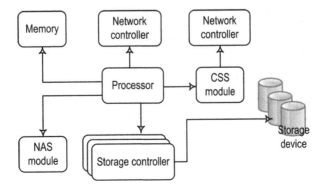

Figure 5. A storage network system (figure redrawn based on source (Brand, 2010))

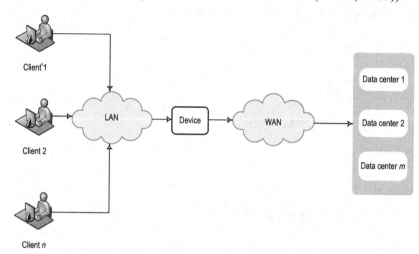

3. There is a group of storage devices for locally storing data in the device
4. There is a CSS module for at least synchronizing data locally stored in the group of storage devices and the data stored in the CSS
5. There is a processor for enabling the group of clients to perform file-based operations on the device using a file sharing protocol

A cloud connector is used to optimize a cloud service. It is a software component integrated with enterprise routing platforms. Some of the commercially available connectors are the products by Etherios, Cisco, and Mulesoft (http://www.etherios.com/, http://www.cisco.com/, http://www.vmware.com/,

Figure 6. A block diagram of a cloud connector (figure redrawn based on source (Brand, 2011))

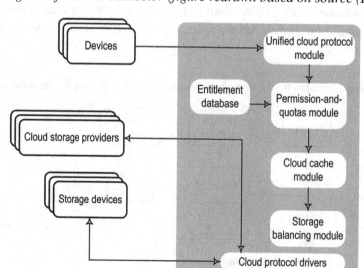

https://www.mulesoft.com/, respectively). Figure 6 shows the CCN block diagram that complies with the following setup rules (Brand, 2011):

1. Communication requires a unified cloud protocol module
2. The communication takes place between the CED device and the NAS device through a cloud transport protocol
3. A group of cloud protocol drivers for interfacing with at least one of a group of storage devices and some cloud storage providers is needed
4. The group of storage devices and the group of cloud storage providers are part of the CSS
5. A permissions-and-quotas enforcement module for enforcing access control is required. The module enforces access to data blocks stored in at least one the group of storage devices and the group of cloud storage providers of the CSS

SUMMARY

Extensive data storage, processing, and distribution are attainable with Cloud Computing infrastructure. Based on the characteristics of the cloud environment, an organization or enterprise may be able to identify the requirement for the infrastructure and framework, the storage resource, and the associated technologies. Interoperability of big data and cloud is now a trend. In selecting an approach to data stream processing for devices with different hardware and software, an organization or enterprise needs to consider the characteristics of interoperability, data models, programming languages and security. Access to cloud architectures and open-source software permits big data processing. To realize the Big Data and cloud interoperability, the transfer of data must take place. A cloud-based worldwide collaboration in projects and remote processing of data require service-oriented architecture. Information leakage on uploading to the servers and stolen of sensitive data are the concerns in Cloud Computing infrastructure.

Cloud-enabled robotic works within the manufacturing infrastructure as a service. Storage of huge data in the cloud environment allows a group of robots to mine relevant data and use them, according to predefined tasks for unique manufacturing operations. In doing so, the data gathered from multiple sets of sensors and transducers belongs to a group robot are uploaded to the storage devices through cloud connectors as shared data or information. Depending on the current operation, a robot that is a member of the group will download packets of data or information from the cloud. The data will then be used to perform preprogrammed tasks or to create decisions for the upcoming sequences of operation.

REFERENCES

Addis, B., Ardagna, D., Capone, A., & Carello, G. (2014). Energy-aware joint management of networks and Cloud infrastructures. *Computer Networks*, *70*, 75–95. doi:10.1016/j.comnet.2014.04.011

Aminzadeh, N., Sanaei, Z., & Ab Hamid, S. H. (2014). Mobile storage augmentation in mobile cloud computing: Taxonomy, approaches, and open issues. *Simulation Modelling Practice and Theory*. doi:10.1016/j.simpat.2014.05.009

Belaud, J.-P., Negny, S., Dupros, F., Michéa, D., & Vautrin, B. (2014). Collaborative simulation and scientific big data analysis: Illustration for sustainability in natural hazards management and chemical process engineering. *Computers in Industry*, *65*(3), 521–535. doi:10.1016/j.compind.2014.01.009

Brand, A. (2010). *Storage device and method thereof for integrating network attached storage with cloud storage services*. Israel: United States Patent and Trademark Office.

Brand, A. (2011). *Cloud connector for interfacing between a network attached storage device and a cloud storage system*. Israel: United States Patent and Trademark Office.

Brand, A. (2013). *Remote access service for cloud-enabled network devices*. Israel: United States Patent and Trademark Office.

Castiglione, A., Pizzolante, R., De Santis, A., Carpentieri, B., Castiglione, A., & Palmieri, F. (2014). Cloud-based adaptive compression and secure management services for 3D healthcare data. *Future Generation Computer Systems*. doi:10.1016/j.future.2014.07.001

Ebejer, J.-P., Fulle, S., Morris, G. M., & Finn, P. W. (2013). The emerging role of cloud computing in molecular modelling. *Journal of Molecular Graphics & Modelling*, *44*, 177–187. doi:10.1016/j.jmgm.2013.06.002 PMID:23835611

Gao, S., Li, L., Li, W., Janowicz, K., & Zhang, Y. (2014). Constructing gazetteers from volunteered Big Geo-Data based on Hadoop. *Computers, Environment and Urban Systems*. doi:10.1016/j.compenvurbsys.2014.02.004

Kourtesis, D., Alvarez-Rodríguez, J. M., & Paraskakis, I. (2014). Semantic-based QoS management in cloud systems: Current status and future challenges. *Future Generation Computer Systems*, *32*, 307–323. doi:10.1016/j.future.2013.10.015

Li, R., Xu, Z., Kang, W., Yow, K. C., & Xu, C.-Z. (2014). Efficient multi-keyword ranked query over encrypted data in cloud computing. *Future Generation Computer Systems*, *30*, 179–190. doi:10.1016/j.future.2013.06.029

Mateo, R. M. A. (2013). Scalable Adaptive Group Communication for Collaboration Framework of Cloud-enabled Robots. *Procedia Computer Science*, *22*, 1239–1248. doi:10.1016/j.procs.2013.09.211

Pagallo, U. (2013). Robots in the cloud with privacy: A new threat to data protection? *Computer Law & Security Report*, *29*(5), 501–508. doi:10.1016/j.clsr.2013.07.012

Qureshi, B., & Koubâa, A. (2014). Five Traits of Performance Enhancement Using Cloud Robotics: A Survey. *Procedia Computer Science*, *37*, 220–227. doi:10.1016/j.procs.2014.08.033

Sultan, N. (2013). Cloud computing: A democratizing force? *International Journal of Information Management*, *33*(5), 810–815. doi:10.1016/j.ijinfomgt.2013.05.010

KEY TERMS AND DEFINITIONS

Big Data Science: The extraction of the knowledge as a basis for intelligent services and decision-making systems is known.

Cloud Collaboration Framework: A message-based mechanism manages the communication.

Cloud Computing Infrastructure: Computer resources arrangement that provides large-scale data storage, processing, and distribution.

Cloud Computing: Sharing of computer resources with the help of servers.

Cloud-Enabled Robotic: The interoperability of software service providers, computers, sensor devices, and robots in a cloud environment.

Interoperability of Big Data and cloud: The exchange of data between the Big Data and Cloud Computing.

Robot Agent: A robot agent is an actual robot shown as a node in a computer program.

Worldwide Collaboration: Using a cloud-based service-oriented architecture for updating and sharing of information through remote processing of data.

Section 2
Big Data:
Management Issues

Chapter 5

How to Engrain a Big Data Mindset into Our Managers' DNA:
Insights from a Big Data Initiative in a French Business School

Kevin Daniel André Carillo
Toulouse University, France & Toulouse Business School, France

ABSTRACT

The industry experts' claim that big data will be the next frontier for innovation, competition, and productivity, has turned from an unfounded omen to an obvious reality. In the looming data-driven business era, data will pervade organizations and will thus affect their nature and functioning. The central role played by data is about to impact the main mechanism that fuels the life of organizations, decision making, which will then gradually redefine the job and function of managers. In May 2014, a French top-ten business school launched a 2-week big data initiative aiming at immersing future managers into a big data simulation and also sensitizing them to the overall cultural shift that big data is about to engender within organizations. Using semi-real data about a French newspaper, 100 graduating students were engaged into a big data serious game which main objective was to use data visualization techniques on a large dataset hosted on a Hadoop cluster in order to derive business recommendations to higher management. By conducting observations, taking field notes, and interviewing participants, important insights could be derived for educational institutions that are contemplating the importance of including big data into their curricula but also for organizations that strive to engrain a big data mindset within their managers.

INTRODUCTION

There is now no doubt that there exists a reality beyond the big data buzz. By realizing that data have the potential to be a key business driver, organizations are gradually shifting towards a new business era in which data will be treated as precious and strategic resources. McKinsey's 2011 claim (Manyika

DOI: 10.4018/978-1-4666-9649-5.ch005

et al., 2011) about big data being the next frontier for innovation, competition, and productivity, has now turned from omen to an understated reality. In this data-driven business era, data will pervade organizations and will thus affect their nature and functioning. As a consequence, the main mechanism that fuels the life of organizations, decision making, will be significantly impacted by the central role played by data. In other words, big data is gradually redefining the job of managers by incorporating data into decision processes.

In May 2014, a French business school launched a 2-week big data initiative aimed at immersing future managers into a big data simulation and engraining into them a big data mindset. Using semi-real data about a French newspaper, 100 graduating students were engaged into a big data serious game which main objective was to use data visualization techniques in order to derive business recommendations from user data hosted on a Hadoop cluster. By conducting observations and interviewing students during the serious game, important lessons could be derived for organizations that strive to engrain a big data mindset within their managers. For instance, the workshop clearly highlighted that the lack of solid database-related skills as well as certain statistical concepts could prevent managers from effectively extracting the business value contained into data. Besides, lessons generated from the workshop can also help business schools and universities to identify pedagogical strategies to sensitize future managers towards the predominant role that big data is going to play as well as to provide them with the necessary skills and mindset.

The chapter particularly targets business schools that are contemplating the decision to integrate big data into their mainstream curricula as well as into specific trainings. It also provides insights about how big data is gradually redefining the function and job of managers. By doing so, this chapter also aims at helping organizations to tailor effective trainings to raise awareness about the transformation of management in the big data era. The public sector, perceived as "the most fertile terrain" for benefitting from entering the data-driven era, is particularly targeted as governments have collected huge amounts of 'siloed' data and have for long suffered from an overall lack of efficiency and performance (Brown et al., 2011).

This book chapter is organized as follows. In a first section, it explains that beyond the big data buzz there exists a big data reality that will globally impact all businesses and our society as a whole. It concludes by contemplating how big data will affect managers, how business schools shall take it into consideration, and how the Information Systems field can play a leading role in developing and delivering adapted curricula. After succinctly presenting the French business school context, the workshop and details about its pedagogical engineering are presented. Based on results drawn from data collected throughout the event, the last section derives insights and recommendations for organizations as well as business schools and universities. A conclusion summarizes the key points raised throughout the chapter.

BIG DATA, BIG CHANGE, BIG SKILL SHORTAGE

The Quest for a 'Good' Big Data Definition

Attempts to determine the origin of the term 'big data' have led to inconclusive results. However, what is sure is that the "big" part of "big data" is ill-chosen as it implies ideas of numbers or quantities omitting more predominant aspects such as its strategic importance or its business relevance. As a result, the connotations around the use of 'big data' tends make companies think in terms of *how big do my data need to be to do some big data? … whereas the key question shall rather be what strategic value can I derive from my data no matter its size?*

Big data definitions abound as big data experts have attempted to delineate the blurry boundaries that surround the big data phenomenon. Realizing that the shared origin of big data among academia, industry and the media had led to ambiguous and contradictory definitions, Jonathan Stuart Ward and Adam Barker (2014) of University of St Andrews (UK) attempted to close the debate by collating the various definitions having gained some consensus and providing a clear and concise definition. Table 1 presents the big data definitions compiled by Ward and Barker as well as other definitions that have been commonly acknowledged in the industry and education.

Table 1. Most commonly acknowledged big data definitions

Source / Author(s)	Big Data Definition
Merriam Webster	An accumulation of data that is too large and complex for processing by traditional database management tools.
Oxford Dictionaries	Extremely large data sets that may be analysed computationally to reveal patterns, trends, and associations, especially relating to human behaviour and interactions: much IT investment is going towards managing and maintaining big data
Gartner's glossary (2014)	Big data is high-volume, high-velocity and high-variety information assets that demand cost-effective, innovative forms of information processing for enhanced insight and decision making.
IDC	Big Data technologies as a new generation of technologies and architectures designed to extract value economically from very large volumes of a wide variety of data by enabling high-velocity capture, discovery, and/or analysis. This definition encompasses hardware, software, and services that integrate, organize, manage, analyze, and present data that is characterized by "four Vs" — volume, variety, velocity, and value (discussed in the sections that follow).
Gartner (2012)	In 2001, a Meta (now Gartner) report noted the increasing size of data, the increasing rate at which it is produced and the increasing range of formats and representations employed. This report predated the term "dig data" but proposed a three-fold definition encompassing the "three Vs": Volume, Velocity and Variety. This idea has since become popular and sometimes includes a fourth V: veracity, to cover questions of trust and uncertainty.
Oracle	Big data is the derivation of value from traditional relational database-driven business decision making, augmented with new sources of unstructured data.
Forrester	The practices and technology that close the gap between the data available and the ability to turn that data into business insight.
Intel	Big data opportunities emerge in organizations generating a median of 300 terabytes of data a week. The most common forms of data analyzed in this way are business transactions stored in relational databases, followed by documents, e-mail, sensor data, blogs, and social media.
Microsoft	Big data is the term increasingly used to describe the process of applying serious computing power—the latest in machine learning and artificial intelligence—to seriously massive and often highly complex sets of information.
The Method for an Integrated Knowledge Environment open-source project	The MIKE project argues that big data is not a function of the size of a data set but its complexity. Consequently, it is the high degree of permutations and interactions within a data set that defines big data.
The National Institute of Standards and Technology	NIST argues that big data is data which "exceed(s) the capacity or capability of current or conventional methods and systems." In other words, the notion of "big" is relative to the current standard of computation.
Jonathan Stuart Ward and Adam Barker	Big data is a term describing the storage and analysis of large and or complex data sets using a series of techniques including, but not limited to: NoSQL, MapReduce and machine learning.

It is striking that nearly all definitions suffer from the same tendency to reduce big data to a technological change in the global economic landscape, rather focusing on the "big" part of "big data". Besides, mentions of the human side of big data: business, organizations, and people are rarely present in the definitions. Even Ward and Barker's definition, which is supposed to be a meta-definition, thus hypothetically more encompassing, is entirely focused on the technical side of big data: *the storage and analysis of large and or complex data sets using a series of techniques including, but not limited to: NoSQL, MapReduce and machine learning*. If big data is such a major phenomenon, what is the societal impact of the use of tools and technologies such as Hadoop, HBase, BigTable, Hive, or NoSQL?

Big Data Is Real

'Selfie' was chosen by the Oxford Dictionaries as the 2013 word of the year as the frequency of the word had increased by 17,000% over the year. If there were an equivalent contest with business terms, there is little doubt that 'big data' would be the winner by far. Indeed, it is nowadays nearly impossible to go a day without encountering some mention of the term 'big data' in the corporate sphere or in the media. Nonetheless, there is a business reality beyond the big data buzz. Since McKinsey's 2011 report (Manyika et al., 2011) that took part in drawing attention on the big data phenomenon, companies are multiplying efforts and investments on big data initiatives. A 2012 Gartner report predicted that IT spending on big data in the U.S. would hit $34 billion and concluded that 64% of the surveyed companies had made such investments (Gartner, 2012a). Previsions for the coming years are even higher. IDC has predicted that the big data market (including infrastructure, services, and software) would reach $16.1 billion in 2014 (Gil Press, 2013) (a growth 6 times faster than the growth of the overall IT market). Behind such a frenzy on investing into big data technologies, big data has a reality that goes beyond the mere idea of a technological revolution. It is a real shift towards a new business era in which data play the central role.

Big Data Talent Shortage for Managers

It is now clearly acknowledged that the global gap between the demand for big data talent and the supply of talent is one of the key challenges that seriously hamper big data implementations across organizations. A 2012 Gartner report predicted that by 2015, the demand for big data related jobs would reach 4.4 million jobs throughout the world while barely a third of those jobs would be filled (Gartner, 2012b). Predictions for the following years are not any better as the gap is foreseen to significantly widen…

Such prediction shot an alarm signal for all universities and business schools, urging them to develop new programs and adapt older ones to urgently answer the demand from organizations. Business schools may be tempted to think that this drastic skill shortage only concerns IT-related jobs. Such a view is absolutely erroneous as it would simply omit the human layer that surrounds the big data technological revolution, and even the entire 'data-transformation' that organizations are about to live.

Peter Sondergaard's words (senior vice president at Gartner and global head of Research) during his 2012 keynote speech of the Gartner Symposium/ITxpo, illustrate how the boundaries of the skill shortage will bridge the IT sphere:

In addition, every big data-related role in the U.S. will create employment for three people outside of IT, so over the next four years a total of 6 million jobs in the U.S. will be generated by the information economy (Sondergaard, 2012).

Meanwhile, Gartner (2012a) predicted a lack of 1.5 million managers and analysts with the skills to understand and make decisions based on the analysis of big data. The reports also foresees a lack of an additional 1.5 million managers and analysts in the United States for skills related to the effective identification and formulation of big data opportunities, and the consumption of their associated analysis. The accuracy of the above numbers is perhaps questionable but it is undoubtable that business schools are in the same boat and must urgently act. Training future managers being the main mission of business schools…

A New Business Paradigm where Data is Digital Oil

The main argument of this book chapter is that big data heralds a major shift towards a new business paradigm that will impact every aspect of organizations. The direction of the link between business and data is gradually shifting. Indeed, data used to be there to support business. Now, organizations have understood that data have the potential to 'drive' business by providing new opportunities, strategies, allowing new business models, and transforming most business processes. Data are becoming the new digital oil that runs through the veins of organizations and that must be cherished in order to keep it pure (accurate and reliable) and valuable. Beyond the technological buzz surrounding the term 'big data' lays a much broader truth: the advent of a new data-driven business paradigm. Back in 2004, Yahoo! was among the first to appoint a Chief Data Officer (Usama Fayyad), this was already announcing the beginning of this new era. Very few people had realized it at that time…

A few years ago, when some organizations started realizing the potential of analyzing big data, they thought that a clever and talented individual could alone unleash the power of big data and do wonders. The quest for the mythical five-legged sheep that master statistics, computer science, and business, started; making the data scientist job one of the sexiest in the world. There is no doubt that there exists extremely talented individuals whose profile is close to the data scientist ideal. Nonetheless, examples showing that the 'data scientist can do it all' model does not work, abound. In this new data-driven business world, it is not one person that must be different but it is rather organizations as a whole and their overall functioning that must change. Data must become an organizational culture rather than technical means that support businesses. Data must become the center of attention for all employees from any hierarchical level as everybody in an organization takes part in the life cycle of data from its generation, storage, to its analysis and consumption. In retail and distribution companies, creating such a 'data culture' starts by making cashiers and employees working in warehouses aware that data are important and precious as these individuals play a crucial role by being at the very beginning of the data lifecycle.

New Skills or New DNA?

Taking into consideration the above arguments, the big data skill shortage shall be seen from two complementary angles. First, such shortage can be seen *vertically*, as big data and the societal phenomenon that surrounds it have engendered new skills and created new functions in organizations.

There is a wealth of new technologies and tools around big data. Highest paying IT jobs ask for specific skills in NoSQL, Apache Hadoop, Python, and even MongoDB, HBase, Hive … Besides, starting from the function of Chief Data Officer, an array of new big data-related jobs have appeared in organizations such as big data scientist, big data analyst, big data visualizer, big data manager, big data solutions architect, big data engineer, big data consultant… to name but a few. However, by considering that behind the big data frenzy hides the looming shift towards a data-driven business era, the big data skill shortage goes way beyond the figures compiled by experts' reports. In this new data-driven business era, big data must become a mindset that is engrained into all employees' DNA. This is all the more important for managers from any hierarchical level as no matter their decisional scope (top, middle or operational), data and big data is becoming an inherent part of the inner mechanisms that govern the functioning of organizations: *decision making*. This is the perspective that is adopted throughout the remainder of the book chapter.

Information Systems Coming to the Rescue of Management Education

Since the alarming 2011 McKinsey report about the looming worldwide shortage in big data / data analytics skills, universities have launched tremendous efforts to improve their existing degree programs and create new offerings. Overall, there has been a worldwide tendency to: (1) Add a Business Analytics/Big Data/Data Science focus to existing MBA programs; and (2) Develop new Master's programs (mainly Master of Science programs) in Business Analytics/Big Data/Data Science. In the United States, the number of MS Analytics programs (combining MSA: Master of Science in Analytics, MSBA: Master of Science in Business Analytics, and MSDS: Master of Science in Data Science) has grown from less than 20 in 2012, to about 30 in 2013, up to more than 60 in 2014 and nearly 80 as of 2015 (Schoenherr and Speier-Pero, 2015). A review of the top MS in Analytics programs performed in 2013 revealed that the content of such programs was split across the three core areas: analytical and modeling tools (44% of the overall content on average), business processes and decision making (24%), and data management (23%) (Schoenherr and Speier-Pero, 2015). There is no doubt that the programs that have been created to answer the big data skill shortage have high academic and practical value. However, it is puzzling to realize that on average only 13% of the delivered content (ranging from 6% to 20%) integrates the three knowledge domains through the realization of "hands-on" projects. The new data-driven business paradigm engenders the fusion of the three domains. As a result, preparing future managers to evolve in such new business environment shall not be by concatenating courses of each of the three fields but rather by merging them in nearly every program unit. Only then, universities will be in a position to claim that they are efficiently preparing managers that will be capable of evolving in the data-driven business paradigm. The academic boundaries between disciplines have no more reason to hold. Big data is the result of the fusion of all three.

The main quest of the Information Systems discipline is to tackle challenges and identify opportunities that can have a long lasting scientific and societal impact (Chen, 2011). Shortly after the publication of the 2011 McKinsey report, the IS field realized the urgent need to revisit existing curricula and launch action plans to provide Business Intelligence (BI) and Business Analytics (BA) education programs that would address the new generation of data/analytics savvy and business students and professionals (Chen et al., 2012). In 2012, the AIS Special Interest Group on Decision Support, Knowledge and Data Management Systems (SIGDSS) and the Teradata University Network (TUN) cosponsored the Business Intelligence Congress 3 conducted surveys to assess academia's response to the growing market need for students with Business Intelligence (BI) and Business Analytics (BA) skill sets with an emphasis on 'big data' (Wixom et al., 2014). The report concluded that the IS field was particularly well positioned to train the next-generation BI/BA workforce.

The most challenging curricular aspects when reflecting on the most efficient means to prepare future managers, is the breadth and depth of skill sets (at the junction of the three expertise domains) that are needed to become a highly capable professional (Schoenherr & Speier-Pero, 2015). Since its early beginnings some 30 to 40 years back, Information Systems (IS) has been an interdisciplinary field in nature and has mastered on trans-disciplinary dialog (Galliers, 2003). If one discipline could claim legitimacy in being the perfect candidate to deliver education programs based on a new knowledge domain that is at the junction of computer science (data/database management), statistics (analytical and modeling tools), and business (business processes and decision making), Information Systems is the first discipline that shall immediately come to mind. The advent of the data-driven business era is an unprecedented opportunity for IS departments to play a central role by leading the education of next-generation professionals.

This chapter also aims at warning organizations that following the big data hive will go beyond gaining big data skills and creating big data functions. The remainder of this chapter is a testimony of a big data initiative that took place at Toulouse Business School in 2014 which main objective was to attempt to engrain such big data mindset into the DNA of future managers. This chapter does not have the pretension to provide lessons to other educational institutions. Indeed, over the last few years, some business schools and universities throughout the world have started launching an array of quality big data programs and trainings. This chapter particularly targets business schools that are in the initial phase of contemplating the relevance to teach big data to future managers.

PRESENTATION OF THE 'BIG DATA BETTER DECISIONS' WORKSHOP

The Big Data Better Decisions workshop was a two-week event that took place at the end of the 2013-2014 university year of the Master in Management program. It involved 100 participants and twelve corporate partners that took part to the different sessions. The objectives of the workshop were to sensitize future managers to the reality of big data, to train them to a big data visualization tool, and to participate in a serious game aiming at simulating a business task in a big data context.

Specificities of French Business Schools

Business schools in France are based on the model of French *grandes écoles*. They are 'elite' higher education entities that lay outside the French university system. *Grandes écoles* ((usually specialized in either engineering, sciences, or business) select students based on national rankings that are established through competitive written and oral exams. Most candidates complete two years of dedicated preparatory classes before taking the different *grandes écoles'* entrance exams even though more and more students are accepted through a parallel admission process (involving an ever increasing number of foreign students). The workshop presented in this book chapter was organized at one of the top ten French business schools that is representative of the French business school system.

Participant Profile

Because the program aimed at sensitizing future managers to the global shift into a data-centric business paradigm, it was important to select participants that represented a broad spectrum of skills and expertise and that had some work experience. Students in the final year of the Master of Management program of the school seemed to be ideal targets. Besides, we selected only students that were following the apprenticeship track of the program which guaranteed a minimum of one to two years of work experience.

All the majors of the business school were represented (marketing, finance, accounting, international business, entrepreneurship, and supply chain management) as well as nearly all possible specializations. The participants, aged between 22 and 25 years old, worked for all types of organizations starting from small and medium-sized companies to large multinational corporations in a variety of sectors such as banking, aerospace, retail, distribution, energy, oil… as well as consulting firms. The workshop was designed for big data neophytes. The degree of knowledge about big data was close to null and limited to having read a few newspaper articles. No single student had worked directly or indirectly on big data issues in their respective company.

Workshop Structure and Content

The main structure of the workshop is presented in Table 2. The first week of the workshop consisted of four half-day sessions on a range of complementary big data topics (see Table 3 for the complete list of the big data sessions and the associated learning objectives), a day session on presenting the serious game and the business concepts surrounding it (social network analysis and customer/user experience data), and two full days for training sessions aiming at mastering the data visualization tool that had to be used for the serious game. A certificate was delivered to participants having demonstrated a good mastery of it by successfully passing two online quizzes. The second week involved four half-day sessions with big data experts, the rest of the time being dedicated to partaking the serious game and working on the case. Three professors and an admin person were there to coach the groups and help with technical problems. Participants also used an online forum to ask questions to the professionals that had taken part in creating the serious game and who had a good understanding of the case and the dataset.

Serious Game: Data Visualization Business Case

Participants were placed into groups of five, ensuring that each group had members from different domains of expertise and work experience in distinct sectors/industries. A full-day session was dedicated to present the business case associated with the serious game as well as the business concepts required to get an in-depth grasp of the specificities of the case. The groups were provided four days to work on the case. The final day consisted of attending the group presentations and evaluating their performance. Four big data experts (who had knowledge about the case and its business context) were invited to partake the final stage of the event.

Table 2. Big data better decisions – Workshop structure

WEEK 1	Monday	Tuesday	Wednesday	Thursday	Friday
Morning	Sessions with big data professionals/ specialists		Serious game presentation	Training/certification	
Afternoon				Data visualization tool	
WEEK 2	Monday	Tuesday	Wednesday	Thursday	Friday
Morning	Sessions with big data professionals/specialists				Student presentations and award ceremony
Afternoon	Serious game (group work and coaching)				

Table 3. Big data sessions: Title, content, and speaker(s)

Session	Theme	Learning Objective(s)	Content	Speaker
1	Introduction to big data	*LO1:* Gain awareness about the advent of the data-driven business paradigm. *LO2:* Understand the nature, size and scope of the big data phenomenon *LO3:* Distinguish big data buzz vs. reality	● Defining big data ● The three/five/seven Vs ● Beyond the Vs, a business paradigm ● Famous big data stories and applications	Information System assistant professor (specialized in big data)
2	Big data challenges, issues, and applications	*LO4:* Understand how the different sectors and industries are (about to be) impacted/ transformed.	● What are the main issues, challenge, and applications of big data? ● Sectors and industries impacted by big data ● Feedback – Project in online retail industry	Big data consultant / CEO of big data startup
3	Story of a big data startup	*LO5:* Understand the business opportunities (including entrepreneurship) engendered by the big data phenomenon *LO6:* Gain insights about what working 'with big data' means through real life examples	● Feedback – Creation of a big data startup (through the school's incubator) ● Demo of the social network analysis tool ● Feedback from various projects	CEO of big data startup (current student of the school)
4	The reality of big data for analytics experts	*LO7:* Know the key players and dynamics of the analytics sector *LO8:* Perceive how analytics solutions can be used by organizations entering the data-driven era	● The big data landscape for firms specialized in analytics ● Big data solutions provided by the company ● Feedback from various projects	Director Business Solutions & Emerging Markets / large multinational company
5	Technological impact of big data / Big data architecture	*LO9:* Understanding the main big data architecture concepts	● Distributed databases / Hadoop ● What are the main technological impacts of big data in firms? ● Feedback – Projects in the aerospace and defense sectors	Managing enterprise architect and big data expert (consulting firm, big data leader in France) + Account manager (American software company, big data solutions)
6	Big data and smart cities	*LO10:* Understand how the public sector can benefit from the big data phenomenon *LO11:* Gain insights about the specificities/complexity of big data project management	● Promises and challenges of smart city projects ● Presentation of the smart city project lifecycle from the provider and the customer's points of view.	CEO of big data startup + digital manager of the city of Toulouse
7	Big data, personal privacy, and intellectual property	*LO12:* Reflect on the societal implications of the data-driven era. *LO13:* Understand the main ethical and legal issues raised by the big data phenomenon	● Big data ownership ● Legal aspects surrounding big data ● Privacy and intellectual property in the big data world	Professor of business law (expert in privacy, intellectual property, and Internet law)
8	Big data strategy: Between jobs, processes, and collective intelligence	*LO14:* Reflect on the new business models engendered by the big data phenomenon *LO15:* Reflect on the organizational changes occurring within organizations that decide to engage the path of data transformation	● Big data strategy and business models ● What are the main organizational impacts of big data in firms? ● Feedback from various projects (how the two startups collaborate)	Head of operations + CEO of two collaborating big data startups

Serious Game Context

The context of the serious game was a French newspaper, specialized in financial and economic news (and leader in the French market). Students were presented the main characteristics and difficulties of the newspaper industry such as the collapse of paper-based newspaper sales, the intense competition with web-based newspapers, and the overall tendency for customers to prefer digital information channels. The participants were presented the two main business objectives of the serious game:

1. Develop the usage of digital information channels (even free of charge) to expand online advertising revenues
2. Increase revenues in terms of memberships (two options), article readership, and content downloads.

To do so, participants had to: first get a good understanding of the dataset using a data visualization tool, identify patterns and potential opportunities, and finally derive business recommendations that are adapted to the context of the company and its industry. Students were not provided any guidance for any the three steps. The rationale behind this approach was to sensitize participants to the insertion of a data component into organizations' decision processes. The task was specifically designed so that students would follow the decision cycle: *business problem/opportunity ⇨ data ⇨ insights ⇨ business decision*.

The learning objectives of the serious game were the following:

- **LO16:** Understand what 'raw data' is about and how business value is in embedded into it.
- **LO17:** Be able to address a real-life business problem using a data-driven approach (by following the decision cycle: *business problem/opportunity ⇨ data ⇨ insights ⇨ business decision*.
- **LO18:** Be able to derive business insights from raw data using visual statistical techniques.
- **LO19:** Be able to efficiently communicate to an audience of experts in a big data context (mastery of big data terms, jargon, and key notions).
- **LO20:** Gain an understanding about how the job/function of managers is impacted in data-driven organizations.

Dataset and Visualization Tool

The dataset was built on semi-real structured data collected from two leading French newspapers on which slight corrections were performed in order to ensure the pedagogical value of the dataset (to make sure that patterns could be identified by students). The data were stored on a simulated Hadoop cluster hosted on an external cloud platform. The database consisted of data from about 3.5 million newspaper users that had been captured for four consecutive months (providing a total of 14 million lines). About a hundred variables were provided to students including:

- **User Characteristics:** Such as gender, location, address, postcode, email address…
- **Membership Characteristics:** Such as membership status in relation to the various newspapers of the associated brand, membership duration, inactivity duration and degree…
- **Behavioral Characteristics:** Website connection numbers, number of received emailing campaign messages, number of downloaded pdf files…

The students were provided a full-day training to master the big data visualization tool (SAS® Visual Analytics) prior to partake the serious game. The demos and tutorial sessions used the dataset of the serious game to make sure that students had the data properly loaded.

The data visualization tool was provided by a leader in analytics solutions. Through a drag-and-drop graphical user interface, it allowed to explore datasets by identifying trends, patterns, and relationships. Basic functions included the manipulation of data such as creating hierarchies, aggregated measures, or joining datasets. Simple visualization functions involved standard descriptive statistical techniques such as bar charts, line charts, box plots, but also heat maps, correlation matrices, and word clouds. Predictive techniques could also be used such as the generation of band plots (based on the notion of confidence intervals) or decision trees (regression models) for instance. Figure 1 presents some of the graphs that can be generated when using the data visualization tool.

Figure 1. Sample of visualization techniques provided by SAS® Visual Analytics

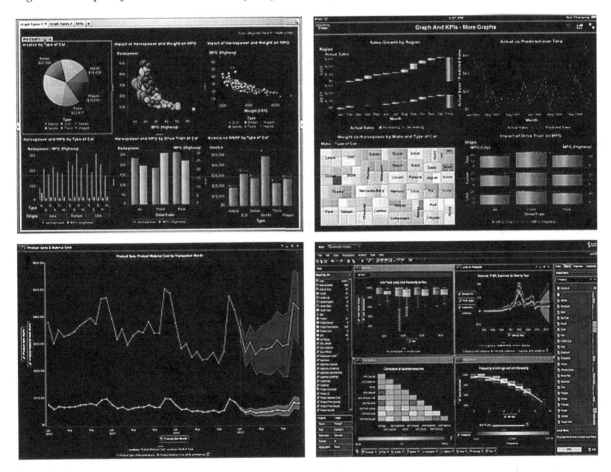

Deliverables and Presentations

The participants were provided four full days to prepare a 25-minute presentation of their main results and recommendations. The tool had two main usage modes: exploration and reporting. Students were given the choice to use the reporting functionality of the data visualization tool for their presentation (using a tablet as a remote) or else more conventional presentation software/ online applications. Four big data experts (the VP innovation of a consulting firm, a big data entrepreneur, a big data project manager, and an information systems professor specialized in big data) took part in evaluating the performance of each group.

An array of visual descriptive statistical techniques were used by participants to explore the various characteristics of the dataset, such as histograms, bar charts, pie charts, or bubble charts (see Figure 2 for sample graphs). More advanced uses included correlation tables, linear regressions, or confidence intervals (see Figure 3). The members of the jury acknowledged that most groups had gained a good understanding of the business case and an in-depth grasp of the dataset and its main patterns: e.g. four to five distinct readership profiles, the relationship between brand proximity and readership type/quantity, as well as factors correlated to revenues (direct or indirect).

LESSONS LEARNT AND BIG DATA INSIGHTS

Following the two-week workshop, debrief sessions were organized with individuals from the business school as well as from the corporate partners that had been involved in the event and its organization. Direct feedback was provided by the participants during the two-week period while feedback forms were completed by all participants and collected at the end of the event. Participant observations were performed by the main organizers while coaching the students during the serious game, field notes were taken during the workshop, and informal interviews were conducted. The collected data allowed to derive insights for the organization of future big data events, courses, and programs. Lessons for organizations that are working towards nurturing a big data culture could also be identified.

Collaborating with the Big Data Ecosystem

Big data is inherently complex. This results in an evolving and interconnected network of actors that interact (and often collaborate) with each other, covering a very wide spectrum of specialization domains such as applications (vertical, log data, ad/media), business intelligence, analytics, visualization, data/ infrastructure as a service, analytics infrastructure, and even traditional structured database specialists. As a result, big data projects usually require the expertise and services from several companies belonging to the overall big data ecosystem that includes all big data actors (including the many big data startups), companies specialized in big data integration and services (usually provided by consulting firms), and open source software projects such as Hadoop, Apache HBase, or MongoDB to name but a few.

From a pedagogical perspective, teaching big data is thus challenging. The complexity and many applications of big data can only be apprehended through direct involvement with the big data ecosystem. In simple terms, big data training programs, courses, and curricula shall be organized in such a way that students shall interact with an array of big data specialists in order to provide them a broad enough picture of the big data landscape. Furthermore, the big data ecosystem evolves quite fast in terms of both

Figure 2. Sample of visual descriptive statistics techniques

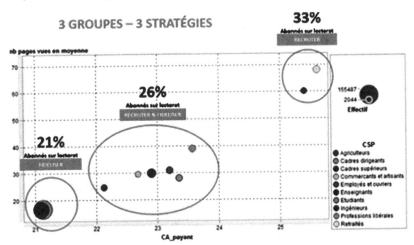

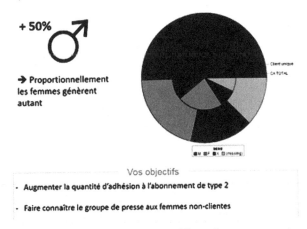

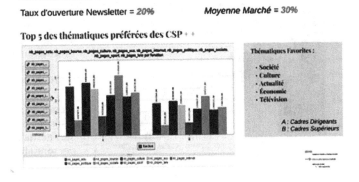

Figure 3. Sample of advanced visual statistics techniques

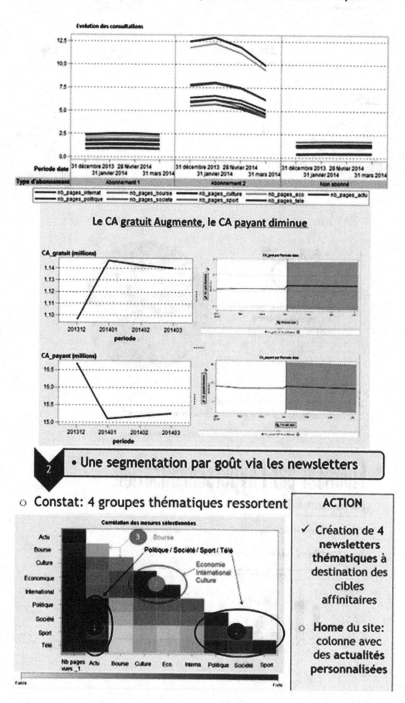

technology and actors. For instance, until the end of October 2013, Hadoop was seen as the breakthrough technology of the big data phenomenon, allowing to manage and transform large quantities of data with performance levels that had never been reached before. In 2014, Apache Spark dethroned Hadoop by allowing to work 100 times faster than Hadoop 1.0, and the trend will continue... The big data sphere is a bubbling ecosystem in which startups keep emerging and growing, and in which the sub-domain leaders are a mix of technology dinosaurs to mere infants with only a few years of existence.

As a consequence, higher education institutions are facing a nearly impossible challenge that is equivalent to being urged to catch a very important train that is already moving and which speed keeps increasing. The only way to tackle such challenge is to close the gap between educational institutions and the world of practitioners and engage into an active collaboration. Teaching big data cannot be efficiently done without being directly 'plugged' into the big data ecosystem. In other words, it is not sufficient to work towards reducing the dramatic big data skill shortage that is foreseen for the next two to three years. Big data is evolving at such a fast pace that new expertise, skills, and technologies keep emerging. It will not be astounding to hear from industry experts about another dramatic big data 2.0 skill shortage within the next few years. In short, the solution is to catch the train and stay in it while its pace increases instead of going down at the next stop and catching another train that goes even faster and is thus harder to catch.

Touching Data to Feel its Business Value

Manipulating data is not a common task for managers who are more used to already digested and formatted information. It was interesting to notice that about a third of the time spent by all participants (the 20 groups) during the serious game was to get acquainted with the dataset and looking at raw data in order to get insights about the type, accuracy, and potential value of each variable. Participants used simple descriptive statistics for each of the variables but more importantly, they dedicated a lot of time displaying raw data and scrolling through the different values associated with each variable. Because there was no instructed sequence of tasks to be performed during the serious game (only the main objectives were provided), it can be argued with a reasonable amount of confidence that this common tendency about the need to 'touch' data naturally occurred. The participants quickly realized that it was simply impossible to derive relevant business recommendations without pulling up their sleeves, going back to data in its raw form, and spending time getting a good grasp of it.

By doing so participants were directly confronted with issues that were new to them but crucial to perform the task such as: dealing with missing variables and understanding the associated meaning, realizing that data sources are more or less reliable, understanding that the degree of accuracy of data sources can vary, realizing that sources can be trusted but not others... Participants gradually entered the world of data scientists and understood that deriving insights and making business decisions based on big data is no easy task. We noticed that the groups which dedicated the largest amount of time to get a good grasp of the dataset were the ones that performed the best (based on the performance scores provided by the members of the jury).

This validated the pertinence of the task that was designed for the serious game which was aiming at sensitizing future managers to the intrusion of data in the traditional decision lifecycle. If one has to define in simple terms what the main mission of business schools is when teaching big data, it can be argued that it is simply to create and consolidate the link between data and business decision in students' conceptual mind maps. The coaching of students during the serious game allowed to clearly observe the gradual understanding from the participants that data contain business value and shall thus be treated as precious resources.

To answer the main question formulated in this chapter title, a sine qua non condition to engrain a big data mindset into our managers' DNA is to get managers acquainted to data and make them apprehend the business value that is embedded into data. This can only be done by touching data, manipulating them, and 'playing' with them.

Playing with Data: Serious Games and Simulations

The big data business paradigm will engender a cultural shift in organizations. Whereas failure is used to be severely condemned in our nowadays highly competitive world, it becomes a positive mechanism in the big data world. Indeed, a big data mindset is characterized by an experiential culture in which one learns from failures and gradually improves through several cycles of experiments and actions. For instance, sentiment analysis modelling is an ever evolving task as language keeps changing: new words keep appearing (such as selfie…) and our society keeps giving birth to new ways of expression. For instance, more than 100 distinct emoticons are officially recognized (to which correspond a combination of two to three characters) and used in digital communication channels to express a broad range of emotions. Developing social media data models is thus an incremental process during which human actions and corrections allow to refine models up to satisfactory levels of accuracy and performance. In short, big data is not about success but rather about experimental failures that eventually lead to success.

Engendering an experiential culture within the mind of managers is a difficult task as it contradicts the basic nature of a manager's job. Time is money and failing costs even more money. To convince (future) managers of the benefits of experimentation in the big data context, the use of serious games or other types of simulation shall be recommended. Indeed, it is only through direct experimentation that one can seize that incremental learning allows to reach higher ends (at least in the big data context). To plant such seed in the mind of managers, well-designed big data simulations shall accompany participants through several loops of a fail-and-learn process and demonstrate the overall benefits of the approach.

The choice to use a data visualization task for a short big data training program (a few weeks) was highly satisfactory and shall be recommended for similar big data training initiatives. Indeed, a one-day training session was sufficient to ensure that participants had enough skills to perform basic but also advanced manipulations on the dataset. The technical barriers of entry were lowered as the drag-and-drop interface of data visualization applications are designed in such a way that users can go straight into the data without having to deal with either database management commands or obscure statistical functions.

Working in close collaboration with the big data ecosystem is crucial in the design of pedagogically effective simulations as their success is directly dependent on the provision of appropriate big data tools but also, and more importantly, on the use of datasets that contain a decent amount of 'pedagogical value'. Indeed, past and current experiences in designing big data events in the business school made us realize that good datasets are rare resources. Big data professionals are keen to provide real datasets (under certain terms) but the inherent complexity of big data renders the task to find quality datasets perhaps the most delicate one. In the case of the workshop presented in this book chapter, the opted solution was to rely on semi-real data that consisted of merging two real datasets (from two French newspapers) and to slightly inflate the patterns that characterized the final dataset (by applying several mathematical formulas on some of the columns and adding some random variation).

Strengthening Statistics and Database Skills

Managers will in no way become data scientists. They will rather be an interface between a team of big data experts (data scientists, data analysts, big data solution architect…) and higher management. They may also be directly involved in big data projects within their organization. As a result, it is necessary that all participating actors shall use a common language and have some shared understanding on a number of basic big data-related concepts. In addition to getting big data engrained into their mindset, managers shall thus develop solid skills in statistics and databases. The workshop allowed to clearly identify the need for the two types of knowledge. The participants that had no prior knowledge on database management and data structure struggled throughout the serious game. Moreover, those that had not acquired a solid basis in business statistics were equally penalized.

Data visualization tools usually use statistical techniques that rely on concepts (such as descriptive statistics, linear regressions or time series…) that are covered in traditional business statistics courses provided by business schools. For instance, correlation is a common concept in a wealth of big data projects. Real-time decision making tools use simple and more advanced correlation techniques to identify insightful patterns that would otherwise remain hidden in exabytes or zettabytes of messy data. Online recommendation systems used by Netflix (Bollier & Firestone, 2010) or Amazon (Linden et al., 2003) look for correlations in users' viewing habits and product features. Making predictions is also an essential big data component and linear regressions (but also confidence intervals) are commonly used. As a result, it is crucial that business schools at least maintain the content of their conventional business statistics course and dedicate extra time and efforts to ensure that the main concepts are thoroughly acquired by students. This is a necessary condition to make sure that future managers will have a sound basis to evolve in a big data environment.

However, big data modelling techniques tend to rely more and more on advanced statistical concepts that are not taught in business schools. Extra efforts shall thus be spent to include them in curricula leading to globally stress out the importance of statistics in the training of future managers.

For example, predictive modeling techniques provided in data visualization tools often rely on generalized linear modeling, logistic regression, or classification trees, as it was the case with the tool used during the workshop. No single participant used such techniques to analyze the data. Cluster analysis and modeling is for instance widely used in online recommendation systems (Linden et al., 2003) but also to identify communities or commonalities within groups of users in social networks, or to identify customer segments to offer finely targeted services/products. Big data can help marketing research in performing simulations (e.g. Monte Carlo) to estimate entry market share for a new product/service, forecast sales, or evaluate the actual market size for a product or service. Finally, big data solutions heavily rely on correlation techniques to identify patterns among sources of data. However, big data experts are raising concern about the validity of such approach as correlation is far from equating causation which is what is usually sought. People such as Chris Anderson, editor-in-chief of Wired magazine claimed that big data had rendered obsolete the scientific method arguing that the analysis of correlation in large datasets would replace it. Big data experts have on the contrary shot an alarm signal at the overuse of correlation techniques and the associated theory-free causal inferences that are made. Spurious correlations abound in our world. A wrong conclusion about the existence of causation can lead to erroneous actions and negative consequences for businesses with ill-used big data tools. Expertise in the design of experiments as well as scientific models can help close the gap between causation and correlation (McAfee et al., 2012) and would be of great help for managers working on big data.

The Google Flu Trend case is one among the many examples of the limits of correlation. Google Flu Trends is a web-based service provided by Google that started in 2008. For several years, the theory-free service accurately predicted influenza outbreaks by correlating search engine terms and the spread of flu. In 2013, confidence in the accuracy of the service was strongly severed as it had drastically overestimated peak flu levels (Lazar et al., 2014). One of the potential explanations was that the media broadcasted a lot of negative 'flu' stories that provoked an increase of 'flu' web searches even by people who were healthy. A pharmaceutical company which would take for granted the predictions of the Google Flu Trend service and act accordingly would have lost a significant amount of money.

A similar argument can be made about the need to develop data structure and database management skills (which are not usually taught as a core course in business schools). This was a striking observation while coaching students during the serious game. For instance, the exploration of multidimensional data usually requires the organization of data into hierarchies allowing to slice and dice data through the use of filters. The participants that did not properly used data hierarchies (or did not use them all) remained at a superficial degree of comprehension of the dataset and provided shallow business recommendations. Difficulties in making the distinction between nominal, ordinal and interval variables, as well as the applicability of the different statistical techniques for each of the variable category, also appeared as an obstacle to perform good analyses. Finally, basic database management knowledge was a plus for the participants that were comfortable with the notions of database, tables, records, and fields, and who had previous experience in relational database management (such as handling SQL queries). The data visualization tool that was used during the workshop had a data builder mode which main functionality was to merge source tables from third-party vendor databases and manage the tables of the entire dataset. Participants who used the data builder module when exploring the dataset and understanding the link between the different tables, provided a much more in-depth analysis that resulted in quality business recommendations.

In conclusion, a necessary condition for business schools that are striving to diffuse big data into their curricula is to adjust the content of their business statistics courses and to emphasize the crucial importance of statistics in the big data context. Key database concepts (including managing and manipulating relational databases) shall also be taught as this provides a sound basis to understand important big data notions such as scalable distributed database systems or NoSQL.

CONCLUSION

This book chapter aims at providing insights to business schools as well as organizations from both the private and the public sector, that are reflecting on the extent to which big data will impact the function and role of managers. Perceived as one of the most fertile terrains for taking advantage from the data transformation, the public sector is particularly targeted in this chapter.

By going beyond the conventional techno-centric view of big data that sees the phenomenon as simply a question of processing too large and too complex datasets, this book chapter adopts a higher-level societal approach that heralds a business paradigm shift in which data will play a predominant role and be a key business driver. A French top-ten business school reflected on how to address the overall big data talent shortage announced by most industry experts, who are also predicting that such skill shortage will also concern millions of managers throughout the world. The school designed a two-week big data workshop with the intention of experimenting a small-scale big data initiative (with 100 graduating students for a master in management program) that would help gain insights for larger-scale initiatives aiming at diffusing big data into the various programs and curricula of the school. In addition to being an overall success by being perceived quite enthusiastically by all participants including the involved practitioners and the organizers, important lessons could be learnt. First, the nature of the big data phenomenon as well as the complexity of the big data landscape render the tight collaboration with the big data ecosystem a key success factor. Second, engraining a big data mindset into our managers' DNA can be effectively done only through the design of courses or programs that make students and trainees touch and manipulate data. Third, serious games and other types of simulation are ideal pedagogical strategies to infuse an experiential culture within the minds of trainees and to demonstrate the link that exists between data, business value, and business decision. Finally, skills in simple and advanced business statistics, but also data structure and database management appear to be crucial in establishing a conceptual and practical basis on which to build a sound understanding of big data in dedicated courses and programs. Considering the degree of commonality between French business schools and other international business schools, we believe that the derived insights and conclusions are also beneficial to any international business school that is at the reflection stage about how curricula shall be impacted by the advent of the data-driven era. We sincerely hope the overall approach as well as the pedagogical engineering presented in this chapter will provide insights to educational institutions and organizations from both the private and the public sector that have launched a similar reflection and have engaged on the path of the big data era.

REFERENCES

Big Data. (n.d.a). In *Merriam-Webster dictionary*. Retrieved October 27, 2014, from http://www.merriam-webster.com/dictionary/big_data

Big Data. (n.d.b). In *Oxford dictionaries*. Retrieved October 27, 2014, from http://www.oxforddictionaries.com/definition/english/big-data

Big Data. (n.d.c). In *Gartner IT Glossary*. Retrieved October 27, 2014, from http://www.gartner.com/it-glossary/big-data

Bollier, D., & Firestone, C. M. (2010). *The promise and peril of big data*. Washington, DC: Aspen Institute, Communications and Society Program.

Brown, B., Chui, M., & Manyika, J. (2011). Are you ready for the era of 'big data'? *The McKinsey Quarterly, 4*, 24–35.

Chen, H. (2011). Design Science, Grand Challenges, and Societal Impacts. *ACM Transactions on Management Information Systems, 2*(1), 1–10. doi:10.1145/1929916.1929917

Chen, H., Chiang, R., & Storey, V. (2012). Business Intelligence and Analytics: From Big Data to Big Impact. *Management Information Systems Quarterly, 36*(4), 1165–1188.

Galliers, R. (2003). Change as crisis or growth? Toward a trans-disciplinary view of information systems as a field of study: A response to Benbasat and Zmud's call for returning to the IT. *Journal of the Association for Information Systems, 4*(6), 337–351.

Gartner, Inc. (2012a). *Gartner Says Big Data Will Drive $28 Billion of IT Spending in 2012*. Retrieved October 27, 2014, from http://www.gartner.com/newsroom/id/2200815

Gartner, Inc. (2012b). *Gartner Says Big Data Creates Big Jobs: 4.4 Million IT Jobs Globally to Support Big Data By 2015*. Retrieved October 27, 2014, from http://www.gartner.com/newsroom/id/2207915

Gil Press. (2013). *$16.1 Billion Big Data market: 2014 Predictions From IDS And IIA*. Retrieved from http://www.forbes.com/sites/gilpress/2013/12/12/16-1-billion-big-data-market-2014-predictions-from-idc-and-iia

Lazer, D., Kennedy, R., & Vespignani, A. (2014). The Parable of Google Flu: Traps in Big Data Analysis. *Science*, *343*(6176), 1203–1205. doi:10.1126/science.1248506 PMID:24626916

Linden, G., Smith, B., & York, J. (2003). Amazon.com recommendations: Item-to-item collaborative filtering. *Internet Computing*, *7*(1), 76–80. doi:10.1109/MIC.2003.1167344

Manyika, J., Chui, M., Brown, B., Bughin, J., Dobbs, R., Roxburgh, C., & Byers, A. H. (2011). *Big data: The next frontier for innovation, competition, and productivity*. Retrieved October 27, 2014, from http://www.mckinsey.com/insights/business_technology/big_data_the_next_frontier_for_innovation

McAfee, A., Brynjolfsson, E., Davenport, T. H., Patil, D. J., & Barton, D. (2012). Big Data. The management revolution. *Harvard Business Review*, *90*(10), 61–67. PMID:23074865

Olofson, C. W., & Vesset, D. (2012). *Big Data: Trends, Strategies and SAP Technology*. Report ICD #236135.

Schoenherr, T., & Speier-Pero, C. (2015). Data Science, Predictive Analytics, and Big Data in Supply Chain Management: Current State and Future Potential. *Journal of Business Logistics*, *36*(1), 120–132. doi:10.1111/jbl.12082

Sondergaard, P. (2013). *Gartner Analyst Opening Keynote Gartner. Symposium/ITxpo 2013*. Retrieved October 27, 2014, from http://www.gartnereventsondemand.com/index.php?t=trailer&e=SYM23&i=K2

Ward, J. S., & Barker, A. (2013). *Undefined By Data: A Survey of Big Data Definitions*. arXiv preprint arXiv:1309.5821

Wixom, B., Thlini, A., Douglas, D., Goul, M., Gupta, B., Iyer, L., & Turetken, O. et al. (2014). The Current State of Business Intelligence in Academia: The Arrival of Big Data. *Communications of the Association for Information Systems*, *34*(1).

KEY TERMS AND DEFINITIONS

(Apache) Hadoop: An open source project that provides a programming framework allowing the scalable and distributed processing of large datasets across a cluster of commodity servers. It is part of the Apache project and sponsored by the Apache Software Foundation.

(Apache) HBase: A column-oriented database management system that is used to provide real-time read and write access to datasets hosted on Apache Hadoop clusters. Apache HBase does not relies on the support a structured query language such as SQL. It is a sub-project of the Apache Hadoop project.

(Apache) Hive: An open source data warehouse system designed to query and analyze large datasets stored in Hadoop files.

(Apache) Spark: An open-source parallel processing framework that allows developers to run large-scale data analytics applications across a cluster of commodity servers. The Spark project fits within the Hadoop community.

(Big) Data Visualization: The implementation of traditional and more contemporary visualization techniques that help identify trends, patterns, and relationships within data.

Machine Learning: A scientific/engineering field that aims at constructing algorithms that can learn from data and at building models that are typically used to make decisions or predictions.

MapReduce: A software framework used at the core of the Hadoop system and allowing developers to write programs for processing large amounts of unstructured data in parallel across a cluster of commodity servers.

MongoDB: An open source project that provides a cross-platform document-oriented database framework. It is among the most popular NoSQL (see definition) database systems.

NoSQL: (also called Not Only SQL): An alternative database environment (as opposed to more conventional relational databases) that allows to design and manage very large sets of distributed data.

Python: An open-source high-level programming language (object-oriented) that is known for being easy to read and simple to implement. It is often used in big data projects.

Chapter 6
Big Data from Management Perspective

Alireza Bolhari
Islamic Azad University, Science and Research Branch, Iran

ABSTRACT

Competency matters. Social media, customer transactions, mobile sensors, and feedback contents are all piled up with data. This might be unstructured and complex data in voluminous quantity, often called Big Data. However, if this Big Data is managed, it might bring competency for organizations. This chapter introduces the must-know concepts and materials for organizational managers who face Big Data. Through the chapter, Big Data is defined and its emergence over the time is reviewed. The four Vs model in Big Data literature and its link to a banking system is analyzed. The chapter concludes by making a managerial awareness concerning ethical issues in Big Data. This is of high priority in public sectors as data relies for every individual in the society.

INTRODUCTION

Without Big Data analytics, companies are blind and deaf, wandering out onto the Web like deer on a freeway (Geoffrey Moore[1]).

Organizations are facing every 18 months with doubled data (Moore, 1965) in unlike formats and in different departments such as marketing, research and development, procurement, warehousing, production, sales, customer satisfaction and retention, etc. These inconsistent, unstructured and massive data- first called "Big Data" by Cox and Ellsworth (1997, p. 235)- must be managed to avoid digital disruption. Managers are responsible for providing necessary infrastructures, hardware, software or applications, and most of all, data analysts who are familiar with massive data concepts.

Although Big Data is introduced in 1997, it is still a popular and developing subject in the field of analytics (Sathi, 2012, p. 73). Complex and massive structured/unstructured data will not be processed due to memory limitations and must be processed in a place other than memory. The best suitable place is where they reside (Prajapati, 2013, p. 4). For instance, around 20 million storage cabinets are needed

DOI: 10.4018/978-1-4666-9649-5.ch006

to file text documents or more than 13 years of video files in high-definition (HD) quality when talking about data in petabytes (Hurwitz, Nugent, Halper, & Kaufman, 2013, p. 15). This size of storage is rarely processed in memory with current available technologies.

This chapter is intended to present a holistic managerial view over Big Data with emphasis on integration issues in public sector. A definition and an overview of the emergence of Big Data are presented. The *4Vs model* introducing variety, volume, velocity and veracity of data is deeply reviewed with examples. Following, Big Data applications and management challenges are discussed and finally, the importance of ethical issues in Big Data management is highlighted.

WHAT IS BIG DATA?

Big Data refers to the storage, management and manipulation of different types of data in vast quantities (Hurwitz, Nugent, Halper, & Kaufman, 2013, p. 1). This includes different types such as text files, images, voices, and videos. By investigating these vast amounts of data, hidden patterns that would lead important changes might be revealed. Hurwitz et al. (2013, p. 16) define Big Data as a process in which huge and different types of data are timely managed to meet real time responsiveness in analytics. Figure 1 illustrates the emergence of Big Data over time. Famous relational databases were introduced in 1980s and 1990s which were or presumably are handling complex data. The exponential growth of data in 2000s led to massive and various data types. This lets very complex and unstructured data to be managed.

This unstructured data will be obtained either from the inside of a corporation or outside. Sathi (2012) defines these two sources as:

Figure 1. How Big Data emerged over time (Mohanty, Jagadeesh, & Srivatsa, 2013)

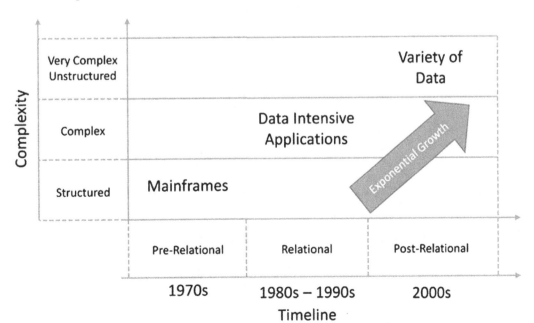

... a fair amount of data within the corporation that ... is increasingly shared. This includes emails, mainframe logs, blogs, Adobe PDF documents, business process events, and any other structured, unstructured, or semi-structured data available inside the organization.

... a lot more data outside the organization—some available publicly free of cost, some based on paid subscription, and the rest available selectively for specific business partners or customers. This includes information available on social media sites, product literature freely distributed by competitors, corporate customers' organization hierarchies, helpful hints available from third parties, and customer complaints posted on regulatory sites.

Accordingly, Big Data requires innovative models to analyze voluminous, various in type and rapidly being generated data (Loshin, 2013, p. 3). This is conducted by following the general cycle of Big Data management (Hurwitz, Nugent, Halper, & Kaufman, 2013, p. 17) shown in figure 2. In the first two steps, data is captured and organized in databases or data warehouses. Due to data variety, data integration is the third step and then, analyzing data is implemented through different techniques. Finally, findings of data analysis define action plans that lead to organizational effectiveness.

Loshin (2013, p. 4) mentions a number of trends that force organizations to look for Big Data platforms, for instance, ever increasing data volume and data growth, increasing data variety, growing need for real time analytics, and etc. When talking about Big Data, various data types are considered such as (not limited to):

- Social media files
- Customer manuals of products
- RFID tags

Figure 2. General cycle of Big Data management

- Mainframe logs
- Geo-tag locations
- Customer transactions
- News feeds
- Blog contents
- etc.

This combination of structured and unstructured complex crowd of data is called "*Big Data*".

Short Case: Big Data in Marketing Industry

Figure 3 presents customer experience in different marketing business areas and their possible sources of data (Arthur, 2013, p. 31). Customer experience, the interaction between customer and company, encompasses different channels and instruments which are all potential data-generators. Every day, every hour, and every second, customer related data are being generated in call center communications (telephone, email, on-line ticketing, etc.), social networks, mobile applications and etc. This remarkably Big Data includes texts, voices, and pictures with valuable information, if exploited.

Big Data, however, may be a driver to change marketing business model. This may be done through the use of information derived from Big Data (Hurwitz, Nugent, Halper, & Kaufman, 2013, p. 1).

Figure 3. Customer experience in marketing industry

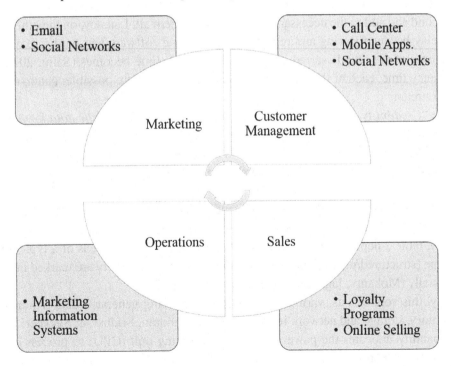

FOUR VS MODEL

In understanding Big Data, the *4Vs model* of variety, volume, velocity and veracity (Sathi, 2012, p. 2) could bring insight for managers:

- **Variety:** In the age of data warehousing, data were typically structured and in least variety. This enabled the extract, transfer, and load (ETL) functions to convert data into data warehouses (Sathi, 2012, p. 4). Big data, on the contrary, comes with unstructured, semi-structured and structured formats, for instance: social media texts, music and video files, news and blog contents, customer transactions, information system logs, and financial and manufacturing records. These data could be from different sources such as comments, photos, and interview videos of a movie (Ming, et al., 2014, p. 140).
- **Volume:** Typical information systems are not capable of analyzing Big Data in a desired time frame. This is duo to the massive volumes of data which are continuously rising. In 2012, a few terabytes were to be Big and it is growing to petabytes[2] and more. Big Data for one company might be dealing with around 10 TB of data. However, this would not be considered Big Data for another company. Dealing with such a voluminous data necessitates manager's considerations before any data-related crises take place (Prajapati, 2013, p. 4). Fortune (2012) reports that the total amount of digital data generated until 2003 was five exabytes, while in 2011 this amount was created in only 2 days (Fortune, 2012). Moreover, until 2020 the volume of data reaches to some 35 zetta-bytes[3] (Fourneau & Pekergin, 2002).
- **Velocity:** Data throughput and latency are the two factors of velocity. Throughput represents the flow of data in transferring channels. Picture, music, video, and text files are transferred every single second and add to the necessary volume to save them all. Latency, on the other hand, stands for the delay between storing and reporting. In the same software and hardware conditions, the more volume of the data is stored, the more the latency time becomes (Sathi, 2012, p. 4). Due to the latency time, each of the following processing methods are possible: batch, near time, real time, and stream.
- **Veracity:** *"Credibility of the data source as well as the suitability of the data for the target audience"* (Sathi, 2012, p. 4) is defined as veracity in Big Data. Source credibility is identified by the trustfulness and accuracy of data derived from a source and audience suitability is the amount of truth to be shared with audience (customers, suppliers, etc.).

According to the 3Vs model (volume, velocity, and variety), table 1 demonstrates the characteristics of Big Data in different industries in selected areas (Mohanty, Jagadeesh, & Srivatsa, 2013, p. 48).

Accordingly, table 2 depicts existence of Big Data in the underlying areas of a typical banking industry. Data type (structured/unstructured) and volume, velocity and variety are marked in each banking system individually (Mohanty, Jagadeesh, & Srivatsa, 2013, p. 54).

Accordingly, this voluminous, various and continuously being-generated data requires processing capability, memory, storage and network infrastructures (Chandran, Sridhar, & Sakkeer, 2014, p. 180). Processing capability indicates the power of central processing unit (CPU) to process data. Memory holds the data which is being processed and the necessary datasets are saved in storage. Network infrastructures prepare data flow between nodes (Loshin, 2013, p. 61).

Table 1. Review of 3Vs model in different industries (Mohanty, Jagadeesh, & Srivatsa, 2013, p. 48)

Industry	Area	Characteristics		
		Volume	Velocity	Variety
e-Commerce	Market Analyzing Programs	✓		✓
	Loyalty Programs	✓		✓
	Supply Chain Logistics	✓	✓	
	Recommender Systems	✓	✓	✓
	Just In Time Service	✓	✓	✓
Financial Services	Risk Management	✓	✓	✓
	Fraud Analysis	✓	✓	✓
	Customer Relationship Management	✓	✓	✓
	Credit Scoring	✓	✓	✓
Health Services	Insurance Control and Fraud Detection	✓	✓	✓
	Brand Management	✓		✓
	Patient Program Analysis	✓		✓
	Research and Development	✓		✓
Communication Technology	Pricing	✓	✓	✓
	Churn Management	✓	✓	✓
	Real Time Call Detail Record	✓	✓	✓
	Customer Loyalty Management	✓	✓	✓
	Social Services	✓	✓	✓
Government Services	Regulatory Management and Analysis	✓	✓	✓
	Fraud and Intrusion Management	✓	✓	✓
	Surveillance	✓	✓	✓
	e-Governance	✓	✓	✓
	Energy Production and Consumption	✓	✓	✓

APPLICATIONS OF BIG DATA ANALYTICS

Conventional analysis models conduct structured analysis as in business intelligence, while other models perform unstructured analysis (Sathi, 2012, p. 58). Factors such as accuracy, completeness, consistency, and uniqueness are measures of data quality in conventional analysis models (Loshin, 2013, p. 41). In Big Data, massive amounts and various types of structured or unstructured data are analyzed. The source of this data would be internal or external (from the outside of the organization). As a result, Big Data makes it sophisticated for managers to either locate the desired piece of data or recognize the hidden patterns. Improving customer marketing, developing new products and services, more efficient supply chains, and better fraud detection are a few samples. In table 3, several Big Data analytics applications are listed in summary (Sathi, 2012, pp. 15-29; Hurwitz, Nugent, Halper, & Kaufman, 2013, p. 23). Every application would be categorized in counting, scanning, modeling, and storing of data (Loshin, 2013, pp. 12-16).

Table 2. Banking systems and 3Vs model (Mohanty, Jagadeesh, & Srivatsa, 2013, p. 54)

Applications / Systems	Area	Data Type	Characteristics		
			Volume	Velocity	Variety
Retail	Branching	S/U	✓		
	Mortgaging	S			
	Credit Cards	S	✓		
	Private Banking	S/U			
Commercial	Credit Risk Analysis	S/U	✓		✓
	Noncredit services	S/U			
	Client Management	S/U			
	Middle Market Lending	S/U			
Capital Markets	Trading and Sales	S	✓	✓	
	Structured Finance	S			
	Non-depository Credit Institutions	S/U			
Assets	Management of Wealth	S			
	Asset Management	S			
	Asset Owner Services	S			
	Investment Products	S			
	Asset Issuer Services	S			
	Asset Reporting	S			
	Investment Deposit Analytics	S			
Enterprise Services	Markets Trading	S	✓	✓	
	Liability Management	S			
	Risk Management	S/U	✓	✓	✓
	Customer Relationship Management	S/U	✓	✓	✓

S: Structured Data, U: Unstructured Data

Short Case: Big Data Application in Police and Traffic Services

A Big Data solution is developed for a Chinese city to prevent illegal attempts and violations in the domain of the traffic control system. Real-time cameras capture images with meta-data such as date and time, car's license (plate) number, color, speed, etc. Images are saved in a central data warehouse and Real-Time Analytics (RTA) system examines every instance of the images and identifies inconsistencies. For instance, if an Alpha model car with license number 999 and blue color is captured as a red car, the alarm is automatically generated for the agent in charge. Likewise, if a single car is captured in two different geographically distributed streets in a short period of time, the alarm rings.

The whole system is equipped with extensive reports containing car owners' data, average speeds, frequent locations of the cars, etc. (Zhong, Doshi, Tang, Lou, & Lu, 2014, p. 99). This integration of several systems works as one whole system and leads to increased public security.

Table 3. Summary of some of the applications of Big Data

Application	Description
Social Media Data Analytics	• Increasing consumer experience • Forecasting future consumer needs • Automating responses in feedback process
Knowledge Base	• Forming a knowledge base/hub from different databases • Accessing to real-time data • Reducing the time of call handling in call centers
Public Safety	• Developing smart systems • Anticipating and preventing public crimes
Product Design	• Tailoring products based on customer experience • Designing personalized products
Geography-Based Services	• Forming a database of customer's locations • Clustering customers • Proposing services and products based on location
Risk Management	• Analyzing Big Data to find fraud patterns • Developing a fraud engine

Short Case: Managing Big Data in Healthcare Industry

Big Data in healthcare industry, as a public and private sector, is of high importance. Various parties are engaged in the process of health-related data generation like governments, healthcare institutes, healthcare providers, insurers, patients, etc. Data are gathered and stored in different formats (texts, images, video, etc.) and levels of sensitivity. No doubt there exists personal data such as name, age, national code, address and very personal data such as previous health records in circulation between health parties (Kambatla, Kollias, Kumar, & Grama, 2014) (see Figure 4).

The underlying challenge is the exploitation of these distributed and different types of Data. This is the main reason why traditional data management systems are not capable of processing Big Data. As an ultimate goal, Costa (2014, p. 433) draws the future of Big Data application in health industry as" *"having personalized medicine programs that will significantly improve patient care"*.

On the other hand, Big Data may be used to prevent fraudulent actions in this industry. Every year in the United States an estimation of 60 Billion dollars are paid by taxpayers to cover fraud costs (Kambatla, Kollias, Kumar, & Grama, 2014). A mechanism to detect these fraudulent actions come true by Big Data applications.

BIG DATA: MANAGEMENT CHALLENGES

Hurwitz et al. (2013, p. 10) state that "when you are dealing with so much information in so many different forms, it is impossible to think about data management in traditional ways". This brings a managerial insight which would lead to a revision in data management strategies and policies. Chang et al. (2013) discuss three types of managerial issues that Big Data addresses. Business issues refer to product pricing, optimal service design, social networking and others. Consumer issues hold segmentation, product design sensitivity, churn management, etc. Finally, support for education, human communication, public

Figure 4. Schematic view the parties of a health system

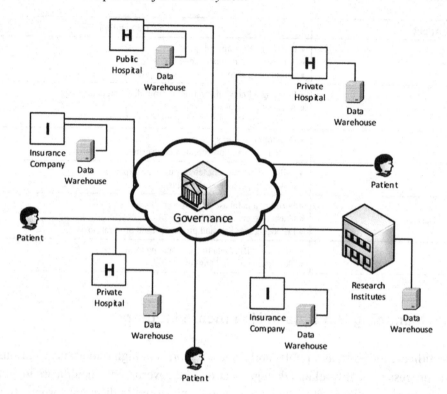

goods management, and so forth are discussed in social issues. Meanwhile, the primary role of information technology managers is to distinct between conventional data in datasets and Big Data. In addition, they should take into consideration organizational readiness for storing and analyzing Big Data in a desired time frame. Figure 5 depicts the level of data penetration in selected industries by text, audio, image and video distinction. As illustrated, managers are faced more complex issues in media rather than in an insurance industry.

Managers would forecast confronting challenges by conducting initial analysis (Table 4). The analysis starts from the feasibility study by focusing on infrastructure, software, skills and organizational environment. These factors should be deeply analyzed independently and in correlation to each other. To be feasible does not mean to be reasonable. As a result, reasonability indicates the logic behind implementation of Big Data. This is in tight reference between value and integrability: does Big Data add value to the organization and stay integrated with current environment? As a final point, sustainability of the Big Data is analyzed to ensure that it would be a surviving plan.

More specifically in the public sector, managers are faced challenges and issues concerning Big Data integration. Basic government services such as public transportation, road maintenance, military, police, prison and security services, healthcare and education systems, etc. are all piled up with structured and unstructured data. Managing this massive data and integration between mentioned services confront government managers with fundamental challenges. In the States, cloud services are considered as a solution. Integrations in cloud are significantly decreasing down-times and operating costs and help reach an integrated and real-time solution based on Big Data (Kambatla, Kollias, Kumar, & Grama, 2014). Accordingly, for a successful implementation of Big Data, Loshin (2013, p. 105) defines the roadmap

Figure 5. Map of data generated by selected industries

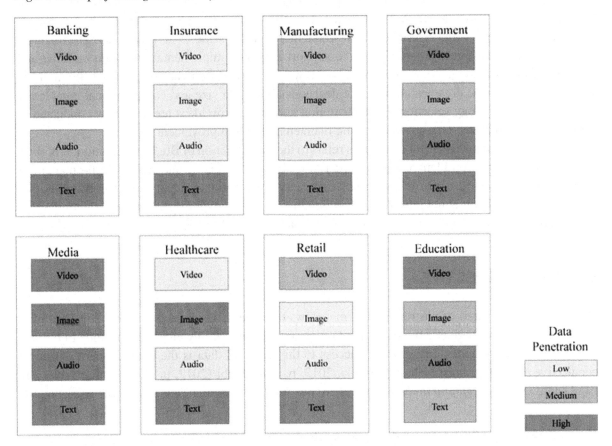

Table 4. Forecasting challenges in Big Data (Loshin, 2013, p. 8)

Area	Description
Feasibility	• Considering infrastructure, software, skills and environment, is the organization ready to implement Big Data?
Reasonability	• According to data types and resource requirements, is it reasonable to implement Big Data? • Does the environment stay constant?
Value	• Does the organization gain value against implementation of Big Data? • How the cost/benefit analysis does reveals values?
Integrability	• What are the possible hinders and constraints that would prevent total integrity? • What would be the solutions towards integrity?
Sustainability	• According to the changing environment, what are the potential plans to survive and continue Big Data?

of Big Data implementation as a "*program management approach*" to arrange an organized situation (Figure 6). The overall roadmap complies with the plan–do–check–action management method with more detailed steps. It starts with needs assessment which thoroughly assesses 3 or 4Vs model. The roadmap continues with management's commitment to support Big Data implementation. Team building and preliminary organizational assessment are the next two steps that follow the commitment. Preliminary assessment enables the organization to make decisions about data size and computational complexity which lead to technology selection. Implementation and integration ideas are somehow conducted in parallel and the final step engages the ongoing maintenance and improvement plans.

The final point in management challenges refers to the identification of Big Data situation. It is obvious that every business problem relating to data is not a Big Data problem and at least the problem must fit the three Vs model. It is worth mentioning that every organization needs its own Big Data solution and a universal solution is not prescribed (Loshin, 2013, p. 105). As a result, the identification of the problem (needs assessment in the above mentioned roadmap) is a key to a successful Big Data.

ETHICAL PERSPECTIVE

Data in either structured or unstructured format flows over the networks and Internet. Big Data platforms and technologies enable the flow of data more readily and rapidly and make it prone to billions of potential network nodes. Inappropriate access to this personal data is the main concern of ethical perspective (Mohanty, Jagadeesh, & Srivatsa, 2013, p. 198). Sathi (2012, p. 5) urges that privacy in Big Data is "*the big elephant in the room*". There has been few researches and concerns regarding the

Figure 6. Roadmap of Big Data implementation, derived from Loshin (2013, p. 105)

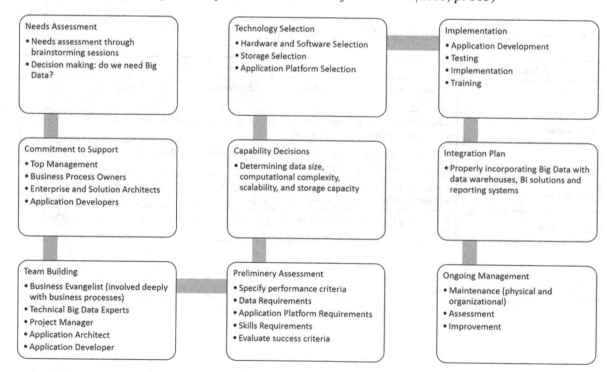

ethical issues. From the ethical perspective, the privacy of Big Data has become a factual concern for both governments and data-holder companies. This concern has led them to set privacy policies (Sathi, 2012, p. 44) to protect the identity of their customers and information policy management to protect organization-wide information. However, by possessing detailed customer data such as name, demographic data, cell-phone number, health-related data, home and work address, bank account numbers, and etc. does privacy policy protect the privacy of the customers? This is still a controversial issue that calls for deeper investigation. In this regard, audit programs, preferably conducted by third parties are valuable to measure the effectiveness of privacy policies (Sathi, 2012, p. 46).

One method to protect sensitive data is data masking. This is somehow a powerful tool to de-identify data which removes customer's identification data from data (Mohanty, Jagadeesh, & Srivatsa, 2013, p. 152). Another method is the database or data warehouse monitoring mechanisms deployed to watch the access of privileged users, their data retrieval jobs, etc. Based on each organization's Big Data solution, numerous other methods are deployed to protect privacy issues and satisfy ethical concerns.

Short Case: Privacy and Data Analysis in Website Browsing

In order to benefit from data analysis in online sales, capturing the behavior of websites' visitors is implemented by browser cookies and other technologies. This is often employed without direct permission of visitors. This data is further analyzed to let users automatically log-into the system (session management), recommend items (products and services) based on previously bought or visited items (personalization), and tracking purposes.

In a recommender system (figure 7), the data gathering phase initiates when a user/customer visits the website. Information about location, time, IP address, form fields, operating system, visited pages and

Figure 7. A simplified Model of a Recommender System

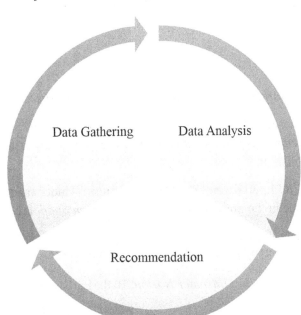

items, purchased items and etc. are gathered either with or without prior permission of the visitor. This brings the privacy issues into consideration: am I permitted to gather these information? Do I have to set a privacy policy and inform the visitor before engaging with my website? This controversial discussion remains open as the benefits of the recommender systems are for both parties: organizations and visitors.

CONCLUSION

Worldwide interests have been dedicated to Big Data behavior and pattern extraction in different industries (Halevi & Moed, 2012; Rousseau, 2012). Big Data makes information processing more efficient and enables existing technologies to deliver faster and on-time results (Miller, 2013, p. 571). In typical information systems, data is normalized and stored in structured tables. However, as discussed, unstructured and various data types should be stored, manipulated and treated differently. Everyday transactions in different departments of organizations and public sectors are samples of this unstructured data as documents, customer experience archives, and social networks. Nowadays with application of business intelligence and data analytics tools, numerous benefits are achieved: increasing revenue, reducing cost, growing market share, and most of all, managers are equipped with a holistic view of the organization in all aspects (operational and analytical dashboards). Meanwhile, with the ever increasing amount of data being created, organizations are facing lack of offline and online analytical tools. Of the world's total data, 90% has been generated in just two years: 2011 and 2012. With the advent of social networks and cloud computing, data is getting complex and unstructured as normal querying does not satisfy the requirements (Sawant & Shah, 2013, p. 1). This urges organizations to implement Big Data solutions. Warden (2011, p. 33) positively illustrates the applications and specifically the technique of data visualization for both organizations (internal usage) and their customers (external usage).

The dark side of Big Data, if neglected, is the ethical concerns. Imagine an organization in public sector which holds health-related data of the citizens. If proper data management instructions or privacy policies are not mandated by managers, serious consequences would emerge.

REFERENCES

Arthur, L. (2013). *Big Data Marketing: Engage Your Customers More Effectively and Drive Value*. Wiley.

Chandran, R., Sridhar, K. T., & Sakkeer, M. A. (2014). *MPP SQL Engines: Architectural Choices and Their Implications on Benchmarking. In Advancing Big Data Benchmarks* (pp. 179–192). Switzerland: Springer International Publishing.

Chang, R. M., Kauffman, R. J., & Kwon, Y. (2013). (in press). Understanding the paradigm shift to computational social science in the presence of big data. *Decision Support Systems*.

Costa, F. F. (2014). Big data in biomedicine. *Drug Discovery Today*, *19*(4), 433–440. doi:10.1016/j.drudis.2013.10.012 PMID:24183925

Cox, A. (1997). *Business Success. In Midsomer Norton*. Bath: Earlsgate Press.

Cox, M., & Ellsworth, D. (1997). Application-controlled demand paging for out-of-core visualization. *IEEE 8th conference on Visualization* (pp. 235-244). Phoenix: IEEE.

Cumbley, R., & Church, P. (2013). Is "Big Data" creepy? *Computer Law & Security Report, 29*(5), 601–609. doi:10.1016/j.clsr.2013.07.007

Fortune. (2012). *What Data Says About Us.* New York: Time Inc.

Fourneau, J.-M., & Pekergin, N. (2002). Benchmark. In M. C. Calzarossa & S. Tucci (Eds.), *Performance 2002* (Vol. 2459). Heidelberg, Germany: Springer.

Gloor, P. (2000). *Making the e-Business Transformation.* London: Springer-Verlag. doi:10.1007/978-1-4471-0757-6

Halevi, G., & Moed, H. F. (2012). The evolution of big data as a research and scientific topic: Overview of the literature. *Research Trends, 30.*

Hurwitz, J., Nugent, A., Halper, F., & Kaufman, M. (2013). *Big Data For Dummies.* Hoboken, NJ: John Wiley & Sons, Inc.

Kambatla, K., Kollias, G., Kumar, V., & Grama, A. (2014). Trends in Big Data Analytics. *Journal of Parallel and Distributed Computing, 74*(7), 2561–2573. doi:10.1016/j.jpdc.2014.01.003

Loshin, D. (2013). *Big Data Analytics: From Strategic Planning to Enterprise Integration with Tools, Techniques, NoSQL, and Graph.* Waltham: Elsevier Inc.

Miller, H. E. (2013). Big-data in cloud computing: A taxonomy of risks. *Information Research, 18*(1), 571.

Ming, Z., Luo, C., Gao, W., Han, R., Yang, Q., Wang, L., & Zhan, J. (2014). *BDGS: A Scalable Big Data Generator Suite in Big Data Benchmarking. In Advancing Big Data Benchmarks* (pp. 138–154). Switzerland: Springer International Publishing.

Mohanty, S., Jagadeesh, M., & Srivatsa, H. (2013). *Big Data Imperatives: Enterprise Big Data Warehouse, BI Implementations and Analytics.* Apress. doi:10.1007/978-1-4302-4873-6

Moore, G. E. (1965). Cramming More Components onto Integrated Circuits. *Electronics Magazine, 4.*

Parka, H. W., & Leydesdorffb, L. (2013). Decomposing social and semantic networks in emerging "big data" research. *Journal of Informetrics, 7*(3), 756–765. doi:10.1016/j.joi.2013.05.004

Prajapati, V. (2013). *Big Data Analytics with R and Hadoop.* Mumbai: Packt Publishing.

Rousseau, R. (2012). A view on big data and its relation Informetrics. *Chinese Journal of Library and Information Science, 5*(3), 12–26.

Sathi, A. (2012). *Big Data Analytics: Disruptive Technologies for Changing the Game.* Boise: Mc Press.

Sawant, N., & Shah, H. (2013). *Big Data Application Architecture Q&A: A Problem - Solution Approach.* New York: Apress. doi:10.1007/978-1-4302-6293-0

Simon, P. (2013). *Too Big to Ignore: The Business Case for Big Data.* Hoboken, NJ: Wiley.

Taylor Shelton, A. P. (2014). Mapping the data shadows of Hurricane Sandy: Uncovering the sociospatial dimensions of 'big data'. *Geoforum*, *52*, 167–179. doi:10.1016/j.geoforum.2014.01.006

Warden, P. (2011). *Big Data Glossary*. Sebastopol, CA: O'Reilly Media.

Zhong, T., Doshi, K., Tang, X., Lou, T., & Lu, Z. L. (2014). *Big Data Workloads Drawn from Real-Time Analytics Scenarios Across Three Deployed Solutions. In Advancing Big Data Benchmarks* (pp. 97–104). Switzerland: Springer International Publishing.

ENDNOTES

[1]   Geoffrey Alexander Moore, Ph.D., an American Organizational Theorist.

[2] 10^{15} bytes of data

[3] 10^{21} bytes of data

Chapter 7

Blending Technology, Human Potential, and Organizational Reality:
Managing Big Data Projects in Public Contexts

Jurgen Janssens
TETRADE Consulting, Belgium

ABSTRACT

To make the deeply rooted layers of catalyzing technology and optimized modelling gain their true value for education, healthcare or other public services, it is necessary to prepare well the Big Data environment in which the Big Data will be developed, and integrate elements of it into the project approach. It is by integrating and managing these non-technical aspects of project reality that analytics will be accepted. This will enable data power to infuse the organizational processes and offer ultimately real added value. This chapter will shed light on complementary actions required on different levels. It will be analyzed how this layered effort starts by a good understanding of the different elements that contribute to the definition of an organization's Big Data ecosystem. It will be explained how this interacts with the management of expectations, needs, goals and change. Lastly, a closer look will be given at the importance of portfolio based big picture thinking.

INTRODUCTION

Big Data is an extremely vast field. Big Data can be all about Hadoop, Map Reduce, Tableau, HANA, Nexidia and Stata. Big Data can be all about crunching and capturing regional specificities. It can be all about statistical modelling, tendency plotting and data supporting technological optimization. Big Data can be and is indeed all of this. But it is also much more: it is about elevating an organization to unexplored reflection paths.

DOI: 10.4018/978-1-4666-9649-5.ch007

To make the deeply rooted layers of catalyzing technology and optimized modelling gain their true value for education, healthcare or other public services, it is necessary to prepare well the Big Data environment in which the Big Data will be developed, and integrate elements of it into the project approach. It is by integrating and managing these non-technical aspects of project reality that analytics will be accepted. This will enable data power to infuse the organizational processes and offer ultimately real added value.

This chapter will shed light on organizational, human and change management actions required on different levels to maximize the unfolding of the Big Data potential. It will be analyzed how this layered effort starts by a good delineation of the different elements of the organization's Big Data ecosystem. It will be explained how the management of expectations, needs and goals is essential for the fit between the silver lining and the technical realization. Lastly, to ensure feasibility and long term contribution, a closer look will be taken at the importance of the bigger portfolio picture.

All together this chapter will illustrate that managing Big Data projects in a public context can only deliver a solid result if the organizational context and the human reality are embraced together with the technical challenges.

BACKGROUND

In the Big Data definition provided by research and advisory firm Gartner (2014) a strong emphasis is put on technology related aspects and the potential contribution to decision making. As indicated by Kobielus (2013), Big Data players like IBM base themselves on 4 Vs to characterize the key elements of Big Data success: Volume, Variety, Veracity and Velocity.

This tendency to focus on the technical aspects is part of a larger reality where the Big Data potential is put in the perspective of the always moving frontier of technological possibilities. With recent estimates of Turner, Reinsel and Gantz (2014) expecting digital data created by humans and devices to increase between 2012 and 2020 by a 50-fold to almost 40ZB, it seems very unlikely that the attention for technological aspects of Big Data will revert soon.

At the same time, research has indicated repeatedly that the majority of projects focusing on data analytics fail because of non-technical reasons, or because they do not deliver the benefits that are agreed upon at the start of the project (Young, 2003; Gulla, 2012; Van der Meulen & Rivera, 2013). As tools and technology are used by people who are working themselves in an organizational context, this technical IT focus of Big Data endeavors should therefore be complemented with other aspects of the reality.

In that context, paying attention for change on the human level and opening the mind to a new way of thinking are part of the 'soft' factors that play a fundamental role in paving the road to success of Big Data projects. There is namely limited added value to provide a hyper-advanced data cruncher to people that only want to execute the very same daily professional routine, and use the tools they have been using for years. If they are not gradually prepared for this change and don't grasp the potential advantages, there will be no 'real' use of the data tool. If they have the impression that they don't have the means to work efficiently anymore, they risk even to blame Big Data for a disruption of service.

Complementarily, managing data projects means being able to look beyond the most exciting Big Data facets, and taking time for the guiding project backbone. Freewheeling on the most stimulating ideas can namely only result in a concrete and valuable outcome if the efforts are framed, planned and guided towards a final goal.

Project Management frameworks exist that provide a sound base for a structured project follow-up. Prince2[1] and PMBOK[2], for instance, have been developed and improved, respectively since 1989 and 1996. They are applied nowadays in different sectors by private and public organizations all over the world.

These frameworks ensure structuring guidance of essential project aspects from the very start till the final delivery. They cover soft and hard matters, ranging from the building of a solid Business Case or the management of Stakeholder dimensions, to a detailed product description or thorough quality reviews.

References to the use of these frameworks are however relatively limited in the context of Big Data. The author wants to translate and include the underlying philosophy into practical advice for Big Data projects, as data management is bound to become a powerful driver, not only of technological evolution, but also for strategic decisions and organizational change, especially in the public-private context.

MANAGING DATA POWER BY BLENDING IN PEOPLE AND ORGANISATION

Issues, Controversies, Problems

Due to its multiple dimensions and constant evolutions, Big Data is often regarded as a technical subject matter. By extension, there is a natural tendency to see Big Data projects as purely technical projects. Omitting to take into account also organizational and human aspects in the management of projects entails however different risks.

Firstly, there is a risk that the delivered results are not in line with what is wanted, even if the outcome is technically very complete and efficient. Senior stakeholders might have had something fundamentally different in mind, which could, if the expectations are not met, lead to a lack of final acceptance or a lack of support for future projects.

For end users, the proposed change in way of working could be perceived as unworkable or unacceptably insurmountable, and therefore without added value.

This resistance could then lead to the outcome being wrongly used (or not used at all). In more severe cases, the project or its outcome could simply be put in the fridge or thrown in the trash bin due to its perceived inadequacy.

Another, more fundamental, risk is that there might be a total misfit between the delivered results and the strategic direction the organization wants to follow. Managing and executing a project from an isolated technical perspective could even result in the organization being refrained from exploring new directions in its current development, or missing evolutions that could have opened doors to the future. On a macro level, this would mean that public bodies miss the opportunity to keep their services to society on par with those offered by private counterparts. In the worst case, this lack of coordinated project advancement could lead to public organizations remaining structurally behind.

Technical possibilities to perfect the unfolding of the Big Data potential are not in scope of this chapter. In this chapter, the author analyzes practical guidelines on the organizational and human level, to be used in complement of the technical foundation. Once these guidelines are structurally integrated in the management of Big Data projects, they will contribute in making the foundation open up towards its true value in the ecosystem for which it is intended.

In combination with representative examples from the public sphere, it will be detailed out how the layered effort starts by a thorough understanding of the different elements of an organization's Big Data ecosystem. It will be explained how this interacts with the management of expectations, the identification and control of the needs, and a consequent big picture thinking on the portfolio level.

All together this chapter will illustrate that managing Big Data projects in a public context can only come to a satisfying result for the entire stakeholder community if the organizational and human reality will be embraced in support of the technical efforts.

SOLUTIONS AND RECOMMENDATIONS

To optimize the benefit public organizations can obtain from their own efforts in optimized modelling and out of the box experimentation, it is indeed necessary to combine data work with guiding thoroughly the non-technical elements of the ecosystem in which Big Data[3] will be developed and used. It is this synchronized interaction between technology and reality that will open the doors to real progress and new insights.

This requires efforts on different levels. It starts by a good definition of the components of the expected Big Data ecosystem. It encompasses the management of expectations, needs, goals and change. Lastly, it involves some big picture thinking, by making sure the Data ambition is compatible with the entire Project Portfolio.

The Elements to Build the Big Data Ecosystem

The socio-economic cycles and the competitive market reality put pressure towards higher efficiency of administrations, stronger decision taking of leaders and more sophisticated technology to keep public services on par with private ones. One of the means of getting there is Big Data, as it is at the intersection of increased data power and reinforced actionability.

Before kick-starting the analysis of the 'real' data, it is fundamental to reflect on the fundamental elements of the larger Big Data ecosystem. Knowing what the organization wants and where the organization wants to go is essential in the shaping of the Big Data initiatives by the project sponsor (in the very beginning) or by the project manager (along the different phases).

Traditionally, these discussions are driven by choices on technology, optimization layers, or expected improvements. From a pure management perspective, however, the categorization that makes most sense is one that fits the angle of the decision taker(s).

This essence focused helicopter view can be articulated around some key drivers. What is the final objective for the organization, and what dimensions are particularly important? Does the organization want to gain experience or target immediately solid transformation? What are the technical and humans means at hand?

Once these fundamentals are clarified, sleeves can be turned up and the management of the Big Data project started.

Possible Objectives

In the public sector, developing data powered decision taking is mostly done with one or more specific benefits and objectives in mind: Internal improvement, Innovation towards external stakeholders, Development of integrated solutions or, depending on the type of public body, eventually Building collaborations with public or private actors.

Projects focusing on Internal Improvement want to have a better view and understanding of the internal functioning of one or more departments or services. The factual data are used to define specific improvements or end-to-end process enhancements. The reason for doing so is to attain budgetary efficiencies, improve the image towards internal or external stakeholders, or, in the end, increase 'customer' satisfaction, for instance to avoid that the community moves away from public services for which private alternatives exists.

Public or semipublic bodies may also desire to identify possibilities for Innovation. It is unlikely that this type of projects will take place in an isolated way, as innovation should not be set in motion for the sole sake of innovation. Such projects will therefore be in complement of the other mentioned categories. This can for instance be in an environment that desires to give itself the means for a significant improvement after many years of technological status quo (see Figure 1).

Environments with a higher Big Data maturity may want to take a leap forward by working on integrated solutions. Rather than working on specific improvements, a combined program will focus on a larger quality injection, by joining complementary initiatives, or focusing on improvements that go beyond departmental borders. City administrations may for example decide to join forces in offering a unique entry point for all questions and administrative obligations of entrepreneurs. Cities like Brussels have this already for entrepreneurs[4]. By working on an integrated data solution that is used as a collaborative platform for the different services and as a smooth front end service by the companies, all concerned parties benefit from this advanced approach.

In specific contexts, the Big Data objective to start or enhance collaborations with public or private actors can be done through above initiatives, or through a dedicated collaboration program, fueled with Big Data information. Such initiatives can bring the additional automation, maturity or strategic value to an organization. This, in turn, can open the door to collaboration with others.

This could potentially be the case if several hospitals are owned by the same local body. In their desire to better allocate their financial resources and offer a better service, it could be beneficial for the different hospitals to reach the same level of data intelligence. The resulting integrated understanding from their shared 'population' would then make it possible to develop a complementary service portfolio. Over time, it could even help to balance peaks within this community for the services that each institution would still provide separately (e.g. emergency treatments, maternity…).

Figure 1. The objective of Big Data projects can be Internal improvement, Innovation towards External parties, the Development of Integrated solutions, or Building Collaborations

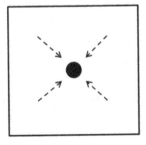 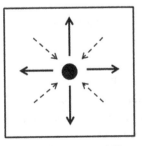 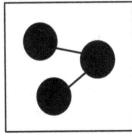

INTERNAL IMPROVEMENT   EXTERNAL INNOVATION   INTEGRATED SOLUTIONS   COLLABORATIONS

Similarly, public transportation companies could be very interested in levelling up in preparation of joint initiatives, for instance in areas where railway transport and urban transport (underground, bus, tram) are managed by different entities. If companies attain a similar quality and granularity of their transportation data, they could optimize their offerings or develop synchronized schedules for dense zones. It is even imaginable to go a step further by sharing the physical customer passes, which would path the way to even more shared optimization initiatives (and eventual cost reductions). In Belgium, different public Belgian transportation companies are exploring this path by gradually using the shared smart travel card MOBIB (Baele & Devraux, 2014). This card, initially used only by one of them, offers in the meantime the possibility for multi-modal use and follow-up.

Overall, knowing and expressing the objectives offers thus a first element of focus. Note that none of these areas of improvement is 'better' or 'more ambitious' from a Big Data angle than others. It is the fit of the project(s) with the organization that is the key to success. As will be explained in one of the coming sections, paving the road to this fit starts by having a clear understanding of the needs, the approach and the available means. Once determined, one can evaluate what initiative is better suited to answer these needs.

Starting Small or Going for a Big Bang

Closely related to the reflection on the objectives, public bodies need to take sufficient time to define the suitable project size and the return on experience that the they want to obtain.

Although each Big Data project should leave some freedom for experimentation (Viaene, 2014), an organization can desire to start with a small project to optimize the return on experience. The driver can be very down to earth, i.e. harvesting low hanging quick win fruit. A more fundamental driver for starting with a limited perimeter can be to gain experience first, for example, before larger projects. This experience development is possible on the technical level on new data modeling techniques, on the use of Hadoop, HANA, Spotfire or Tableau, on new types of hardware and the like. It is advised to manage the project in such a way that technical experimentation is stimulated, with a cascading of the experience on the overall stakeholder community.

The gaining of experience can also be focused on the human level. A small project can for instance have the advantage to develop concrete use cases to create the necessary awareness and change in mind-set amongst stakeholders. This will reduce a possible reluctance and resistance that can arise in a more profound, disruptive context.

Besides the technical and human dimension, starting small can offer valuable experience on the managerial level. It can provide the necessary lessons learned to adapt or fine-tune the way of working for subsequent projects, highlight the skills that need to be improved, and the like.

Instead of kicking-off a small focus with specific added value (or after having started small), one may decide to go for a full blown Big Bang. The reason to do so can be that the desired level of experience is already present, or that important windows of opportunity cannot be missed for organizational, economic or political reasons. If well prepared and managed, Big Bang projects have the potential advantage to bring higher informational return.

In public bodies, the order-of-magnitude of this 'big' can be expressed in terms of impacted processes, the number of internal people, the size of the (external) community, or the level of overall disruption compared to the existing situation.

Altogether, small projects offer thus the occasion for focused gain of experience, whereas large projects offer potentially larger results, but require more coordination.

In both scenarios, it is important to keep in mind that a Big Data project is not only an IT project, but also an organizational and human journey requiring the necessary preparation, follow-up and guidance. The better the initial choices are made and the better the actions are supported, the higher the likelihood that the initiative will be embraced by everyone, and offer the necessary transformational value.

At the same time, both small and large projects need to be 'prepared for success'. Initiatives delivering the expected results with the necessary visibility can initiate a demand for an extended use to other departments, or for additional analytical models in different contexts. It is therefore advised, both for small and for large projects, to foresee the necessary room for capacity growth, in terms of technical and human means, skills and budget. This aspect will be discussed in more detail in one of the next sections.

Types of Data

In complement of the preliminary reflection on the objective and the size of the Big Data initiative, it is important to do an assessment of the desired and available data. No matter if it concerns a pilot project that is 'only' intended to gain experience, or a 'real' full-fledged one, data can be grouped from two different angles.

A first categorization focuses from the technical angle on the distinction between structured data and non-structured data. Structured data are 'traditional' data, like databases, spreadsheets, or statistical analytics. Non-structured data come from less conventional data sources like free-text payment descriptions, content of social media and blogs, emails, news feeds, instant messages and the like.

A second approach consists of gaining insights through a division in Human/Social data, Location data, Market Data, Machine related data and Smart Data (Yasuda, Yasuharu, & Yoshida, 2014). This distinction of the data opens the door to more 'contextual' reflections on the project scope.

Human and Social Data result from initiatives intended to obtain data on the human body or to study collective human social behavior. On the medical level, this can provide insights on individual habits or the evolution of certain variables. In the US, for example, the government funded private organization UNOS[5] is using he outcome of Big Data initiatives to continuously improve the algorithms used in the optimization of waiting lists for organ transplants.

On the level of (sub)societal dynamics, the Social Data provide insights on patterned habits and recurring interactions between groups of individuals. Public transportation companies or healthcare programs like healthcare.gov[6] (also known as 'Obamacare') could bring significant improvements to their online services by completing attractiveness focused redesign initiatives (Paskin, 2014) with intelligent mining of all information on the time people spent on specific pages, the type of information they search for and the like. This information will not only help in optimizing the general layout and perceived efficiency of the services. It could also be the trigger for providing additional information that would fit to queries done simultaneously by other people in the same area. This could appear to be very useful in periods of seasonal issues, extreme climatological problems or pandemic concerns.

Using Human and Social data in the public sector requires paying attention to two subtle 'traps'.

A first one is the data security. No public body wants to announce that it has lost control on the citizens private information. This is applicable on all types of data, but is a more sensitive matter for human, social and health related information. As hospitals are, for instance, hacked more and more (Orcut, 2014), public bodies want to dedicate additional attention to this dimension to avoid that citizens move from public to private services, due to (the impression of) weak data protection. For details on this matter, the author refers the reader to specialized literature.

A second attention point is avoiding to be regarded as Orwellianly scary by using these data. Public bodies need to reflect well on how sensitive or 'intrusive' the use of certain data is. This may lead to a fractional or gradual use until sufficient public acceptance and trust is available.

In certain exceptional cases, the opposite may be true. The advantages that the pooled use of medical or genetic information can offer, prevail then over the impact on privacy. This is the case in Iceland, where the medical records and genealogical and genetic data of most Icelanders were, until some years ago, all present in a common database, deCODE[7]. As the population is rather small and most citizens have Icelandic roots, the initiative wanted to provide the keys to solving eventual general health issues impacting the entire Icelandic population. In the meantime, the attempts to make an Icelandic Health Sector Database out of it have been stopped (Gertz, 2004). The outcome is used, amongst others, as basis for Íslendingabók[8] (literally 'the Book of Icelanders'), a search engine that allows Icelanders to know if they are dating distant family members.

In the same data pooling train of thought, an initiative was launched by Sage Bionetworks[9]. This nonprofit organization promotes open science, and has developed the ethical procedures needed to create an open database of anonymized health and genetics related data from many sources. Dutcher (2014) argues that the compilation of test results in one location would turn genetic info into Big Data, giving scientists new insights that could accelerate findings, and strongly influence the current approach to healthcare research.

Location Data result from initiatives intended to obtain information on the location of people, based on mobile technology, radio frequency or GPS powered devices like phones, computers, cars or public transport. The patterns that become apparent through the analysis of location data are used to steer (or adjust) business decisions and marketing initiatives. If translated intelligently, they are then experienced as quality enhancing services by the targeted people.

In a series of cases, this information is used by private companies. Local governments can however benefit very much of this information, for example, to optimize the fluidity of the traffic. A noteworthy example on this level is under development in Finland. Inspired by a master thesis written in 2014 (Heikkilä, 2014), the city of Helsinki is planning to create a 2.0. transportation system by 2025. The goal is to have all types of public and private traffic synchronized through the combination of transport sharing, solid technology to guarantee streamlined, affordable payment, and ambitious localization programs (see Figure 2).

Figure 2. Data can be categorized in different groups: Human/Social Data, Location Data, Market Data, Machine Data, Smart Data. For all types, dedicated attention is needed for data security.

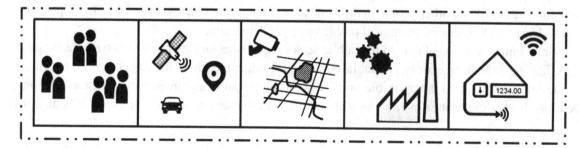

Market Data result from initiatives intended to collect and analyze the visual data collected in public spaces. Although the use of visual data is subject to specific legislation in each country, it does offer public bodies useful information. Instead of using GPS data, cities could for instance use Market Data to optimize traffic light synchronization or optimize road cleaning schedules in function of the visually observed traffic density.

For certain niches of the public sector, Machine related data and Smart Data are increasingly important, for instance in the improvement of (sub)processes for the healthcare sector or in a leanified running of Utilities or other (semi)public facilities.

Machine Data result from initiatives intended to obtain operational knowledge of the (often real time) functioning of machines. These data are generated by monitoring industrial devices. They are used to optimize machines and maintenance, with the real aim of improving business processes, service quality or safety.

In the public Sector, these data can be potentially obtained through healthcare equipment, IT hardware, school infrastructure, traffic lights, public transport vehicles, mining or manufacturing machines and the like.

Smart Data result from smart infrastructure used by private or (semi)public actors. Whereas machine data are used to optimize efficiency of machines and equipment, smart data are focusing on gaining insights on usage patterns or potential infrastructure optimization. This concerns for instance equipment used by telecom companies, or in industries like specific financial services, mining or energy distribution or supply (Ala-Kurikka, 2010).

Although smart data are mostly generated and used by private or semipublic companies (like utility companies), it is worth noticing that smart data can be used also in more 'traditional' public environments. In certain countries, data warehousing powered vending machines are currently already gathering consumption and machine data in real time to increase their stock management and product freshness (Honaman, 2010). According to Nelson (2014), Coke's Freestyle dispensing machines go a step further. They have the bold purpose to grasp better the consumption profiles and tastes of the customers in the different locations where people are longing to their daily drink.

Currently, these data are privately owned by the Coca-Cola Company. But when taking into account that the vast majority of public schools have vending machines, it is not unthinkable that educational bodies start similar initiatives to have more information on consumption habits, or to build and improve health awareness programs for children and students.

The evaluation of the different types of data does not imply that an organization needs to choose and focus solely on one category of data – quite the contrary. In practice, the power of Big Data projects lays exactly in obtaining most from a constellation of data – be it from a range of interlinked (sub)categories or from a variety of categories where the interconnections seem less straightforward.

Determining the dataset(s) can even imply going beyond the traditional borders. Whereas past initiatives would focus on improving the use (and outcome) of existing data and in house algorithms, it is now possible to maximize the value from own sources by combining them with public and private third party data, made available to a larger audience.

New York City, for instance, set up the Mayor's Office of Data Analytics (MODA)[10] to tackle the challenges of rapid urbanization. Through this vehicle, a series of local government agencies share openly their data. By 2018, all city agencies of New York will have to have their data openly shared. In October 2014, data streamed into MODA resulted already in more than 300 data sets. This allows each agency to work on different dimensions of urbanization (such as crime, public safety, overcrowding, road incidents, and pollution), by benefitting from information that was previously not directly available.

A similar potential exists beyond the collaboration with local sister organizations. The EU[11], the US[12], the OECD[13], the Worldbank[14] and many governments have made large amounts of data available, that could significantly improve the granularity and power of data initiatives.

Although private open data initiatives are regularly under discussion (Herzberg, 2014), one can have the same collaborative advantage in some crossover platforms. Algorithmia[15], for instance, builds a bridge between people that have developed algorithms for which they see specific possibilities, and organizations or companies that are looking for algorithms that solve certain problems or provide specific information. Similar collaborations exist between academic and non-academic actors. Reviewing such open initiatives can contribute to having a resized scope and move forward more quickly.

Assessing Means and Skills

Private companies embrace the potential of new technologies to stay ahead in the competition. Certain public bodies or (semi) public companies might want to do the same with one of the aforementioned objectives in mind. At the same time, the preliminary review of the desired and available data might reveal that it is too challenging to do, due to a lack of means or skills. Healthy ambition requires however that an organization gives itself the necessary means to succeed.

Crossing the river that meanders between the as-is and to-be banks without going to the very end is rarely interesting. Therefore, three options are at hand. A first one is to increase the technical, human or financial means. A second option is to limit the scope (without necessarily limiting the reflection process), and to do the rest once sufficient means are at disposal. Lastly, the commitment can be taken that the final goal will be attained, but by building upfront a phased plan.

The last option was chosen in the earlier mentioned transportation project in Helsinki. Initially, the city had only access to the public transportation data. To solve this in due time, it increased its technical means by building collaboration platforms like Traffic Lab[16] and plans to extend existing initiatives to integrate gradually (by 2025) all desired data of the private transportation companies, taxis, and car sharing pools.

Besides a lack of means, there might be a (temporary or structural) shortage of qualified skills. In such situations, the scope or the project planning needs to be adapted, knowledge needs to be 'transferred', or reinforcement needs to be foreseen with the help of additional resources.

A non-negligible side note for knowledge transfer or resource reinforcement is the time needed for a new (internal or external) resource to be up to speed. It may indeed require a significant amount of time before a person understands sufficiently the practical or technical specificities of an organization.

It is therefore advisable to foresee a solid scaling and contingency margin when evaluating the resource needs and the time needed for the different phases. An alternative is to foresee the transition of internal resources from other projects. This has, however, an impact on the project portfolio. This aspect will be discussed in a dedicated section.

Note that securing the necessary human means and technical skills might require the set-up of new teams, or new collaborative combinations within the existing organizational framework. It might require people to change their way of working or the way they are organized. It might even involve the investment in talent and the development of new skills. Given these potential reorganizations, it is advised to foresee the skill-based analysis upfront, eventually in collaboration with the concerned HR manager(s) of the respective units (see Figure 3).

Figure 3. Assessment of human, technical, financial or knowledge means may reveal a need of resizing, reallocation of means, or adaptation of scope

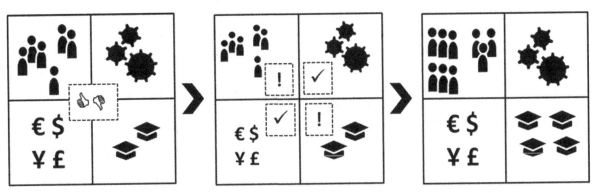

The skill and resource constraints can occur, for instance, in projects in an educational context. Every student corresponds to a lot of (continuously growing) information in the files of the school. A school – or an association of schools – may decide to optimize the use of these data for educational purposes. Such initiatives may trigger privacy concerns from parental associations, for example due to fear for misuse or selling of this information to third parties. Set aside the privacy concern, schools may be faced with an important expertise problem in the realization of the data project. Many schools lack namely the technical abilities to structure efficiently these data, and, especially, the skills to manage the databases and the related infrastructure.

Similar challenges can happen in healthcare contexts. Such initiatives require, in addition to budget, the availability of skilled people to prepare the set-up of the infrastructure and train the practitioners, people available during the trainings to ensure the continuity of activities and services, and the necessary staff to actively use this information, while keeping a critical eye on potential improvements. Developing such data empowered projects requires therefore the necessary sizing.

In 2012, a British hospital benefitted from supercomputers usually used by the McLaren group in monitoring hundreds of variables and thousands of health indicators from their Formula 1 drivers. During this period, the hospital got to enrich its traditional follow-up with predictive early warnings through increased, real-time analytical power (The Health Foundation, 2012). A project with a similar potential exists in New York City, at the Mount Sinai Hospital. They are injecting Big Data power into their daily functioning to forecast potential diseases and reduce the number of hospital visits (Mount Sinai Hospital, 2014).

Ambiguously enough, such an issue may arise also in environments with a strong track record of following data sets. A data rich environment can namely lead to an informational flow or data structure that requires even more means than already at disposal. In those cases, it is advised to evaluate if focusing on sub-segments of information (rather than on the full set) can bring sufficient catalytic value to the management in support of the envisioned changes or decisions. The inclusion of other segments can then be planned for an eventual later phase.

On that level, reality has shown that improvement initiatives involving potentially zealous amounts of data have encountered big successes as well as significant failures.

During the last ten years, several European governments launched ambitious data projects, mostly with the goal of optimizing their internal functioning and improving their service to the citizens (Bové,

2013). One of the means was to have groups of data mapped and interconnected, to obtain more precious information for courts of justice, tax departments or financial collection divisions.

Quite illustrative are the attempts made by the Belgian federal government since the early 2000's. Inspired by success in the Netherlands and driven by encouraging results of the 'eHealth' platform of the Belgian Ministry of Health, the plan was to realize a similar initiative for the Ministry of Justice: building a web portal able to deliver efficient services and data exchange, fueled (amongst others) by cross-combined data sources and strong analytics. During the first ten years, cluster-projects with inspired names like Phoenix and Cheops turned out to be vast disasters (Bové, 2014 ; Vanleemputten, 2013), partially due to the high ambitions and the important complexity. Based on these lessons, the scope was reviewed and a new project started in 2014, JustX (Peumans, 2014). It aims at bringing all data dynamics up to speed in the near future.

Overall, it is thus needed to do an aggregated evaluation of the means that are available and scale in accordance to the organization's ambitions. If assessed correctly and put together with the other pieces of the Big Data ecosystem, one will have a good view of the type of project that is actually at stake. The understanding of this big picture will be valuable throughout the subsequent steps of the project lifecycle.

Managing Projects, the Before and After Included

The goal of increasing the use of Big Data in public services is to develop or refine different types of information that contribute to the operational efficiency. This dynamic turns fractional information into multidimensional results that allow to grasp a bigger picture, analyze more precise tendencies, and drive the strategic decision making process.

As indicated earlier, the level of contribution is preconditioned by the components of the desired Big Data ecosystem: the nature of the data that will be analyzed, the quality of the delivered information, and the supporting means.

It depends, however, at least as much – if not more – on a clear vision and strategy on the way forward. It is this vision and strategy that will create the fit between analytical ambition, technological power and organizational reality.

In essence, five major steps should be followed to ensure that the data dynamic will be embraced and bring the necessary value: Preparing the mindset, Determining the Business Case, Planning & Realizing the flow, Analyzing & Steering, and Guiding the Change (see Figure 4).

Figure 4. Five major steps should be followed: 1. Preparing the mindset,2. Determining the Business Case, 3. Planning & Realizing the flow, 4. Analyzing & Steering, and 5. Guiding the Change

Preparing the Mindset

Organizations are led by people that either take decisions based on the analytic power of their tools, or based on experience and (interaction enriched) intuition. In both cases, it will take time to change these habits. It is therefore important that the sponsor(s) or the initiator(s) of the project prepare early the mindset of the future data powered decision takers, ideally already at the Ideation stage.

Decision takers need to understand what Big Data is really all about. They need to understand that it is not solely about adding a sexy App on the governmental servers and gaining extra insights by pushing a button. It is about setting in motion an organizational transformation journey in a structured way, based on revisited analytics through technical improvements on different levels, leading potentially to insights that could trigger real game changers in the envisioned field(s) of activity (Van Driessche, 2014).

This is possible - even before really kicking off the project and its larger change management process - by focusing on correct understanding, preparing for dedication and ensuring enriched thinking.

Firstly, empowering decision takers to support the project needs to be done with a sense of realism. They need to understand that success stories from other countries cannot necessarily be transposed as such. Transportation projects like LIVE Singapore![17] in Singapore or Traffic Lab in Helsinki (Heikkilä, 2014) will not have the same influence in New York, Brussels or Mumbai. The education focused hackathons in Boston[18] may be inspiring, but the outcome will not be bluntly applicable in Hong Kong, Buenos Aires or Johannesburg.

The contextual caution is even needed in the same geographical sphere. Projects in, for example, healthcare are not necessarily transposable in education or transport, and vice versa, due to diverging realities. Even within the same geographical and operational area, one should take time to regard reference examples with sufficient caution, as the intrinsic maturity or the economical ecosystem may be incomparable.

In addition to realism on the management level, is essential to have managerial dedication. Regular communication and collaboration with the different concerned parties is therefore key when bending the data in the correct shape.

In case of green field projects, for instance, project sponsors can be very enthusiastic, because of the high exposure and/or the 'innovative' nature of the project. This type of project will therefore require close follow-up to ensure that the taken direction fits to the (wild) plans of the fascinated sponsor. More traditional brown field projects, on the other hand, might require more steering, due to more mature context, and the eventual existence of more ambitious initiatives.

Thirdly, in preparing the mindset awareness should be created about the fact that a Big Data projects go beyond the sole providing of traditional data. The Big Data reality can offer much richer information than the existing view that some hospitals, governmental departments or educational working groups have. Managers should be aware and support the fact that Big Data can – and should - lead to a different way of thinking (see Figure 5).

The earlier mentioned UNOS activities, for instance, do not only focus on improving the organ donor's waiting list with new names. The work is done with a focus on creating more detailed ways to define the fit between donors and receivers. These different angles may lead to exploring new data paths that, if intelligently combined, lead to a more powerful granularity, and, in the end, improve the fit.

Likewise, Helsinki does not only want to have a better traffic management with Traffic Lab (Heikkilä, 2014). It wants to create a new way of living. This will be enabled by a vast source of data. But some

Figure 5. Preparing the mindset starts with a clear explanation to the stakeholders of what Big Data really is about, goes through the active involvement of senior members in the project support, and in looking to unveil the Big Data potential through a new way of thinking

of these data are triggered by intermediate changes in behavior that the town wants to initiate amongst its citizens.

Note that the need to prepare the mindset (by building on a realistic mindset, ensuring focus on communication and collaboration, and making sure that the high potential of big data is really understood) can also be true for the non-managerial stakeholders, like the technical teams. People often look at the new problem through the frame of reference of previous experiences or old problems (Janssens, 2002). To unveil the full potential, it is however important to be also open-minded enough on the technical level. This can mean pushing for trying and exploring new technologies (Mac Gregor, 2014; Van Driessche, 2014), new architectures or new technical catalysts that will stimulate the novel human way of thinking.

Overall, the expectations of the project's team should thus be aligned on the fact that Big Data are not only about 'plug and play' or brushing the existing. Going for Big added value requires Big implication from the very beginning by everyone, and should embrace the true potential of Big Data: going beyond the current frames of reference of the organization, with a sense of realism.

Determining the Business Case

For all endeavors, having a clear view on the final goal is a precondition to gauge success. This is also valid for Big Data projects. Generally speaking, it is advised to prepare beforehand a definition of the expected benefits. This will be a valuable backbone for the preparation of the project and the evaluation of the completed outcome.

To do so, the managers and senior users who will be using the data need to define the value in regards of their targets. From a methodological point of view, Kobielus (2014) advises to pay attention to 4 Vs of Big data: Volume, Velocity, Variety and Veracity.

Although not excluding the latter, the value definition can be done from a complementary, more pragmatic angle with a Business Case. This includes a reflection on the reasons and objectives of the project, having an aligned view on the stakeholders and impacted users, as well as evaluating the expected return, the payback period and the exact scope. It is advised to align the budgetary dimension well with the reality the concerned public body of and the policy in place.

Table 1. Major due diligence elements for writing the Business Case or related deliverables

	Attention Points
1	Scope of the project
2	Reasons of doing the project
3	Objectives of the project
4	Costs, including TCO and impacted stakeholders
5	Benefits, including ROI and impacted stakeholders
6	Cost of not doing the project
7	Timeline
8	Project stakeholders
9	Relative importance of time, cost, scope, quality
10	Possible contribution to the Organizational strategy
11	Risks, dependencies, constraints, assumptions

Classically, important indicators are also evaluated. This will take relative expectations into account for the project delivery in terms of time, cost, scope and quality; and assess the project environment on risks, dependencies, constraints and assumptions (see Table 1).

To ease this reflection, it is worth to have a closer look at how the project could contribute to the organization's objectives.

A public bank or insurance company, for instance, could be interested in reproducing a project that has been reported to provide significant results in lowering the fraud detection time for a specific private institution[19], or 'simply' try to reproduce the Big Data Leadership strategy taken by a competing private bank (ING, 2015).

If the institution reviews the above mentioned points before kicking off a Big Data initiative, they could come to the conclusion that it is not the right moment to start the project because the government wants to significantly cut public expenses for the financial sector, or prefers to allocate the budget to more down to earth initiatives that differentiate them from private actors.

Similarly, such a due diligence could show that most aspects can be managed, but that the perception certain stakeholders have of Big Data requires a significant review of the timing or the scope. On the other hand, the Business Case could also conclude that the envisioned project can and should be started quickly, to avoid some strong constraints linked to a possible decisional status quo resulting from upcoming elections or evolving international liquidity regulations.

Note that it can happen that people expect to estimate the return for the business case only at completion of the data project. The rationale behind this approach is that key stakeholders can have a convicted gut feeling that improved analytical power on certain groups of data could lead to interesting information, which, if confirmed, would then open the door to reflection paths for actions and belonging value estimates. If this situation takes place in an organization with limited Big Data experience, the project will then have to be sliced in a smaller pre-project to prepare the data, and a second 'full-fledged' project, that focuses on the real value dimension. Environments with a track record should be able to evaluate the potential value and build the business case based on prior experience.

If the business case shows that the success of the project requires some key decision takers to feel first more comfortable with the Big Data dynamic at large, it might be useful to set up a best practice sharing or experience sharing with other organizations or departments. This will help to benefit from lessons learned with a critical eye.

It is, for example, imaginable that major cities would want to anticipate city focused data initiatives by gaining first insight on the road already travelled by similar projects like the MODA project, the London Data Store[20], or the Brussels' Smartcity[21] platform.

If the goal of the initiative is to come to a compatibility level with a sister organization, experience sharing can have a beneficial influence on the set up of the Big Data initiative, and on the shaping of foundations for future collaboration.

Overall, one should be cognizant in every context of the fact that obtaining an agreement on the business case means that a balanced choice will have to be made. The potential decision power will be directly impacted by the level of allocated means – or the lack of.

Planning and Realizing the Big Data inflow

With the expectations being clear and the business case agreed upon, it is very tempting to start directly the technical realization: working on the crunching core, adapting the external visualization layer, or - as Big Data projects without eye candy offer rarely a lasting outcome – finding an optimal combination of both. Still, it is essential to be aware that the real level of complexity (and the speed to start) does not only depend on the technical choices, but also on the way the work is managed and organized.

ETL projects involving limited data sources, for instance, are technically speaking less complex than projects involving also the creation of new data bases, cleansing of existing sources, the development of new algorithms or the preparation of hardware upgrades (Willinger & Gradl, 2008). But if there is no clarity on matters like project ownership, deadlines and risks, even traditional ETL projects can become a challenge.

For the technical side of the distillation of the essence of the data, the author refers the reader to dedicated chapters and additional reading.

For the management aspect, it is advised to foresee a solid preparation.

In the ideation or project initiation stage, it is essential to develop a structured project plan. It will be the base to come to a shared view and understanding of all elements necessary to attain the goal: the project time line, the resources and the budget, the work breakdown and belonging schedule, plans for stakeholder management and communication, project governance and the like.

In addition, a good preparation needs to result in a transparent view on the as-is and a blueprint of the to-be situation. This is especially true for Big Data projects, as they are prone to open contexts with dynamic requirements gathering. This preparation includes detailed technical inventories, extended data mapping and qualitative technical specifications. One will also want to document clearly the impact of the data change on the decisional process, as well as the future data ownership (Madrid, 2009; Merz, Hügens, & Blum, 2015).

During the realization itself, it is essential to keep the stakeholder(s) closely involved, and foresee sufficient managerial feedback on the technical work. If the preparation is done too much behind closed doors, there is namely a real risk that the outcome will not fit to the expectations, or that key decision makers will lose interest and support (see Figure 6).

Figure 6. Projects can be managed through waterfall phases, or as work packages in scrum sprints. Both approaches require regular follow up and feedback loops.

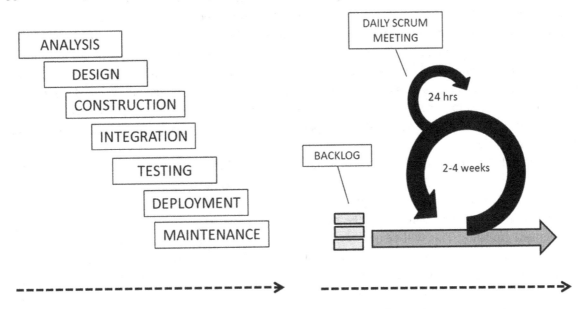

The feedback and follow-up loops are particularly important. The number of loops depends on the vastness of the scope and the adopted project approach. For details on waterfall methodologies or agile scrum approaches, the author refers to dedicated literature[22]. The different project sizes can however already provide a good indication.

For small projects or projects intended to bring quickly Big Data experience, it may be preferable to work with sprints, as they tend to deliver swift results, compared to a traditional methodology with more formal periodic reviews. This being said, the structural fluidity one might associate with scrum and other agile methodologies, requires a significant level of maturity and discipline of the key actors, and an unconditional availability of decision takers towards rapid feedback. A balance has therefore to be made during the setup between pros and cons of each methodology.

Besides the fact that the quantity of loops depends on the project approach, it is essential that they aim at quality. The real goal of these loops goes beyond trying to obtain some rubber stamping. In the interest of the organization - and the people involved - these feedback rounds should be regarded as stage gates, offering incremental quality to each step of the process foreseen in the overall planning, until the completion of the project.

Analyzing. Using. Staying Critical.

Depending on the fact if the goal of the Big Data project is to have straightforward and clear 'final' data, or rather an outcome that will be a base for different interpretative scenarios, Big Data projects can – and will mostly - require additional analysis and interpretation of the information. But in the end, the data will be the feeding influx for action focused initiatives.

From an organizational and managerial point of view, the delivery of new tangible information is therefore regarded as the most exciting stage, especially in the expectation of previously unthinkable insights. The excitement after the long preparation journey is however also exactly the reason why this stage requires a critical mindset and a sound quality review of the delivered results.

To start the quality review, the easiest is to re-assess the main expectations defined in the business case in terms of time, cost, scope and quality. This will offer a relatively good view on the project execution.

If there is real desire to go beyond a 'one off' initiative, one should also evaluate the contribution of the project to the overall Big Data dynamic. To do so, the adaptability and reusability of the solution are relatively good indicators, as well as the organizational acceptance and the actualized payback period.

Combined with latter, one might also want to include the review of the total cost of ownership over 3 to 5 years, as this provides an additional perspective into time, compared to the 'basic' review of the actuals of the project.

The adaptability of the solution can be evaluated in terms of the use of open formats, the respect of governance defined standards, or the ease of use of the front end layer.

The organizational acceptance can be evaluated through interviews and questionnaires of senior users and key stakeholders. This should be part of more general project work, focusing on the change management guidance. This will be discussed more in detail in subsequent sections.

Note that a complete assessment report does not close the door to differentiated managerial decisions. If a big bang project delivered only a part of the expected results, for example, one can still decide to be positively satisfied, because the project provided a solid experience, a positive change climate or a specific technology base for further initiatives.

What really matters in the end is that criteria are set in the beginning, and evaluated at the end. What comes afterwards is a matter of managerial decision taking.

Guiding the Change

Once the mindsets are aligned, the needs clear, the realization work done and the outcome used in an intelligent way, one could expect that the organization is in motion and the circle therefore closed. In reality, this the phase of the project requiring increased attention to have the 'technical' leap forward accepted and handled correctly by everyone. In other words: making sure that the changes are adopted and accepted as evolution, in preparation of an eventual revolution.

Although organizational change management actions should be initiated from the early beginning of the project, this dimension is often overlooked, or at least underestimated as Big Data projects tend to be regarded as technical – or reporting focused at best.

This is quite contradictory to the spirit of Big Data. As explained earlier, tools offering power through advanced analytics are not a goal on itself; they are a means to more.

The only exception are projects that focus only on the intermediate reinforcement or increased automation of existing data mining tools. Such initiatives will not necessarily change the span or depth of the decisional process, but 'only' speed up the existing situation. In such contexts, the need of solid change management is less important, and will mainly ensure that the people collecting the data in the existing situation understand correctly the functioning of the new data feed. Eventual calculation- or usage related assumptions that were taken to build the feed need to be documented and shared to avoid the (wrong) perception of biased data. In complement, sufficient time should be taken to ensure that the concerned people trust the data (as they are created without 'control' of the concerned person).

Set aside such cases, the outcome of Big Data projects is thus a means to more. As these means need to be used mostly by people, organizational acceptance and guided change of the results of the project are a conditio sine qua non to reap the fruits from the increased decisional intelligence.

A noteworthy example in the public sphere is the journey of the non-profit corporation inBloom. Founded in 2012 by a group of American educators, and co-funded by the Gates and Carnegie foundations, the company has been active in the educational field. Its goal was the creation of an open source computer system for schools, to offer a structured and efficient management of the data related to the students. The deeper purpose was to provide insights in potential improvements for learning and teaching.

Mid 2014, inBloom announced it had to stop its activities, after strong protests of parents and privacy lawyers. One of the main reasons that this project failed was thus not IT or technology related, but more human, given that the schools were not able to combine their role of 'customer' of inBloom, with their role of change agent towards parents and the like.

Streichenberger (2014), the group's CEO, phrased it as following in his closing letter:

It is a shame that the progress of this important innovation has been stalled because of generalized public concerns about data misuse, even though inBloom has world-class security and privacy protections that have raised the bar for school districts and the industry as a whole. (...) We stepped up to the occasion and supported our partners with passion, but we have realized that this concept is still new, and building public acceptance for the solution will require more time and resources than anyone could have anticipated.

Generally speaking, organizations or public bodies that have the ambition to launch a Big Data project with a large impact will have to follow a structured approach. For change management matters, this can be summarized in a gradual process (see Figure 7).

Figure 7. Change Management is a structured but gradual process

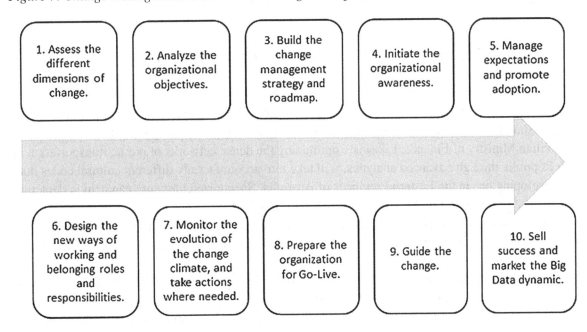

The success and efficiency of the change management guidance depends on different factors.

First of all, change management actions have to be taken up early in the process. Ideally, this is already clearly highlighted and planned at the beginning of the project, and translated in a clear change management strategy. This strategy will then be the starting point for a change management plan, for subsequent communications, and for training plans. In small projects, this preparatory responsibility is taken up by the project manager or owners of the concerned processes. For large projects, it is advised to have a dedicated change manager or change management team.

Secondly, guiding change requires a down to earth sense of realism and vision, as transformational matters implying human change are usually faced with resistance. Smoothening the road to acceptance is traditionally done through information and guidance, and complemented by training sessions and follow-up. The final goal of these initiatives is making sure that the concerned people fully accept and understand the new tools, use them correctly, and, in the end, really own them.

The target 'audience' of these initiatives can be relatively large, as it concerns the different groups of internal stakeholders that will contribute to the success. This includes three major groups. Firstly, there are the people offering the necessary senior support and structural (and/or political) oxygen to make the project work. They need to understand the purpose of the project and need to be prepared to play their role of internal change agent towards the different levels of the organization.

A second group consists of the people realizing the Big Data flow. They are less impacted by the final change as such. But to design the technical layers appropriately, they need to be given a view on the way the data will be used.

Last but not least, the change initiatives focus on the end users of the information. In some cases, these end users are analysts working with the data. It can also include their management, who will (have to) base their decisions on the analyst's reports.

When preparing and guiding the Change Management process, change agents need to take into account the impact of their words and their actions. As communicators they need to pay additional attention to the fact that their audience may have a totally different understanding due to their specific background (Pietrucha, 2014) or their organizational culture. It would be regretful to leave this unnoticed as having powerful analytics is good, but worth nothing if it is translated or used incorrectly due to a skewed understanding.

The organizational culture is strongly influenced by the tendencies and macro-evolutions in the field of activity, eventually by specific factors that relate to the identity of certain departments, and by cultural habits of the region or country.

Initiating a Big Data project in the financial department of the (government owned) oil and gas company Statoil, for instance, requires another mindset and way of working than data initiatives for the Brazilian Ministry of Finance. Likewise, optimizing the dense networks of public transportation in Czech Republic through advanced analytics, will take into account totally different cultural codes than when developing one in the Eastern Provinces of Australia. Specialized literature can help in depicting these specific geographical influencing factors (Kogut, 2012; Moll, 2012).

Including differences in perception and reaction in the change process can even be needed on an intra-organisational scale. Some departments can, for instance, be more open to data sharing than others, for human or historical reasons.

Different tools and techniques are available to grasp the essential elements of the overall culture (Cameron & Quinn, 2011; Campens, 2011; HBR, Kotter, Kim, & Maubergne, 2011). The author will focus on the distillation of three dimensions: the Climate for Change, the Mindset of the Stakeholders, and the

Impact of the Project. All these elements are traditionally assessed through interviews of stakeholders at different levels. A more detailed explanation of these techniques can be found in the dedicated section.

Change Management Tools

Periodically, research and articles evaluate the main reasons of failure of major IT transformation projects. Unsurprisingly, they highlight the lack of proper management, absence of real leadership and underestimated planning or cost estimates. At the same time, attention is also drawn to the importance of good understanding, communication, and change management.

In 2003 already, Gartner - the research and advisory firm - expressed the trend as follows (Young, 2003):

Collectively and individually, human beings respond to change in predictable ways. This predictability lends itself to a fairly standard, simple set of change tactics that can build systematic support for change initiatives and radically reduce their risks.

Research consistently demonstrates that initiatives, investments and enterprise responses requiring high levels of organizational compliance or agility fail more than 90 percent of the time, and that the drivers of failure are not found in the nature of the change decision itself, but in how it's implemented – that is, leadership's failure to recognize and manage the magnitude of the change and its effects on those who must adapt.

More recently, IBM estimated that only 3% of project failures are attributed to technical challenges (Gulla, 2012). In 2013, Gartner estimated that more than 50% of the projects focusing on data analytics fail because they are not completed in time or on budget, or because they fail to deliver the benefits that are agreed upon at the start of the project (Van der Meulen & Rivera, 2013).

One of the essential ingredients of successful data projects is thus the anticipation and preparation of the organization for the upcoming change. Different tools and techniques exist to facilitate this process. Most of them focus on building the bigger picture through the evaluation of three fundamental drivers: the Climate for Change, the Mindset of the Stakeholders, and the Impact of the Project. Each of them is traditionally built through interviews or questionnaires of stakeholders.

The evaluation of the Change Management Climate gives an indication of the recent exposure to change in function of the past track record. The track record is influenced by elements like the quality of the internal communication, the way resistance to change is usually managed, priority setting habits, the presence of change agents, the span of the eventual politicized environment, and the like. The results give a strong indication of the organizational zones requiring additional attention. This can range from a clear need for consistent trainings for each project, to strong efforts needed on the management level in priority setting, or consistency in the decision-taking process.

The Stakeholder assessment evaluates the willingness to change versus the capability to do so for a series of individual stakeholders. Usually, different persons are interviewed in each group of stakeholders. This helps in identifying eventual change agents capable to mentor their colleagues or bring significant support to the initiative. Adversely, the assessment might shed light on the departments that are most resistant to change. They will require specific change management attention. Note that the outcome can be aggregated per organizational unit to understand differences per site or department.

The Project Impact assessment evaluates who will feel the biggest impact. The impact can be seen from different angles. It can come from having to work in a different way with data. It can also relate to changes that the Big Data outcome may trigger amongst the management, for example in contexts where the (conclusions on the) data will be the enablers for internal improvements or external collaborations.

Contrary to the evaluation of the Change Climate and the Stakeholders that are plotted on a two-dimensional axis, the outcome of the Project Impact assessment is translated into a web diagram. In case of a pentagram, the five angles can be Organization, Governance, Culture, Technology and Business Processes.

In Figure 8, the Change diagnostics have been done for an organization desiring the put in place a joint data project for its different departments. The Change climate has been evaluated by the Executive Director of the organization through an assessment of 50 statements, to be evaluated on a scale from 1 (strongly agree) to 5 (strongly disagree). The answers on the questions result automatically in an update of the graph.

The Stakeholder assessment has been obtained through a (different) self-assessment, completed by the senior managers of each division, resulting each in a divisional image. The aggregated picture shows the final graph. The Project Impact assessment is based on the feedback of the Executive Director.

Figure 8. Change Management climate, Stakeholder assessment, Project Impact assessment

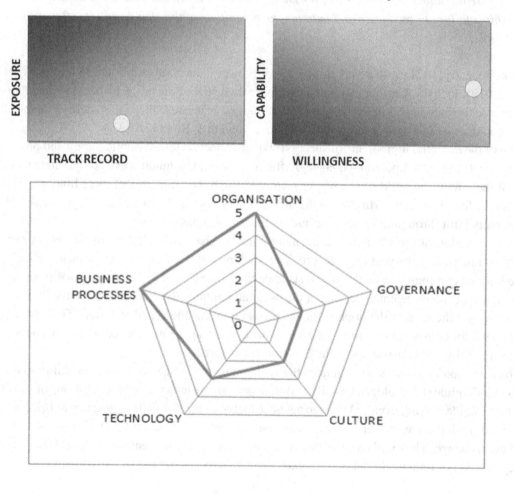

The combination change diagnostic illustrates a project in an environment with a limited exposure to change and a limited change track-record; a moderately positive stakeholder support; and the highest impact of the project being expected on business processes and organizational fluidity.

To take this change management climate into account, one will have to capture the outcome from previous projects and make a selective use of good practices or recognized experts, focus on quick-wins to reassure and involve users, and put extra focus in communication, business involvement and transparent reporting.

The stakeholder assessment illustrates that the project will take place in an environment that is favorable to change management, but with a strong need to guide the change management awareness that is latently present. Based on the aggregated assessment of the stakeholders, a part of the department appears to be composed by people able to support the initiative from a change management angle, if they receive some additional support. In their position of change agent, they appear to be appropriate to promote the project to key users or, at least, have a positive influence on the local promotion of change.

As the project is likely to impact more business processes and organizational fluidity, one will have to dedicate reinforced attention to these aspects – or to the expectations stakeholders have on this level. On the other hand, it is an indication that the stakeholders have their feet well on the ground concerning the possibilities of the Big Data power. This will make it easier to embed the technological changes in a fitting environment.

For more detailed guidelines on Change Management in IT Transformation projects and specific information on (sub)organizational models, the authors advises the reader to consult dedicated literature.

Taking into Account the Portfolio

'Early data projects' tend to focus on obtaining quick wins, on fueling a very specific set of decisions, or on gaining experience. Subsequent waves of similar initiatives will use the outcome of these first projects to nourish larger ones. Big Data analysis is thus rarely a one-shot action. It is rather the start of a broader process, intended to deliver products or services with higher value to customers and society.

At the same time, these projects are also embedded in a larger reality, where a project runs in parallel with the daily activities or with other projects. To make this portfolio reality function efficiently (including the earlier mentioned evaluation of resources and means), the management needs to set a strong silver lining.

Senior leaders should prepare a time phased roadmap upfront to give a contextual meaning to the portfolio reality. The roadmap should indicate what sets of information are used now, what information is under rework through other projects, and what sets of information will be included when in what future initiatives. This will offer a clear sense of direction and reality to collaborators. In addition, it will comfort the people that are eventually deceived by a limited scope of early Big Data projects.

In parallel with thinking holistically and setting a clear direction, a portfolio requires a gradual preparation of the cumulated technical and organizational change that will come out of the portfolio of Big Data initiative(s). With the help of the Enterprise Architect and the IT Architects, reflections need to take place on the evolution in data and application architecture, and what it means for other projects and services.

One of the important discussions in that context will be about the impact on the use of existing strategic analytical tools, like Business Intelligence applications based on ERP systems (SAP, Cognos, Oracle, Odoo and the like) (see Figure 9).

Figure 9. Communicating on the roadmap is essential to understand the direction in which the portfolio of projects, tools and data will evolve over time

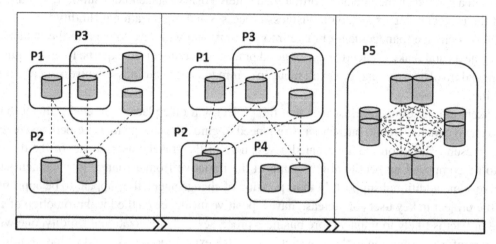

Choices might have to be made, for example, in a context where Big Data and Business Intelligence are used in the same perimeter. Big Data and Business Intelligence have both their own pros and cons. Business Intelligence through ERPs can be much faster and much more precise than Big Data powered reports. On the other hand, Big Data is much more powerful to draw tendencies out of huge volumes of data. In other words: despite a valid series of potentially overlapping tasks, both can and should be used for their own strengths.

As there is no general preference of Big Data vis-à-vis Business Intelligence (Breugelmans, 2014), ERP data will thus be impacted to a larger or a lesser extent, depending on the span and the scope of the Big Data project(s). The success of this symbiosis (or cohabitation) implies therefore a preliminary review of the impacts of the data related project portfolio on existing processes.

In such a review, a non-ambiguous understanding is needed of all taken assumptions. Ideally, these assumptions should be documented in the business case of each project.

It could, for example, be decided to implement SAP HANA to 'improve the analytical power' of the organization. The understanding of this power could diverge, as HANA is driven by three core components (parallel, in-memory relation query techniques, columnar stores, and improved compression technology) (Plattner & Zeier, 2012). Some will opt for it because of the possibilities the high compression rates offer, others for the speed of data retrieval, or for the fact that it can process queries via HANA and other Hadoop like tools. As the reasons to choose for this product may differ, the realization might differ. Consequently, the impacts may differ as well.

In complement of doing a sound transversal portfolio review, it is essential to create a climate that determines consistently what source of information will be used as single source of truth for what type of decision. This is especially useful in case of applications with (temporarily) overlapping data. Confusion could for instance occur when variables with similar names are used, but with a slightly different meaning; or when two applications use exactly the same variable, but with a synchronous/asynchronous delay. An additional advantage of such a climate is that it will limit the tendency to cruise back to Excel islands, and reinforce the focus on shared operational dashboards.

Hence, a sound preparation of Big Data initiatives requires that one takes the entire portfolio of activities, projects and data tools into account. The portfolio view and time based roadmap will allow everyone to see to what extend they will be impacted by the data crunching applications as such, by the evolving way of thinking, or by the shifting organizational approach. If, in addition, clarity is safeguarded on the different sources of truth, the chances are real that the fruits of this preparation will be used at their true value for all elements of the portfolio.

FUTURE RESEARCH DIRECTIONS

Big Data is in the midst of a period where the technical possibilities and the number of implementations are experiencing a continuous growth. According to outlooks of Gartner and IBM (Gulla, 2012; Van der Meulen & Rivera, 2013), this tendency will continue during the years to come.

Given this constant inflow of new projects, it is important to bring Big Data initiatives to a higher maturity level. One of the possibilities is to capitalize on past experiences by integrating not only the lessons learned and incremental quality gains on the technical level, but also those that take the organizational and human dimensions into account.

Currently, the consequent inclusion of a structural approach that reconciles the technological potential and the contextual reality is still going through a crystallization process, despite the fact that elaborated project management methodologies exist.

To improve this, several aspects could be further explored.

From the methodological point of view, the project management toolbox has to be further enriched with specific best practices. This best practice dynamic will have to dedicate specific attention to Change and Stakeholder Management during Big Data projects, and return on experience after the Go-Live. This will not decrease the important structuring role of project management frameworks. On the contrary, it will make it easier for the continuously growing number of Big Data projects to truly embrace the project methodologies and apply them appropriately.

Similarly, it would be valuable to build a best practice base for specific sub-sectors of the public sphere. By building on lessons learned, it is imaginable to strengthen data projects in key domains like education, health or city management. Indirectly, this experience base could even stimulate future improvements of the general project management frameworks.

Obviously, best practices will require regular revisiting as the Big Data world is in constant evolution. But the author believes that the recurring efforts will be largely compensated by the advantages in quality and outcome of the data projects.

Lastly, future research should explore ways to use the potential of the public-private force field. Using private experiences to improve the public reality is indeed only a part of the Big Data journey. The real satisfaction and added value will come when public organizations are able to think ahead of their private counterparts. To do so, a management approach needs to be developed that brings the current inspirational relation to a higher, more catalytic level, in combination with the structured project follow-up.

CONCLUSION

Three fundamental aspects need to be taken into account in the management of projects that intend to unveil the true potential of Big Data in the public sector, especially if they have the ambition to nourish the organization with new insights.

Firstly, it is essential to shape the building blocks of the Big Data ecosystem from the very beginning. To do so, one needs to define from the decisional angle what objective the data will have to support. This can be Internal improvement, Innovation towards external stakeholders, the Development of integrated solutions or eventually Building collaborations with public or private actors. In complement, one has to decide if the idea is to go for a small project, or a larger Big-Bang. It has been explained that an important factor in choosing between both is the extent to which the organization wants to focus on experimentation and the development of human and technical experience.

With these aspects in mind, it will have to be evaluated what types of data are desired, in addition to existing ones. Public bodies will also want to pay additional attention to the integrity and security of these data.

To complete the base outline, an evaluation is needed of the means that are available on the human, technical and financial level. They need to be scaled in accordance to the organization's ambitions. Ideally, this scaling should go slightly beyond the actual ambitions, in order to be prepared for strong demand, resulting from the project's success.

If assessed correctly, the combined configuration will offer a good view of the type of project that is actually at stake. This improved view and understanding will be valuable in the 'real' preparation, the shaping and the management of the project throughout the entire lifecycle.

A second essential element in managing a Big Data project is being prepared to go beyond the follow-up of the technical creativity with Hadoop, HANA and the like. Project management should not only encompass the different degrees of freedom of the project or the need to follow the progress closely. Big Data projects are about developing new possibilities that can bring public organizations on par with services offered by private counterparts- or even ahead of them.

This is done by changing the frames of reference and setting the foundations of a new way of thinking. To ensure that this added value gets captured efficiently, Big Data changes need to be embedded in a larger process. Effective management starts therefore already at the ideation of the project with the preparation of the mindset of the organizational sponsors. In combination with the clear definition of the business case, it should be evaluated if all elements of the public context feel right to launch the Big Data project in the envisioned circumstances. Once this is indicator is green, managing will require further follow-up through a solid planning, iterative follow-up loops with different stakeholders and the necessary change management until the organizational acceptance after the project.

The change management tools at hand are diverse. It has been illustrated that a multidimensional understanding can be built by evaluating the Stakeholders' capability and willingness to change, the Climate for Change and the Project Impact. The resulting bigger picture will offer a complementary indication of the change management reality. On the one hand, it will bring clear indications of the different aspects that require specific attention. At the same time, one will also have a better view on the possibilities of the organization, and the eventual presence of active change agents.

Last but not least, the management of Big Data projects needs to be done with a holistic view. The entire portfolio of activities, projects and data tools needs to be assessed, prepared and aligned upfront. This will bring a synchronized, contextual and functional coherence to otherwise loose pieces. Doing so will benefit the data landscape and the internal functioning, and therefore the final outcome.

In the end, data management, Big Data and traditional decision taking are bound to converge through a cross-fertilizing interaction, also for public bodies. Organizations should therefore see Big Data projects as an opportunity to enter with both feet in a new era of possibilities. Managing it with a clear vision, a good knowledge of the day-to-day reality and a layered approach will therefore contribute to a stable continuity of existing services, while assuring the transition of the existing organization to future evolutions.

REFERENCES

Ala-Kurikka, S. (2010). *Enel: Italy reaping first-mover benefits of smart meters.* Retrieved May 30, 2015, from http://www.euractiv.com/italy-reaping-first-mover-benefits-smart-meters-enel

Baele, E., & Devreux, H. (2014, December). MOBIB: the card of the future. *Eurotransport.* Retrieved May 30, 2015, from http://www.eurotransportmagazine.com/

Boone, R. (2013). Er is geen blauwdruk voor de informatisering van Justitie. *Legal World.* Retrieved July 7, 2014, from http://www.legalworld.be/

Bové, L. (2012, February 24). Justitie prutst met miljoenenclaim over computers. *De Tijd.* Retrieved Aug 19, 2014, from http://www.tijd.be/

Bové, L. (2013, August 29). België scoort slecht in informatisering justitie. *De Tijd.* Retrieved July 7, 2014, from http://www.tijd.be/

Breugelmans, J. (2014). *Big Data vs Business Intelligence.* Retrieved May 24, 2014, from http://visual-intelligence.nu/

Dutcher, J. (2014). *John Wilbanks: Let's Pool Our Medical Data.* Retrieved August 21, 2014, from http://datascience.berkeley.edu/john-wilbanks-lets-pool-medical-data/

Gartner. (2014). *IT Glossary.* Retrieved June 12, 2014, from http://www.gartner.com/it-glossary/?s=big+data

Gulla, J. (2012, February). Sevens Reasons IT Projects Fail. *IBM Systems Magazine.* Retrieved May 13, 2014, from http://www.ibmsystemsmag.com/

Herzberg, B. (2014). *The Next Frontier for Open Data: An Open Private Sector.* Retrieved June 21, 2014, from http://blogs.worldbank.org/voices/next-frontier-open-data-open-private-sector

Kobielus, J. (2013). *Measuring the Business Value of Big Data.* Retrieved July 11, 2014, from http://www.ibmbigdatahub.com/blog/measuring-business-value-big-data

Mount Sinai Hospital. (2014). *Fast Company names Icahn School of Medicine as one of world's top ten most innovative companies in big data.* Press Release. Retrieved September 21, 2014, from http://www.mountsinai.org/about-us/newsroom/press-releases/fast-company-names-icahn-school-of-medicine-as-one-of-worlds-top-ten-most-innovative-companies-in-big-data

Nelson, F. (2014). *Coca-Cola Drinks In New Social Data.* Retrieved September 3, 2014, from http://www.networkcomputing.com/networking/coca-cola-drinks-in-new-social-data/d/d-id/1100837

Orcutt, M. (2014). Hackers Are Homing in on Hospitals. *Technology Review.* Retrieved September 15, 2014, from http://www.technologyreview.com/news/530411/hackers-are-homing-in-on-hospitals/

Paskin, J. (2014). Sha Hwang, the Designer Hired to Make Obamacare a Beautiful Thing. *Business Week*. Retrieved May 14, 2014, from http://www.businessweek.com/

Peumans, K. (2014). *Informatisation de la Justice: de l'âge de la pierre au 21e siècle*. Press Release. Retrieved July 7, 2014, from http://justice.belgium.be/fr/ordre_judiciaire/reforme_justice/nouvelles/news_pers_2014-03-14.jsp

Streichenberger, I. (2014). *Press release (par. 3, par. 5)*. Retrieved August 7, 2014, from https://www.inbloom.org/

The Health Foundation. (2012). *Birmingham Children's Hospital NHS Trust: Continuous remote monitoring of ill children*. Retrieved May 30, 2015, from: http://www.health.org.uk/areas-of-work/programmes/shine-eleven/related-projects/birmingham-children-s-hospital-nhs-foundation-trust/

Turner, V., Reinsel, D., & Gantz, J. F. (2014). *The Digital Universe of Opportunities: Rich Data and the Increasing Value of the Internet of Things*. Retrieved September 3, 2014, from http://www.emc.com/leadership/digital-universe/index.htm

Van der Meulen, R., & Rivera, J. (2013). *Gartner Predicts Business Intelligence and Analytics Will Remain Top Focus for CIOs Through 2017*. Press Release. Retrieved September 3, 2014, from http://www.gartner.com/newsroom/id/2637615

Vanleemputten, P. (2013, August 29). Informatisation de la Justice: la Belgique parmi les plus mauvais élèves. *Datanews*. Retrieved May 20, 2015, from http://www.datanews.be/

Viaene, S. (2014). Zorg ervoor dat je technologie mee kan. *Business Bytes*. Retrieved May 15, 2015, from http://business.telenet.be/nl/artikel/zorg-ervoor-dat-je-technologie-mee-kan

Young, C. M. (2003). *Driving Organizational Change: Key Issues*. Retrieved July 19, 2014, from https://www.gartner.com/doc/383466

KEY TERMS AND DEFINITIONS

Agile: Project management methodology, in which the development is characterized by the breakdown of tasks into short periods, with frequent reassessment of work and plans. Used in software related projects.

Big-Bang: Term used in project management to identify a project in which most of the changes are operated at once, contrary to a phased implementation.

Business Case: Cost benefit analysis used for the justification of a significant expenditure at the initiation of a project.

Change Management: Management of changes impacting an organization by enabling changes while ensuring minimal impact on the organization or its stakeholders. Involves the definition and implementation of new values and behaviour in an organization, the management of expectations, the building of consensus, and the management of organisational changes.

Lean(ification): Approach that focuses on the optimization of processes by the elimination of waste in terms of time and resources.

Non-Structured Data: Data coming from non-structured data sources. Can be encountered as free-text communications in payments, or unmapped information from external data sources or social media.

Scrum: Iterative and incremental product development framework used in agile projects.

Stakeholder Management: Management of all people who have an interest in an organization or project, or that could be impacted by its activities, targets, resources or deliverables. This can include the management of customers, suppliers, vendors, shareholders, employees and senior management. Closely related to change management.

Structured Data: Data coming from structured data sources. Can be encountered as structured payment data or transactional data in internal, data model based ERP systems.

Waterfall Project Methodology: Sequential project management methodology, in which project progress is regarded as a downwards process. Originally described as consisting of phases for Requirement Specifications, Design, Construction, Integration, Testing, Installation and Maintenance, variations exist on the naming and number of phases. Used in software related projects.

ENDNOTES

[1]   For more information on Prince2, the author refers the reader to: http://www.prince-officialsite.com/

[2]   For more information on PMBOK, the author refers the reader to: http://www.pmi.org/PMBOK-Guide-and-Standards.aspx

[3]   For a detailed definition of Big Data, the author refers the reader to Gartner (2014)

[4]   For more information on the Entrepreneurs Desk, the author refers the reader to: http://www.beci.be/services/je_cree_ma_societe/guichet_d_entreprises/enterprise_desk/

[5]   For more information on UNOS, the author refers the reader to: http://www.unos.org/

[6]   For more information on Healthcare.gov, the author refers the reader to: https://www.healthcare.gov/

[7]   For more information on deCODE, the author refers the reader to: http://www.decode.com/

[8]   For more information on Islendingabok, the author refers the reader to: https://www.islendingabok.is/Leidbeiningar.jsp

[9]   For more information on Sagebase, the author refers the reader to: http://sagebase.org/

[10]   For more information on MODA, the author refers the reader to: http://www.nyc.gov/html/analytics/html/home/home.shtml

[11]   For more information on the Open Data from the European Union, the author refers the reader to: https://open-data.europa.eu/en/data/

[12]   For more information on the Open Data from the USA, the author refers the reader to: https://www.data.gov/

[13]   For more information on the Open Data from the OECD, the author refers the reader to: http://data.oecd.org/

[14]   For more information on the Open Data from the Worldbank, the author refers the reader to: http://data.worldbank.org/

[15]   For more information on Algorithmia, the author refers the reader to: https://algorithmia.com/

[16]   The aim of the local authorities is to install Traffic Lab devices in more than 50 000 vehicles by 2015. When ready, the data will be made available to any interested party, in order to continue to

crunch the data and have the new transport up and running by 2025. For more details on Traffic Lab, the author refers the reader to: http://trafficlab.fi/

[17]   For more information on LIVE Singapore!, the author refers the reader to: http://senseable.mit. edu/livesingapore/

[18]   For the Big Data events in Boston, the author refers the reader to: http://www.massbigdata.org/ events/

[19]   For more information on data driven fraud detection, the author refers the reader to the Big Data insight of the Association of Certified Fraud Examiners: http://www.acfe.com/

[20]   For more information on the London Data Store, the author refers the reader to: http://data.london. gov.uk/

[21]   For more information on the Brussels Smartcity initiative, the author refers the reader to: http:// smartcity.bruxelles.be/

[22]   For details on waterfall methodologies, the author refers the reader to: http://www.pmi.org/PMBOK-Guide-and-Standards.aspx (PMBOK), http://www.prince-officialsite.com/ (Prince2). For scrum, the author refers to https://www.scrum.org/ and to https://www.scrumalliance.org/.

Chapter 8
On Efficient Acquisition and Recovery Methods for Certain Types of Big Data

George Avirappattu
Kean University, USA

ABSTRACT

Big data is characterized in many circles in terms of the three V's – volume, velocity and variety. Although most of us can sense palpable opportunities presented by big data there are overwhelming challenges, at many levels, turning such data into actionable information or building entities that efficiently work together based on it. This chapter discusses ways to potentially reduce the volume and velocity aspects of certain kinds of data (with sparsity and structure), while acquiring itself. Such reduction can alleviate the challenges to some extent at all levels, especially during the storage, retrieval, communication, and analysis phases. In this chapter we will conduct a non-technical survey, bringing together ideas from some recent and current developments. We focus primarily on Compressive Sensing and sparse Fast Fourier Transform or Sparse Fourier Transform. Almost all natural signals or data streams are known to have some level of sparsity and structure that are key for these efficiencies to take place.

1. INTRODUCTION

The scientific community as well as the intelligence agencies have traditionally led the field in collection and compilation of vast amounts of electronic data. Search engines (such as Google, Yahoo!, and Microsoft) and e-commerce started amassing exponentially increasing amounts of data starting in the early 2000's. After social networks, like Facebook or Twitter arrived, with hundreds of millions of users, electronic data collection increased to a level beyond imagination.

Deriving actionable information from the data collected has challenged the best minds in many disciplines. Efficient storage and retrieval of data on demand needed new thinking. From this need, many new technologies including the "Hadoop – MapReduce" ecosystem, with an ever increasing number of components was born. There are several scientific communities and commercial or public entities hard at

DOI: 10.4018/978-1-4666-9649-5.ch008

work to exploit this newest opportunity in spite of the unforeseen challenges in doing so. The traditional analysis of digital data was limited to one's own computing domain, often represented by an academic or corporate structure. However, with the advancement of computing and networking technologies that lead to big data, there seems to be a paradigm shift in what we even consider to fit the definition of "data".

The word "data" is readily conceptualized my most of us. However these concepts vary widely. Even most current dictionaries have generic and varying definitions of the term. According to Oxford dictionary, data means, "Facts and statistics collected together for reference or analysis". Oxford goes on to specify it meaning in Computing as, "the quantities, characters, or symbols on which operations are performed by a computer, being stored and transmitted in the form of electrical signals and recorded on magnetic, optical, or mechanical recording media" and its meaning in Philosophy as, "things known or assumed as facts, making the basis of reasoning or calculation." Merriam-Webster defines data as "facts or information used usually to calculate, analyze, or plan something or as information that is produced or stored by a computer". However, with the introduction of the World Wide Web in the early nineties and its success in providing connectivity to digital information everywhere (and the subsequent development of unforeseen levels of acquisition, storage, and analysis capabilities of digital information) one may wonder whether these definitions suffice what we consider as data.

Useful data can generally be considered as information of any kind that may evoke any of our senses about past or present. Such information often is embedded with high levels of sparsity and redundancy, especially in one or other of its alternate representations. Any event that has occurred or is occurring and could lead to some form of sensation or thought in one or more of us can be regarded as source of useful data. Data sources that interest us can perhaps be divided into two broad categories: data that can be attributed to humans, and data that can be attributed to non-humans.

Some examples of the first kind are e-mails, internet searches, tweets, articles (scientific or otherwise), creative works including audio and video, commercial transactions and the census. In this case since humans act as both the source and recipient, we have complete control of how the related data is perceived or interpreted. The second kind can be sourced mostly to observations of natural phenomena around us, as in oceanography, seismology, geology and meteorology, astronomy, high energy physics, biology, and chemistry. This type of data allows us perhaps our own impression or interpretation of what actually is taking place.

Analytics on both types of data holds promise. But strategies for analysis, however, may differ. The former will always be discrete and finite in size and dimension, no matter the volume, velocity, variety, or any other characteristics. At least theoretically, it may not need as much processing in acquisition, storage, and retrieval. The latter, on the other hand tends to be continuous and infinite in size and perhaps in dimension but full of sparsity and redundancy.

Regardless, analytics to divulge meaningful information from any data has better potential when they are used collectively through aggregation, composition, or integration. For example, individual transactions by themselves are unlikely targets for analytics (although perhaps with information gathered from analytics one can and may go back to subsets or individual data.)

Analytics, even after identifying patterns visually or otherwise, will largely have to be based more and more on principles of computational techniques, whether mathematical or statistical. Much of the information content in any type of data depends on the amount and type variation contained in it (Rudder, 2014). Identifying this would require on data in non-quantitative forms, (here forth we will assess only digital data regardless of source,) whether structured, unstructured, or qualitative, be transformed into quantitative. After all, analytics on big data is only promising if the analytical techniques used can reveal patterns or trends that the "naked eye" cannot discern on its own. That is why, at the core of many scientific techniques, the Fourier transform and its related techniques loom large. Such technology, roughly speaking, allows us to glean the intrinsic character of the data or signal in question by transforming it from a "time domain" to a "frequency domain" and gives us an opening for all kinds of analysis and synthesis on the content. It all requires efficient acquisition of the data or signal of interest and its successful recovery.

This is exactly where the developments such as compressive sensing (CS) come in. In a nutshell, CS promises a way to acquire the data, with sparsity and structure, proportional to its useful content only and recover it. For decades, the gold standard has been the Shannon-Nyquist theorem, which roughly states that to guarantee exact recovery of information one has to keep up with the fastest frequency (variation) component in the data. And that may not have anything to do with the amount of information content. One can then appreciate the promise of CS: it eases the complexities of volume and velocity, acquiring only the necessary data by avoiding sparsity and exploiting structure.

Donoho (2006) in his seminal article on the topic asks "If much of the data that is acquired are thrown away later why acquire them in the first place?" He goes on to present guarantees for exact recovery or at least probabilistic estimates for it, from a significantly reduced set of signal samples provided the signal is sparse (see Figure 1, for example.) About the same time, Candice, Romberg, and Tao in their groundbreaking work on the topic, provide many results that spurred a large amount of work in the area now called compressive sensing, which provides for efficient sampling and robust recovery methods.

Figure 1. Sparsity: A one megapixel (1,000,000) picture on the left next to one that is reconstructed from 25,000 wavelet coefficients on the right. The difference is hardly noticeable. It turns out that the original picture can perfectly be reconstructed from just 96,000 measurements alone according to Candès in "Undersampling and Sparse Signal Recovery"

Another group (Indyk & Kapralov 2014) apparently independent of compressive sensing developments, were coming up with surprisingly efficient algorithms for Discrete Fourier Transform that they called sparse Fast Fourier Transform (sFFT) in order to achieve similar goals.

At the core of all these efforts is the desire to reduce conventional signal sampling frequency requirements so that sampling is proportional to content (in a natural or a transformed form) and not only provide recovery guarantees but also hold the computational time for sampling and recovery to a minimum. There also are several other recent important developments, seemingly independent of the aforementioned, for efficient acquisition and recovery. Some examples are the techniques applied to streaming data, such as sketching (Cormode, Garofalakis, Haas, & Jermaine, 2012) and compressed counting (Ping, & Zhang, 2011)., which are beyond the scope of this chapter.

In this chapter, we are concerned primarily with the discussion of basic developments that holds promise in dealing with big data as a whole. We do not attempt to discuss existing technologies, systems, specific issues, and their resolutions as is done in other chapters.

This chapter is organized into two main sections. First, Section II discusses big data and provides a general overview and context for the key section that follows. It is divided into subsections on big data opportunities that are still being discovered, as well as the increasing challenges presented by it. Second, Section III deals with the efficient acquisition, processing, and recovery of data with the two properties: sparsity and structure. This is quite a different from the characterization of big data in terms of three or more V's. In this section, also divided into subsections, we outline recent and somewhat parallel developments that may help alleviate many challenges associated with big data even before the data is acquired by reducing the volume and perhaps the velocity aspects of it. This section is meant to be a brief and non-technical survey of some of the recent advancements that are relevant in this regard.

2. BIG DATA

2.1. What is Big Data?

There seems to be no complete consensus on a definition for big data. However literature and research on big data itself is exploding for understandable reasons. Some notable attempts on a definition: "Big data' refers to datasets whose size is beyond the ability of typical database software tools to capture, store, manage, and analyze." - from a report by McKinsey Global Institute in June 2011 (McKinsey Global Institute, 2011.) "Big data is a resource and a tool" - from an essay titled: The Rise of Big Data: How It's Changing the Way We Think About the World by K. Cukier & V. Mayer-Schoenberger (2013). "Big data is being generated by everything around us at all times. Every digital process and social media exchange produces it. Systems, sensors and mobile devices transmit it. Big data is arriving from multiple sources at an alarming velocity, volume and variety. To extract meaningful value from big data, you need optimal processing power, analytics capabilities and skills." – from the IBM website (October 2013.) "Big data is a popular term used to describe the exponential growth and availability of data, both structured and unstructured. And big data may be as important to business – and society – as the Internet has become. Why? More data may lead to more accurate analyses." – from the SAS website (October 2014)

Perhaps the more recognized interpretation is the one that came from the title of Doug Laney's article in 2001 entitled "3D Data Management: Controlling Data Volume, Velocity and Variety" (Laney, 2001). Ever since, big data has been characterized by the 3V's: Volume, Velocity and Variety. Recently other V's have been added to these three; however there seems to be no agreement on how many more nor on which ones should be added. We will keep in mind a more holistic way of looking at big data, as discussed in introduction.

The proceedings of the ACM SIGKDD international conference on Knowledge Discovery and Data mining, (most recently held in August 2014 in New York City, NY) serve as a key benchmark display for various scientific and technological advancements made in making sense of big data.

2.2. Opportunities and Challenges

The variety of data being collected seems to have no end. It is hard to even classify the types of data along clear boundaries any more. Google, Facebook, Amazon, Twitter, and security agencies are just a few global entities that are likely to have access to vast amounts of human generated data (the first type discussed in the introduction.) Other entities include research labs, academic institutions, and public and government agencies. Growth in the data collection rate always seems to outpace increasing storage and processing capabilities.

One common and basic way of categorizing data is into structured data and unstructured data. Many of the theories and techniques developed in the past apply exclusively to structured data. However, the need for techniques to deal with unstructured data is incredibly pertinent as the variety of data collected becomes more and more complex. Just consider tweets, for example, from different parts of the world with different socioeconomic conditions, customs, political structures, and different languages.

Here are some common challenges faced today:

1. Collecting that includes cleaning and integrating before storage
2. Organizing and storing data into scalable modern databases (such as the Cloud)
3. Ensuring privacy and security
4. Computational power for retrieving and analyzing at will
5. Analytics: extracting actionable information/intelligence

Examples of big data use are prolific. The two following sample examples (one public and the other private) demonstrate entities that have unlocked the potential of big data to overcome the challenges mentioned above.

First, Dr. Lee, who placed the foundational architecture for the University of Pittsburg Medical Center's (UPMC) new enterprise data warehouse, writes, "the integration of data, which is the goal of the enterprise data warehouse, allows us to ask questions that we just simply couldn't ask before". Indeed, Pitt researchers recently were able to electronically integrate for the first time clinical and genomic information on 140 patients previously treated for breast cancer (UPMC, 2013.)

Second, Uber's rapid development and popularity amongst the millennial generation stems partially from its ability to reliably integrate a plethora of data and extract from that data a link between individual drivers and consumers of the service Uber provides (Uber, 2014). "Uber owns no cars and hires no drivers. In many ways, the whole company is a data play. Its systems know where you've come from, your favorite haunts and how you pay. The company's 'Math department,' as Kalanick calls it, collects user behavior over time into a 'God view' that allows them to know exactly which neighborhood will need more cars on a rainy day.'" (Scola & Peterson, 2104.)

3. EFFICIENT ACQUISITION AND RECOVERY

The celebrated Shannon-Nyquist theorem on sampling, guarantees full recovery of a signal from its samples provided that the sampling rate is greater or equal to twice the highest frequency (Nyquist rate) in the signal (Shannon, 1949). However with the advent of big data, the demands of the Nyquist rate sampling on hardware, potential storage, and on the fly retrieval and analysis is becoming harder to meet. Therefore, it is natural to look for alternate possibilities. It is quite timely that Donoho poses the question "Why go to so much effort to acquire all the data when most of what we get will be thrown away? Can't we just directly measure the part that won't end up being thrown away?" (Donoho, 2006)

The origin of the mathematical ideas behind compressive sensing appears decades old. In fact, in the 1970's, seismologists were already utilizing precursors of this idea to spot oil underground. There have been two significant developments that perked up interest in compressive sensing within the last decade or so. First, let us consider the advances made in sublinear sampling and recovery of certain signals with the work of Candès, Romberg, and Tao (2006a) between 2004 and 2006. Remarkably they conclude, "the resolution of an acquired image is not controlled by the number of pixels (conventional wisdom) but proportional to the information content." In fact, that is the way it ought to be, isn't it? "Information content" in this context refers specifically to non-sparse data in some convenient representation (such as a in "wavelet basis") but not necessarily in natural or standard form.

These results have then been followed by promising advances made in processing sparse signals called sparse Fast Fourier Transform (sFFT), remarkably, in sublinear time by (Hassanieh, Indyk, Katabi, & Price, 2012) and others. Sublinear time roughly means that computation time may be less than the signal length!

3.1. Compressive Sensing

"Finally, in some important situations the full collection of n discrete-time samples of an analog signal may be difficult to obtain (and possibly difficult to subsequently compress). Here, it could be helpful to design physical sampling devices that directly record discrete, low-rate incoherent measurements of the incident analog signal. (This) suggests that mathematical and computational methods could have an enormous impact in areas where conventional hardware design has significant limitations." (Candès & Wakin, 2008.)

At an abstract level the compressive sensor is a matrix $\mathbf{\Phi}$ that does not just take N sample measurements of the signal x of the same length but uses compressing techniques to only take (significantly less) $M \ll N$ samples $y = \mathbf{\Phi}x$. From this reduced sample y the original signal x needs to be either recovered completely or approximated sufficiently well. The tradeoffs in making such recovery possible are, roughly speaking, requirements of sparsity and structure in the signal. It turns out a great many natural signals have either one or both of these characteristics to a varying extent. Often the signal x itself may not manifest its sparsity, but generally upon transformation to an appropriate basis (such as wavelets or sinusoids) it will. Suppose that $x^* = \psi x$, where ψ_{NXN} is a matrix (such as wavelet transformation), be the transformed signal and that is what really being sampled. So $y = (\phi\psi)x = \mathbf{\Phi}x$, where ϕ is takes the samples, is an M dimensional vector from which we are to recover x. The hope is even if M is significantly less in length than the signal N, under certain requirements on x, it can be reconstructed exactly or sufficiently well. The classic Nyquist condition requires that $M \geq 2F$, F being the highest frequency in x. With these new developments initiated by Donoho (2006), Candès et al. (2006) and Hassanieh et al. (2012) we may by-pass sampling frequency requirements. The key difference here is that it is not the frequency but the information content (sparsity and structure) that drives the sampling requirements.

Let us now take a little closer look. The sample vector,

$$y = (\phi\psi)x = \Phi x$$

where Φ_{MXN} represents both transformation and sampling from x. Note that in most of the literature the difference between ϕ and Φ is not spelled out as compressing a signal using basis ψ, such as wavelets or Fourier, and is somewhat well understood, and with many assuming x to be natively sparse.

It is crucial to understand though that the chances of recovery will not be good if the ϕ and ψ are coherent. Somewhat of a variation of this *incoherence* requirement is that Φ has the *restricted isometry property* (RIP) which roughly states that any subset ϕ and ψ be close to orthogonal (notice that they are not going to be orthogonal as there are more columns than rows.) In other words the sampling basis ϕ must have columns that are as nearly orthogonal as possible to the compressing basis ψ.

With $M << N$, recovering x from y is an ill-posed problem and will not present a unique solution in general. Under the sparsity (or near sparsity) and incoherence or RIP requirements, it can be shown that out of the possible solutions, the sparsest one, the one with the least non-zero entries is the actual solution (or has very good probability of being it.) Finding such solution though is an l_0 minimization problem (Duarte & Eldar, 2011). The l_0 and l_1 norms of a vector x are $\left\| x \right\|_0 = \left\| x_1, x_2, x_3, \ldots, x_n \right\|_0 = \sum_{i=0}^{N} x_i^0$ (this is really not a norm in the mathematical sense, but is an accepted convention and simply counts nonzero entries) and $\left\| x \right\|_1 = \left\| x_1, x_2, x_3, \ldots, x_n \right\|_1 = \sum_{i=0}^{N} \left| x_i \right|$. Finding l_0 solution to this problem would amount to finding $\min_{y=\frac{1}{2} x} \left\| x \right\|_0$. This happens to be a combinatorial problem with high computational cost. Surprisingly though, the higher the dimension of the solution the more likely the sparse solution from l_0 is the same as that of l_1 minimization: $\min_{y=\frac{1}{2} x} \left\| x \right\|_1$. Here the advantage is that, this minimization amounts to convex linear programming problem that has well developed, efficient, algorithmic solution strategies. Such l_1 minimizations are also robust even in the presence of signal noise that is a reality in practical sampling implementations (Candès, et al., 2006a).

Further refinements of l_1 minimizations in the form of iterative algorithms started appearing soon. This sequence of algorithms that were proposed to improve the computational complexity is a combination of l_1 minimization and "greedy algorithms" that refine the choices step-by-step and are called orthogonal matching pursuits. Significant improvements in efficient recovery were achieved by these.

One of the few practical applications compressive sensing that researchers Baraniuk and Kelly's (2007) team at Rice University came up with is now the well-known single pixel camera (SPC). A schematic diagram is in Figure 2 (*Courtesy of Rice University and used with permission*)

What actually happens here is that the signal (an image in this case) of the scene is focused on an array of small mirrors each of which can be randomly positioned to either reflect the signal to the single pixel camera or elsewhere. This random positioning of the mirrors makes the signal received by the pixel an average of a randomly sampled image. The SPC sequentially takes *Klog(N/K)* samples of the scene (K-sparse). The reconstructed image thus recovered just from *Klog(N/K)* is quite comparable with that from N samples in conventional means.

Candès (2008) sketches a potential "analog-to-information conversion" architecture is another example of bringing CS theory to practice. Healy and Brady (2008) discuss them further in their article.

3.2. sFFT (or SFT): Sparse Fourier Transform

"The sparse Fourier transform (SFT) addresses the big data setting by computing a compressed Fourier transform using only a subset of the input data, in time smaller than the data set size." (Gilbert, Indyk, Iwen, & Schmidt, 2014)

SFT methods attempt to calculate (estimate) discrete Fourier Transform (DFT) of K-sparse (compressible) N-length signals in sublinear *K log(N)* time. All the SFT techniques essentially proceeds as follows: first divide the problem of identifying frequencies involved in the sparse signal into sub-problems until each frequency is basically isolated into narrow bands called bins; second, identify (or at least estimate) the frequency by its position and value in each bin which can be done with just two samples. For the case of frequencies that are close to each other and thus hard to separate, use a random permutation technique to move the positions of the frequencies around and then repeat isolating and recovering those frequencies. Repeat these processing with different random permutation and subsequent isolation until all K frequencies are isolated. At the end we will have a process that is of the order roughly of *K log(N)*. There are several implementations of this method and the reader is referred to a survey such as (Gilbert et al., 2014) for more details.

Figure 2. Schematic diagram of single pixel camera (SPC)

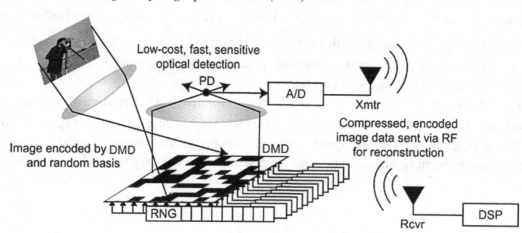

In (Gilbert et al., 2014) the authors points out that SFTs also can be considered compressive sensing in a broader sense as these also recover (or estimate) frequency-sparse signals from a reduced set of samples in sublinear time.

4. CONCLUSION

Through compressive sensing and other related technology, great advancements have been made towards extracting only the minimal information required to recover and reconstruct data signals received. In terms of timing, these advancements couldn't have been better, insofar as many are now experiencing the complexities of a deluge of data. It is logical that compressive sensing type of technologies will be helping alleviate the volume and velocity, and perhaps other aspects of big data in near future.

These advances are exciting because hardware based on conventional sampling will be limited due to Nyquist - Shannon sampling requirements. That will impede our ability to sample and acquire digital data as fast as we desire. But even if we circumvent that issue the enormity of the captured data poses major challenges. Compressive sensing makes a two-fold promise regarding its potential to revolutionize data analytics. First, hardware limitation issues will be turned into mathematical and algorithmic issues related to recovery and processing speed. These in turn, eventually become software design issues. Second, CS promises a potentially significant reduction in volume and velocity of data for us to deal with.

Despite the aforementioned, significant future research needs to be done in bringing the promises of CS technology to fruition. First, we are still waiting for implementations of this compressive sensing technology that can simultaneously transform and sample analog signals into discretized and compressed form at the acquisition stage itself. Second, our ability to utilize such sampled (perhaps even transformed) data across all phases, access during cleaning and integration just for example, of big data processing has to be realized yet.

REFERENCES

Baraniuk, R. G. (2007). Compressive sensing. *IEEE Signal Processing Magazine*, *24*(4), 118–121. doi:10.1109/MSP.2007.4286571

Candès, E. J., Romberg, J. K., & Tao, T. (2006a). Robust uncertainty principles: Exact signal reconstruction from highly incomplete frequency information. *IEEE Transactions on Information Theory*, *52*(2), 489–509. doi:10.1109/TIT.2005.862083

Candès, E. J., Romberg, J. K., & Tao, T. (2006b). Stable signal recovery from incomplete and inaccurate measurements. *Communications on Pure and Applied Mathematics*, *59*(8), 1207–1223. doi:10.1002/cpa.20124

Candès, E. J., & Wakin, M. B. (2008). An introduction to compressive sampling. *IEEE Signal Processing Magazine*, *24*(2), 21–30. doi:10.1109/MSP.2007.914731

Committee on the Analysis of Massive Data et al. (2103). *Frontiers in Massive Data Analysis*. The National Academies Press.

Cormode, G., Garofalakis, M., Haas, P., & Jermaine, C. (2012). *Synopses for Massive Data: Samples, Histograms, Wavelets and Sketches.* doi:10.1561/1900000004

Cormode, G., & Muthukrishnan, S. (2005). Improved data stream summaries: The count-min sketch and its applications. *Journal of Algorithms, 55*(1), 58–75. doi:10.1016/j.jalgor.2003.12.001

Cukier, K., & Mayer-Schoenberger, V. (2013). *The Rise of Big Data: How It's Changing the Way We Think About the World.* Retrieved from http://www.foreignaffairs.com/articles/139104/kenneth-neil-cukier-and-viktor-mayer-schoenberger/the-rise-of-big-data

Donoho, D. L. (2006). Compressed sensing. *IEEE Transactions on Information Theory, 52*(4), 1289–1306. doi:10.1109/TIT.2006.871582

Duarte, M., & Eldar, Y. (2011). Structured Compressed Sensing: From Theory to Applications. *IEEE Transactions on Signal Processing, 59*(9), 4053–4085. doi:10.1109/TSP.2011.2161982

Foucart, S. & Rauhut, H. (2013). *A Mathematical Introduction to Compressive Sensing, Applied and Numerical Harmonic Analysis.* Springer Science + Business Media.

Gilbert, A., Indyk, P., Iwen, M., & Schmidt, L. (2014). A compressed Fourier transform for big data. IEEE Signal Processing Magazine, 31(5), 91 - 100

Han, J., Wang, C., & El-Kishky, A. (2104). Bringing structure to text: mining phrases, entities, topics, and hierarchies. *Proceedings of the 20th ACM SIGKDD international conference on Knowledge discovery and data mining.* ACM.

Hassanieh, H., Indyk, P., Katabi, & Price, E. (2012). Nearly Optimal Sparse Fourier Transform. *ACM-SIAM Symposium on Discrete Algorithms.* ACM.

Healy, D. D., & Brady, D. J. (2008). Compression at the Physical Interface. IEEE Signal Processing Magazine, 25(2)

IBM Website. (2014). Retrieved from http://www.ibm.com/big-data/us/en/

Indyk, P., & Kapralov, M., (2014, October). Sample-Optimal Sparse Fourier Transform in Any Constant Dimension. *FOCS.*

Laney, D. (2001). *3D Data Management: Controlling Data Volume, Velocity and Variety.* Retrieved from http://blogs.gartner.com/doug-laney/files/2012/01/ad949-3D-Data-Management-Controlling-Data-Volume-Velocity-and-Variety.pdf

Mackenzie, D. (2009). *Compressed Sensing Makes Every Pixel Count.* Retrieved from http://www.ams.org/samplings/math-history/hap7-pixel.pdf

McKinsey Global Institute. (2011). *Big data: The next frontier for innovation, competition, and productivity.* Retrieved from http://www.mckinsey.com/~/media/McKinsey/dotcom/Insights%20and%20pubs/MGI/Research/Technology%20and%20Innovation/Big%20Data/MGI_big_data_full_report.ashx

Ping, L., & Zhang, C. (2011). *A new algorithm for compressed counting with applications in Shannon entropy estimation in dynamic data.* COLT.

Rudder, C. (2014). *Dataclysm, Who we Are*. Crown Publishers.

Scola, N., & Peterson, A. (2014). *Data is Uber's business. But protecting it may be its biggest weakness*. Retrieved from https://www.washingtonpost.com/blogs/the-switch/wp/2014/11/18/data-is-ubers-business-but-protecting-it-may-be-its-largest-weakness/

Shannon, C. E. (1949). Communication Theory of Secrecy Systems. *The Bell System Technical Journal, 28*(4), 656–715. doi:10.1002/j.1538-7305.1949.tb00928.x

SmartAmerica. (2014). Retrieved from http://nist.gov/el/smartamerica.cfm

Uber. (2014). Retrieved from https://www.uber.com/about

UPMC. (2013). Retrieved from http://www.upmc.com/media/newsreleases/2013/pages/upmc-big-data-tech-breast-cancer-research.aspx

Section 3
Big Data:
Health Care Issues and Applications

Chapter 9
Application of Big Data in Healthcare:
Opportunities, Challenges and Techniques

Md Rakibul Hoque
University of Dhaka, Bangladesh

Yukun Bao
Huazhong University of Science and Technology, China

ABSTRACT

This chapter investigates the application, opportunities, challenges and techniques of Big Data in healthcare. The healthcare industry is one of the most important, largest, and fastest growing industries in the world. It has historically generated large amounts of data, "Big Data", related to patient healthcare and well-being. Big Data can transform the healthcare industry by improving operational efficiencies, improve the quality of clinical trials, and optimize healthcare spending from patients to hospital systems. However, the health care sector lags far behind compared to other industries in leveraging their data assets to improve efficiencies and make more informed decisions. Big Data entails many new challenges regarding security, privacy, legal concerns, authenticity, complexity, accuracy, and consistency. While these challenges are complex, they are also addressable. The predominant 'Big Data' Management technologies such as MapReduce, Hadoop, STORM, and others with similar combinations or extensions should be used for effective data management in healthcare industry.

INTRODUCTION

The healthcare industry is one of the most important, largest, and fastest growing industries in the world. It has historically generated large amounts of data, "Big Data", related to patient healthcare and well-being (Nambiar, 2013). These data include clinical data from clinical decision support systems, patient data in electronic patient records, physician's prescriptions, pharmacies, insurance, administrative data, sensor data, social media posts, blogs, web pages, emergency care data, news feeds, and articles in medical journals (Bian et al., 2012; Raghupathi & Raghupathi, 2013). International Data Corporation, a global

DOI: 10.4018/978-1-4666-9649-5.ch009

market research firm, estimates that the amount of digital data will grow from 2.8 trillion gigabytes in 2012 to 40 trillion gigabytes by 2020 (IDC, 2012). A recent study estimates that over 30% of all data stored in the world are medical data and this percentage is expected to increase rapidly. In 2012, the volumes of worldwide healthcare data were 500 petabytes and are projected to reach 25,000 petabytes in 2020 (Feldman et al., 2012).

It is widely accepted that Big Data can transform the healthcare industry by improving operational efficiencies, the quality of clinical trials, and optimizing healthcare spending from patients to hospital systems (Koh & Tan, 2011). The potential for Big Data analytics in healthcare leads to better outcomes by analyzing patient characteristics and outcomes of care. It identifies the most clinically and cost effective treatments and offers analysis and tools. Big Data can assist patients to determine regimens or care protocols by collecting and publishing data on medical procedures. For example, broad scale disease profiling helps to identify predictive events and support prevention initiatives; and, implementing much nearer to real-time by aggregating and synthesizing patient clinical records. Moreover, licensing data can assist pharmaceutical companies to identify patients for inclusion in clinical trials.

The doctors will be able to understand which tests are not necessary and patients will be able to access information on the doctors for specific procedures with Big Data analytics (Chawla & Davis, 2013). The Big Data analytics can avoid errors, diagnostic accuracy and improve coordination of care by using high-quality data. In USA, the Obama Administration has invested USD 200 million for Big Data Research and Development initiative to transform the use of Big Data for biomedical research (STP, 2012). The government proposed "Health 2.0" to manage hospitals, patients, insurance and government efficiently. The U.S. healthcare alliance network, Premier, has more than 2,700 members, hospitals and health systems, 90,000 non-acute facilities and 400,000 physicians. It has assembled a large database of clinical, patient, financial, and supply chain data to generate comprehensive and comparable clinical outcome measures. The Korean government plans to operate the National DNA Management System which will offer customized diagnosis and medical treatment to patients (NICT, 2011).

However, the health care sector lags far behind other industries in leveraging their data assets to improve efficiencies and make more informed decisions. While other industries such as the insurance, banking and retail sectors are far advanced in leveraging Big Data techniques, health care remains poor at handling the flood of data. Researchers have raised concerns about how to ensure that Big Data has central role in a health system's ability to secure improved health for its users (Ohlhorst, 2012). Big Data entails many new challenges regarding security, privacy, legal concerns, authenticity, complexity, accuracy, and consistency.

There is increasing concern that millions pieces of important data are lost every day due to traditional storage technologies. This is problematic, as it does not allow health services to adapt to the needs of patients or diseases, as there are currently no tools being utilized that are capable of storing and managing so much information, although the technology exists (Diaz et al., 2012). While these challenges are complex, they are also addressable. Mass data storage in real-time technologies is needed. The predominant 'Big Data' Management technologies such as MapReduce, Hadoop, STORM, and others with similar combinations or extensions should be used for effective data management in healthcare industry.

Big Data in Healthcare

About 2.5 quintillion bytes of data are generated every day and almost 90% of the existing global data has been created during the past two years (IBM, 2013). In 2011 alone, 1.8 zettabytes of data were created globally. This volume of data equates to 2 hours long HD movies, which one person would need 47 million years to watch in their entirety (Hoover, 2013). In addition, this volume of data is expected to double each year. On the other hand, Social Networking users generate large amounts of data. For instance, Facebook users generate 90 pieces of contents (notes, photos, link, stories, posts), while 600 million active users of social platforms spend over 9.3 billion hours a month on the site (McKinsey, 2011). Every minute 24 hours of video is uploaded and more than 4 billion view per day onto YouTube, while Twitter users send 98000 tweets per minute (HP, 2012).

International Data Corporation (IDC) has forecasted that the Big Data market is expected to grow from $3.2 billion in 2010 to $16.9 billion in 2015. This represents a 40 per cent compound annual growth rate (CAGR) and about seven times that of the overall information and communications technology (ICT) market (McAfee et al., 2012). A recent study predicts that the number of specialist Big Data employees in big organization will increase by more than 240% over the next five years in the UK alone (Power, 2014).

Nowadays, many organizations are collecting, storing, and analyzing massive amounts of data. These data are commonly referred to as "Big Data" because of the volume and velocity with which it arrives, the variety of forms it takes, and the value it realizes (Kaisler et al., 2013). Using this definition, the characteristics of Big Data can be summarized as the four Vs, i.e., Volume (great volume), Variety (various modalities), Velocity (rapid generation), and Value (huge value but very low density). The US Congress defines Big Data as "a term that describes large volumes of high velocity, complex, and variable data that require advanced techniques and technologies to enable the capture, storage, distribution, management, and analysis of the information" (Hartzband, 2011, p.3).

Big Data is a collection of large and complex data sets which are difficult to process using common database management tools or traditional data processing applications. According to Gartner "Big Data is high-volume, high-velocity and high-variety information assets that demand cost-effective, innovative forms of information processing for enhanced insight and decision making" (Gartner, 2013). Elbashir et al. (2013) use the term Big Data to refer to "the technology used to collect, process, store, share, and analyze huge volumes of data such as text, documents, videos and pictures".

Big Data, however, differs from data-warehousing and data mining. Data mining can handle only limited amounts of data and usually focuses on abnormal data or errors and discover interesting patterns from previous data stored (Yoo et al., 2012). On the other hand, Data warehousing refers to simple data storage in a central repository of information from multiple sources. It stores current and historical data for further analysis through Big Data technology or data mining (Kantardzic, 2011).

In the global economy, the Big Data revolution has begun and is now available to many industries. The healthcare industry is part of this revolution and it is anticipated that Big Data will transform this industry by increasing accessibility and availability of information (Groves et al., 2013). Big Data in healthcare means large and complex electronic health data sets which are very difficult to manage with traditional hardware, software and data management tools and methods (Sun & Reddy, 2013). The key sources of Big Data in the healthcare industry are the following: Electronic Health Records (EHRs) from healthcare service providers; clinical trials data; population health management data; new diseases trend analysis; research and development data; and data from insurance agencies (Mancini, 2014). In the last few years, Big Data related to health has been referred to by multiple terms, including e-Health, digital health, health information technology, mHealth, health 2.0, e-medicine, and among many other terms (Barrett et al., 2013).

Big Data in healthcare is overwhelming because of its volume, diversity of data types, and the speed at which it must be managed. In the healthcare sector, a single patient generates thousands of data elements, including diagnoses, medications, medical supplies, digital image, lab results, procedures, and billing (Liu & Park, 2014). The sources of external health data such as social media, use of smartphones or wearable sensor information on patients' heart rates, sleep patterns, brain activity, temperature, muscle motion, and numerous other clinically useful data are also generated by patients outside the care provider facilities (Liu et al., 2012). Moreover, the e-Health communication, Health Information Network, Health Information Organizations, associates parties of insurance, government reporting and so on also generate large volumes of data in the healthcare industry.

Recently, the healthcare industry has been trying to understand all the innovative uses things that can be made done with Big Data. Data from multiple sources, data collection techniques and technologies, will promote Big Data to generate new and innovative solutions to healthcare. Healthcare stakeholders in developed and developing countries have realized that the ability to manage and create value from today's large volume of data, from various sources and in many forms (i.e. structured, semi-structured, unstructured), represent the new competitive differentiation (Jee & Kim, 2013). Therefore, most of the governments, especially in developed countries, and the healthcare industry are currently operating Big Data projects or are in the planning stage. All Big Data projects in healthcare industries have common goals, such as better citizens' healthcare services, easy and equal access to public health services, and the improvement of medically related concerns (Raghupathi & Raghupathi, 2014). Side by side, each country or healthcare industry has its own priorities, opportunities, and threats, based on that country's unique environment (e.g., healthcare expenditure, inefficient healthcare systems, regional disparities), which Big Data projects should address.

Many white papers and business reports confirmed that Big Data could be used to guarantee public health by appropriate treatment for patients, monitor safety of healthcare, managerial control and health systems accountability (Jee & Kim, 2013). Healthcare industry already captured the value from Big Data. For example, Kaiser Permanente can now exchange data across all medical facilities and achieved USD 1 billion in savings by implementing a new computer system, HealthConnect. Blue Shield of California, in partnership with NantHealth, improved healthcare delivery, by developing integrated technology system. They can now provide evidence-based care to patients. AstraZeneca have developed more than 200 innovative health-care applications, in partnership with WellPoint's data and analytics subsidiary, HealthCore to provide economical treatments for some chronic illnesses and common diseases (Kayyali et al., 2013).

In recent years, the healthcare industry has applied Big Data Analytics tool to detect diseases and medical treatment. A number of healthcare organizations are applying Big Data tools to address multiple healthcare challenges, assist in diagnosis diseases and support research (i.e. genomics). DNAnexus provides cloud based platform for storing, managing, analyzing and visualizing next generation DNA sequencing (Fieldman et al., 2012). Genome Health Solution, network of physicians and technology providers, integrate personal genomics and streamline care for patients with cancer and other diseases. Aggregating individual medical data into Big Data algorithm helps physician to provide evidence-based medicine to patients (Groves, 2013).

Opportunities of Big Data in Healthcare

Big Data is creating a new generation of decision support data management. Healthcare sectors are recognizing the potential value of this data and are putting the technologies, people, and processes in place to capitalize on the opportunities. Big Data is the key factor in competition and particularly relevant in areas such as growth, innovation, productivity, efficiency and effectiveness of organization (Chen et al., 2012). Organizations are currently addressing enhanced customer experience, process efficiency using Big Data (Bughin et al., 2010). It is also not uncommon that some organizations are engaging in more game-changing activities and developing new products and business models, and producing valuable information directly through Big Data.

The Gartner, IT research firm, conducted a survey on 720 of the company's Research Circle members worldwide. They found nearly 64 percent of organizations investing or planning to invest in Big Data technology, 30 percent have already invested in Big Data technology, 19 percent plan to invest within the next year, and rest of 15 percent plan to invest within two years. The respondents of organizations already invested in Big Data, report that investments in Big Data will exceed $10 million in 2013, rising to 50% by 2016. The 32% executives of the organizations that have already tested the Big Data waters, reported that their Big Data initiatives are fully operational, in production across the corporation (Eddy, 2013).

Worldwide Forecasts & Analysis (2013 – 2018) states that demand of Big Data applications, growth of consumer and machine data, and growth of the unified appliances are playing a key role in shaping the future of Big Data market (Nirmala, 2014). From a regional point of view, North America continues to lead investments and have invested in technology specifically designed to address the Big Data challenge. Big Data market in Europe is projected to grow at a compound annual growth rate (CAGR) of 31.96 percent over the period 2012-2016. Big Data's ability to analyze data to forecast future accurately is the key factors contributing to this market growth.

Many organizations including healthcare in Asia-Pacific region is notably ambitious to invest during the next two years. Big Data market is expected to grow from $258.5 million in 2011 to $1.76 billion in 2016, 46.8 percent five year annual growth rate, in Asia-Pacific region (Cerra et al., 2012). This market will grow 20 percent or more over the next 24 to 36 months. Big Data adoption among Chinese companies are fast gaining momentum, adding that the adoption rate is 21 percent, compared with 20 percent for Singapore and Indonesia and 19 percent for the Malaysia. The same study forecast that Big Data business in China could touch $806 million by 2016 (Schönberger & Cukier, 2013). Cisco Systems Inc, global networking major, conducted a survey among Chinese and overseas companies. This study showed that more than 60 percent of the respondents believed that Big Data is essential for businesses to improve decision-making. More than 90 percent of the respondents from China expressed their confidence in using Big Data technology (Jing & Yingqun, 2014).

For Big Data, 2013 is treated as the year of early deployment and experimentation. Big Data investment and planned investment led by media and communications, banking, healthcare and services industries. Planned investments during the two years are highest for transportation (50 percent), health care (41 percent) and insurance (40 percent) (Davenport, & Dyché, 2013). Governments and healthcare sectors in developed and developing countries have recognized that Big Data can be a fundamental resource for discovering useful information to enhance social and economic growth. Moreover, Big Data can produce a wide range of innovations for personalized care, making health care more preventive, new wave of efficiency and productivity, improve the quality of health care delivery, clinical and health policy decision making, and improved patient engagement (Schouten, 2013). Big Data has also emerged as essential tool for the improvement of e-Health.

Big Data has unlimited potential for effectively storing, processing, analyzing, and querying healthcare data which profoundly influence the human health. It can transform health care by providing information directly to patients, enabling them to play a more active role (Groves et al., 2013). Currently, patients' records with health care professionals, putting the patient in a passive position. In the future, medical records may reside with patients. Big Data offers a chance to integrate the traditional medical model with the social determinants of health in a patient-directed fashion by linking traditional health related data (eg, medication list, treatment history and family history) to other personal data found on other sites (eg, income, education, diet habits, exercise schedules, and forms of entertainment), all of which can be retrieved without having to interview the patient with an extensive list of questions (Murdoch & Detsky, 2013)

Big Data will be used to analyze the line of treatment by using relevant patient medical information and past experience from the database. It will be beneficial to decide on line of treatment for deadly diseases like Cancer, HIV, etc. Moreover, Patient's past history and bio-informatics analysis will be used for personalized medicine if required. Analysis will also help to advice appropriate diagnostics thereby assisting fast tracking of diseases and its cure. Big Data will also reduce the length of hospital stay and treatment because of effective Big Data management (Michele, 2012).

Big Data provides new opportunities to index and store previously unstructured, siloed and unusable data for additional uses by health care stakeholders. In the health care sector, access to Big Data is enabling stakeholders to exploit the potential of previously unusable data (Khorey, 2012; Srinivasan & Arunasalam, 2013). Big Data creates new business value by transforming previously unusable data into actionable knowledge and new predictive insights. It is estimated that the health care sector in US could create savings of more than USD 200 billion every year, reducing healthcare expenditure by about 8 percent, if they use Big Data creatively and effectively (Kayyali et al., 2013).

Healthcare data is continuously and rapidly growing containing abundant information values which help in decision making process (Joseph & Johnson, 2013). Data-driven firms who effectively use Big Data analytics in their decision-making processes derived five to six per cent better "output and productivity" than if they had not used Big Data analytics. If we use this same five-six per cent average for Big Data Analytics for health care in Canada, it would translate into $10 billion in cost savings annually which comprising five per cent of $207 billion healthcare expenditures in 2012 (Wallis, 2012).

It is widely believed that the use of Big Data can reduce the cost of health care while basing it on more extensive continuous monitoring. With minimum length of stay, appropriate investigations and best line of treatment reduces the healthcare services cost. An effective use of Big Data can not only reduce the cost of healthcare but also rightly considered crucial to improve health services. McKinsey & Company estimates that $300 billion to $450 billion can be saved in the healthcare industry in the world from Big Data Analytics (Chris, 2012).

Recently, health care organizations ranging from single-physician offices to multi-provider groups, accountable care organizations, and large hospital networks by digitizing, combining and effectively using Big Data. It helps to improve the quality and efficiency of health care delivery; detecting diseases at earlier stages, managing specific health populations; and detecting health care fraud more quickly and efficiently. In the last few years there has been a move toward evidence-based medicine instead of traditionally used Physicians judgment when making treatment decisions. Big Data help evidence-based medicine which involves systematically reviewing clinical data and making treatment decisions based on the best available information (LaValle et al., 2014). Moreover, aggregating individual medical data sets into Big Data algorithms offers the healthiest evidence that helps physicians, patients, and other healthcare stakeholders identify value and opportunities. Health care providers are using Big Data to identify patients at high-risk for certain medical conditions before major problems occur.

It is claimed that Big Data discover population health patterns, identify non-traditional intervention points and predict long-term conditions by linking petabytes of raw information to health records, demographic data and genetic information. Many white papers and business reports focusing on healthcare have claimed that Big Data could be used to guarantee public health, support clinical improvement, determine appropriate treatment paths for patients, monitor the safety of healthcare systems, and promote health system accountability to the public (Burghard, 2012). Disease prevention is now achievable and Big Data are used as better diagnostic tools which increased access to healthcare. Important application areas of Big Data are nutrition, accidents and injury, chronic and infectious diseases, mental health, environmental health, and social health (Cambria et al., 2013).

Recently, Big Data is also used to find causes of, and treatments for diseases; actively monitor patients so clinicians are alerted to the potential for an adverse event before it occurs (Pentland et al., 2009). In recent times, the healthcare sectors used Big Data to detect diseases in better way and aid medical research. For example, HIV researchers in the European Union worked with IBM, applying Big Data tooling to perform clinical genomic analysis. IBM Big Data tooling played a crucial role in helping researchers understand clinical data from different countries in order to discover treatments based on accumulated empirical data.

Challenges of Big Data in Healthcare

Still, not too many people including patients, doctors in healthcare realize they are part of the Big Data generation process. Although Big Data holds out enormous opportunities for improving health systems, there are also dangers that must be avoided. In particular, Big Data entails many new challenges regarding its privacy and security risks, ownership issues, complexity, as well as the need for new technologies and human skills.

Privacy issues will continue to be a major concern of Big Data in healthcare. The inappropriate use of personal data, due to linking of data from multiple sources, is great public fear regarding Big Data. Managing privacy is a problem in healthcare because Big Data has to be addressed from both technical and sociological perspectives (Agrawal et al., 2011). There is also risk of misuse of putting so much personal data in the hands of either government or companies. The privacy of healthcare data is only increases in the context of Big Data.

Several researchers have argued that it is very difficult to ensure the security of Big Data in health systems to secure improved health for its users (Lodha et al, 2014; Feldman et al., 2012). Although new computer programs can freely remove names and other personal information from records being transported into large databases, stakeholders across the industry still worried about potential problems as more information becomes public. In most of the cases, Big Data software has no safeguards which have serious negative consequences (Villars et al., 2011). It is very difficult for healthcare industry to ensure that the data in Big Data operations itself is secured.

Data usability and ownership have been identified as major concern, especially with respect to healthcare decision making. Eighty per cent of medical data is unstructured as images, documents, and transcribed notes which make it difficult to access for effective analytics (Grimes, 2012). When physicians can read narrative text within an Electronic Health Record (EHR), most current analytics applications cannot effectively utilize this unstructured data. Another important challenge of Big Data is data ownership issues. Important questions are being raised over who will own certain forms of health information for what purpose, how and by whom that information can be used. It is also challenging for healthcare organization how to store their data, and how and when to delete and/or archive their data. Moreover, the unfamiliar and correlational nature of Big Data increases the probability of misinterpretation that can cause serious harm.

Big Data also pose internal IT challenges. Big Data deployments require new IT staff and application developer skill which are likely to be in short supply for quite some time. There is already a worldwide skills shortage in the data scientist and data analyst. McKinsey Global Institute predicts that the U.S. alone will face a shortage of 140,000 to 190,000 people with deep analytical skills as well as 1.5 million managers and analysts to analyze Big Data and make decisions by 2018 (Manyika et al., 2011). Existing staff in many healthcare organizations may not have the required skills and competencies to execute Big Data. Moreover, sometimes existing team members will be highly sought after by competitors and Big Data solutions providers.

Although there are serious issues involved in the ethics of online data collection and analysis, little is understood about the ethical implications of the healthcare research being done in Big Data (Ess, 2002). Still, many ethics boards do not understand the processes of mining and anonymizing Big Data. Finally, it is not surprising that Big Data creates a new kind of digital divide: the Big Data poor and the Big Data rich.

Big Data Technologies

Facing the challenges and advantages derived from collecting and processing vast amounts of medical data, a new technological schema is highly needed to address the every need arising from the Big Data applications. First, the sheer size of the data generated may require more powerful data storage technologies, which advocates the distributed file systems. And consequently, Second, the manipulation of the massive data stored implies the need for new database management systems capable of manipulating structured and unstructured data, which has to be relying on the corresponding distributed file systems. Third, large data sets may allow for more insightful explorations to reveal some valued patterns hidden, which drives the development of new analytics tools.

In this section, some emerging technologies in Big Data will be described in three categories including file systems, data management systems and analytics tools. In recent years, file systems, data management and analytics tools are widely used in healthcare industry (Russom, 2011). Healthcare service provider can provide better care to patients, get more valuable insights, faster fraud detection, and reduce administrative cost by using data analytics tools such as spark, MapReduce. They can store, analyze, and correlate various data sources to extrapolate knowledge by using Big Data technologies (Basu, 2014). It should be noted that most of the technologies described here can't work alone and always appear as one component of a Big Data technical schema. Sometimes, the functionalities of them are overlapped or without crisp boundaries. Another note is that the development of related Big Data technologies is very fast, and it might be impossible to capture every new track of the corresponding technology in this chapter.

File Systems

Hadoop Distributed File System

Hadoop is an open-source software framework for distributed storage and distributed processing of Big Data on clusters of commodity hardware. Its Hadoop Distributed File System (HDFS) splits files into large blocks and distributes the blocks amongst the nodes in the cluster. For processing the data, the Hadoop Map/Reduce ships code (specifically Jar files) to the nodes that have the required data, and the nodes then process the data in parallel. This approach takes advantage of data locality, in contrast to conventional HPC architecture which usually relies on a parallel file system (compute and data separated, but connected with high-speed networking) (IBM, 2014).

Since 2012, the term "Hadoop" often refers not to just the base Hadoop package but rather to the Hadoop Ecosystem, which includes all of the additional software packages that can be installed on top of or alongside Hadoop, such as Apache Pig, Apache Hive, Apache HBase, Apache Spark, and others (Yahoo, 2012).

The Hadoop distributed file system (HDFS) is a distributed, scalable, and portable file-system written in Java for the Hadoop[1] framework. HDFS stores large files (typically in the range of gigabytes to terabytes across multiple machines. It achieves reliability by replicating the data across multiple hosts, and hence theoretically does not require RAID storage on hosts (but to increase I/O performance some RAID configurations are still useful). A Hadoop cluster is the mainly working unit which usually has a single name node along with a cluster of data nodes. Each data node serves up blocks of data over the network using a block protocol specific to HDFS. The internal communication among blocks/clusters are through TCP/IP and the external one is conducted by remote procedure call (RPC) sent by users.

HDFS was designed for mostly immutable files and may not be suitable for systems requiring concurrent write-operations (White, 2009). HDFS can be mounted directly with a File system in User space (FUSE) virtual file system on Linux and some other Unix systems. File access can be achieved through the native Java API, the Thrift API to generate a client in the language of the users' choosing (C++, Java, Python, PHP, Ruby, Erlang, Perl, Haskell, C#, Cocoa, Smalltalk, and OCaml), the command-line interface, browsed through the HDFS-UI webapp over HTTP, or via 3rd-party network client libraries.

HDFS evolved to be more mature as times goes. In May 2012, it was equipped with added the high-availability capabilities, as letting the main meta data server (the Name Node) fail over manually to a backup. HDFS Federation, a new addition, aims to allow multiple name spaces served by separate name nodes. In general, HDFS contributes as the footstone of any Hadoop systems/packages.

The potential for Hadoop in healthcare and healthcare data is exciting. Recently, Raghupathi and Raghupathi (2014) reported that the Hadoop is the most significant data processing platform for Big Data analytics in healthcare. The Hadoop can opens up the platform for new research domains. Researcher can now use air quality data with asthma admissions, genomic data to speed drug development using Hadoop.

Google File Systems

Google File System (GFS or GoogleFS) is a proprietary distributed file system developed by Google for its own use (Carr, 2006; Ghemawat, 2003). It is designed to provide efficient, reliable access to data using large clusters of commodity hardware.

GFS is enhanced for Google's core data storage and usage needs (primarily the search engine), which can generate enormous amounts of data that needs to be retained. Google File System grew out of an earlier Google effort, "Big Files", developed by Larry Page and Sergey Brin. Within GFS, files are divided into fixed-size chunks of 64 megabytes, similar to clusters or sectors in regular file systems, which are only extremely rarely overwritten, or shrunk; files are usually appended to or read. It is also designed and optimized to run on Google's computing clusters, dense nodes which consist of cheap,

Figure 1. GFS Architecture

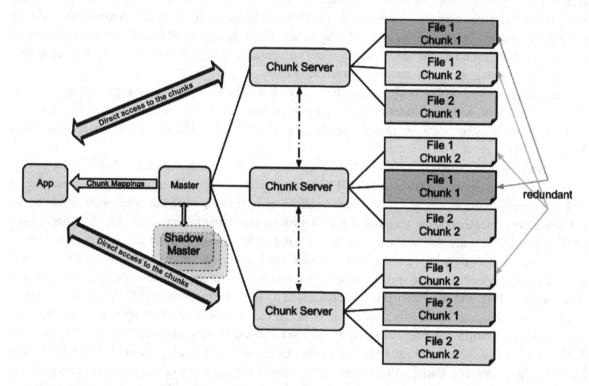

"commodity" computers, and thus precautions must be taken against the high failure rate of individual nodes and the subsequent data loss. Fig.1 depicts the general structure of GFS.

A GFS cluster consists of a single master and multiple chunk servers, and is accessed by multiple clients, as shown in Figure 1. Each of these is typically a commodity Linux machine running a user-level server process. It is easy to run both a chunk server and a client on the same machine, as long as machine resources permit and the lower reliability caused by running possibly flaky application code is acceptable.

A GFS cluster generally consists of one Master node and a large number of Chunk servers. Files are divided into fixed-size chunks. Chunk servers store these chunks. Each chunk is assigned a unique 64-bit label by the master node at the time of creation, and logical mappings of files to constituent chunks are maintained. Each chunk is replicated several times throughout the network, with the minimum being three, but even more for files that have high end-in demand or need more redundancy. Chunk servers store chunks on local disks as Linux files and read or write chunk data specified by a chunk handle and byte range. For reliability, each chunk is replicated on multiple chunk servers. By default, users can designate different replication levels for different regions of the file name space. The master maintains all file system meta data. This includes the name space, access control information, the mapping from files to chunks, and the current locations of chunks.

The Master server does not usually store the actual chunks, but rather all the meta data associated with the chunks, such as the tables mapping the 64-bit labels to chunk locations and the files they make up, the locations of the copies of the chunks, what processes are reading or writing to a particular chunk, or taking a "snapshot" of the chunk pursuant to replicate it (usually at the instigation of the Master server, when, due to node failures, the number of copies of a chunk has fallen beneath the set number). All this meta data is kept current by the Master server periodically receiving updates from each chunk server ("Heart-beat messages").

Data Management Systems

BigTable

Bigable is a compressed, high performance, and proprietary data management system built on Google File System, which is capable of storing large amounts of data in a semi-structured manner. BigTable development began in 2004 and has been used by a number of Google applications, such as web indexing, Google Maps, Google Book Search, "My Search History", Google Earth, Blogger.com, Google Code hosting, Orkut, YouTube, and Gmail. Google's reasons for developing its own database include scalability and better control of performance characteristics. Following Google's philosophy, BigTable was an in-house development designed to run on commodity hardware. BigTable allows Google to have a very small incremental cost for new services and expanded computing power (they don't have to buy a license for every machine, for example).

BigTable maps two arbitrary string values (row key and column key) and timestamp (hence three-dimensional mapping) into an associated arbitrary byte array. It is not a relational database and can be better defined as a sparse, distributed multi-dimensional sorted map. BigTable is designed to scale into the petabyte range across "hundreds or thousands of machines, and to make it easy to add more machines to the system and automatically start taking advantage of those resources without any reconfiguration"(Chang, et al., 2006).

Each table is a multi-dimensional sparse map. The table consists of rows and columns, and each cell has a time version. There can be multiple copies of each cell with different times, so they can keep track of changes over time. In his examples, the rows were URLs and the columns had names such as "contents:" (which would store the file data) or "language:" (which would contain a string such as "EN"). Tables are optimized for Google File System (GFS) by being split into multiple tablets – segments of the table are split along a row chosen such that the tablet will be ~200 megabytes in size. When sizes threaten to grow beyond a specified limit, the tablets are compressed using the algorithm BMDiff and the Zippy compression algorithm publicly known and open-sourced as Snappy. The locations in the GFS of tablets are recorded as database entries in multiple special tablets, which are called "META1" tablets. META1 tablets are found by querying the single "META0" tablet, which typically resides on a server of its own since it is often queried by clients as to the location of the "META1" tablet which itself has the answer to the question of where the actual data is located.

Hive

Hive is a data warehouse infrastructure built on top of Hadoop for providing data summarization, query, and analysis. While initially developed by Facebook, Hive is now used and developed by other companies such as Netflix (Venner, 2009).

Hive supports analysis of large datasets stored in Hadoop's HDFS and compatible file systems such as Amazon S3 file system. It provides an SQL-like language called HiveQL with schema on read and transparently converts queries to map/reduce, Apache Tez and in the future Spark jobs. All three execution engines can run in Hadoop YARN. To accelerate queries, it provides indexes, including bitmap indexes. By default, Hive stores metadata in an embedded Derby database, and other client/server databases like MySQL can optionally be used.

HBase

HBase is an open source, non-relational, distributed database modeled after Google's BigTable and written in Java. It is developed as part of Apache Software Foundation's Apache Hadoop project and runs on top of HDFS (Hadoop Distributed Filesystem), providing BigTable-like capabilities for Hadoop. That is, it provides a fault-tolerant way of storing large quantities of sparse data (small amounts of information caught within a large collection of empty or unimportant data, such as finding the 50 largest items in a group of 2 billion records, or finding the non-zero items representing less than 0.1% of a huge collection).

HBase features compression, in-memory operation, and Bloom filters on a per-column basis as outlined in the original BigTable paper (George,2011).Tables in HBase can serve as the input and output for MapReduce jobs run in Hadoop, and may be accessed through the Java API but also through REST, Avro or Thrift gateway APIs.

HBase is not a direct replacement for a classic SQL database, although recently its performance has improved, and it is now serving several data-driven websites, including Facebook's Messaging Platform.

Analytics Tools

MapReduce

There are several tools that have been designed to address Big Data analytics problems. Among them, the most popular one is the MapReduce. MapReduce is a programming model and an associated implementation for processing and generating large data sets with a parallel, distributed algorithm on a cluster (Zikopoulos et al, 2011).

A MapReduce program is composed of a Map() procedure that performs filtering and sorting (such as sorting students by first name into queues, one queue for each name) and a Reduce() procedure that performs a summary operation (such as counting the number of students in each queue, yielding name frequencies). In short, "Map" is used for per-record computation, whereas "Reduce" aggregates the output from the Map functions and applies a given function for obtaining the final results. The model is inspired by the map and reduce functions commonly used in functional programming, although their purpose in the MapReduce framework is not the same as in their original forms. The key contributions of the MapReduce framework are not the actual map and reduce functions, but the scalability and fault-tolerance achieved for a variety of applications by optimizing the execution engine once. As such, a single-threaded implementation of MapReduce (such as MongoDB) will usually not be faster than a traditional (non-MapReduce) implementation, any gains are usually only seen with multi-threaded implementations. Only when the optimized distributed shuffle operation (which reduces network communication cost) and fault tolerance features of the MapReduce framework come into play, is the use of this model beneficial (Lämmel, 2008; Grzegorz et al, 2014).

MapReduce libraries have been written in many programming languages, with different levels of optimization. A popular open-source implementation is Apache Hadoop. The name MapReduce originally referred to the proprietary Google technology, but has since been genericized.

The growth of medical data including image need parallel computing and algorithm optimization for analysis and indexing to scalable solution. The MapReduce framework is used to speed up medical data processing such as parameter optimization for lung texture segmentation using support vector machines, content based medical image indexing, and three dimensional directional wavelet analysis for solid texture classification (Markonis et al, 2012).

Spark

In addition to MapReduce, Spark (Karau etc, 2014) is a new system developed to overcome data reuse across multiple computations. It supports iterative applications, while retaining the scalability and fault tolerance of MapReduce, supporting in-memory processes. This latter emergent technology aspires to be the new reference for the processing of massive data.

Spark was initially started by Matei Zaharia at UC Berkeley AMPLab in 2009, and opened sourced in 2010 under a BSD license. In 2013, the project was donated to the Apache Software Foundation and switched its license to Apache 2.0. In February 2014, Spark became an Apache Top-Level Project. In November 2014, the engineering team at Databricks used Spark and set a new world record in large scale sorting

In contrast to Hadoop's two-stage disk-based MapReduce paradigm, Spark's in-memory primitives provide performance up to 100 times faster for certain applications. By allowing user programs to load data into a cluster's memory and query it repeatedly, Spark is well suited to machine learning algorithms. Spark can interface with a wide variety of file or storage systems, including Hadoop Distributed File System (HDFS), Cassandra, OpenStack Swift, or Amazon S3.

Spark is one of the most actively developed open source projects. It has over 465 contributors in 2014, making it the most active project in the Apache Software Foundation and among Big Data open source projects.

The Spark project consists of multiple components. Spark Core is the foundation of the overall project. It provides distributed task dispatching, scheduling, and basic I/O functionalities. The fundamental programming abstraction is called Resilient Distributed Datasets, a logical collection of data partitioned across machines. RDDs can be created by referencing datasets in external storage systems, or by applying coarse-grained transformations (e.g. map, filter, reduce, join) on existing RDDs.

The RDD abstraction is exposed through a language-integrated API in Java, Python, Scala similar to local, in-process collections. This simplifies programming complexity because the way applications manipulate RDDs is similar to manipulating local collections of data.

Spark SQL is a component on top of Spark Core that introduces a new data abstraction called SchemaRDD, which provides support for structured and semi-structured data. Spark SQL provides a domain-specific language to manipulate SchemaRDDs in Scala, Java, or Python. It also provides SQL language support, with command-line interfaces and ODBC/JDBC server.

Spark Streaming leverages Spark Core's fast scheduling capability to perform streaming analytics. It ingests data in mini-batches and perform RDD transformations on those mini-batches of data. This design enables the same set of application code written for batch analytics to be used in streaming analytics, on a single engine.

Machine Learning Library (MLlib) is a distributed machine learning framework on top of Spark that because of the distributed memory-based Spark architecture is ten times as fast as Hadoop disk-based Apache Mahout and even scales better than Vowpal Wabbit. It implements many common machine learning and statistical algorithms to simplify large scale machine learning pipelines, including summary statistics, correlations, stratified sampling, hypothesis testing, random data generation, SVMs, logistic regression, linear regression, decision trees, naive Bayes, collaborative filtering, k-means, singular value decomposition (SVD), principal component analysis (PCA), optimization primitives and so on. GraphX is a distributed graph processing framework on top of Spark. It provides an API for expressing graph computation that can model the Pregel abstraction. It also provides an optimized runtime for this abstraction.

The Spark-based approach to healthcare data processing produces very accurate data marts which are used by statisticians and epidemiologists in the occurrence of some diseases (i.e. AIDS, leprosy, and tuberculosis). The spark, a tool of in-memory facility, scalability, and ease of programming, can link disparate databases with socioeconomic and healthcare data, serving as a basis for decision making processes and assessment of data quality (Pita et al., 2015).

STORM

Storm is a distributed computation framework written predominantly in the Clojure programming language. Originally created by Nathan Marz and team at BackType, the project was open sourced after being acquired by Twitter. It uses custom created "spouts" and "bolts" to define information sources and manipulations to allow batch, distributed processing of streaming data.

A Storm application is designed as a topology in the shape of a directed acyclic graph (DAG) with spouts and bolts acting as the graph vertices. Edges on the graph are named streams, and direct data from one node to another. Together, the topology acts as a data transformation pipeline. At a superficial level the general topology structure is similar to a MapReduce job, with the main difference being that data is processed in real-time as opposed to in individual batches. Additionally, Storm topologies run indefinitely until killed, while a MapReduce job DAG must eventually end. Storm can provide real-time analytics, continuous computation and online machine learning to healthcare industry data analysis. It is fault-tolerant, scalable and guarantees healthcare data will be processed, and is easy to set up and operate (Hu et al., 2014).

CONCLUSION

The health care industry undergoes tremendous pressure to deliver quality service to patients across the globe. Big Data application in healthcare is the drive to capitalize on growing patient and health system data availability to generate healthcare innovation. By making smart use of the ever-increasing amount of data available, we can find new insights by re-examining the data or combining it with other information. In healthcare this means not just mining patient records, medical images, bio-banks, test results, etc., for insights, diagnoses and decision support advice, but also continuous analysis of the data streams produced for and by every patient in a hospital, a doctor's office, at home and even while on the move via mobile devices. Many governments and healthcare provider has already increased the transparency by making decades of stored data, searchable and actionable healthcare data. However, healthcare Big Data has different values and attributes which poses different challenges. Addressing the challenges associated with biomedical Big Data must of necessity engage all parts of the Big Data ecosystem. Although all Big Data project in healthcare industries have similar common goals such as, better citizens' healthcare services, equal access to public services and improvement of quality medical services, each government or healthcare stakeholder has its own priorities based on nation's unique environment. The government and healthcare stakeholder should collaborate with entities that possess a great deal of technologies and expertise. They should develop strategies and policies on how Big Data could be best managed. The government and healthcare service provider should explore advanced analytics, legislation, privacy, security technologies for real-time analysis of Big Data in healthcare. The Big Data research in healthcare requires knowledge about standards, filters, meta-data, techniques for storing, finding, analyzing, visualizing and securing data, and sector-specific editing of data. The researcher and practitioner should carefully look to determine the best ways of using Big Data in healthcare.

REFERENCES

Agrawal, D., Bernstein, P., Bertino, E., Davidson, S., Dayal, U., Franklin, M., ... Widom, J. (2011). *Challenges and Opportunities with Big Data 2011-1*. Academic Press.

Barrett, M. A., Humblet, O., Hiatt, R. A., & Adler, N. E. (2013). Big Data and disease prevention: From quantified self to quantified communities. *Big Data*, *1*(3), 168–175. doi:10.1089/big.2013.0027

Basu, A. (2014). *Real-Time Healthcare Analytics on Apache Hadoop using Spark and Shark*. White Paper Intel Distribution for Apache Hadoop Software, Big Data Analytics Healthcare.

Bian, J., Topaloglu, U., & Yu, F. (2012, October). Towards large-scale twitter mining for drug-related adverse events. In *Proceedings of the 2012 international workshop on Smart health and wellbeing* (pp. 25-32). ACM. doi:10.1145/2389707.2389713

Bughin, J., Chui, M., & Manyika, J. (2010). Clouds, Big Data, and smart assets: Ten tech-enabled business trends to watch. *The McKinsey Quarterly*, *56*(1), 75–86.

Burghard, C. (2012). *Big Data and Analytics Key to Accountable Care Success*. IDC Health Insights.

Cambria, E., Rajagopal, D., Olsher, D., & Das, D. (2013). Big social data analysis. *Big Data Computing*, 401-414.

Carr, D. F. (2006). *How Google Works*. Retrieved from http://www.baselinemag.com/c/a/Infrastructure/How-Google-Works-1/

Cerra, A., Easterwood, K., & Power, J. (2012). *Transforming Business: Big Data, Mobility, and Globalization*. John Wiley & Sons.

Chang, F., Dean, J., Ghemawat, S., Hsieh, W. C., Wallach, D. A., Burrows, M., ... Gruber, R. E. (2006). *Bigtable: A Distributed Storage System for Structured Data*. Google.

Charles, D., Furukawa, M., & Hufstader, M. (2012). Electronic Health Record Systems and Intent to Attest to Meaningful Use Among Non-federal Acute Care Hospitals in the United States: 2008-2011. *ONC Data Brief*, *1*, 1–7.

Chauhan, R., & Kumar, A. (2013, November). Cloud computing for improved healthcare: Techniques, potential and challenges. In E-Health and Bioengineering Conference (EHB), 2013 (pp. 1-4). IEEE.

Chawla, N. V., & Davis, D. A. (2013). Bringing Big Data to personalized healthcare: A patient-centered framework. *Journal of General Internal Medicine, 28*(3), 660–665. doi:10.1007/s11606-013-2455-8 PMID:23797912

Chen, H., Chiang, R. H., & Storey, V. C. (2012). Business Intelligence and Analytics: From Big Data to Big Impact. *Management Information Systems Quarterly, 36*(4), 1165–1188.

Chris, P. (2012). *Centralizing healthcare Big Data in the cloud.* Retrieved from http://blogs.computer-world.com/cloud-computing/20488/centralizinghealthcare-big-data-cloud

Czajkowski, G. (2014). *Sorting Petabytes with MapReduce - The Next Episode.* Google.

Davenport, T. H., & Dyché, J. (2013). *Big Data in Big Companies.* International Institute for Analytics.

Diaz, M., Juan, G., & Oikawa Lucas, A. R. (2012). *Big Data on the Internet of Things. Sixth International Conference on Innovative Mobile and Internet Services in Ubiquitous Computing.* doi:10.1109/IMIS.2012.198

Eddy, N. (2013). *Big Data Adoption, Investment Plans Grow.* Gartner, Inc. Retrieved from http://www.eweek.com/small-business/big-data-adoption-investment-plans-growgartner.html#sthash.ypLZZpMk.dpuf

Elbashir, M. Z., Collier, P. A., Sutton, S. G., Davern, M. J., & Leech, S. A. (2013). Enhancing the Business Value of Business Intelligence: The Role of Shared Knowledge and Assimilation. *Journal of Information Systems, 27*(2), 87–105. doi:10.2308/isys-50563

Feldman, B., Martin, E. M., & Skotnes, T. (2012). Big Data in Healthcare Hype and Hope. *October 2012. Dr. Bonnie, 360.*

Gartner. (2013). *Gartner IT Glossary Big Data.* Retrieved from http://www.gartner.com/it-glossary/big-data

George, L. (2011). *HBase: The Definitive Guide.* O'Reilly Media.

Ghemawat, S., Gobioff, H., & Leung, S. T. (2003). The Google file system. In *Proceedings of the Nineteenth ACM Symposium on Operating Systems Principles - SOSP '03.* ACM.

Github. (2013). *Storm Codebase.* Github.

Grimes, S. (2012). *Unstructured data and the 80 percent rule.* Retrieved from http://clarabridge.com/default.aspx?tabid=137&ModuleID=635&ArticleID=551

Groves, P., Kayyali, B., Knott, D., & Van Kuiken, S. (2013). The 'Big Data' revolution in healthcare. *The McKinsey Quarterly.*

Hartzband, D. D. (2011). *Using Ultra-Large Data Sets in Health Care.* e-healthpolicy.org.

Hoover, W. (2013). *Transforming Health Care through Big Data Strategies for leveraging Big Data in the health care industry.* Institute for Health Technology Transformation.

HP. (2012). *Big security for Big Data.* Retrieved from http://www.hpenterprisesecurity.com/collateral/whitepaper/ BigSecurityforBigData0213.pdf

Hu, H., Wen, Y., Chua, T. S., & Li, X. (2014). Toward scalable systems for big data analytics: A technology tutorial. *Access, IEEE, 2*, 652–687. doi:10.1109/ACCESS.2014.2332453

Huai, Y., Lee, R., Zhang, S., Xia, C. H., & Zhang, X. (2011, October). DOT: a matrix model for analyzing, optimizing and deploying software for Big Data analytics in distributed systems. In *Proceedings of the 2nd ACM Symposium on Cloud Computing* (p. 4). ACM. doi:10.1145/2038916.2038920

IBM. (2013). *IBM's smarter cities challenge: Syracuse.* Armonk, NY: IBM Corporate. Available from: http://smartercitieschallenge.org/ executive_reports/SmarterCities-Syracuse.pdf

IBM. (2014). *What is the Hadoop Distributed File System (HDFS)?.* IBM.

IDC. (2012). *Worldwide Big Data Technology and Services 2012-2015 Forecast.* International Data Corporation. Retrieved from http://www.idc.com

Jee, K., & Kim, G. H. (2013). Potentiality of Big Data in the medical sector: focus on how to reshape the healthcare system. *Healthcare Informatics Research, 19*(2), 79-85.

Jing, L., & Yingqun, C. (2014, April 21). When Big Data can lead to big profit. *The China Daily.* Retrieved from http://www.chinadailyasia.com/business/2014-04/21/content_15131425.html

Joseph, R. C., & Johnson, N. A. (2013). Big Data and Transformational Government. *IT Professional, 15*(6), 43–48. doi:10.1109/MITP.2013.61

Kaisler, S., Armour, F., Espinosa, J. A., & Money, W. (2013, January). Big Data: Issues and challenges moving forward. In *System Sciences (HICSS), 2013 46th Hawaii International Conference on* (pp. 995-1004). IEEE.

Kantardzic, M. (2011). *Data mining: concepts, models, methods, and algorithms.* John Wiley & Sons. doi:10.1002/9781118029145

Karau, H., Konwinski, A., Wendell, P., & Zaharia, M. (2014). *Learning Spark: Lightning Fast Big Data Analytics* (1st ed.). O'Reilly Media.

Kayyali, B., Knott, D., & Van Kuiken, S. (2013). *The big-data revolution in US health care: Accelerating value and innovation.* Mc Kinsey & Company.

Khorey, L. (2012). Big Data, Bigger Outcomes. *Journal of American Health Information Management Association, 83*(10), 38–43. PMID:23061351

Koh, H. C., & Tan, G. (2011). Data mining applications in healthcare. *Journal of Healthcare Information Management, 19*(2), 65. PMID:15869215

Lam, C. (2010). *Hadoop in Action.* Manning Publications.

Lämmel, R. (2008). Google's Map Reduce programming model — Revisited. *Science of Computer Programming, 70*(1), 1–30. doi:10.1016/j.scico.2007.07.001

LaValle, S., Lesser, E., Shockley, R., Hopkins, M. S., & Kruschwitz, N. (2013). Big Data, analytics and the path from insights to value. *MIT Sloan Management Review, 21.*

Liu, W., & Park, E. K. (2014, February). Big Data as an e-Health Service. In *Computing, Networking and Communications (ICNC), 2014 International Conference on* (pp. 982-988). IEEE. doi:10.1109/ICCNC.2014.6785471

Liu, W., Park, E. K., & Krieger, U. (2012, October). eHealth interconnection infrastructure challenges and solutions overview. In *e-Health Networking, Applications and Services (Healthcom), 2012 IEEE 14th International Conference on* (pp. 255-260). IEEE.

Lodha, R., Jain, H., & Kurup, L. (2014). Big Data Challenges: Data Analysis Perspective. *International Journal of Current Engineering and Technology*.

Mancini, M. (2014). Exploiting Big Data for Improving Healthcare Services. *Journal of e-Learning and Knowledge Society, 10*(2).

Markonis, D., Schaer, R., Eggel, I., Muller, H., & Depeursinge, A. (2012). Using MapReduce for large-scale medical image analysis. In *2012 IEEE Second International Conference on Healthcare Informatics, Imaging and Systems Biology* (p. 1). IEEE. doi:10.1109/HISB.2012.8

Mayer-Schönberger, V., & Cukier, K. (2013). *Big Data: A revolution that will transform how we live, work, and think*. Houghton Mifflin Harcourt.

McAfee, A., Brynjolfsson, E., Davenport, T. H., Patil, D. J., & Barton, D. (2012). Big Data. *The management revolution. Harvard Business Review, 90*(10), 61–67. PMID:23074865

McKinsey Global Institute. (2011). *Big Data: The next frontier for innovation, competition, and productivity*. Retrieved from http://www.mckinsey.com/mgi/publications/big_data/pdfs/MGI_big_data_full_report.pdf

Michele, O. C. (2012, October). Big Data, Bigger Outcomes Enterprise Systems and Data Management. *Journal of American Health Information Management Association, 83*(10), 38–43.

Murdoch, T. B., & Detsky, A. S. (2013). The inevitable application of Big Data to health care. *Journal of the American Medical Association, 309*(13), 1351–1352. doi:10.1001/jama.2013.393 PMID:23549579

Nambiar, R., Bhardwaj, R., Sethi, A., & Vargheese, R. (2013, October). A look at challenges and opportunities of Big Data analytics in healthcare. In *Big Data, 2013 IEEE International Conference on* (pp. 17-22). IEEE. doi:10.1109/BigData.2013.6691753

NICT. (2011). *President's Council on National ICT Strategies. Establishing a smart government by using Big Data*. Seoul, Korea: President's Council on National ICT Strategies.

Nirmala, M. B. (2014). A Survey of Big Data Analytics Systems: Appliances, Platforms, and Frameworks. *Handbook of Research on Cloud Infrastructures for Big Data Analytics*, 392.

Ohlhorst, F. J. (2012). *Big Data analytics: turning Big Data into big money*. Hoboken, NY: John Wiley & Sons. doi:10.1002/9781119205005

Pentland, A., Lazer, D., Brewer, D., & Heibeck, T. (2009). Using reality mining to improve public health and medicine. *Studies in Health Technology and Informatics, 149*, 93–102. PMID:19745474

Pita, R., Pinto, C., Melo, P., Silva, M., Barreto, M., & Rasella, D. (2015). A Spark-based workflow for probabilistic record linkage of healthcare data. In *the Workshop Proceedings of the EDBT/ICDT 2015 Joint Conference (March 27, 2015, Brussels, Belgium) on CEUR- WS.org*.

Power, D. J. (2014). Using 'Big Data'for analytics and decision support. *Journal of Decision Systems*, *23*(2), 222–228. doi:10.1080/12460125.2014.888848

Priyanka, K., & Kulennavar, N. (n.d.). *A Survey On Big Data Analytics In Health Care*. Academic Press.

Raghupathi, W. (2010). Data Mining in Health Care. In S. Kudyba (Ed.), *Healthcare Informatics: Improving Efficiency and Productivity* (pp. 211–223). Taylor & Francis. doi:10.1201/9781439809792-c11

Raghupathi, W., & Raghupathi, V. (2013). An Overview of Health Analytics. *J Health Med Informat*, *4*(132), 2.

Raghupathi, W., & Raghupathi, V. (2014). Big Data analytics in healthcare: Promise and potential. *Health Information Science and Systems*, *2*(1), 3. doi:10.1186/2047-2501-2-3 PMID:25825667

Russom, P. (2011). *Big data analytics*. TDWI Best Practices Report, Fourth Quarter.

Schouten, P. (2013). Big Data in health care. *Healthcare Financial Management: Journal of the Healthcare Financial Management Association*, *67*(2), 40-42.

Srinivasan, U., & Arunasalam, B. (2013). Leveraging Big Data Analytics to Reduce Healthcare Costs. *IT Professional*, *15*(6), 21–28. doi:10.1109/MITP.2013.55

STP. (2012). *Office of Science and Technology Policy, Executive Office of the President of the United States. The Obama administration unveils the "Big Data" initiative: announces $200 million in new R&D investments*. Washington, DC: Executive Office of the President.

Sun, J., & Reddy, C. K. (2013, August). Big Data analytics for healthcare. In *Proceedings of the 19th ACM SIGKDD international conference on Knowledge discovery and data mining* (pp. 1525-1525). ACM. doi:10.1145/2487575.2506178

Venner, J. (2009). *Pro Hadoop*. Apress. doi:10.1007/978-1-4302-1943-9

Villars, R. L., Olofson, C. W., & Eastwood, M. (2011). *Big Data: What it is and why you should care*. White Paper, IDC.

Wallis, N. (2012). *Big Data in Canada: Challenging Complacency for Competitive Advantage*. IDC.

White, T. (2009). *Hadoop: The Definitive Guide*. O'Reilly Media.

Yahoo. (2014). *Continuuity Raises $10 Million Series A Round to Ignite Big Data Application Development Within the Hadoop Ecosystem*. Retrieved from finance.yahoo.com

Yoo, I., Alafaireet, P., Marinov, M., Pena-Hernandez, K., Gopidi, R., Chang, J. F., & Hua, L. (2012). Data mining in healthcare and biomedicine: A survey of the literature. *Journal of Medical Systems*, *36*(4), 2431–2448. doi:10.1007/s10916-011-9710-5 PMID:21537851

Zikopoulos, P. C., Eaton, C., deRoos, D., Deutsch, T., & Lapis, G. (2011). *Understanding Big Data - Analytics for Enterprise Class Hadoop and Streaming Data* (1st ed.). McGraw-Hill Osborne Media.

ENDNOTE

[1] The term "Hadoop" often refers not to just the base Hadoop package but rather to the Hadoop Ecosystem, which includes all of the additional software packages that can be installed on top of or alongside Hadoop, such as Pig, Hive, HBase, Spark, and others.

Chapter 10
Big Data Paradigm for Healthcare Sector

Jyotsna Talreja Wassan
University of Delhi, India

ABSTRACT

The digitization of world in various areas including health care domain has brought up remarkable changes. Electronic Health Records (EHRs) have emerged for maintaining and analyzing health care real data online unlike traditional paper based system to accelerate clinical environment for providing better healthcare. These digitized health care records are form of Big Data, not because of the fact they are voluminous but also they are real time, dynamic, sporadic and heterogeneous in nature. It is desirable to extract relevant information from EHRs to facilitate various stakeholders of the clinical environment. The role, scope and impact of Big Data paradigm on health care is discussed in this chapter.

INTRODUCTION

Health care data are valuable resource which may consists of patient's demographics (age, sex etc...), treatment plans provided by a clinician, medical history of a patient, laboratory reports, radiology reports, billing data, insurance claiming requests etc. But the electronic storage, management and retrieval of health care data are difficult tasks as the health data are complex, voluminous, dynamic, sporadic, unstructured and heterogeneous (Wasan, S. K., Bhatnagar.V & Kaur, H., 2006). The activity of health care systems is reaching to terabytes even to petabytes and more in various cases. It is important to store such Big Data in an efficient distributed manner over computing nodes. Big Data analytics has the potential to improve health care at lower costs by gaining insights and discovering associative patterns within real time health care data. The aim of this chapter is to review a trial on modelling of big data analytics to expedite the large scale processing of electronic health data for various stakeholders.

DOI: 10.4018/978-1-4666-9649-5.ch010

BACKGROUND

The Big Data revolution is nascent and there is a lot of scope for new innovations and discoveries. It has set the path of rapid change in technological world. The Big Data is impacting various areas like social networking, online education etc. including health industry. The major 5 V's associated with Big Data (Figure1) are listed as follows (Marr, B., and February 2014):

1. **Volume:** Health Care data is enormous.
2. **Velocity**: Health Care data is delivered at various speeds and is dynamic.
3. **Variety**: Health Care data is heterogeneous.
4. **Veracity:** Health Care data is enormous; thus it is important to maintain its relevance and trust-worthiness to give best possible benefits to the patients.
5. **Value:** Health Care data is rich source of information and is useful if could be turned into valuable knowledge.

Various Big Data platforms may prove beneficial for decision-making process in treatment plans under digitized health care systems. The applications of real-time health care systems e.g. detecting viral infections as early as possible, identifying various symptoms and parameters swiftly, reducing patient morbidity and mortality etc. electronically would revolutionize healthcare.

Premier analyzes data various healthcare providers and enabling its members with high-performance, integrated and trusted information. *University of Ontario Institute of Technology (UOIT)* is using IBM big data technology to capture and analyze real-time data from medical monitors, alerting stakeholders to potential health problems for patients (Retrieved from http://www-01.ibm.com/software/data/bigdata/industry-healthcare.html). Various repositories such as *Microsoft Health-Vault, Dossia* are supporting health data analytics (Steinbrook, R., 2008). Various technology driven applications based on big data paradigm such as *Asthma-polis* developed for asthmatic patients for monitoring via GPS enabled tracker

Figure 1. V's of big data technology (IGI, 2014)

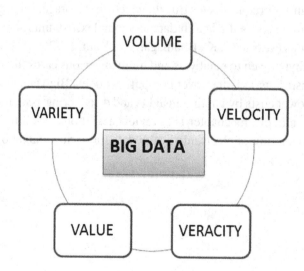

are emerging online. The *dashboard* technology is also emerging and *RiseHealth* is one such example of dashboards (Groves, P., Kayyali, B., Knott, D., & Van Kuiken, S., 2013).*Wiki-Health* is an emerging personal health training application.

Cost reduction for health care services managed electronically (as few mentioned above) based on big data paradigms is a promising feature.

MAIN FOCUS OF THE CHAPTER

Big Data platforms supporting distributed computing provide storage capacity and computing power over high speed networks, to extract valuable information from large medical data sets. Big Data basically deals with two main concepts of data storage and data analytics. The main focus of the chapter is to propose how data storage with Big Data stores and analytics with MapReduce paradigm, may be performed on simulated health data.

Issues, Controversies, Problems

The structure and nature of health industry possess some challenges in concepts supporting Big Data. It is difficult to easily share and distribute data over various health service providers due to privacy and security concerns regarding patients (Ash, J. S., & Bates, D. W., 2005). The issues and problems are there due to semantic and legal barriers. Many times even the data in the same hospital is provided only to concerned department due to lack of integration support for big data platforms. Also the lack of public support related to privacy and security issues has hindered the progress of Electronic Health Records with big data needs. Thus it's important to abide by stringent privacy protection while accessing EHRs. Many people feel comfort zone in traditional evidence based care instead of accepting technology driven models in health care, being sensitive area. Also data standardization, costing and ease of use factors are needed to be taken care off for accessing EHRs globally. Today various medical standards (like HL7 etc.) are coming up to accelerate the global usage of EHRs. Measures like Health Insurance Portability and Accountability Act (HIPPA) have been created which enforce privacy rules accounting to patient's health information (Cheng, V. S., & Hung, P. C., 2006). It's important to aim for clear understanding of health care data source and providing a best possible solution.

ELECTRONIC HEALTH RECORDS

Healthcare industry is many times impacted by various challenges, like high costs, rising expenditures, inconsistent quality care, and delays in providing care and limited access in various areas across the world. It is widely believed that the use of information technology in health care over paper based phenomena can reduce the cost of health care while improving its quality. Electronic health records (EHRs), have been thought to be possible solutions to these problems as they store all the information about a patient and make it interoperable and shared among different health care providers. Thus EHRs are longitudinal collection of electronic health information about patients and is capable of being shared across various stakeholders to provide better health care (Yina, 2010).

All healthcare stakeholders, patients, health care providers, payers, researchers, governments, etc. are being impacted by analysis of data stored in EHRs, which may help in predicting how these players are likely to act. As the populations across countries are increasing; health related data stored in EHRs is also increasing. EHRs aid in representing this data in comprehensive summarized form, including demographics, medical history, medication and allergies, immunization status, laboratory test results, radiology images, and billing information etc. The following ways emphasize on how electronic data available in large amounts will enable the healthcare industry to reduce costs and improve quality:

1. **Improved Care:** The integration and application of big data tools promote evidence-based care for patients as all health care providers have the same information about a given patient and are working towards a common goal. This can improve outcomes, reducing medical errors. EHRs can also provide drug recommendations; verify medications and dosages to ensure right drug for the patient. Big Data analysis can help in matching the skills and specializations of the health care provider with the requirements of the patient. Service providers can identify patients who are due for preventive visits and screenings etc. and can monitor how patients measure up to certain parameters, such as vaccinations, sugar levels and blood pressure readings etc.

2. **Improved Standard of Living:** Knowledge from large amounts of data available online can help patients to play an active role in monitoring their own health, not only treating and managing their current conditions, but also taking precautions for future ones by getting informative recommendations online and following them. Today there are many patient portals that provide online interaction with health service providers.

3. **Improved Value:** Big data can be used to ensure cost-effectiveness of healthcare through different methods, such as better health insurances, patient-medical reimbursements and eliminating frauds and wastages in the health systems.

4. **Improved Personalized Care:** Patients are empowered through day to day life style measures and their personnel care such as diet, exercise, and medication adherence to control their health issues. EHRs provide a means to share information so that patients and their families can more fully take part in decisions about their health care.

There is estimated a 300-450 billion dollar reduction in U.S. healthcare costs via big data interventions (statistics available on http://rockhealth.com). The data available on http://www.healthit.gov/ has reflected evidence of advantages of EHR adoption; few examples as listed on the website are quoted as follows:

- "Researchers at the Center for IT Leadership (2010) Web Site Disclaimers studied the U.S. Department of Veterans Affairs, estimated the savings of $4.64 billion from preventing adverse drug events."
- "In Indianapolis, Finnell and Overhage (2010) found medical professionals have been benefited from access to pre-existing health information like medication lists, allergies, and medical histories— via quick electronic exchange. This also proved useful in cases of emergency."
- "Shapiro et al. (2011) examined health information exchange projects in 48 States which depicted enormous potential for improving public health reporting and investigation, emergency response, and communication between public health officials and clinicians besides some financial and technical hurdles."

- "Persell et al. (2011) found that EHRs can use information on patients' medical histories to improve quality significantly by providing best methods of care for specific patients."

The true potential of digitized information lies in big data and EHRs are built to provide structured output. EHRs play a major part in the healthcare reform and can be mined to detect fruitful health related patterns using big data analytics tools and techniques. Health care providers with busy practicing and patients with busy live schedules appreciate convenience in their health care transactions provided by EHRs.

HEALTH DATA STREAMS

Health data sets which grow and expand continuously in rapid manner over time are pertinent form of clinical data collected via digitized treatment plans for patients whether they are clinical notes or laboratory reports etc. Various medical domains comprise of health sensors or information systems generating real time data. Also in many of the medical situations, monitoring of constant real-time data is utmost important e.g. heart beat monitoring etc. Clinicians make use of large amounts of time sensitive data while providing effective medication to patients. Because of real time huge data, traditional sequential systems are not efficient to use. Dealing with large continuous flows of health care data, require big data management and processing. Health Data Stream Analytics (HDSA) could play important role in clinical decision system (Zhang, Q., Pang, C., Mcbride, S., Hansen, D., Cheung, C., & Steyn, M., 2010). The ultimate goal is to provide best treatment plan to the patient at reduced cost in real time manner. Streaming is increasingly gaining importance as new paradigms of Big Data analytics are emerging to produce best results in reasonable time as incremental tasks.

One of the IBM Stream Computing press releases states the following example of stream analytics (http://www-03.ibm.com/press/us/en/pressrelease/42362.wss):

Emory University Hospital is using software from IBM and Excel Medical Electronics (EME) for a pioneering research project to create advanced, predictive medical care for critical patients through real-time streaming analytics. Emory is exploring systems that will enable clinicians to acquire, analyze and correlate medical data at a volume and velocity. The research application developed by Emory uses IBM's streaming analytics platform with EME's bedside monitor data aggregation application to collect and analyze more than 100,000 real-time data points per patient per second. The software developed by Emory identifies patterns that could indicate serious complications like sepsis, heart failure or pneumonia, aiming to provide real-time medical insights to clinicians.

Accessing and drawing insights from real-time data can mean life and death for a patient," says Tim Buchman, MD, PhD, director of critical care at Emory University Hospital. "Through this new system we will be able to analyze thousands of streaming data points and act on those insights to make better decisions about which patient needs our immediate attention and how to treat that patient. It's making us much smarter in our approach to critical care." Emory's vision of the "ICU of the Future" is based on the notion that the same predictive capabilities possible in banking, air travel, online commerce, oil and gas exploration and other industries can also apply in medicine.

As the medical community increasingly embraces the power of technology to help improve health outcomes for patients, predictive medicine is finally becoming reality," says Martin S. Kohn, MD, chief medical scientist at IBM. "The ability to pull actionable insights from patient monitors in real-time is truly going to transform the way doctors take care of their sickest patients.

SOURCES OF BIG DATA IN HEALTH CARE

Big data in healthcare can come from *Electronic Health Records, Clinical Decision Support Systems,* laboratories, pharmacies, medical claim and insurance companies in multiple formats (text, images, graphs etc.) and can be geographically distributed. The various sources are listed as follows:

1. Logs of clickstream and interaction data on social networks discussing about health care (e.g. discussions on Facebook, Twitter or various blogs.). It can also include Health Care Apps on electronic devices.
2. Readings from devices having health sensors and information systems.
3. Billing Data in semi structured format, provided by medical insurance agencies electronically.
4. Genomic Data
5. Biometric Data
6. Clinical notes provided electronically by physician.
7. Imaging Data like scans/ultrasounds etc. of various patients.

MHEALTH: GENERATING BIG DATA STREAMS

mHealth deals with generation and dissemination of health information via mobile or wireless devices. With the advancement in technology, mobile apps and devices are proving them useful in collaborating with clinicians and patients to provide more personalized, preventive care. This data also has the potential to enable a 'learning health system' to anticipate health risks before they become a problem. Using mobile devices to monitor patient activity can help clinicians and patients in saving time and making patients healthier by providing instant solutions for health issues. The massive amount of data being collected on mobile healthcare devices may lead to big data initiatives amongst various stakeholders. Many people today are tracking their levels of daily activity and health statuses like blood pressure, body temperature etc. and clinicians may increasingly use this data to improve levels of health care. The ubiquitous mobile devices are presenting opportunities to improve health services with clinical efficacy. This may prove effective in realizing remote patient monitoring and providing better healthcare if used judiciously. There may be some privacy and security concerns for which it is needed to follow health standards.

BIG DATA PARADIGM FOR EHRs

Big Data platforms focus primarily on three aspects; one is large amount of data storage and secondly data analytics and thirdly a supporting query language for data retrieval (Figure 2). Various NoSQL data stores like Hadoop, MongoDB, and Cassandra etc. are emerging to *acquire, manage, store and query* big data.

Figure 2. Big data stack for EHRs (IGI, 2014)

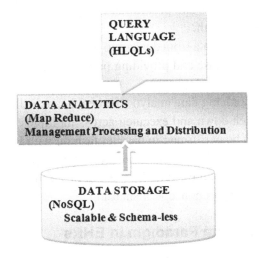

NoSQL stands for "Not Only SQL" or "Not Relational". The movement of developing schema less data stores, parallel programming models and various analytical platforms due to increasing amounts of data is known as NoSQL movement. NoSQL platforms work on distributed environment and are horizontally scalable. These platforms may aid in aggregating and storing patient information in dynamic form enhancing portability and accountability across hospitals. Various NoSQL stores are emerging to support Big Data paradigm. Few of them are listed in Table1.

All these NoSQL data stores could be explored for storing and analyzing health care data. Big data storage and analytics provide more accurate knowledge about patients, clinicians, and diagnostic or insurance claim operations for EHRs. By processing a large stream of health care data real-time or static data with different Big Data tools and techniques, clinicians can monitor emerging trends, can make time sensitive decisions better and can drive on new better health opportunities. Big data could help greatly in following domains:

1. Creating more clinically relevant and cost-effective treatment plans and diagnostic measures.
2. Analyzing patient records to identify symptoms, responses, best suited vaccines etc. for them and providing them with best services..

Table 1. NoSQL Data stores (Source: http://nosql-database.org/ last seen on October 2014)

Category	Databases
Key-Value Data stores	DynamoDB, Riak,Redis,Aerospike, Azure Table Storage,FoundationDB,LevelDB,GenieDB, Chordless,Scalaris,Voldemort, Dynomite, Maxtable, Pincaster, RaptorDB, OpenLDAP, LSM
Document Data stores	MongoDB,Elasticsearch,Couchbase Server, CouchDB,RethinkDB,RavenDB, Clusterpoint Server, Terrastore, SisoDB, djondb,EJDB,densodb
Column Data stores	Hadoop / HBase, Cassandra, Hypertable, Amazon SimpleDB, Cloudata, Stratosphere, Cloudera, HPCC
Graph Data stores	Neo4J, Infinite Graph, InfoGrid, HyperGraphDB, DEX, GraphBase, BrightstarDB, Meronymy

3. Improving Public Health surveillance.
4. Analyzing medical claim requests and preventing frauds and wastages.
5. Identify risks for a patient's health.
6. Capturing real time health care data from devices to monitor health parameters and predicting risks for developing a particular disease and providing preventive care.

The conceptual framework for a big data analytics in healthcare is different from traditional ones as for big data, processing is broken down and executed across multiple computing nodes instead of one machine and their analytics can be performed in parallel fashion with help of MapReduce, for making better-informed health-related decisions. Furthermore, open source platforms such as Hadoop/MapReduce, MongoDB etc. are available on the cloud, have encouraged the application of big data analytics in healthcare. These platforms support concept of sharding.

Advantages of Using Big Data Paradigm in EHRs

Big Data is a nascent technology. It has set the platform for innovating, experimenting and analyzing data in almost every domain including EHRs.

The advantages of using Big Data are listed as follows:

1. Big Data platforms are cloud friendly.
2. They are easy to scale and works well in distributed environment to provide more efficiency.
3. The Big Data paradigm gives both speed and capacity for cloud storage.
4. No fixed schemas are required in most Big Data platforms such as MongoDB, as was the case in traditional database systems.
5. They may prove cost effective.
6. They may support dynamic queries engines over Big Data stores.
7. The new wave may aid greatly in generating new health care opportunities.

MAP-REDUCE MODELLING FOR BIG DATA WORLD

Google devised an approach called MapReduce (Dean, J., & Ghemawat, S., 2008) to deal with exponentially growing Web data. The MapReduce model as shown in Figure 3 is designed to work with a massively distributed file system. MapReduce became motivation for an open source technology called Hadoop, along with an associated file system called HDFS (Borthakur, 2007) and various other such platforms as listed in Table2.Map/Reduce framework is capable of taking a big task and divide it into small discrete tasks that can be performed in parallel manner.as illustrated in Figure 3. The *Map* and *Reduce* functions of *MapReduce* are both defined with respect to data structured in (key, value) pairs.

Map Function: It accepts an input pair and produces a set of intermediate key/value pair's.
Map: (key$_1$, value$_1$) → list (key$_2$, value$_2$)

Figure 3. MapReduce framework (IGI, 2014)

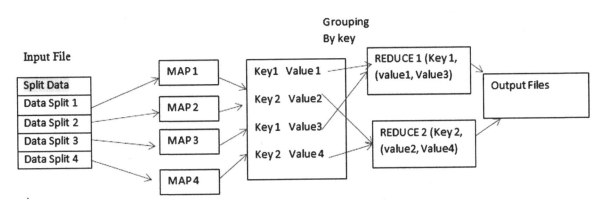

The *Map* function is applied in parallel to every pair in the input dataset which produces a list of pairs for each call. After that, the MapReduce framework collects all pairs with the same key from all lists and groups them together, thus creating one group for each one of the different generated keys.

Reduce Function: This function accepts an intermediate key and a set of values for a particular key.
Reduce: $(key_2, list (key_2, value_2)) \rightarrow value_3$

The Reduce function is applied in parallel to each group, which in turn produces a collection of values in the same domain.

Thus the MapReduce framework transforms a list of (key, value) pairs into a list of values.

An efficient scenario could be achieved by running many Map tasks and many Reduce tasks in parallel. Health care data being big; may also use MapReduce framework in various activities and may achieve significant improvement in its implementation. This paradigm could effectively be used in analyzing EHRs as discussed in later sections.

QUERYING BIG DATA WORLD

Big Data paradigms also support various HLQL (higher-level query languages) to simplify both the specification of the MapReduce operations and the retrieval of the result. Several of these HLQL's like HiveQL, Pig Latin, and JAQL (Stewart, R.J. et al., 2011) etc. have emerged to query Big Data stores.

Table 2. Attributes and their granularities

Attribute	Type	Domain	Granularity
I Measuring Value for a disease	Numeric	1-100	**4** ([0-25],[25-50],[50-75],[75-100])
II Symptoms of disease	Categorical	say a, b, c, d	**4**

HiveQL etc. are like SQL of traditional database systems. All of them can also translate higher level jobs into MapReduce jobs. Many platforms like MongoDB also provide their own query languages for retrieving the results.

DATA MINING FOR EHRs

Data Mining deals with extracting relevant patterns or items of interests from heterogeneous data sets.

EHRs are useful in capturing and utilizing health care data but it is also important to extract useful information for supporting good medical health care and medical research using EHR data. Mining of Electronic Health Records (EHRs) has the potential for finding relevant patterns and for establishing new clinician, patient or disease correlations. It also helps in evaluation of effectiveness of treatment plan, customer relationship management, and the detection of fraud insurance claims etc.

Data Mining may also involve predictive modelling w.r.t health care data. The purpose is to transform information into knowledge to be utilized in health care industry. Data mining approaches could be characterized into two main classes: i) Supervised Learning, ii) Unsupervised Learning. The modelling of data in both the cases is different. A supervised learning approach deals with data set of classified labels from which a model is derived to predict future labels from the existing features. Examples are: classifiers such as naive Bayes; artificial neural networks etc. Unsupervised methods, such as clustering algorithms, take unclassified data set and try to group data vectors on the basis of similarity features. Another important aspect for data mining is correlation mining. Association Rule Mining (ARM) is an example of correlation mining. It tries to uncover hidden or previously unknown connecting patterns. A rule in the form of X=>Y denotes an implication of element Y by an element X i.e. how two items (X and Y) are co-related with each other. This usually tends to find simple if-then rules in any data set for formulating hypothesis to study further. The subsequent section mainly focuses on modelling of clustering technique on health streaming data. In computer science, data stream clustering is defined as the clustering of data that arrive continuously such as data from social networks, online health records etc. Data stream clustering aims at constructing a good clustering (grouping) of the stream i.e. given sequence of input data points, using reasonable amount of resources such as memory, time etc. Data stream clustering has recently attracted attention for emerging applications that involve large amounts of streaming data. The algorithm for data stream clustering must be able to detect changes in evolving data streams and grouping data points representing a cluster.

PROPOSED MAP-REDUCE MODELLING FOR CLUSTERING HEALTH DATA STREAMS

The real time analysis of digitized health data requires large volumes of multi-dimensional data at higher data rates. The processing of this kind of data needs to be efficient to provide real time care to the patient. Thus modelling of scalable clustering on multidimensional data as per the user real time requirements is preferable for providing better health care. Clustering may form coherent group of patients on the basis of similarity of symptoms they are embracing. To solve the clustering problem on multidimensional health care data streams in an exclusive manner, scalable paradigm is preferable. One of the basic structures that could be used for storing the multi-dimensional data coming from real time health care application data stream is *GRID*. The proposed approach maps the incoming data stream into grid cells and then clusters the grid cells to find similar or coherent patients. The basic flow of the proposed algorithm is shown in Figure4.

The approach has been simulated on dummy two dimensional data for consideration. Table 2 shows sample dummy data with two attributes and their respective domains and chosen granularities.

Attribute I is discretized as per user-defined granularity, g = 4 and categorical attributes are assigned granularities according to distinct values in respective domain sets. An incoming data point is inserted in the appropriate cuboid of the Grid using its dimensional values. In this way, all data points within physical proximity of each other are placed together in same cuboid region. The input sample data file is shown in Table3.

The input file consists of data points and record of their arrival times as the last parameter. The parameter of arrival time is used to calculate the speed of the stream which will be averaged out (aatc) to measure the recency of the data points. Also assumed a *threshold* value to be associated with GRID (each cell) to see whether a grid cell is dense and will be considered for clustering or not. If weight of the grid cell is greater than the predefined threshold then only it will be considered for clustering.

Considering above definitions, the input file (as shown in Table1) is mapped to a GRID and create an output file as shown in Table 3 with the help some data transformation (here PERL SCRIPT was used). The output sample data file is shown in Table4.

Figure 4. Flow of Proposed Algorithm (IGI, 2014)

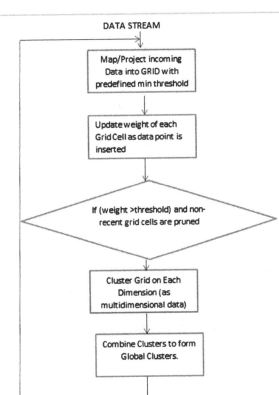

179

Table 3. Sample input data file

d1 a 12 0.25
d2 b 14 0.5
d3 c 40 0.75
d4 d 60 1
d5 a 40 1.25
d6 a 62 1.5
d7 b 45 1.75
d8 c 18 2
d9 d 42 2.25
d10 a 89 2.5
d11 b 63 2.75
d12 c 72 3
d13 d 09 3.25
d14 b 92 3.5
d15 c 98 3.75

Table 4. Sample output data file

gID: grid_1 Dim1:1 Dim2:1 Weight:1 aatc:1 Recent:0
gID:grid_2 Dim1:1 Dim2:2 Weight:2 aatc:1.875 Recent:9.375
gID:grid_3 Dim1:1 Dim2:3 Weight:7 aatc:2.32142857142857 Recent:0.678571428571429
gID:grid_4 Dim1:1 Dim2:4 Weight:7 aatc:2.25 Recent:0.571428571428571
gID:grid_5 Dim1:2 Dim2:1 Weight:5 aatc:2.15 Recent:2.2
gID:grid_6 Dim1:2 Dim2:2 Weight:2 aatc:1.875 Recent:8.75
gID:grid_7 Dim1:2 Dim2:3 Weight:7 aatc:2.39285714285714 Recent:0.785714285714286
gID:grid_8 Dim1:2 Dim2:4 Weight:7 aatc:2.32142857142857 Recent:0.642857142857143
gID:grid_9 Dim1:3 Dim2:1 Weight:7 aatc:2.35714285714286 Recent:0.714285714285714
gID:grid_10 Dim1:3 Dim2:2 Weight:2 aatc:1.875 Recent:8.25
gID:grid_11 Dim1:3 Dim2:3 Weight:2 aatc:1.875 Recent:8.125
gID:grid_12 Dim1:3 Dim2:4 Weight:7 aatc:2.39285714285714 Recent:0.75
gID:grid_13 Dim1:4 Dim2:1 Weight:7 aatc:2.32142857142857 Recent:0.607142857142857
gID:grid_14 Dim1:4 Dim2:2 Weight:7 aatc:2.25 Recent:0.535714285714286
gID:grid_15 Dim1:4 Dim2:3 Weight:5 aatc:1.8 Recent:2.05
gID:grid_16 Dim1:4 Dim2:4 Weight:2 aatc:1.875 Recent:7.625

Clustering approach proposed (illustrated in Figure 5), involves firstly the creation of local clusters and subsequently global clusters are generated. Considering a 2D Grid example, firstly grid cells that have the same dimension value are clustered; with respect to both the axis i.e. X and Y respectively. If two local clusters contain the same grid cell, they form a global cluster. If two global clusters contain the same local cluster or global cluster, these two global clusters form a larger global cluster. For instance, if {$g1, g2$} ⊆ Local Cluster l1 and {$g2, g3$} ⊆ Local Cluster l2, then {$g1, g2, g3$} ⊆ Global Cluster GC1 (Sun, X., & Jiao, Y., 2009).

The implementation of the discussed clustering approach could be done using three Mappers and reducers under MapReduce framework. Initial sample input to first Map-Reduce is shown in Table3. Each MapReduce process changes the <key, value> input. The output of each MapReduce process is the input of the next one. The three MapReduce functions are discussed as follows:

1.   The initial mapper works for mapping and emitting the *<Dimension, {gridIndex, Dimensions, weight, aatc, recent}>* pairs of the grid. The output of first MapReduce process is a list of *Grid ID's* (i.e., *<g1, g2 etc. >*) and their corresponding local cluster ID's after applying pruning of the grid cells on the basis of comparison of weight of the grid cell with the minimum threshold and recency factor with aatc factor in the Reduce function . Reduce function will consider a grid cell if its weight is greater than the threshold value and recency factor is greater than aatc.

2.   The second MapReduce clusters the grids into local clusters and produce list of local cluster ID's corresponding to the GRID ID's.

Figure 5. Clustering approach (IGI, 2014)

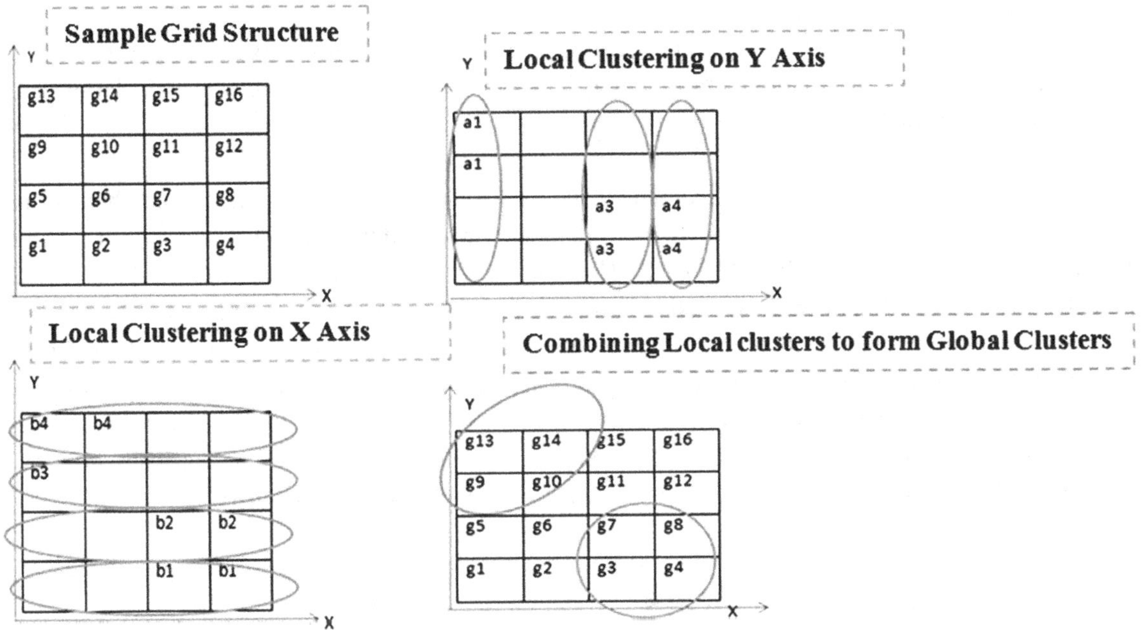

3. The third MapReduce combines the local clusters into global clusters according to the fact that if two local clusters contain the same grid cell, they form a global cluster.

The proposed approach is being implemented in MongoDB platform on virtual machine and the results are shown in Table5.

The above results reflect that g4,g 8,g3 and g7 grid cells area having similar kind of patients and hence grouped into one cluster. Similarly for all clusters; we have combination of coherent data. Clustering health data could help in numerous other ways depending on input data set.

SOLUTIONS AND RECOMMENDATIONS

All stakeholders have unique role in accessing health data. It is important to leverage comprehensive information amongst each stakeholder to understand potential features of accessing EHRs. Also Big Data paradigm has great potential to transform health care industry into electronic world. The following recommendations are proposed to share and work on EHRS:

1. Designing Big Data governing models to manage and share health data across organizations for making health care efficient and balancing health care and costs.
2. Ensuring consistent data storage by using Big Data stores and successful distributed environment for sharing EHR data.
3. Designing use cases based on big data analytics to facilitate each stakeholder of health data.

4. Building base models based on Big Data technology to ensure research and development in medicine and health care domain.
5. Establishing efficient commination between various health care providers in EHR systems.
6. Analyzing health data streams using efficient data mining algorithms w.r.t clustering, classification or association rule mining.

Exploring platforms for big data management and analysis for EHRs to design effective health paradigm is useful. These platforms include NoSQL databases MongoDB, Hadoop, programming models like MapReduce, architectures like ASTERIX (Borkar, V. R., Carey, M. J., & Li, C., 2012)etc. which are different from traditional SQL based database systems and support heterogeneously structured voluminous data with its management and access. The decision may depend on choosing an architecture (e.g. distributed, clustered machines) for storing the data and programming models for development of data parallel, distributed applications for big data considering factors like scalability limits, query speed etc. It is important to also focus on cost effectiveness and real time support for data from strategy to implementation. Big data analytics also requires governance, privacy, and security.

FUTURE RESEARCH DIRECTIONS

Many hospitals have started embracing the meaningful use of EHRs; but now the concern is to facilitate ease of use of EHRs for patients and interoperability of data they are using. It is beneficial to aim for two main areas: i) good and easy to use user interface for patients accessing EHRs and ii) performing data analytics on EHR data. Since EHR is big data; MapReduce could prove to be a very efficient paradigm for analytics. The continuous efforts taken for building timely and cost-effective management over "Big Data" are appreciable and could form the basis of key ingredient for success in managing health records electronically. We must aim for designing and usage of more appropriate and efficient future big data tools for gaining insight of their usage in medical industry. This may aid in reducing costs, saving time and enabling quick access to patient records for efficient health care. Also various data mining techniques could be implemented via big data analytic procedures of MapReduce, aggregation etc. to facilitate ease of access with efficiency. Computing over cluster of nodes instead of utilizing the capability of one main sever is the future of various industries and this could help online medical records too. Big Data is new paradigm to explore and underpinning many futuristic ways of innovation and experimentation with vast amount of data. Futuristic research proposals in-cooperate evaluating proposed approach of stream clustering with various metrics and implementing various other algorithms to solve problems with scalable distributed environment.

CONCLUSION

Both EHRs and the techniques for storage, management and analysis of big data are emerging. EHRs have played role in moving health records from paper based information into electronic one. Big Data has become a ubiquitous technology. It could prove useful in generating new knowledge in health care industry too by analyzing heterogeneous, unstructured and schema less health care data unlike traditional database management systems. Big Data Analytics in the form of MapReduce distributed paradigm

Table 5. Results after applying MapReduce

(d) (e) Results of MAP REDUCE 1
With Respect to X axis
{ "_id": 1, "value": { "grid_id": ["g3", "g4"], "loccluster_id": "b1" } }   { "_id": 2, "value": { "grid_id": ["g7", "g8"], "loccluster_id": "b2" } }   { "_id": 3, "value": { "grid_id": ["g9", "g12"], "loccluster_id": "b3" } }   { "_id": 4, "value": { "grid_id": ["g13", "g14"], "loccluster_id": "b4" } }
With Respect to Y axis
"_id": 1, "value": { "grid_id": ["g9", "g13"], "loccluster_id": "a1" } }   "_id": 2, "value": { "grid_id": ["g14"], "loccluster_id": "a2" } }   "_id": 3, "value": { "grid_id": ["g3", "g7"], "loccluster_id": "a3" } }   "_id": 4, "value": { "grid_id": ["g4", "g8", "g12"], "loccluster_id": "a4" }
(f) Results of MAP REDUCE 2
{ "_id": "g13", "value": { "loccid": ["a1", "b4"], clusterstage: gclust } }   { "_id": "g14", "value": { "loccid": ["a2", "b4"], clusterstage: gclust } }   { "_id": "g3", "value": { "loccid": ["a3", "b1"], clusterstage: gclust } }   { "_id": "g4", "value": { "loccid": ["a4", "b1"], clusterstage: gclust } }   { "_id": "g7", "value": { "loccid": ["a3", "b2"], clusterstage: gclust } }   { "_id": "g8", "value": { "loccid": ["a4", "b2"], clusterstage: gclust } }   { "_id": "g9", "value": { "loccid": ["a1", "b3"], clusterstage: gclust } }
(g) Results of MAP REDUCE 3
{ "_id": "gclust", "value": { "globlclust": [("g4", "g8", "g3", "g7"),("g9", "g13", "g14")] } }

allows various stakeholders of EHRs to develop efficient models for health care domain. This could facilitate access of health data at speeds and in cost effective manner. Various monitoring devices, clinicians, patients access platforms etc. under health domain are generating flow of thousands of data per unit time known as Health Streams. Health Data Stream Analytics (HDSA) with help of MapReduce or aggregation framework could play important role in clinical decision system. EHRs, the electronic health records have vast scope for clinical practices and data mining paradigms implemented via big data technology could utilize this scope well in today's world of information overload. It may prove beneficial in implementing good clinical practices and high degree of correlations amongst clinicians and patients. Big Data is accelerating the usage of products and services of medical domain amongst each stakeholder by sharing over networks unlike paper based healthcare records which were not accessible though networks across the world. Another advantage is that various Big Data platforms are open-source and freely available to use. Big Data paradigms are also supporting easy, dynamic and high level query languages over big data stores.

REFERENCES

Ash, J. S., & Bates, D. W. (2005). Factors and forces affecting EHR system adoption: Report of a 2004 ACMI discussion. *Journal of the American Medical Informatics Association*, *12*(1), 8–12. doi:10.1197/jamia.M1684 PMID:15492027

Borkar, V. R., Carey, M. J., & Li, C. (2012). Big data platforms: What's next? *XRDS: Crossroads. The ACM Magazine for Students*, *19*(1), 44–49. doi:10.1145/2331042.2331057

Borthakur, D. (2007). *The Hadoop Distributed File System: Architecture and Design*. Academic Press.

Cheng, V. S., & Hung, P. C. (2006). Health Insurance Portability and Accountability Act (HIPPA) Compliant Access Control Model for Web Services. *International Journal of Healthcare Information Systems and Informatics*, *1*(1), 22–39. doi:10.4018/jhisi.2006010102

Dean, J., & Ghemawat, S. (2008). MapReduce: Simplified data processing on large clusters. *Communications of the ACM*, *51*(1), 107–113. doi:10.1145/1327452.1327492

Duan, L., Street, W. N., & Xu, E. (2011). Healthcare information systems: Data mining methods in the creation of a clinical recommender system. *Enterprise Information Systems*, *5*(2), 169–181. doi:10.1080/17517575.2010.541287

Ebadollahi, S., Coden, A. R., Tanenblatt, M. A., Chang, S. F., Syeda-Mahmood, T., & Amir, A. (2006, October). Concept-based electronic health records: opportunities and challenges. In *Proceedings of the 14th annual ACM international conference on Multimedia* (pp. 997-1006). ACM. doi:10.1145/1180639.1180859

Feldman, B., Martin, E. M., & Skotnes, T. (2012). Big Data in Healthcare Hype and Hope. *October 2012. Dr. Bonnie, 360*.

Groves, P., Kayyali, B., Knott, D., & Van Kuiken, S. (2013). The 'big data 'revolution in healthcare. *McKinsey Quarterly*. Retrieved from http://www-01.ibm.com/software/data/bigdata/industry-healthcare.html

Jensen, P. B., Jensen, L. J., & Brunak, S. (2012). Mining electronic health records: Towards better research applications and clinical care. *Nature Reviews. Genetics*, *13*(6), 395–405. doi:10.1038/nrg3208 PMID:22549152

Koh, H. C., & Tan, G. (2011). Data mining applications in healthcare. *Journal of Healthcare Information Management*, *19*(2), 65. PMID:15869215

Lee, C. O., Lee, M., Han, D., Jung, S., & Cho, J. (2008, July). A framework for personalized Healthcare Service Recommendation. In *e-health Networking, Applications and Services, 2008. HealthCom 2008. 10th International Conference on* (pp. 90-95). IEEE.

Lee, K. K. Y., Tang, W. C., & Choi, K. S. (2013). Alternatives to relational database: Comparison of NoSQL and XML approaches for clinical data storage. *Computer Methods and Programs in Biomedicine*, *110*(1), 99–109. doi:10.1016/j.cmpb.2012.10.018 PMID:23177219

Lomotey, R. K., & Deters, R. (2013, June). Terms extraction from unstructured data silos. In *System of Systems Engineering (SoSE), 2013 8th International Conference on* (pp. 19-24). IEEE. doi:10.1109/SYSoSE.2013.6575236

Manyika, J., Chui, M., Brown, B., Bughin, J., Dobbs, R., Roxburgh, C., & Byers, A. H. (n.d.). *Big data: The next frontier for innovation, competition, and productivity*. Retrieved from http://www.mckinsey.com/Insights/MGI/Research/Technology_and_Innovation/Big_data_The_next_frontier_for_innovation

Nash, D. B. (2014). Harnessing the power of big data in healthcare. *American Health & Drug Benefits, 7*(2), 69.

Patra, D., Ray, S., Mukhopadhyay, J., Majumdar, B., & Majumdar, A. K. (2009, December). Achieving e-health care in a distributed EHR system. In *e-Health Networking, Applications and Services, 2009. Health-com 2009. 11th International Conference on* (pp. 101-107). IEEE. doi:10.1109/HEALTH.2009.5406205

Rajaraman, A., & Ullman, J. D. (2011). *Mining of massive datasets*. Cambridge University Press. doi:10.1017/CBO9781139058452

Ramakrishnan, N., Hanauer, D., & Keller, B. (2010). Mining electronic health records. *Computer, 43*(10), 77–81. doi:10.1109/MC.2010.292

Schafer, J. (2009). The Application of Data-Mining to Recommender Systems. Encyclopedia of Data Warehousing and Mining, 1, 44-48.

Stewart, R. J., Trinder, P. W., & Loidl, H. W. (2011). Comparing high level mapreduce query languages. In *Advanced Parallel Processing Technologies* (pp. 58–72). Springer Berlin Heidelberg. doi:10.1007/978-3-642-24151-2_5

Strauch, C., Sites, U. L. S., & Kriha, W. (2011). *NoSQL databases. Lecture Notes.* Stuttgart Media University.

Sun, X., & Jiao, Y. (2009). *pGrid: Parallel Grid-Based Data Stream Clustering with MapReduce.* Report. Oak Ridge National Laboratory.

Wang, F., Ercegovac, V., Syeda-Mahmood, T., Holder, A., Shekita, E., Beymer, D., & Xu, L. H. (2010, November). Large-scale multimodal mining for healthcare with mapreduce. In *Proceedings of the 1st ACM International Health Informatics Symposium* (pp. 479-483). ACM. doi:10.1145/1882992.1883067

Wasan, S. K., Bhatnagar, V., & Kaur, H. (2006). The impact of data mining techniques on medical diagnostics. *Data Science Journal, 5*, 119–126. doi:10.2481/dsj.5.119

Yina, W. (2010, April). Application of EHR in health care. In *Multimedia and Information Technology (MMIT), 2010 Second International Conference on* (Vol. 1, pp. 60-63). IEEE. doi:10.1109/MMIT.2010.32

Zhang, Q., Pang, C., Mcbride, S., Hansen, D., Cheung, C., & Steyn, M. (2010, July). Towards health data stream analytics. In *Complex Medical Engineering (CME), 2010 IEEE/ICME International Conference on* (pp. 282-287). IEEE. doi:10.1109/ICCME.2010.5558827

KEY TERMS AND DEFINITIONS

Clustering: Clustering deals with grouping of objects based on some similarity measure. Items in the same group (called a cluster) are more similar to each other than to those in other groups (clusters).

Data Analytics: Analysis of data is a process of inspecting, cleaning, transforming, and modeling data with the goal of discovering useful information, suggesting conclusions, and supporting decision making.

Data Intensive Domain: It is a classified area supporting various parallel computing applications, that use a data parallel approach to process huge volumes of data like terabytes or petabytes in size and referred to as Big Data.

Data Mining: Data Mining is an analytic process designed to explore data for extracting interesting and relevant patterns.

Distributed System: It consists of autonomous machine nodes connected in a network to, share and coordinate their activities via message passing to achieve a common system goal.

Hadoop: Apache Hadoop is an open-source software framework that supports data-intensive distributed applications, licensed under the Apache v2 license. It supports the running of applications on large clusters of commodity hardware. Hadoop was derived from Google's MapReduce and Google File System (GFS) papers. It implements MapReduce paradigm.

HLQL: High Level Query languages designed for extracting data from Big Data stores.

MapReduce: MapReduce is a parallel programming architecture, proposed by Google and is used to process large data sets via distributing data over cluster of machines maintaining load balancing, parallel processing and sharing of data.

NoSQL: NoSQL systems are also called "Not only SQL" to emphasize non-adherence to fixed schema structures like traditional relational systems. NoSQL systems are simple to use, dynamic and support various big databases via sharding.

Sharding: It is a principle supporting horizontal database partitioning to separate very large datasets into smaller, faster, easily manageable chunks known as shards.

Chapter 11
Towards an Intelligent Integrated Approach for Clinical Decision Support

Rajendra Akerkar
Western Norway Research Institute (Vestlandsforsking), Norway

ABSTRACT

Nowadays, making use of big data is becoming mainstream in different enterprises and industry sectors. The medical sector is no exception. Specifically, medical services, which generate and process enormous volumes of medical information and medical device data, have been quickening big data utilization. In this chapter, we present a concept of an intelligent integrated system for direct support of decision making of physicians. This is a work in progress and the focus is on decision support for pharmacogenomics, which is the study of the relationship between a specific person's genetic makeup and his or her response to drug treatment. Further, we discuss a research direction considering the current shortcomings of clinical decision support systems.

INTRODUCTION

Everyone's talking about the value of big data in medical sector. However, as the data piles up – most of it is isolated in different silos, and health systems are struggling to turn big data from a concept into a reality. By definition, big data in medical sector refers to electronic health data sets so large and complex that they are difficult to manage with traditional software and/or hardware; nor can they be easily managed with traditional or common data management tools and methods (Akerkar, 2013a). Gradually, health-related data will be generated and accumulated, resulting in an enormous *volume* of data. The current medical data includes personal medical records, radiology images, clinical trial data FDA submissions, human genetics and population data genomic sequences, etc. Moreover, new types of big data, such as 3D imaging, genomics and biometric sensor readings, are also stimulating this exponential growth.

Predictably, it takes over 10 years and a billion dollars to develop a new medical treatment for a specific disease. This is because most medications that look promising turn out not to work for many

DOI: 10.4018/978-1-4666-9649-5.ch011

Figure 1. Every person is unique, and drugs that are beneficial for some turn out to be ineffective or unsafe for others

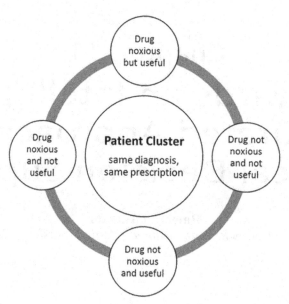

of the patients, and, even worse, some of the patients are harmed by certain drugs (see Figure 1). 50% of medication is prescribed sub-optimally, because it has no effect in particular clusters of people. A sizable fraction of this variability in medication efficacy and safety can be accounted for by individual differences in the 'code' that drives the human organism: the genome. This is addressed by an R&D domain of rapidly increasing importance and popularity: pharmacogenomics (Shin et al., 2009). The promise of pharmacogenomics is to know personal drug response in advance, optimizing the efficiency of medical treatments and avoiding harm. The term pharmacogenomics is often used interchangeably with pharmacogenetics. Although both terms relate to drug response based on genetic influences, pharmacogenetics focuses on single drug-gene interactions, while pharmacogenomics encompasses a more genome-wide association approach, incorporating genomics and epigenetics while dealing with the effects of multiple genes on drug response (Shin et al., 2009).

However, understanding a human genome is not trivial. The genetic code of each of us is made up of three billion letters. How can we help medical doctors and drug developers understand what the three billion letters in each patient's genetic code mean and what the implications of these characters are for finding the best possible medical treatments?

It is becoming increasingly easier and cheaper to obtain the individual genetic code of individual patients. Advances in genetic sequencing in the last decade have made it possible to extract this code faster and cheaper than ever before. Figure 2 shows the cost for sequencing a full human genome since 2001 on a logarithmic scale. It is clear that the cost of sequencing a full human genome is, since 2007, decreased rapidly than exponentially.

Unfortunately, the interpretation of the large quantities of data generated by genetic testing is still associated with many difficulties and costs. This led commentators to speculate that while the $1,000 personal genome has been reached, the current methods for interpreting the data could cost $100,000 for each patient, rendering it infeasible for clinical practice (Mardis, 2010). Furthermore, it is becoming

Figure 2. The cost of sequencing an individual patient genome has fall at surprising rate. (Source: http://www.genome.gov/sequencingcosts/)

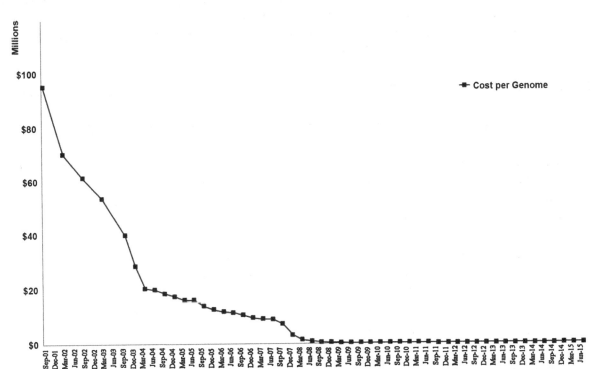

clear that physicians cannot keep all necessary knowledge on the thousands of genetic variants and their effects in their brains.

To realize the promises of personalized, genetic medicine, and the associated reduction in medical treatment costs due to less experimentation before the optimal treatment is found, the development of trustworthy, quick and user-friendly systems for the medical interpretation of large-scale, personal genetic data is of fundamental importance. The interpretation of genetic tests is often hindered by the large amount and the complexity of data they contain. This makes it necessary to provide sophisticated, intuitive tools for rapidly exploring, visualizing and understanding clinically relevant genetic variants in the genome of patients. Furthermore, the use of personal genetic data for medical decision making opens many important questions about the privacy and security of medical data, which need to be addressed.

To be able to make use of pharmacogenomics effectively, we propose a decision support system (HelseDSS) that, given the characteristics of a patient, will suggest the optimum dosage within a few seconds and based on up-to-date evidence. The development of HelseDSS is still in progress. The recommendation made must be fully transparent and verifiable. In many cases, existing clinical information systems do not meet the needs of the user (Feldman, 2010), and may even harm the patient (Han et al., 2005). The systems have yet to fulfil the promise of genomics and personalized medicine (Scheuner et al. 2009, Green & Guyer, 2011), as well as decision support (Sittig et al., 2008).

Outline of the remaining chapter is as follows: Next section 2 describes the datasets to be handled in the proposed system. Then section 3 lists some important existing shortcomings of clinical decision support systems. In section 4, a novel intelligent decision support in 21st century healthcare is presented illustrating our approach to providing evidence based medical decision support and typical use cases. It will allow effective evidence based decisions on drug use based on genetic and other information about patients to be made, as well as new knowledge from the analysis of big medical and clinical data, to be discovered. Major research challenges and issues in developing the suggested approach are discussed in section 5. Finally, section 6 concludes the chapter.

Medical and Clinical Datasets

In general, the types of data foreseen to be available for use by big data analytics include:

- **Genomic data:** Represents significant amounts of new gene sequencing data being made available through new investments, analytics capabilities and business models.
- **Streamed data:** Home monitoring, tele-health, handheld and sensor-based wireless and smart devices are new data sources and types. They represent significant amounts of real time data available for use by the health system.
- **Web and social networking-based data:** Web-based data comes from Google and other search engines, consumer use of the Internet, as well as data from social networking sites.
- **Health publication and clinical reference data:** This includes text-based publications (clinical research and medical reference material) and clinical text based reference practice guidelines and health product (e.g., drug information) data.
- **Clinical data:** Eighty per cent of health data is unstructured as documents, images, clinical or transcribed notes. These semi-structured to unstructured clinical records and documents represent new data sources.
- **Business, organizational and external data:** Data which previously has not been linked, such as financial, billing, scheduling, administrative, external and other non-clinical and non-health data

The type of data to be handled in HelseDSS includes: public biomedical databases, genomic information (e.g., micro-arrays, genotypes), and electronic health records (EHRs) containing demographic info (e.g., age, origin of a person), clinical information (e.g., signs and symptoms), clinical narratives, and other medical data (e.g., laboratory results, drug treatments). An integrated decision support system will integrate this data into knowledge bases (both private and available for research use) to allow more effective use of the data for research and clinical decision support.

To give an idea of the amount of data that exists and will be generated, the output of a gene sequencer typically is a file of around 29 TB. This is then reduced to a sequence reference file (SRF) of around 2TB. An interpreted gene sequence fills around 90GB, and a file showing the deviation from an arbitrary standard sequence around 20GB.

Furthermore, many structured datasets and ontologies have been identified for integration and alignment with the HelseDSS Linked Data infrastructure. These datasets and ontologies is shown in the Table 1.

Examples of some important datasets are: Pharmacogenomics Knowledge Base (PharmGKB), Open Genomes, 1000 Genomes Project, Personal Genome Project, NCBI dbSNP, NCBI ClinVar, SNPedia, OMIM, GEN2PHEN Knowledge Center, HuGE Navigator, SwissVar, Entrez-Gene/GeneRiFs, Gene Ontology Association (GOA), DrugBank and PharmaADME.

Quality control will be a major challenge when dealing with the data (Akerkar, 2013b), in particular for text and sequence-derived data. In both cases, the interpretation pipeline is complex and requires strict methodological processes. Thus, web harvested data require de-duplication, as alerts tend to generate

Table 1. Examples of relevant ontologies and terminologies

Type	Name	Description
All of translational and personalized medicine	Translational Medicine Ontology (TMO)	An ontology covering key aspects of the entire spectrum of translational and personalized medicine, developed by participants of the W3C Heath Care and Life Science Interest Group.
Anatomy	Foundational Model of Anatomy (FMA)	Ontology for the canonical, anatomical structure of an organism.
Chemical	ChEBI	Chemical Entities of Biological Interest (ChEBI) is a dictionary of molecular entities focused on 'small' chemical compounds.
Clinical descriptors	SNOMED CT	The broadest coverage medical nomenclature.
Clinical descriptors for Patient Summary and e-Prescription	epSOS'MVC	The epSOS meta-thesaurus, aggregating subsets of 45 different clinical terminologies including ICD-10, LOINC andWHO-ATC.
Diagnosis	ICD	The WHO International classification of diseases.
Gene products	Gene Ontology	Molecular functions, Subcellular locations and biological processes.
Gene products	NextProt Terminology	Human anatomical entity (body parts, cells, tissues, gestational structures)
Gene products	GO evidence codes	Qualitative tracking of evidences for manual curation and automatic annotation of proteins
Laboratory	Logical Observation Identifiers Names and Codes (LOINC)	An established coding system for clinical lab results. Contains many identifiers for results of genetic.
PGx	Suggested Ontology For Pharmacogenomics (SO-Pharm)	A complex ontology that represents phenotype, genotype, treatment and their relationships in groups of patients. SO-Pharm has been designed to guide knowledge discovery in pharmacogenomics.
Medicinal products	WHO-ATC	The WHO Anatomic, Therapeutic and Chemical classification for medicinal chemistry.
Phenotype	Disease Ontology	Ontology of human diseases.
Phenotype	Phenotypic Quality Ontology (PATO)	A general ontology of qualities that can be used to describe phenotypes
Safety	Medical Dictionary for Regulatory Activities (MedDRA)	A terminology currently for safety reporting (mandated in Europe and Japan for safety reporting, standard for adverse event reporting in the U.S.).
Safety	WHO-ADR	The WHO Adverse Drug Reaction Terminology, the international legacy reporting system for post market surveillance.

sizeable echoes. Further, data cleansing is a key problem with web contents as the focus of the alert is often surrounded by significant noise (site map, facets, table of contents, related and less related news…). Similarly, data generated by modern sequencers (e.g., Illumina) require careful tuning and sometimes expert interpretation (polymorphisms vs. mutations…) out of source image files. Similarly, the massive quantities of data generated by high-throughput sequencers (Illumina, Solid, IonTorrent etc.) provide particular challenges for quality evaluation and the algorithms are evolving rapidly. There is currently a conflict between the desire to retain as much quality information as possible (raw data), or to reduce the storage size by irreversibly interpreting the sequence and including quality annotation (FASTQ and similar formats). A secondary level of interpretation is the functional evaluation of sequence changes (pathogenic and predicted severity, versus benign). This currently requires a high degree of expert curation although some algorithms are becoming progressively more commonly used (SIFT and PolyPhen, among others).

Table 2 lists some datasets that will be incorporated into the HelseDSS Linked Data infrastructure.

We conclude this section with an assessment of the characteristics of big medical data. This assessment is illustrated in Table 3.

Shortcomings of Healthcare Decision Support Systems

Existing clinical decision support systems suffer from shortcomings that are difficult to overcome (Akerkar & Sajja, 2010; Varonen, 2008; Castaneda, 2015). There is a vital need for high-quality, efficient means of designing, developing, presenting, implementing, evaluating, and maintaining different types

Table 2. Externally available structured datasets

Name	Description
1000 Genomes Project	Genome sequences of over 1000 volunteers. http://www.1000genomes.org/data
Cochrane Library	A reference digital library for clinical practice guidelines. http://www.cochrane.org/
dbGaP	Results of studies that have investigated the interaction of genotype and phenotype. http://www.ncbi.nlm.nih.gov/gap
DrugBank	A knowledge base for drugs. http://drugbank.ca/
Entrez-Gene/GeneRiFs	Mapping between author-submitted Gene Ontology descriptors and short textual passages extracted from full-text articles (identified by PubMed Identifiers, or PMID). http://www.ncbi.nlm.nih.gov/projects/GeneRIF/
Gene Ontology Association (GOA)	Mapping between all Gene Ontology annotation and gene products, with evidence codes and PubMed Identifiers (PMID) when available. http://www.ebi.ac.uk/GOA/
Genetic Association Database (GAD)	Diseases associated with genetic variants. http://geneticassociationdb.nih.gov
Genotator	Aggregated gene-disease relation data containing an integrated view over other datasets. http://genotator.hms.harvard.edu/geno/
GET-Evidence	Automatically annotated and then manually curated information about the impact of genetic variations. http://evidence.personalgenomes.org/
International HapMap project data	Catalog of common genetic variants that occur in human beings. http://hapmap.ncbi.nlm.nih.gov/
Genome Consortium data	Comprehensive catalogues of genomic abnormalities (somatic mutations, abnormal expression of genes, epigenetic modifications) in tumours from 25 different cancer types. http://tcga-data.nci.nih.gov/tcga/
HuGE Navigator	Genetic variants, gene-disease associations, gene-gene and gene-environment interactions, and evaluation of genetic tests. http://www.hugenavigator.net/

Table 3. 5V in medical sector

Volume	- Massive datasets from electronic health records (EHRs) - Large drug datasets - Huge R&D datasets, e.g. genomics
Variety	- Quantitative data, e.g. laboratory values - Qualitative data, e.g. text documents, medical images, demographics - Transactional data, e.g. records of medical delivery
Velocity	- Patient monitoring, especially in intensive healthcare
Veracity	- Improve data quality - Detection of inconsistencies and anomalies - Combination of medical data
Value	- Knowledge creation from the analysis of EHRs - Improved access to data, e.g. clinical guidelines - Improving efficiency and reducing operational costs

of clinical decision support capabilities for physicians, patients and consumers. Within broad categories, we identified important shortcomings, which we briefly describe below.

1. A lack of publicly available formally represented biomedical and clinical knowledge associating clinical findings with treatment recommendations. Genetic data is not taken into account in medical care, even though this is expected to be affordable soon, and extremely affordable within 5 years.
2. A lack of robust, reliable, evidence-based clinical decision support value model.
3. A lack of integration of decision support systems into existing workflows. In order to be successful, systems must not require time-pressured medical professionals to launch new software, or jump between screens of computers to input data to benefit from the system.
4. Most clinical care guidelines for condition or medication management ignore the fact that the majority of elderly patients have multiple co-morbidities and medications that must be addressed by their patient care team (Boyd, 2005). There is a lack of mechanisms to identify and eliminate redundant, contraindicated, potentially discordant, or mutually exclusive guideline-based recommendations for patients presenting with co-morbid conditions or multiple medications.
5. A lack of actionable patient data in electronic health record systems.
6. A lack of standardized ways of representing clinical data and findings, e.g., allergies, drug intolerance, phenotypic features, disease occurrence in close family members.

DECISION SUPPORT SYSTEM

Our approach is to develop a clinical decision support system that translates genetic, clinical and research information into accurate advice on choice and dosage of medical treatment, in order to reduce the number and impact of adverse drug reactions and other side effects. The service must be accessible every time a physician makes a decision about drug treatment of a patient.

Research databases associating genotypes with phenotypes (including clinically relevant phenotypes) are growing at an enormous pace, and HelseDSS merges and links these databases with anonymized clinical data to facilitate the use of these findings for improving medical decision making. Access and privacy control for clinical data will be implemented.

A single test (genotyping, sequencing) can yield a very large amount of clinically relevant data for each person. HelseDSS takes genetic information into account in mining the data to locate genotype-phenotype correlations. This could be used to optimize future treatment decisions in a wide variety of unanticipated ways.

The HelseDSS approach to providing the required evidence-based medical decision support is illustrated in the following Figure 3.

HelseDSS processes and functions are based on a service oriented, standards-based and semantically enabled architecture that makes it as easy as possible to connect to existing IT solutions that are routinely used in hospital settings. HelseDSS deals with storing and processing a huge amount of data at multiple sites, as well as replicating and synchronising a large central knowledge base to multiple sites. Both data-centred and component-centred integration approaches will be adopted. When the system is used on resources available for research purposes ("Outside World"), the data-centred integration will result in the creation of a research knowledge base integrating a large number of resources. Behind a firewall ("Hospital"), the data-centred integration will create a private knowledge base populated from the private data of the institution. The key step in the data-centred integration occurs now: the research knowledge base will be regularly replicated behind the firewall and integrated with the private knowledge base. As not all research results are directly applicable to healthcare (they could be observations, validated research finding or clinically validated findings), the system cannot perform a completely automated integration of research and private data. The system will therefore flag any potentially interesting results to the relevant responsible person, who will have to make the decision on whether to include the research results or not in the integrated knowledge base. The data in the combined private and research knowledge base now

Figure 3. The approach to providing evidence based HelseDSS

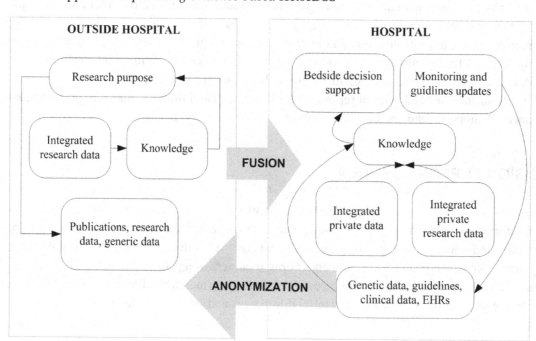

forms that basis for the decision support system for physicians to use at the patients' bedsides. Entries that the physicians make in the EHRs will flow into the private knowledge base in a virtuous cycle. It will also be possible to use the visual analytics tools developed in HelseDSS to analyse the data in the knowledge bases to identify trends and new knowledge within the institution. The final link between the

"Hospital" and the "Outside World" will be the carefully controlled and monitored transfer of de-identified and anonymised EHRs into the "Outside World" to enhance the clinical knowledge available for researchers. The component-centred integration will be done using a Service-Oriented Architecture (SOA) approach. This approach is very effective at solving the problem of integrating a set of diverse software components. Scalability to the processing of huge amounts of data in a reasonable time will be attained through the deployment of the processes on a cloud infrastructure, as well as by the use of software frameworks supporting distributed computing, such as Hadoop and MapReduce.

All diagnoses and treatment decisions entered into the EHR are interpreted and evaluated silently and automatically by the HelseDSS system, with alerts and recommendations only being given when ideal clinical practiceis not being performed.

HelseDSS advances the use of Linked Data technologies and datasets as the basis for automated decision support by filling existing gaps between clinical guidelines, which are stored in texts, and computerized physician order entry, which operates on structured data.

Further, HelseDSS uses a user-centered design process to ensure that the system is designed with guidance and inputs from physicians and hospital staff.

Typical Use Cases

We now describe typical representative and challenging pharmacogenomics use cases. These diverse use cases will ensure that the HelseDSS solution is not a narrow solution for one clinical department in a single hospital (which is often the case with existing decision support systems), but that it is a single framework applicable in departments practicing different medical specialities in varied locations (with different data formats and systems), and extensible to even more. Use case 1 focuses on a specific drug, while Use Cases 2 and 3 focus on wider domains based on medical conditions instead of individual drugs.

Use Case 1: It focuses on pharmacogenomics for the dosage of a single clinically-important drug, Warfarin, on which there already exist many publications on which to base the decision support system.
Use Case 2: focuses on cardiovascular diseases, some of which are potentially treatable by Warfarin – this use case can therefore make direct use of results from Use Case 1, but in the wider domain of all cardiovascular diseases and all drugs used to treat them.
Use Case 3: focuses on a different area, that of renal transplantation. It is a specific area of high importance on which the probability of a clinically useful outcome from HelseDSS is extremely high.

Getting new technology implemented in hospitals is not straightforward. In order to create a decision support system that physicians will use, a user-centered design process should be adopted. The clinical process of problem statement, information gathering, hypothesis forming, decision on action and planning involves information on and knowledge of drugs in several phases. The phases are themselves fragmented by changing actors, division of medical specialties and advanced investigation modalities and changes in patient state. Also, the clinical work is performed in different organizational settings and geographical locations, within various levels of health care and with various time frames of planning. This means that the primary user will need access to the service in a multitude of contexts with a multitude of mindsets. The analysis involved in user-centered design typically utilizes *personas* (i.e. fictional characters or roles for which the design is made for), *scenarios* (i.e. 'daily life' stories about how a persona performs common tasks, and the context they are performed in) and *Use Cases* (i.e. structured descriptions of desired interactions between and individual and the system or environment).

RESEARCH DIRECTION

There are many technical challenges that must be addressed to realize the full potential of big medical data. The problem in healthcare is not the lack of data but the lack of information that can be used to support decision-making, planning and strategy. These data need to be validated, processed and integrated into a large data source to enable meaningful analysis. Outlined below are some of the specific research challenges in HelseDSS.

Mining Big Healthcare Data

Access to medical information by physicians is mostly done using the standard approach of typing search terms into a search box and returning a list of relevant documents.

In the market there exist several medical decision support systems (Zhang, 2012). However, many systems are based on conventional technologies, such as decision tree, Bayesian network and neural network. These technologies are stable and reliable, but they all required consuming the data as static database. Each model reviving has to go through the entire dataset again. There are very few systems that adopt data stream mining algorithms. Data Stream Mining is the process of extracting useful information from continuous, rapid data streams. It is a wide concept and it involves many technical areas such as classification, detection, and clustering. Mining big data streams faces three key challenges: volume, velocity, and volatility. Volume and velocity require a high volume of data to be processed in limited time. Starting from the first inward instance, the amount of available data constantly increases from zero to potentially infinity. This requires incremental approaches that incorporate information as it becomes available, and online processing if not all data can be kept (Gama, 2010). Volatility, instead, relates to a dynamic environment with ever-changing patterns. However, in real-world applications these three challenges often coincide with other, to date insufficiently considered ones.

In HelseDSS, focus is on developing methods targeted at extracting information, including semi-structured contents (biomedical databases, libraries, and medical reports), genetic sequences, Linked Data and targeted numerical information specific to the domain of translational medicine, this emerging borderline area where healthcare meets with post-genomic medicine. Such a move requires the development of more precise algorithms able to access a deeper understanding of textual contents. In particular, the following research directions are envisaged (see Figure 4):

1. Entity recognition, i.e. biomedical entities will be recognized to be able to exploit linked data repositories (e.g., generic, specific concepts). This recognition will work on very specific concepts in the area of pharmacogenomics, and will demonstrate specialization of entity recognition to a narrow domain;

Figure 4. Relevant datasets are captured in the HelseDSS Linked Data infrastructure. These linked datasets are used as the basis for the creation of clinical decision support system which can reason over individual patient data at critical time points in the care process, e.g., when medical professionals are prescribing drugs.

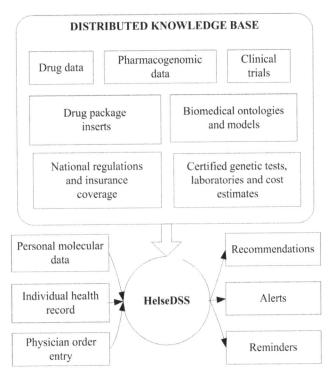

2. Reconciliation of Biomedical entities (e.g., biological entities such as phenotypes or drug dose must be "connected" to clinical entities such as respectively diagnosis and adverse effects);

3. The document/passage retrieval model will evolve towards answer retrieval, i.e. possible answers to a user question will be computed at query-time without human intervention;

4. Answers must be re-computed/adapted as new document flows are added to the document repository;

5. The arbitrary separation between structured (relational or linked databases) and unstructured data (texts, sequences…) will be replaced by seamless multimodal interactions;

6. Background knowledge will be articulated with time-series to separate between relevant and irrelevant answers, but also between trivial and context-pertinent answers (e.g., in an infectious disease department, respiratory pathology symptoms should be more likely associated with pathogen-induced pneumopathies while the same symptoms should more likely be associated with asthma in an allergy service).

In information retrieval, we are going beyond the search box paradigm by removing the necessity for physicians to formulate and enter questions or search queries in their day-to-day work. Techniques will be developed so that the system will, in the background, retrieve pertinent information based on documents that the physician is looking at (such as an EHR), information on the current activity in the physician's workflow (e.g., diagnosis or prescription) and results of decision support and prediction algorithms. It will indicate the availability of the information and display it if requested, also using visualization instruments to highlight possible deviations and significant trend changes. It requires automatic query generation, which has been done for generating queries from patents for patent search (Xue & Croft, 2009), but will be extended in HelseDSS to handle the more complex EHRs. Modifying automatically generated queries and documents retrieved based on the current activity in a workflow is a particularly challenging task that has received little attention so far, as feed-back loops tend to rely on the user intervention. In HelseDSS, its application in a clinical setting will be developed. For example, for physicians working in a diagnosis step, the system could retrieve genes potentially associated with symptoms occurring in the EHR to guide the choice of a genetic test as listed in databases such as Orphanet; once the genetic test results are back, the system could extract the relevant sections of guidelines to assist the physician in interpretation.

The work in HelseDSS will focus on the automated query and question generation, as well as on the continuous generation of updates and possibly alerts.

Linked Data

The Semantic Web (SW) provides ample amount of structured interconnected data. As increasingly RDF data is contributed to the SW, questions arise on how the user can access this body of knowledge in a natural manner. Linked Data-driven question answering systems have caught much attention recently, as these systems allow users, even with a limited familiarity of technical systems and databases, to pose questions in a natural way and gain insights of the data available. Linked data gained popularity as a platform for integration because its capabilities to translate heterogeneous information into a common web accessible model. Linked Data (Bizer, 2009) uses the Web as the information space to publish structured data rather than documents on the Web. In Linked Data, Uniform Resource Identifiers (URIs) are used to identify resources and Resource Description Framework (RDF) is used to describe resources. URIs are to data as what Uniform Resource Locators (URLs) are to web pages, providing identifications to resources; and RDF is to data as what HTML is to documents, providing descriptions about a resource in a machine-processable representation format.

While the distributed nature of the linked data model looks very attractive and largely addresses many of the problems related to data ownership and licensing, it often fails to match the requirements for a high-performance data access. In response to this challenge the SPARQL language specification now supports extended functionality that describes service federation. The new language constructs provides a non-transparent way of combining data between endpoints and greatly reduce the query optimization task. Still, the performance of SPARQL queries executed against remote endpoints spread over Internet will be slower than the local solutions due the lack of network latency and supposedly the tighter protocol and implementation integration allowing better data statistics usage.

There is a need for study on how to efficiently integrate and manage private and public research knowledge with linked data technologies. For instance, efforts towards combining and evaluating a mix of integration patterns include:

1. Warehousing of public or private, heterogeneous data, which will require data cleaning and transformation.
2. Replication of large and complex RDF datasets between public and private warehouse

3.   Reliable federated queries between endpoints, where query complexity allows it and the dataset license requires it.

Pattern Recognition

Machine learning and pattern recognition are well established in various different domains. In today's environment, healthcare industry must balance between the often conflicting goals of cost reduction and enhancing quality of care. With growing costs and rising populations comes an inevitable paradigm shift towards liable care where organizations are aiming on cost reduction, standardized care and quality improvement like never before. In addition, with the information overload in medical literature coupled with the difficulty in inferring evidence from clinical trials to real world settings, providers find it difficult to select appropriate therapy for each patient. Thus far, healthcare has lagged behind other industries in improving operational performance and adopting technology-enabled process improvements.

It is possible to address these challenges by emulating and implementing best practices in health care by analyzing large amount of available information (extensive electronic health records recording patient conditions, diagnostic tests, labs, imaging exams, genomics, proteomics, treatments, outcomes, claims, financial records, clinical guidelines and best practices etc.). This data contains tremendously valuable hidden information relevant both for clinical and non-clinical decision support. At the heart of healthcare analytics is the ability to recognize (identify, classify and discover) patterns from the information available. As such, pattern recognition plays a crucial role in the future of healthcare, specifically in healthcare analytics.

Many algorithms in this area work on relatively simple data structures, such as vector and numerical data. However, over the past two decades and particularly in the biomedical domain, a plethora of knowledge bases with more complex data structures have emerged. These knowledge bases use logical languages such as OWL, have well-defined semantics and the underlying data often has a graph-like structure, i.e., there are relationships and dependencies between different entities in a knowledge base.

Accompanying this trend, machine learning approaches for analyzing data that display such richness (e.g., Inductive Logic Programming approaches such as Aleph and Statistical Relational Learning) have been developed. An inherent challenge when applying those approaches is the size of the search space they have to tackle: More complex target languages, such as expressive description logics or first order logics, lead to an increased search space. Even when incomplete or approximate inference mechanisms are employed in those algorithms, this challenge remains.

One particular type of algorithm, which has been researched in the context of the Semantic Web, is concept learning methods for description logics (DLs). Starting from the early 90s, there have been a number of different approaches to learn in DLs. A common problem of those approaches was that they generated classifiers which are hard to understand by humans due to their syntactic. It provides a range of different algorithms, which scale better than previous approaches, because of using approximate reasoning, knowledge fragment selection and statistical sampling. They were also extended to cover more expressive description logics, e.g., those underlying OWL. Those approaches were applied to various benchmarks in the biomedical domain, such as predicting whether chemical compounds cause cancer. However, a weakness of those approaches is that they still fail to find very complex patterns. Furthermore, those approaches classify by learning a single concept. So we need to extend this to, e.g., learning several clues in favor or against certain treatment options to give the practitioner a better overview and to better be able to assess the uncertainty associated with each treatment option. The immediate research innovations required are:

1. Development of frequent pattern analysis methods as pre-processing step for concept learning algorithms.
2. Extension of existing learning algorithms to richer target languages, such as description logics.
3. Extension of the standard binary learning problem to learning clues for classification. E.g., instead of only giving a single reason on why a treatment may be suitable, we will extend this to provide several (weighted) clues, leading to more fine-grained and precise classifiers with little computational overhead.

Evidence and Risk Computation

The statistical data can be represented as a large graph that encompasses knowledge on the interactions between evidence and risks. In current machine learning literature, such graphs are often encoded with the framework of Bayesian networks and Decision Graphs (Jensen and Nielsen, 2007). Bayesian Networks have been used profoundly in the biomedical literature for purposes as diverse as gene expression analysis (Friedman et al., 2000) and cancer probability modelling (Burnside et al., 2006). In addition, comorbidity networks such as the Hudine network have been used to study the effect of the co-occurrence of illnesses amongst large populations of patients.

Yet, while these approaches have been used all across biology, the combination of Network Learning and comorbidity networks is still rather new (Strong and Oakley, 2011). No approaches for the analysis of large-scale networks that combine large evidence vectors for each node has been implemented so far to the best of our knowledge.

In order to combine large multi-layer comorbidity networks obtained from data including genotypic, demographic and phenotypic data with the idea of Bayesian networks to enable multi-level decision support. For implementing novel and scalable algorithms for the time-efficient assessment of risks based on our multi-layered networks, we must lead to:

1. Development of efficient storage solutions for large-scale multi-layered comorbidity networks
2. Transformation approaches for converting multi-layered networks into Bayesian networks
3. Development of active learning approach for the training of large-scale networks.
4. Development of scalable (incomplete) approach for the time-efficient computation of risks based on the evidence data given by medical doctors.

Visual Analytics

While huge amounts of data are available from EMRs, it is critical to develop new methods for extracting knowledge from this data in order to optimize treatments, improve the quality of patient care, and increase the likelihood of positive patient outcomes. The solution to bridge the gap between available data and improved patient care and outcomes lies in using computational methods combined with visual representations of data and data analytics. The symbiotic coupling of analytics and visualization can be achieved using Visual Analytics (VA) techniques. Visual Analytics denotes the science of analytical reasoning facilitated by interactive visual interfaces and appropriate visualization techniques (Thomas and Cook, 2005). User interactions are one of the most important elements in visualization, and are even more important in Visual Analytics, as studies like (Saraiya, 2006) showed: users preferred inferior visualizations with interaction over superior static visualizations. Furthermore, visual representations provide only an initial direction to the data and its meaning, but through the combination of visual representations and appropriate interaction mechanisms, the users achieve insights into large and complex data sets. Analysis methods are commonly defined as the application of algorithms to extract useful structures from large volumes of data. It is a multidisciplinary field integrating work from areas including Statistics, Machine Learning, Information Retrieval, Database technology, and Neural Networks. Thus, key research challenges are:

1. Presenting the information is a way that physicians can use to make rapid but informed decisions, and the medical researchers can use to gain deep insight into the results.
2. Large and complex data sets cannot be visualized as a whole. So, one has to design and develop task-specific interaction methods, so that physicians and researchers can explore these data sets.
3. Another way to overcome the information overload is the tight integration of interactive visualization and analysis methods.
4. Designing Visual Analytics methods for particular users using particular data (or datasets) and performing particular tasks or achieving particular goals.
5. Avoiding complex user interfaces and data structures; giving users a rapid overview of information that is available, but also about information that is *not* available.

Privacy and Reliability

In addition to the above challenges, privacy and security are critical issues. Privacy in particular raises many concern as big data could be used to re-identify privacy-sensitive data even when this data has been anonymized. Also big data can be used to create profiles of user groups that may be used for discriminating specific groups of individuals or even single individuals. In this respect, population privacy is as crucial as personal privacy.

Moreover, data streams present new challenges and also opportunities with respect to protecting privacy and confidentiality in data mining. Privacy preserving data mining has been researched for over a decade (Agrawal & Srikant, 2000). The key goal is to develop such data mining techniques that would not uncover information or patterns which compromise confidentiality and privacy obligations. Modeling can be done on original or anonymized data, but when the model is released, it should not contain information that may violate privacy or confidentiality. This is usually achieved by controlled distortion of sensitive data by modifying the values or adding noise. We identify two main challenges for privacy preservation in mining data streams. The first challenge is incompleteness of information. Data arrives in portions and the model is updated online. Therefore, the model is never final and it is difficult to judge privacy preservation before seeing all the data. The second important challenge for privacy preservation is concept drift. As data may evolve over time, fixed privacy preservation rules may no longer hold. Hence, one of the important directions for future research is to develop adaptive privacy preservation mechanisms, which would diagnose such a situation and adapt themselves to preserve privacy in the new circumstances.

Today's biomedical domain is characterized by the ever growing amounts of data produced. Therefore IT systems are an absolute necessity to handle EHRs, genome information, or other types of medical data. These IT systems not only provide storage and processing mechanisms, they also facilitate data sharing and thus help to improve patient care. However, keeping these vast amounts of information secure has become a major challenge. In the biomedical domain, security is not limited to the traditional security properties of confidentiality, integrity, and availability. When sensitive personal data are involved, privacy is also of a big concern. Legal acts such as the Health Insurance Portability and Accountability Act (HIPAA) or the Directive 95/46/EC regulate the usage and disclosure of sensitive information, but are often not properly implemented. Although generally accepted as critical, applying security and privacy-enhancing mechanisms is still regarded as necessary nuisance. As a result, concepts such as security and privacy are usually considered at the end of the development process and related measures are implemented as add-ons, often leading to considerable impairment in the system performance and efficiency. Another side effect of this practice is that some aspects can be overlooked. Thus security gaps may still exist.

State-of-the-art authentication and authorization mechanisms are important to ensure that only valid users are granted access to the system, and privacy-enhancing technologies are properly installed to protect data both at rest and in-motion. Anonymisation and pseudonymisation techniques are necessary when creating the large scale knowledge base in order to prevent unintended information leakage and ensure unlinkability, while still preserving data expressiveness and usefulness. The involvement of genomic information, both in raw form as well as in processed forms such as single nucleotide polymorphisms, adds to the complexity of the privacy problem due to its identifying nature.

CONCLUSION

The leveraging of Big Data is accelerating in medical sector. What is required for further advancement of healthcare is analysis based on integrated data, such as clinical data and genomic analysis data, life data including SNS and other data, and data collected from home medical devices for remote medical care and disease management.

Most medications turn out not to work for many patients, and, even worse, some patients are harmed by certain medications. 50% of medication is prescribed suboptimally, because it has no effect in particular groups of people. A sizable fraction of this variability in medication efficacy and safety can be accounted for by individual differences in the genome. Based on current trends, it will cost $1000 to sequence the human genome from 2014, leading to the increased use of full genome sequencing in daily medical treatment. However, due to the size of the data, the current methods for interpreting the data could cost €100,000 for each patient, rendering them infeasible for clinical practice. To realize the promises of personalized, genetic medicine, and the associated reduction in medical treatment costs due to less experimentation before the optimal treatment is found, the development of trustworthy, quick and user-friendly systems for the medical interpretation of large-scale, personal genetic data by physicians is of fundamental importance.

To realize the promises of personalized, genetic medicine, and the associated reduction in medical treatment costs due to less experimentation before the optimal treatment is found, the development of trustworthy, quick and user-friendly systems for the medical interpretation of large-scale, personal genetic data by physicians is of fundamental importance.

As the basis of the decision support system, discussed decision support approach will convert very large and complex datasets into actionable medical insight by dynamically integrating, correlating, fusing and analyzing extremely large pharmacogenomic resources, including anonymized genetic data, anonymized patient data and scientific publications to create a large semantically enabled pharmacogenomic research knowledge base.

REFERENCES

Agrawal, R., & Srikant, R. (2000). Privacy-preserving data mining. *SIGMOD Record, 29*(2), 439–450. doi:10.1145/335191.335438

Akerkar, R. (2013a). *Big Data Computing*. Chapman and Hall/CRC. doi:10.1201/b16014

Rajendra Akerkar (2013b). Improving Data Quality on Big and High-Dimensional Data. *Journal of Bioinformatics and Intelligent Control, 2*(1), 155-162.

Bizer, C., Heath, T., & Berners-Lee, T. (2009). Linked data - the story so far. Int J Semantic Web Inf Syst. *Special Issue on Linked Data, 53*(3), 1–22.

Boyd, C. M., Darer, J., Boult, C., Fried, L. P., Boult, L., & Wu, A. W. (2005). Clinical practice guidelines and quality of care for older patients with multiple comorbid diseases: Implications for pay for performance. *Journal of the American Medical Association, 294*(6), 716–724. doi:10.1001/jama.294.6.716 PMID:16091574

Burnside, E. S., Rubin, D. L., Fine, J. P., Shachter, R. D., Sisney, G. A., & Leung, W. K. (2006). Bayesian network to predict breast cancer risk of mammographic microcalcifications and reduce number of benign biopsy results: Initial experience. *Radiology, 240*(3), 666–673. doi:10.1148/radiol.2403051096 PMID:16926323

Castaneda, C., Nalley, K., Mannion, C., Bhattacharyya, P., Blake, P., Pecora, A., & Suh, K. S. et al. (2015). Clinical decision support systems for improving diagnostic accuracy and achieving precision medicine. *Journal of Clinical Bioinformatics, 5*(1), 4. doi:10.1186/s13336-015-0019-3 PMID:25834725

Feldman, E. (2010, December 22). A piece of my mind. The day the computer tried to eat my alligator. *Journal of the American Medical Association, 304*(24), 2679. doi:10.1001/jama.2010.1805 PMID:21177498

Friedman, N., Linial, M., Nachman, I., & Pe'er, D. (2000). Using Bayesian Networks to Analyze Expression Data. *Journal of Computational Biology, 7*(3/4), 601–620. doi:10.1089/106652700750050961 PMID:11108481

Gama, J. (2010). *Knowledge Discovery from Data Streams*. Chapman & Hall/CRC. doi:10.1201/EBK1439826119

Green, E. D., Guyer, M. S., Green, E. D., Guyer, M. S., Manolio, T. A., & Peterson, J. L. (2011, February 10). Charting a course for genomic medicine from base pairs to bedside. *Nature*, *470*(7333), 204–213. doi:10.1038/nature09764 PMID:21307933

Jensen, F. V., & Nielsen, T. D. (2007). *Bayesian Networks and Decision Graphs. Information Science and Statistics series* (2nd ed.). Springer. doi:10.1007/978-0-387-68282-2

Mardis, E. R. (2010, November 26). The $1,000 genome, the $100,000 analysis? *Genome Medicine*, *2*(11), 84. doi:10.1186/gm205 PMID:21114804

Rajendra Akerkar. (2010). *Priti Sajja*. Knowledge Based Systems, Jones & Bartlett Pub.

Saraiya, P., North, C., Vy Lam, , & Duca, K. A. (2006). An Insight-Based Longitudinal Study of Visual Analytics. *IEEE Transactions on Visualization and Computer Graphics*, *12*(6), 1. doi:10.1109/TVCG.2006.85 PMID:17073373

Scheuner, M. T., de Vries, H., Kim, B., Meili, R. C., Olmstead, S. H., & Teleki, S. (2009, July). Are electronic health records ready for genomic medicine? *Genetics in Medicine: Official Journal of the American College of Medical Genetics*, *11*(7), 510–517. doi:10.1097/GIM.0b013e3181a53331 PMID:19478682

Shin, J., Kayser, S. R., & Langaee, T. Y. (2009). Pharmacogenetics: From discovery to patient care. *American Journal of Health-System Pharmacy*, *66*(7), 625–637. doi:10.2146/ajhp080170 PMID:19299369

Sittig, D. F., Wright, A., Osheroff, J. A., Middleton, B., Teich, J. M., Ash, J. S., & Bates, D. W. et al. (2008, April). Grand challenges in clinical decision support. *Journal of Biomedical Informatics*, *41*(2), 387–392. doi:10.1016/j.jbi.2007.09.003 PMID:18029232

Strong, M., & Oakley, J. (2011). Bayesian Inference for Comorbid Disease Risks Using Marginal Disease Risks and Correlation Information From a Separate Source. *Medical Decision Making*, *31*(4), 571–581. doi:10.1177/0272989X10391269 PMID:21212441

Thomas, J. J., & Cook, K. A. (2005). *Illuminating the Path: The Research and Development Agenda for Visual Analytics*. IEEE Computer Society.

Varonen, Kortteisto, & Kaila. (2008). What may help or hinder the implementation of computerized decision support systems (CDSSs): a focus group study with physicians. *Family Practice, 25*(3), 162-167. doi:10.1093/fampra/cmn020

Yong, Y. (2005, December). Unexpected Increased Mortality After Implementation of a Commercially Sold Computerized Physician Order Entry System. *Pediatrics*, *116*(6), 1506–1512. doi:10.1542/peds.2005-1287 PMID:16322178

Xue, X., & Croft, W. B. (2012). Automatic query generation for patent search. In *Proceedings of the 18th ACM conference on Information and knowledge management* (CIKM '09). Academic Press.

Zhang, F. Fiaidhi, & Mohammed. (2012). Real-Time Clinical Decision Support System with Data Stream Mining. *Journal of Biomedicine and Biotechnology*. doi:10.1145/1645953.1646295

KEY TERMS AND DEFINITIONS

Analytics: Using software-based algorithms and statistics to derive meaning from data.

Big Data: Big Data refers to the new technologies and applications introduced to handle increasing Volumes of data while enhancing data utilization capabilities such as Variety, Velocity, Variability, Veracity, and Value.

Data Analytics: The application of software to derive information or meaning from data. The end result might be a report, an indication of status, or an action taken automatically based on the information received.

Health Record: Historically, the definition of a legal medical record seemed straightforward. The contents of the paper chart formed the provider of care's legal business record.

Healthcare Decision Support System: It is an electronic system designed to aid directly in medical decision making, in which characteristics of individual patients are used to generate patient-specific assessments or recommendations that are then presented to clinicians for consideration.

Linked Data: A pattern for hyperlinking machine-readable data sets to each other using Semantic Web techniques, especially via the use of RDF and URIs. Enables distributed SPARQL queries of the data sets and a browsing or discovery approach to finding information (as compared to a search strategy). Linked Data is intended for access by both humans and machines. Linked Data uses the RDF family of standards for data interchange (e.g., RDF/XML, RDFa, Turtle) and query (SPARQL). If Linked Data is published on the public Web, it is generally called *Linked Open Data.*

Remote Patient Monitoring: monitoring of patients outside of conventional clinical settings (e.g. in the home), which may increase access to care and decrease medical delivery costs; a type of ambulatory healthcare that allows a patient to use a mobile medical device to perform a routine test and send the test data to a medical professional in real-time.

Scalability: The ability of a system or process to maintain acceptable performance levels as workload or scope increases.

Semantic Web: A project of the World Wide Web Consortium (W3C) to encourage the use of a standard format to include semantic content on websites. The goal is to enable computers and other devices to better process data.

Semi-Structured Data: Data that is not structured by a formal data model, but provides other means of describing the data and hierarchies.

Structured Data: Data that is organized by a predetermined structure.

Section 4
Big Data:
Other Application

Chapter 12
Information Processing for Disaster Communications

Yuko Murayama
Iwate Prefectural University, Japan

Dai Nishioka
Iwate Prefectural University, Japan

Nor Athiyah Binti Abdullah
Iwate Prefectural University, Japan

ABSTRACT

This chapter presents the issues on disaster communications. The Great East Japan Earthquake on March 11th, 2011 caused severe damage to the northern coast of the main island in Japan. We report our support activities in Iwate prefecture as well as our findings and experiences. We call disaster communications in this chapter. disaster communications. Following the requests from many organizations and groups of people, we started our support for the disaster area with a few of us in the department of Software and Information Science, Iwate Prefectural University ten days after the disaster. Through our support activities we came across an interesting issue concerning collaboration with people from heterogeneous backgrounds. Disagreements and distrust happened quite easily. We found that trust plays an important role in such communications. In our chapter, we introduce disaster communications as an area for research and practice as well as our trials on the recovery phase after the emergency response.

INTRODUCTION

In this chapter, we introduce the issues on disaster communications. The Great East Japan Earthquake and Tsunami on March 11th, 2011 caused severe damage to the northern coast of the main island in Japan. 15892 people died, 2576 are missing and 6152 are injured (National Police Agency of Japan, 2015). The disaster also caused more global problems due to the nuclear power plant incidents. Following the requests from many organizations and groups of people, we started our support for the disaster area with a few of us in the department of Software and Information Science, Iwate Prefectural University ten days after

DOI: 10.4018/978-1-4666-9649-5.ch012

the disaster. Our activities included collecting local information on requirements for IT equipment and internetworking services in the affected area as well as distributing IT equipment donated by industry. We got the information on such needs by communicating with people in the various local government entities and with a volunteer center in Iwate Prefecture. We also set up a mailing list with those people and sent a daily reports on what we did. Most of our activities lasted for four and a half months from March to the end of July during the initial emergency response. By the end of July, most shelters were closed and the people moved to temporary housing constructed by local governments.

Through our support activities we came across an interesting issue concerning collaboration with people from heterogeneous backgrounds. Those people who worked on the disaster response came from different backgrounds and most of them were doing quite different tasks from what they usually did before the disaster. Disagreements and distrust happened quite easily. We call this problem disaster communications (Murayama, et. al., 2013). We found that trust plays an important role in such communications.

In our chapter, we introduce disaster communications as an area for research and practice as well as our trials on the recovery phase after the emergency response (Murayama, 2014) as follows:

1. Trust issues in disaster communications
2. Misinformation dissemination in disaster communications through SNS
3. Office environments suffering from Tsunami
4. Support for temporal housing and recovery housing
5. Observing recovery progress with live camera
6. Passing the disaster threat information from generation to generation

Finally the chapter discusses these issues with their potential for big data processing.

TRUST ISSUES IN DISASTER COMMUNICATIONS

Just after the Great East Japan Earthquake and Tsunami, industry in the Tokyo area wanted to provide the affected areas with PCs and printers, but did not know who would like to have them. Academic and industrial groups of engineers wanted to provide internet connection services but again did not know where the services were most needed. With requests from such organizations and groups of people, we started our support with a few of us in the department of Software and Information Science, Iwate Prefectural University ten days after the disaster. Our activities included collecting local information on requirements for IT equipment and internetworking services in the affected area as well as arranging to receive, store and manage incoming IT equipment. We got the information on such needs by communicating with people in the various local government entities and with a volunteer center in Iwate Prefecture. We also set up a mailing list with those people and sent a daily reports on what we did.

Most of our activities lasted for four and a half months from March to the end of July during the initial emergency response. By the end of July, most shelters were closed and the people moved to temporary housing constructed by local governments. Gradually we went back to our normal work.

Through our support activities we came across an interesting issue concerning collaboration with people from heterogeneous backgrounds. Those people who worked on the disaster response came from different backgrounds and most of them were doing quite different tasks from what they usually did before the disaster. Disagreements and distrust happened quite easily. We call this problem disaster communications in this paper. We found that trust plays an important role in such communications.

In this section we report our experiences during our support activities and the trust issue in disaster communication.

REPORT ON OUR ACTIVITIES IN IWATE

We received a request from people in Tokyo indicating that some companies located in the Tokyo area would like to know where they could possibly send PCs and printers for use in disaster support. A group of engineers from academia and industry also offered to help set up data networking in the affected area. They needed to know where they could provide the equipment and network services. We contacted the emergency response headquarter of Iwate prefecture for information and suggestions about providing the coast area with network services and PCs. Moreover, we came to know the people in the large volunteer center (VC) in Tohno City located next to the affected coastal cities. Tohno City did not suffer as much from the Tsunami and was useful to support the disaster locations.

In the end, we organized a loosely coupled federation of projects, the Iwate Disaster IT support project, organizations and people. Fig. 1 shows this.

Information about lifeline needs such as electricity and 3G communication links was collected by the prefectural office for regional development from local governments and telephone companies. We used their information mainly but when we needed to be sure about the lifeline status of a specific place, we asked the local governments directly. In this way we started communicating with local government offices so that we could get more information on their requirements. The requirements in the affected area were collected by volunteers in the Tohno Volunteer Center as well. One of our graduates was working there and introduced his fellow volunteers to us. We also got requirements directly from officers in local government in the affected area.

Figure 1. Support organization: A loosely coupled federation

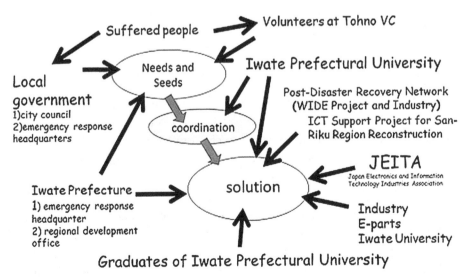

We got requests for connecting networks mainly from the medical team of the prefectural emergency response headquarters at the Iwate Prefecture office located in Morioka near our university. We communicated with one another almost every day by email as well as by face-to-face meetings. The prefectural emergency response headquarter was an ad-hoc organization composed mostly of personnel from other organizations than Iwate Prefecture, such as the Japan Self Defense Forces, the Japan Coast Guard, Maritime Self-Defense Force, local police and medical doctors; the medical team was controlled by the doctors from the local medical school, Iwate Medical University as well as its hospital. In contrast, the prefectural office for regional development that provided us with lifeline information is one of the ordinary Prefectural offices.

The network connecting services were provided by the Post-Disaster Recovery Network project, run by a team of engineers from academia and industry including the WIDE project (WIDE, n.d.), and by the ICT Support Project for San-Riku Region Reconstruction run by Iwate prefectural University researchers with local industry people. PCs, printers and the other devices from industry were offered by the Japan Electronics and Information Technology Industries Association (JEITA) Information and Communication Supporter project (JEITA, 2011). Used PCs were collected and provided through three organizations, Iwate University which is a national university in Iwate, NPO E-parts (E-parts, n.d.), and local industry.

We set up a mailing list including most of the people with whom we communicated. We sent a daily report to them so that we could share whatever happened. Iwate Prefecture provided us daily with information on communication related issues such as states of 3G links in all the affected areas in Iwate. This information was based on reports from local governments and the other sources such as telephone companies. As those reports could be delayed due to the shortage of local staff, we needed to give a call directly to a local government office to ensure the state of a certain site.

Iwate Prefecture encompasses 5,899.02 square miles, slightly larger than the state of Connecticut (5,543 sq mi). We are located in Takizawa Village next to Morioka City. During the disaster recovery we supported mainly four cities and two towns on the coast from Miyako to Rikuzentakata.

During the initial four months after the disaster, we have supported the followings:

1. Information acquisition and provision:
2. Networking for information infrastructure:
3. Shelter information management
4. Volunteer Support

We report each of the above supports as follows.

1. **Information Acquisition and Provision:** For safety information, initially we did not have any network connectivity in shelters. One of our graduates, working as a volunteer at the volunteer center, created an off-line system for people search. Another graduate in Tokyo created software for mobile phone access. The safety information was provided by local police; the information was also available on Iwate Prefecture's home page.

For safety information, we had an interesting technology deployment in Japan for this disaster: the use of broadcast services. People in shelters appeared on TV with a piece of paper on which their names were written, saying where they were staying as well as any other comments such as whom they were seeking. Iwate Broadcast Company (IBC) converted such information on their TV and radio services into the digital form and provided them at their web site. The problem was that the IBC digital form was different from the one provided by the police. We merged those two types of information for the search system on the mobile phone.

For visualizing lifeline information, we mapped road conditions, transport, electricity, water supply and so on. For road conditions, the information was provided by use of GPS car navigation systems. The system was originally created by a car company (HONDA, 2011). Now the information was integrated into major web search systems.

We set up a portal site of disaster information (Iwate Disaster IT support, 2011). We provided all the above information and also information such as radioactivity levels, because in the beginning some people including the volunteers in the Volunteer Center (VC) did not know this because they were too busy every day to look at the news.

2. **Networking for Information Infrastructure:** For Networking for information infrastructure, we supported the engineers for internetworking by providing information where to set up the network with communication links. Accordingly, we provided an IT environment with PCs and printers in shelters and other sites such as city halls in which networks were set up. Networking was hard due to the size of Iwate Prefecture. For instance travel takes nearly three hours from Morioka to Rikuzentakata, the city located in the south of the prefecture. It took almost one day for network engineers to go to Rikuzentakata from Morioka and set up networks. They worked so hard and were exhausted.

We consulted the prefectural emergency response headquarters for which sites to be connected in the beginning and asked the network engineers to set up when communication links and electricity could be made available.

The engineers researched each site thoroughly by visiting and seeing what type of communication links should be set up such as a 3G link or a Satellite Communication link. Gradually, those network engineers knew the affected areas much better than we or engineers in the prefecture's headquarter in Morioka did. In the end, the field engineers were deciding where to set up networks independently by talking directly with the local government officers.

Through our joint work the major shelters were connected onto the network and we provided around 200 PCs and 50 printers in total.

3. **Shelter Information Management:** Shelter information management was required from the beginning, however, we were asked to help with it one month later, in the middle of April. What happened was that goods and foods sent to Iwate prefecture were stored in the central warehouse near Morioka then they were delivered to shelters at the coast. However, the requirements from each shelter were not reported precisely enough and many shelters received some unnecessary goods. Initially, the requirements were collected manually and sent to the prefecture's emergency response headquarters by fax.

A management system with a good communication system was required. We came across the people working on the Sahana system (Currion & Van de Walle, 2007) and introduced them to the prefecture's emergency response headquarter. A group of programmers from industry and Sahana Japan (2011) got together and to create a new system for distribution.

It took a while to produce a system customized for use in Iwate, and it was ready for use in the end of May. It was slightly late for many shelters because in a month's time people would start moving from shelters to temporary housing and shelters were to be closed, Moreover, even though the shelter managers had only poorly-designed tools and procedures, once they got used to them, it would have been hard for them to change.

4. **Volunteer Support:** We also provided information on shopping and other daily-life-related tasks for newcomers to the Volunteer Center. We were asked to set up a Volunteers' site for sharing information. In the VC, they were not capable or too busy to set up a server. Moreover, a physical system would have been hard for them to maintain.

We set up their site using a cloud service. We found it very practical. The cloud services are sustainable in that they do not suffer any damage such as blackout or physical damage to the server from local disaster. One does not have to worry about maintenance. Compared to physical servers, cloud services were much more flexible and easier to set up.

Disaster Communications

Throughout our activities we faced to many blocks. We introduce some of them in this section and identify the needs for disaster communications in this section.

In the beginning of our support activities, most of us working in the information science and engineering area had an assumption that information and communication technology would be required desperately, however, the truth is that it is not so. We presumed in the providers' viewpoint. What was needed in the first place was support personnel and cars with drivers; possibly the people who would listen to.

One day we were asked to set up the networks by the prefecture's emergency response headquarter, we gave a call to the shelter, one of the management personnel from the local city answered and told us to bring cars and support personnel. The person told me that they did neither need any network nor PCs at all. We kept listening to the person and proposed we could arrange a volunteer person to help out. The answer was no, again. What they needed was an experienced person who could manage the shelter for a few months whereas a volunteer would stay temporarily for a week or so. They would stay too short to work for management. Our solution was to provide this shelter an experienced volunteer who lived nearby so that he could come and help for quite a while. Next they asked us for a photo copier and we sent a printer which would be used as a copier. Then next, they asked for input information. Deliberately they asked for information processing which we were capable to support.

We learnt that emergency response support needs many aspects of support. Whatever was requested, when we show our intention to solve, trust would be generated. That way we could have a better communication onwards.

Problems with Governmental Organizations

Organizational problem is this. At disaster, emergency response headquarter is settled by at least three different levels of governmental organizations --- i.e. 1) city and town, 2) prefecture (identical to state) and 3) nation. All of them operated independently.

For instance, when we asked the prefecture emergency response headquarter, they told us that we should set up a network connection in one of the shelters in a city, in which a medical team needed it. We asked the network engineers from Tokyo to go and set up, so they did. After they set up, they were questioned by the local city officers why they set up the network at that particular shelter whereas another shelter would need it more. This case shows two issues as follows:

1. We would have needed to have asked the two following local government organizations for the admission for setting up a network connection:
    a. city
    b. city's emergency response headquarter
2. Prefecture's emergency response headquarter is a temporary section of the prefecture composed of people from many different organizations such as local police, the Japan Self Defence Forces, Japan Coast Guard, medical doctors and local government officers.

Regarding 1 above, at emergency, the decision making in city is done independently from the prefecture. Before an action is made one would need to negotiate with the local government who manages a shelter or any building in which networking would be needed. Although the prefecture-wide decision is made by the prefecture, the local management is controlled heavily by the most local government. Networking in a shelter is the matter of a management of a shelter and it should be admitted by the local town or city, neither by the prefecture nor by the nation.

For 2, the prefecture emergency response headquarter is such a temporary section that its decision could not have been accepted thoroughly by the local city officers.

Problems with Decision Making on Networking

As we described in Section 2.3.2, networks were set up the engineers all over the prefecture. In the beginning, we asked where to set up the networks, however, later the engineers communicated with the local government officers and the other local people, so that they knew much better about the local requirements than us.

As any decision was made mainly by the engineers, we were not sure why those sites were selected. They were too busy to explain. We ended up having little communication. They did not like to report to us because they felt to be controlled. They did not like to have any suggestion or comment at all.

Problem Description

We need to study what sort of communication would be required just after disaster. According to National Research Council (1989), risk communications is "an interactive process of exchange of information and opinion among individuals, groups, and institutions." Risk communications have been studied to a great extent (Reynolds & Seeger, 2005), but focused mainly on the future risks.

Disaster communications are more practical to deal with real incidents and considered as a part of emergency management (Hilz, Van de Walle and Turoff, 2009).

Disaster communications include many different entities such as sufferers, volunteers, administrative offices and supporters from organizations or by individual. All of them have different viewpoints and different background. For disaster support, they need to discuss the issues on the same table. They would have the same purpose but it might be hard to cooperate with each other. From our experiences, disaster communications have the following nature:

1. Heterogeneity of people
2. Most of us are novices
3. Communications with unknown people
4. Need for decision-making in changing circumstances
5. None knows the true needs
6. Don't expect appreciation

For 1 in the above, we have to communicate with the people with different in many aspects such as background from the ones we usually deal with. One might be tired and such fatigue may well cause a different reaction from the usual cognitive behavior. One may work on a volunteer basis while the others may be more business oriented.

For 2, most of us are novice on what we would be asked to do. For instance, the civil servants would need to deal with supply chain management for goods distribution.

For 3, due to fatigue and one need to do things always in rush, it is hard to communicate with the people whom one has never met before. It would be easy for us to misunderstand.

For 4, since we would face to make a decision on what we are inexperienced matter quickly, one could not expect the best optimized solution. Since the people in need would often ask multiple sites for help, even if one would come up to them with a great effort to help out, the trouble might have been sorted out by someone else.

For 5, we would get requests, but we need to be sure none knows the true needs, even a person who makes such a request. That is why even if we solve the problem, we could not expect the best solution as the original request itself would not be true indeed. We provide solutions in terms of IT but we need to be sure that it was a part of solution. We need to try and understand the real needs, but it would be hard.

For 6, we should not expect appreciation from the others in disaster communications. People have no time because things keep happening one after another. One needs to deal with multiple issues to deal with at the same time, so that even if one would like to thank to the other, next time he or she would be preoccupied with another matter and miss the chance to show the appreciation and forget. Although this is true, the supports would always expect to some appreciation. We would need an easy and timely way to express such a positive feeling. Perhaps some kind of communication tool would be of help.

Moreover, from our experience, what we needed for disaster communications included speed, rhythm and trust. We needed speed, because everyone expects a prompt reply. When we were asked for an information system for goods and foods distribution, we were asked to produce such a system in three days. That was impossible. Accordingly we cannot fulfill the requests so fast, but what we could do is to start process whatever was requested and inform the request on it, so that the requester would feel fine.

We need rhythm in our activity in that even when we receive almost impossible request, there would always be a way to deal with. We need to watch out what could be possible. In the above example, soon after we asked for the information system in three days, we came across the sahana system which looked worth trying. We received many requests for the use of systems and tools from their creators. Although not all of them were in use this time, it would be important to get such information as much as possible so that we might find a solution. We need a match making between requesters and suppliers.

As we need to deal with different kind of people whom we have never met, we need to generate trust between each other. We shall discuss this issue in the next section.

Needs for Trust

The previous section pointed out the need in disaster communications to deal with matters with which one has little experienced, to communicate strangers and to make decisions in such circumstances. To better understand the implications of operating in this space we look to the Elaboration Likelihood Model (ELM) from psychology (Petty & Cacioppo, 1981). Figure 2 shows the model. According to the model, when we receive *Persuasive Communication*, such as a commercial message for a car, if we are interested in knowing more about the car in question (*Motivated to Process*) and knows much about cars (*Ability to Process*), we could decide to accept the initial message or not by ourselves (*Process with Central route*). However, if one is not interested in the car, or does not know much about cars, then one would not look back at the initial message content, but would decide to accept the message or not according to environmental issues such as who sent this message or the way in which it is presented (*Process with Peripheral Route*).

For disaster communications we often need to process with the peripheral route and so need to be able to assess our trust in the source.

Trust has been researched as a multi-disciplinary concept. It has been researched in psychology, sociology and economics for long a long time. From psychological viewpoint, Deutsch (1960) defined trust in an interpersonal context. Gambetta (1988) defined trust as a particular level of one's subjective probability that another's action would be favorable to oneself [16]. Lewis and Weigert (1985) identified two aspects of trust, the cognitive and emotional parts of trust.

Cognitive trust has been most identified with the factors with competence, integrity and benevolence (Chong, Yang and Wong, 2003; Luo and Najdawi, 2004). Earle and Cvetkovich (1995) presented Salient Value Similarity (SVS) to include integrity and benevolence.

Slovic (1993) presented the asymmetry principle of trust; it is hard to gain trust from the others, but is easy to lose it. In disaster communications it is easy to generate distrust in others and while becoming over confident in oneself. We need to work on how possibly we could get over distrust and overconfidence so that we could have a continuous disaster communications in a productive way.

Trust plays an important role in decision making. Stephens (2004) gives design elements, such as page layout, navigation, and graphics which affect the development of trust between buyers and sellers in e-commerce. According to Riegelsberger, Sasse and McCarthy (2003), affective reactions influence consumer decision-making. They presented a trust model based on the vast amount of literature survey (Riegelsberger et. al., 2005) in which what sort of signal (message) and reaction one needs to exchange between two entities to construct trust. We could use this model for disaster communications in future.

Related Work on Emergency Management

Disaster communications are part of emergency management (Hilz,et. al., 2009). According to the integrated disaster management cycle, it is involved in both immediate response and sustained response to a disaster. Indeed, most of what we reported from our support activities is listed. Our contribution would be to introduce the importance of trust using ELM.

Figure 2. The elaboration likelihood model (ELM)

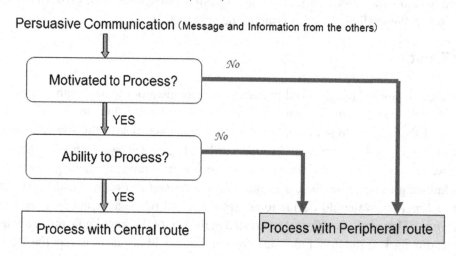

Turoff (2002) introduced the historical background of emergency management information systems. White, Plotnick,, Kushma,, Hiltz, and Turoff (2009). looked into the use of Social Network Services(SNS) for emergency management.

We might need to use SNS for disaster communications to generate trust.

Summary

In this section, we reported our experiences from our support activities just after the Tohoku earthquake and tsunami on March 11th, 2011 and our initial work on disaster communications derived from our experiences. Quite often officers in local governments as well as some in the prefectural emergency response headquarters office, regard that fairness is most important in the management of support. From our experiences what we required was speed, rhythm and trust in disaster communications. Even if it would not be fair to everyone, we found that our prompt and timely support worked out when we provided the affected places with PCs and printers.

We also showed that trust plays an important role in disaster communications using the Elaboration Likelihood Model from psychology. More work is required on ways we could implement trust issues in disaster communications.

From a sociological viewpoint, Yamagishi (1998, 2008) gave Japanese oriented characteristics compared to the concept of trust. In disaster communications we might need to consider such cultural differences.

We need to have further study on disaster communication to proceed as exploration in terms of social science (Stebbins, 2001).

MISINFORMATION DISSEMINATION IN DISASTER COMMUNICATIONS THROUGH SNS

The Great East Japan Earthquake with magnitude 9.0 struck the north east of Honshu island on March 11, 2011 triggered tsunami, nuclear power plant incident, and led to huge loss of human life with severe structural and infrastructure damage. During the disaster, cellular communication and landline service are disrupted and jammed due to the surge of network activity. However, Internet services via 3G network are available. Twitter, Facebook and Mixi are top three listed forms of social networking sites used during and after the disaster (Jung, 2012; Mobile Marketing Data Labo., 2011). In Japan, it is reported that the amount of tweets on the day of the March 2011 Tohoku earthquake was 1.8 times larger than usual (Jung, 2012).

In recent years, several studies have focused on the potential use of social media sites for mass collaboration in emergency response and rescue during emergency situation (White et al., 2009; Raue, Azzopardi and Johnson, 2013; Gupta, Lamba, Kumaraguru and Joshi, 2013). There are several studies in the literature reporting and discuss the effectiveness of social media on supplying information during disaster such as during Haiti Earthquake (Dugdale, Van de Walle, and Koeppinghoff, 2012), The Great East Japan Earthquake (Peary, Shaw and Takeuchi, 2012; Acar and Muraki, 2011), and Hurricane Sandy (Gupta, et al., 2013). However, although social networking sites (SNS) or social media proved to be an important communication and information tools during disaster, information credibility (White et al., 2009; Raue et al., 2013; Chatfield, Scholl and Brajawidagda, 2014) and misinformation spreading through social media (Gupta, et al., 2013; Tanaka, Sakamoto and Matsuka, 2012) raised an important issue to be concerned. Although rumoring during extreme events is not a new phenomenon, the social media facilitate the transmission of these rumors and misinformation to broad audience in a short time. This issue also captured the Japanese government attention as it might lead to other serious social problems and panic situation to public during disaster (Tanaka et al., 2012).

Table 1 provide the example of misinformation tweets spread after the Great East Japan Earthquake 2011 (Mukai, 2012). As we can see, the number of "Favourite" and retweet numbers are quite high although it is not an accurate information.

Recent study by Chen & Sakamoto also highlight the need to investigate user behavior towards crisis information and reveals the relationship between user`s feeling and information sharing behavior during emergencies (Chen and Sakamoto, 2014). Thus, our research is motivated by the need to understand individual behaviour of information diffusion, focusing on the citizen who may or may not directly affected in disaster on spreading information in Twitter environment.

Table 1. Summary of misinformation tweets spread after the earthquake

Example of Tweets	Favourite	RT
The harmful rain because of the fire of industrial complex in Chiba.	19	750
The content is same as above. (but with different user ID)	8	336
Bleeding of the abdomen because of the rack collapse in the company.	83	601
Shinjuku Bunka Gakuin is open for victims.	10	196
Donation of 1.5 billion yen from manga author, "One Piece".	24	470
The content is same as above. (but with different user ID)	68	374
Relief supplies from aerial delivery is impossible.	210	1090
Donation of 10 billion yen from Turkey.	206	329

The User Survey

Accordingly, we conduct a user survey to investigate one action after they read retweet message, the message that have been retweeted and circulated in Twitter network, and why people choose to continue spreading it. The survey was held on 10 and 11 December, 2012 with a total of 133 respondents who are Twitter user (mean age = 20.5, male = 94) from Iwate Prefectural University, Japan. For the analysis part, we perform Exploratory Factor Analysis (EFA) with maximum likelihood method. Factor analysis is used for data reduction and to group a large set of inter-correlated variables together under a small set of underlying variables. After eliminate the problem question items from EFA, we perform Confirmatory Factor Analysis (CFA) with Structural Equation Modeling (SEM) to specify the relationship between variables and factors.

Findings

As a result, we extracted 3 factors on user`s action towards retweet messages, and reason to spread the retweet messages as reported in papers (Abdullah, Nishioka, Tanaka and Murayama, 2014, 2015) as summarized in Figure 3 as below.

The result of the factor analyses on the user`s action after they read the retweet messages indicate 3 factors: 1) Desire to spread the retweet messages as it is considered important. 2) Mark the retweet messages as favorite using Twitter "Favorite" function. 3) Search for further information about the content of the retweet messages.

Then, we further analyzed the first factor on desire to spread the retweet messages and we extracted another 3 factors related to why user makes decision to spread the retweet message which are: 1) Need to retweet. 2) Interesting tweet content. 3) Tweet user. Table 2 and table 3 shows the factor loadings for the first and second factor analyses phase, respectively.

Figure 3. Summary of user`s action and reason to spread retweet messages

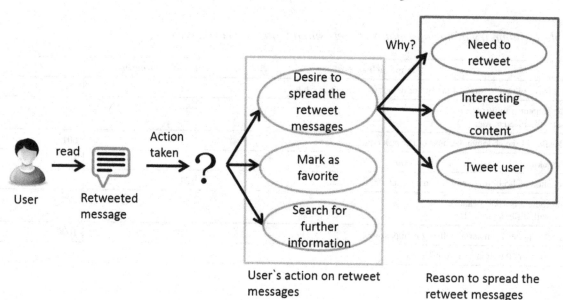

Table 2. The factor loadings of first analyses phase

No.	Question Items	F1 (α = .930)	F2 (α = .862)	F3 (α = .787)
40	I read the retweet messages that has been retweet by some of my following.	.853	-.287	.005
35	I will retweet if the retweet messages were from reliable original author.	.797	-.042	-.012
28	I will retweet if the retweet messages are a call to action for people to read it.	.770	.048	-.021
38	I will retweet of the one who post the retweet messages have a good follower's relation.	.695	-.206	.139
31	I will retweet if the retweet messages are related to my situation.	.687	.085	-.003
26	I will retweet if the retweet messages are positive things.	.661	.124	.002
27	I will retweet if the retweet messages are negative things.	.658	.081	-.074
42	I will decide to retweet or not after I check the retweet messages.	.645	-.034	.127
41	I will decide to retweet or not after I see who (followers) have retweet it.	.633	-.077	-.032
9	I will open the URL in retweet messages if it is available and I know the URL destination.	.613	-.137	-.016
32	I will retweet all retweet messages displayed continuously (related with each other)	.581	.245	-.131
30	I will retweet if the retweet messages contain [Pls spread] written in it.	.576	.117	-.185
36	I will retweet after I determine the retweet message's author.	.565	-.157	.094
16	I check the retweet messages if there is from trusted source of information, for example from television or newspaper. If the content is same, then I will retweet it.	.563	.153	.014
34	I will retweet if the retweet messages were from the official Twitter account of an organization or company.	.547	.082	-.022
5	I feel trigger to take an action after I read the retweet messages.	.460	.146	-.009
17	I do not know the retweet messages in details. But if I think the information is important, I will retweet.	.442	.299	-.007
20	I read the retweet messages now, and it captures my interest, so I retweet it.	.426	.215	.223
29	I will retweet if the retweet messages are for fun or joke.	.423	.106	.273
24	I will decide the trustworthy of the retweet messages, whether it is true or false when I retweet it.	.414	-.024	.128
8	I access all URL link in retweet messages if it is available.	.382	.049	.023
13	I mark the retweet messages as favorite and then I retweet it.	-.067	.940	.020
14	I mark the retweet messages as favorite but I did not retweet it.	-.195	.861	.039
15	I mark the retweet messages as favorite but I do not know whether I want to retweet it or not.	.032	.739	.056
18	My interest on the retweet messages increase now after I read it. So, I want to search for further information.	-.081	-.067	1.054
19	I have the interest on the particular topic, and the retweet messages are same with that I want to know, so I search for further information.	-.050	.104	.825
12	I see the original author's tweets (other tweets) after I read the retweet messages.	.123	.129	.368
7	I think the retweet messages I have read may not be true. I check the author's profile after I read it.	.152	.134	.276
	Cumulative %	37.882	45.792	52.415
	Factor correlation matrix F1	1.00	-	-
	F2	.554	1.00	-
	F3	.521	.477	1.00

Table 3. The factor loadings of second analyses phase

No.	Question Items	F1 (α= .875)	F2 (α= .875)	F3 (α= .765)
17	I do not know the retweet messages in details. But if I think the information is important, I will retweet.	.808	.032	-.170
30	I will retweet if the retweet messages contain [Pls spread] written in it.	.673	.000	-.075
31	I will retweet if the retweet messages are related to my situation.	.607	.169	.053
32	I will retweet all retweet messages displayed continuously (related with each other)	.691	-.212	.311
34	I will retweet if the retweet messages were from the official Twitter account of an organization or company.	.503	.014	.150
35	I will retweet if the retweet messages were from reliable original author.	.499	.182	.172
27	I will retweet if the retweet messages are negative things.	.400	.139	.239
16	I check the retweet messages if there is from trusted source of information, for example from television or newspaper. If the content is same, then I will retweet it.	.392	.097	.254
29	I will retweet if the retweet messages are for fun or joke.	.095	.782	-.195
38	I will retweet of the one who post the retweet messages have a good follower's relation.	-.184	.741	.186
26	I will retweet if the retweet messages are positive things.	.171	.620	.030
20	I read the retweet messages now, and it captures my interest, so I retweet it.	.419	.547	-.231
42	I will decide to retweet or not after I check the retweet messages.	.107	.593	.100
28	I will retweet if the retweet messages are a call to action for people to read it.	.373	.440	.069
36	I will retweet after I determine the retweet message's author.	.033	-.068	.703
40	I read the retweet messages that has been retweet by some of my following.	-.251	.514	.583
41	I will decide to retweet or not after I see who (followers) have retweet it.	.082	-.092	.767
	Cumulative %	46.901	54.971	61.854
	Factor correlation matrix F1	1.00	-	-
	F2	.698	1.00	-
	F3	.558	.615	1.00

The following conclusions can be made from these findings: 1) User`s action to search for more information or verifying the information they get from Twitter before they retweet is important to reduce the spread of unverified or misinformation in SNS, and 2) Twitter environment, including the tweet content and the Twitter user whether the informer, the original tweet author and the tweet that individual evaluate as important to be spread influenced people decision to spread information in Twitter.

Summary

In conclusion, as citizen communication and social media plays an important role as disaster communication tools, the misinformation spreading issue through SNS should not be neglected. In case of disaster, people often retweet and spread tweets they find in twitter trending topics, regardless of whether they follow the user or not (Hagar, 2012). People tend to spread any messages that they think is important for others to know. However, not all information is accurate during disaster. Further research in this area is important to encourage effective use of social media in emergency situation for better disaster response and disaster communication tools for future event.

OFFICE ENVIRONMENTS SUFFERING FROM TSUNAMI

While we have had various documents of personal damage records (Yoshimura, 2004), it is hard to find records of damages of offices equipped with Information Technology such as personal computers. Our university has some officers who used to work at the disaster areas at the Great East Japan Earthquake and Tsunami. We have had an interview with one of them and report what they experienced.

One of the officers used to work for Iwate Fisheries Technical Center which was located by a bay in Kamaishi City which is in the disaster area in Iwate Prefecture. The center is the prefectural organization, conducts research and provides information and support for fishery in Iwate. The office was suffered from Tsunami on 11th March 2011.

The center building s two story high and the office members evacuated to the rooftop of the building, from which they saw Tsunami coming and going. According to the officer who told us what had happened, at disaster one should be prepared to have anything much bigger than what is expected. Waves moved towards difference directions in complicated ways. In Japan we have had various natural disasters since March 2011 and those disasters were indeed were more than one would have expected; e.g. damages from a landslide triggered by a typhoon at Oshima Island, Tokyo in October 2013, a landslide triggered by heavy rain at Hiroshima in August 2014, the eruption of Mt. Ontake in September 2014 and the debris flow after the earthquake at Hakuba village in November 2014.

After Tsunami terminated, the people came down to a room on the upper floor, which had a potbelly stove. It was still cold in March in Iwate and the heater was definitely needed. The potbelly stove was useful because it does not depend lifeline such as electricity and gas. After that, they install this type of stoves in the other rooms in the center.

After the disaster they tried to equip various emergency supplies. The center members raised a question about life jackets because they did not have enough time to put them as well as helmets on at this time. Life jacket might not be practical when one would float in the water fulfilled with rubbles. On the other hand, helmets would be useful to protect from falling objects. Moreover, boots with a thick sole were useful to walk on the ground full of rubbles. The problem was how much space one could get to squeeze those goods in an office.

The ground floor of the center was flooded with seawater and computers and IT equipment were soaked in the water. As the research center had a system to produce distilled water, hard discs were washed with such water. Some of them were recovered data successfully but the others were not. Among various methods to recover the data, a traditional USB stick memory with a cap protected data almost perfectly. In our support project, we had many requests for data recovery from memory and PCs soaked with seawater. We shall well need IT support from such hardware viewpoints as well as some distributed information management making use of cloud computing services.

At the center, they had many documents in paper. They were soaked with seawater but saved. After some time, they got moldy and smelly too much to be used. The documents would need to be digitalized in this view point. Also, at the disaster area, there was popular voluntary work to wash and save personal photographs which were soaked with seawater. One could develop a way how to clean and preserve the paper documents at an office.

SUPPORT FOR TEMPORAL HOUSING AND RECOVERY HOUSING

As the location of temporary housing is decided presumably according to the availability of space in which a hundred small houses could be built, they are located far from town without easy access to shops and transport services in disaster area. Survivors living at such housing found it inconvenient for daily shopping. Mobile shop services are coming once or twice a week. Some could go and buy good at supermarket by car. Many cars and drivers have gone this time. Elderly women without driver's license are left.

We tried and solve this problem by setting up a self-service system with a prepaid card. An experimental system has been running in our laboratory environment for several years for a use by students. The interface is a bar cord reader with which prepaid card would be read as well as the ones for items at a store. Figure 4 shows the store in a temporary housing with 74 families at Aka Mae, Miyako City.

The system includes the front end servers for a store as well as the management client system at our university site. The information on goods would be input at the university and sent it to the server at Aka Mae. The goods are sent from the university to Aka Mae by use a delivery service. The system is located in Aka Mae at the common room in the temporary housing. The manager of temporary housing offers voluntarily as the shop manager at Aka Mae.

Firstly we had an experimental operation from 3rd November 2012 for four weeks, and saw that the system works and the store was highly useful for the residents. On the other hand, there were two issues as follows:

1. Transportation time for the management of goods locally to take two and a half hours drive to visit Aka Mae
2. Hesitation by elderly people to use PC to but goods

It was reluctant for us to go and visit Aka Mae once a week to manage goods such as register each item into the system and place them in the shop shelves. We solved the problem to have remote management over the internet. Nevertheless we visit the place once a month still now to communicate with the local manager and customers to hear their requests. We do the followings at the university:

- Purchase items
- Register items' information to the server
- Produce price tags for items and send them to the local manager at Aka Mae

Figure 4. Our experimental store at Aka Mae, Miyako, Iwate

- Produce prepaid cards
- Inventory management

We send a pack of items once two weeks now.
The local manager at Aka Mae does the followings:

- Place the items sent from us at the shop shelves with price tags
- Sell the prepaid cards to customers

In 2014, with a request from a regional coordinator in Kamaishi City, we install the second store in recovery housing in Kerobe, Tohni, Kamaishi City. The size of the market is relatively small as eleven families mostly elderly. We are trying to install such a store into more places in Iwate. The management of goods distribution could be solved by cooperating with local merchants and we started working on it.

As this type of store heavily depends on trust in a community to avoid losing goods, we need a careful survey whether this store could be used in any other environments. One of them could be a disserted area as well as in an office such as the one run by a confectionary company in Japan (Ezaki Glico Co. Ltd., n.d.).

The work presented in this section is funded by the Iwate Prefectural University as well as Sanriku Fund, Iwate Prefecture at the moment.

OBSERVING RECOVERY PROGRESS WITH LIVE CAMERA

It may well take quite some time such as ten years or so to recover and reconstruct the towns and cities at disaster area. Meanwhile the interests into such recovery would be lost outside the area. We came up with an idea on a recovery watcher to keep people being aware of what is happening.

In the beginning, we used the u-stream service and located a camera at the town hall of Yamada, Iwate. It takes some bandwidth, so we implemented an image-base system and record images in a calendar (Saito, Fujihara and Murayama, 2012). We also located the system in Kamaishi City as well. We found a security problem that in the beginning we had an internet access by making use of a city hall but gradually we could not make use of such network as our system is outside the management of the local city. Accordingly we needed an independent network access for such services.

Currently a system only presents an image as in Figure 5, but in future, we would need to incorporate more sophisticated social media service so that viewers can leave their comments.

Elevant (2014) is working on sharing weather information. Presumably natural disaster could be considered a kind of the weather, so that a service for sharing weather information could be used at disaster. Indeed, one of our findings was that at disaster people would not use a new interface of a system; they prefer an interface which they get used to. If we provide a service to share weather information for a daily use, we could possibly make use of it for passing disaster warning information to the others such as new people who come to the disaster area or to the residents in the future generations.

For a long run, we could use this sort of sharing service to convey the warning information at disaster. One of the big issues at the disaster was that one needed to get out of Tsunami as soon as possible without caring your family members --- i.e. we needs to help ourselves first. This old wisdom was not

Figure 5. Recovery watcher with photo images

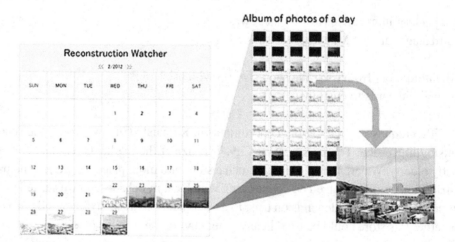

passed correctly from generation to generation and brought the tragedy again. The Sanriku district was attacked by Tsunami once thirty to fifty years again and again. The question is how one can convey such a warning to remind people daily. One of the solutions could be such a weather sharing site. We need more research on sustainability of information delivery sites.

PASSING THE DISASTER THREAT INFORMATION FROM GENERATION TO GENERATION

Touhoku region in Japan are attacked by a tsunami once thirty to fifty years, "Meiji Sanriku Earthquake" of June 15th, 1896, "Showa Sanriku earthquake" of March 3rd, 1933 and "Chilly Earthquake" of May 23th, 1960. Nevertheless, the Great East Japan Earthquake and Tsunami on March 11th, 2011 caused severe damage to Touhoku region in Japan. One of the reason that suffer repeated severe damage from tsunami, lack of information transmission between generations is cited as a possible cause. Currently, on the Internet, many of recording information about the Great East Japan Earthquake are integrated. However, this information also may be forgotten over time when the next tsunami will come after 30-40 years. In this study, we propose an information time capsule which transmits information from generation to generation.

An information time capsule is to realize a concept of time capsule on the Internet. A time capsule would be buried in the ground to put something of the day in a container. It is intended to open after a certain date. In an information time capsule, when burying an information time capsule is "current", and when opening an information time capsule is a "future". An information time capsule users use this system in several users. One user is an administrator of an information time capsule. Administrator creates an information time capsule and conveys it to other users. Other users access an information time capsule created by the administrator, and upload information. Then, the administrator sets the time to open an information time capsule, to be buried an information time capsule. When burying an information time capsule, users and administrators until the specified time cannot open an information time capsule. After the time to open an information time capsule, this system performs the user authentication, to allow access to an information time capsule to allowable users. When the users who accessed it is allowable users, the users can download the information that users uploaded in the past.

When accessing information, in general, users use the ID and password. However, the users have a problem that forgets the ID and password as time ticks away. To solve this problem, Thorpe, MacRaAmirali and Salehi-Abari (2013) have proposed an authentication system for the password to the selected location on the map. Therefore, we decided to use the map information in the access control. In this system, we use user name and administrator name as ID and location information as a password in access control.

An information time capsule is composed of four functions. These functions is "creating a time capsule function", "information upload and download function", "access control function based on time" and "authentication function using the map". We explain the process of registering to register ID and a password. First, the administrator decides the location information to bury an information time capsule using map and register its own administrator name. Second, the users register its own user name when users upload the information. Next, we explain the process of access to an information time capsule. First, user input the user name and administrator name. Second, user selects the location information on map. Third, when user selects the location information, user can access an information time capsule when an information time capsule is buried in the vicinity of the input the location information.

We have created an information time capsule to convey the information from generation to generation. However, we do not verify the strength of the password and user can memorize the ID and password. Therefore, in this future work, we verify the strength of the password and evaluate whether user can memorize the ID and password for a long time.

BIG DATA ISSUES

The Great East Japan Earthquake and Tsunami on March 11th, 2011 caused severe damage with the number of the dead, 15892 and the number of missing 2576 (National Police Agency of Japan, 2015). On the other hand, the possibility of a much larger-scale earthquake along the Nankai Trough has been anticipated in Japan these years. The disaster area will span from Tokai to Shikoku Regions (Government of Japan, 2015a). The number of dead and missing is expected up to 320000 at the worst case. That would be 17 times bigger damage. If that is the case, we may well need to provide more supports.

For instance, the number of evacuees was 124594 as of June 2, 2011 and 87963 as of July 28, 2011 at the earthquake and tsunami in 2011. Many of them stayed in shelters, some of them in other accommodations such as hotels, relatives' houses, temporary housing and so on. Indeed, many of them moved to temporary housing from shelter by the end of June or July. On the other hand, in the case of the Nankai Trough earthquake, we may have 17 times more evacuees. The management of shelters need to accommodate automatic management for counting of evacuees as well as support goods supplies.

For SNS, the number of messages will be much larger. The unit sales of smartphones world-wide in 2011 were 470 million whereas those in 2016 would be expected as 1300 million, 22.5 percent growth (Government of Japan, 2015b). Accordingly more users would make use of such devices for SNS, and at emergency we would expect more messages and information. It would be a serious problem to deduce the correct information out of vast amount of messages.

Moreover, for recovery watcher we would well need to accommodate hundreds of disaster sites all over the world to share the information. Each site has loads of photographs and we shall need to how to analyze them. There could be another model of such a service by collecting photographs and videos from the others. Each smartphone users could register as reporters. Local governments could make use of it to get the local information at once and respond to the situations such as disasters and incidents.

CONCLUSION

In this chapter, we have introduced some of our work for disaster communications. The damage caused by the Great East Japan Earthquake and Tsunami was huge in terms of the lives and infrastructures of communities. If we had such a disaster in the urban area such as Tokyo. The number of people to be rescued and supported would be more than ten millions. We will need a shelter information management to be dealt with such big data. Also, the use of SNS would be much popular in the urban areas and the number of messages to be analyzed would be so big and we need to prepare how to deal with such big amount of data to be processed to get though at a future disaster. For shopping support stores, when the number of shops increases we need a scalable management of stores and possibly to apply the supply chain methods as well as to seek out a method for the management of ad-hoc stores at temporary housing.

For recovery watcher we would well need to accommodate hundreds of disaster sites all over the world to share the information. Each site has loads of photographs and we shall need to how to analyze them. For the information time capsule system, we will need to manage millions of time capsules in future.

REFERENCES

Abdullah, N. A., Nishioka, D., Tanaka, Y., & Murayama, Y. (2014). A Preliminary Study on User's Decision Making towards Retweet Messages. *Proceedings of 29th International Conference on ICT Systems Security and Privacy Protection (SEC2014)* (pp. 359-365). doi:10.1007/978-3-642-55415-5_30

Abdullah, N.A., Nishioka, D., Tanaka, Y., & Murayama, Y. (2015). User's Action and Decision Making of Retweet Messages towards Reducing Misinformation Spread during Disaster. *Journal of Information Processing, 23*(1), 31-40.

Acar, A., & Muraki, Y. (2011). Twitter for crisis communication: Lessons learned from Japan's tsunami disaster. *International Journal of Web Based Communities, 7*(3), 392–402. doi:10.1504/IJWBC.2011.041206

Chatfield, A. T., Scholl, H. J., & Brajawidagda, U. (2014). #Sandy Tweets: Citizens' Co-Production of Time Critical Information during an Unfolding Catastrophe. *Proceedings of the 47th Hawaii Int. Conference on System Sciences (HICCS-47)*, (pp. 1947-1957). doi:10.1109/HICSS.2014.247

Chen, R., & Sakamoto, Y. (2014). Feelings and Perspective matter: Sharing of Crisis Information in Social Media. *Proceedings of the 47th Hawaii Int. Conference on System Sciences (HICCS-47)*, (pp. 1958-1967). doi:10.1109/HICSS.2014.248

Chong, B., Yang, Z., & Wong, M. (2003). Asymmetrical impact of trustworthiness attributes on trust, perceived value and purchase intention: a conceptual framework for cross-cultural study on consumer perception of online auction. *Proceedings of the 5th international conference on Electronic Commerce(ICEC2003)*, (pp. 213-219). doi:10.1145/948005.948033

Currion, P., Silva, C., & Van de Walle, B. (2007). Open source software for disaster management. *Communications of the ACM, 50*(3), 61–65. doi:10.1145/1226736.1226768

Deutsh, M. (1960). The effect of motivational orientation upon trust and suspition. *Human Relations, 13*(2), 123–139. doi:10.1177/001872676001300202

Dugdale, J., Van de Walle, B., & Koeppinghoff, C. (2012). Social media and SMS in the haiti earthquake. *Proceedings of the 21st Int. Conference on World Wide Web (WWW '12 Companion)*. ACM. doi:10.1145/2187980.2188189

E-parts. (n.d.). Retrieved from http://www.eparts-jp.org/

Earle, T. C., & Cvetkovich, G. (1995). *Social trust: Toward a cosmopolitan society*. Westport, CT: Praeger Press.

Elevant, K. (2014). Who wants to "share weather"? The impacts of off-line interactions on online behavior. In *Proceedings of the 47th Hawaii Int. Conference on System Sciences (HICCS-47)*, (pp. 1884- 1893).

Ezaki Glico Co. Ltd. (n.d.). *Office Glico*. Available: http://www.glico.co.jp/en/corp/officeglico.html

Gambetta, D. (1988). Can we trust trust? In D. Gambetta (Ed.), *Trust: Making and breaking cooperative relations* (pp. 213-237). Department of Sociology, University of Oxford. Available online from the following site: http://www.sociology.ox.ac.uk/papers/gambetta213-237.pdf

Government of Japan. (2015a). *Disaster Management in Japan*. Cabinet Office. Available: http://www.bousai.go.jp/1info/pdf/saigaipamphlet_je.pdf

Government of Japan. (2015b). *White Paper 2014*. Ministry of Internal Affairs and Communications. Available: http://www.soumu.go.jp/johotsusintokei/whitepaper/ja/h24/pdf/n2020000.pdf

Gupta, A., Lamba, H., Kumaraguru, P., & Joshi, A. (2013). Faking Sandy: Characterizing and identifying fake images on Twitter during Hurricane Sandy. *Proceedings of the 22nd International Conference on World Wide Web (WWW 2013 Companion)*, (pp. 729–736). Academic Press.

Hagar, C. (2012). Crisis informatics: Perspectives of trust–Is social media a mixed blessing? *Student Research Journal, 2*(2). Available: http://scholarworks.sjsu.edu/slissrj/vol2/iss2/2/

Hilz, S. R., Van de Walle, B., & Turoff, M. (2009). The domain of emergency management information. In Information systems for emergency management (pp.3-20). M.E. Sharp.

HONDA. (2011). *News Release*. Available: http://www.honda.co.jp/news/2011/4110428.html

Iwate Disaster IT Support. (2011). Available: www.go-iwate.org

JEITA. (2011). *Information and Communication Supporter*. Available: http://www.jeita.or.jp/ictot/

Jung, J. (2012). Social Media Use & Goals after the Great East Japan Earthquake. *First Monday, 17*(8), 8–6. doi:10.5210/fm.v17i8.4071

Lewis, D. J., & Weigert, A. (1985). Trust as a social reality. *Social Forces, 63*(4), 967–985. doi:10.1093/sf/63.4.967

Luo, W., & Najdawi, M. (2004). Trust-building measures: A review of consumer health portals. *Communications of the ACM, 47*(1), 108–113. doi:10.1145/962081.962089

Mobile Marketing Data (MMD) Labo. (2011) Survey on social media use after the Great East Japan Earthquake. *MMD SurveySummary*. Available: http://mmd.up-date.ne.jp/news/detail.php?news_id=799.html (in Japanese)

Mukai, M. (2012). *Research on a Model for Decision Making in Retweet which caused Spreading of False Rumor in Emergencies*. (Master Dissertation). Iwate Prefectural University. (in Japanese)

Murayama, Y.(2014). Issues in Disaster Communications. *Journal of Information Processing, 22*(4). doi:10.2197/ipsjjip.22.558

Murayama, Y., Saito, Y., & Nishioka, D. (2013). Trust Issues in Disaster Communication. *Proceedings of HICSS-46*, 335–342.

National Police Agency of Japan. (2015). *Damage Situation and Police Countermeasures associated with 2011Tohoku district - off the Pacific Ocean Earthquake*. Emergency Disaster Countermeasures Headquarters. Available: http://www.npa.go.jp/archive/keibi/biki/higaijokyo_e.pdf

National Research Council. (1989). *Improving risk communication*. National Academy Press.

Peary, B. D. M., Shaw, R., & Takeuchi, Y. (2012). Utilization of Social Media in the East Japan Earthquake and Tsunami and its Effectiveness. *Journal of Natural Disaster Science, 34*(1), 3–18. doi:10.2328/jnds.34.3

Petty, R. E., & Cacioppo, J. T. (1981). *Attitudes and persuasion: Classic and contemporary approaches*. Dubuque, IA: William C. Brown.

Raue, S., Azzopardi, L., & Johnson, C. W. (2013). #trapped!: Social media search system require-ments for emergency management professionals. *Proceedings of the 36th International ACM SIGIR Conference on Research and Development in Information Retrieval*, (pp. 1073–1076). doi:10.1145/2484028.2484184

Reynolds, B., & Seeger, M. (2005). Crisis and Emergency Risk Communication as an Integrative Model. *Journal of Health Communication, 10*, 43–55. doi:10.1080/10810730590904571 PMID:15764443

Riegelsberger, J., Sasse, M. A., & McCarthy, J. D. (2003). Privacy and trust: Shiny happy people building trust? Photos on e-commerce websites and consumer trust. *Proceedings of CHI2003, 5*(1), 121-128.

Riegelsberger, J., Sasse, M. A., & McCarthy, J. D. (2005). The mechanics of trust: A framework for research and design. *International Journal of Human-Computer Studies, 62*(3), 381–422. doi:10.1016/j.ijhcs.2005.01.001

Sahana Japan. (2011). Available: http://www.sahana.jp/

Saito, Y., Fujihara, Y., & Murayama, Y. (2012). A Study of Reconstruction Watcher in Disaster Area. *Proceedings of CHI2012*, 811–814.

Slovic, P. (1993). Perceived risk, trust, and democracy. *Risk Analysis, 13*(6), 675–682. doi:10.1111/j.1539-6924.1993.tb01329.x

Stebbins, R. A. (2001). Exploratory Research in the Social Sciences. *Sage (Atlanta, Ga.)*.

Stephens, R. T. (2004). A framework for the identification of electronic commerce design elements that enable trust within the small hotel industry. *Proceedings of ACMSE*, (pp. 309-314). doi:10.1145/986537.986613

Tanaka, Y., Sakamoto, Y., & Matsuka, T. (2012). Transmission of Rumor and Criticism in Twitter after the Great Japan Earthquake. *Proceedings of the 34th Annual Conference of the Cognitive Science Society*, (pp. 2387-2392).

Thorpe, J., MacRaAmirali, B. & Salehi-Abari, A. (2013). Usability and Security Evaluation of GeoPass: a Geographic Location-Password Scheme. In *Proceedings of the Ninth Symposium on Usable Privacy and Security (SOUPS '13)*, (pp. 1-14). doi:10.1145/2501604.2501618

Turoff, M. (2002). Past and future emergency response information systems. *Comm. of the ACM, 45*(4).

White, C., Plotnick, L., Kushma, J., Hiltz, S. R., & Turoff, M. (2009). An online social network for emergency management. *International Journal of Emergency Management*, 6(3-4), 369–382. doi:10.1504/IJEM.2009.031572

WIDE. (n.d.). *Post-disaster Recovery Internet Project*. Available: http://msg.wide.ad.jp/pdrnet/

Yamagishi, T. (1998). *The structure of trust: The evolutionary games of mind and society*. Tokyo: University of Tokyo Press. Retrieved from http://toshio-yamagishi.net/english/books/index.cgi

Yamagishi, T. (2008). *Why Isn't Japan a Safe Place Anymore?* Tokyo: Shueisha International. (In Japanese)

Yoshimura, A. (2004). *Sanriku Kaigan Otsunami (Sanriku Offshore Great Tsunami)*. Tokyo: Bungei Shunju. (in Japanese)

Chapter 13
Big Data and National Cyber Security Intelligence

A. G. Rekha
Indian Institute of Management Kozhikode, India

ABSTRACT

With the availability of large volumes of data and with the introduction of new tools and techniques for analysis, the security analytics landscape has changed drastically. To face the challenges posed by cyber-terrorism, espionage, cyber frauds etc. Government and law enforcing agencies need to enhance the security and intelligence analysis systems with big data technologies. Intelligence and security insight can be improved considerably by analyzing the under-leveraged data like the data from social media, emails, web logs etc. This Chapter provides an overview of the opportunities presented by Big Data to provide timely and reliable intelligence in properly addressing terrorism, crime and other threats to public security. This chapter also discusses the threats posed by Big Data to public safety and the challenges faced in implementing Big Data security solutions. Finally some of the existing initiatives by national governments using Big Data technologies to address major national challenges has been discussed.

1. INTRODUCTION

With the availability of large volumes of structured and unstructured data and with the introduction of new tools and techniques for analysis, the security analytics landscape has changed drastically. To face the challenges posed by cyber-terrorism, espionage, cyber frauds etc. Government and law enforcing agencies need to enhance the security and intelligence analysis systems with big data technologies. There are two different approaches regarding security in the big data context. One is leveraging Big Data for enhancing the national security systems and second is to secure the national data itself. Intelligence and security insight can be improved considerably by analyzing the under-leveraged data like the data from social media, emails, telecommunication systems, web logs etc. By providing timely and reliable intelligence, big data analytics can help in properly addressing terrorism, crime and other threats to public security.

Nowadays more volume of significant data is available with the security officials as well as with the criminals and hence big data provides both opportunities and threats for national security and critical

DOI: 10.4018/978-1-4666-9649-5.ch013

infrastructures. Security systems need to be able to make use of information from a wide variety of sources including human and software applications in order to exploit the big data and to get value out of it. At the same time data ownership and privacy concerns are also to be taken into account. In light of the growing number of incidents of cyber terrorism and cases of threats to public security, in this chapter we will explore the national security implications of Big Data including opportunities, threats and challenges. The rest of the chapter is organized as follows: Section 1 will discuss Big Data opportunities for national cyber intelligence, section 2 will discuss threats of Big Data to National Security environment. Section3 will cover challenges in exploiting Big Data for national security. In section 4 we will discuss the role of Big Data Analytics for Critical Infrastructure Protection (CIP). Section 5 will discuss some of the tools and techniques available in the big data context and section 6 will discuss about some of the major initiatives taken by governments for national security. Section 7 concludes this chapter.

2. BIG DATA OPPORTUNITIES FOR NATIONAL CYBER INTELLIGENCE

This section will give an overview of how Big Data technologies can complement cyber security solutions. Law enforcement agencies can utilizes Big Data to ensure public safety by capturing and mining huge amounts of data from multiple sources. For example, there are systems which collect data related to travel, immigration, suspicious financial transactions etc. Linking previously unconnected datasets can remove anonymity of individuals and analyzing this data can reveal patterns of connections among persons, places or events. These patterns could then be used for proactive policy making to ensuring public safety. Big Data tools can provide actionable security intelligence by reducing the time for correlating, consolidating, and contextualizing information, and also correlate long-term historical data for forensic purposes. For instance, the WINE platform and Bot-Cloud allow the use of MapReduce to efficiently process data for security analysis. (Ardenas, 2013). Now we will discuss some of the opportunities of Big Data in the security landscape.

2.1. Efficient Resource Management to Set a Holistic Strategy

By integrating and analyzing huge amounts of structured and unstructured data from various sources we can have efficient security assessment and thereby support national security agencies to set a holistic strategy for public safety. Leveraging all sources of available data can present great opportunities for a more efficient resource management and thereby provide new insights and intelligence. Using big data logs from multiple sources could be consolidated and analysed. This provides a better security intelligence compared to analyzing in isolation.

2.2. Crime Prediction and Mitigation

Discovering hidden relationships and detecting patterns from data gathered from sources such as internet, mobile devices, transactions, email, social media etc. can reveal evidence of criminal activity. For example by correlating real time and historical user activity we can uncover abnormal user behavior and fraudulent transactions.

2.3. Enhanced Security Intelligence

Analyzing massive amount of data in real time can enhance security intelligence by providing insights into new associations. For example by analyzing network traffic in real time, attacks could be detected or by intercepting text and voice communications carried over the internet could provide intelligence about terrorist groups.

2.4. Intelligence Sharing

Big Data technologies can help in enhancing sharing of intelligence more frequently and intensively among different nations. The ability to analyze this data more effectively and quickly can produce high quality intelligence. Sharing of data between various industry sectors and with the national security agencies is also needed.

The following case study presented by Zions Bancorporation shows how Hadoop and BI analytics powered for better security intelligence.

2.4.1. Case Study: Zions Bancorporation (Source: Zions, 2015)

According to Preston Wood, CSO at Zions and the moderator of a panel of his Zion team members, the institution has been trying to move to a more data-driven approach to its security practice during the past several years. But it was finding that it was continually running into the limitations of its traditional SIEM tools.

In order to drive deeper forensics and to train statistical machine-learning models, Zions found it needed months or even years of data before it became functionally useful. This quantity of data and the frequency analysis of events was too much for SIEM to handle alone.

"We [knew] we'd be bumping our heads against the ceiling with SIEM fairly early on," Wood said. "The underlying data technology just couldn't handle it."

What's more, the analysis itself was watery. The team was swimming in data but had a hard time turning that into action.

"The SIEM is good for telling the data what to do," Wood said. "But who is telling us what to do?"

The pivotal point came with Hadoop, which allowed the company to use data in a new, more effective way. Open-source Hadoop, when coupled with Google's MapReduce, has made life much different for Zions.

"The crux of the system is the distributed file system," said Mike Fowkes, director of fraud prevention and analytics for Zions. The file system makes it easy for administrators to run Java-based queries that will then run against data spread across multiple systems. This allows more timely analysis of a greater sum of data than was before possible.

Zions' results have been dramatic. In an environment where its security systems generate 3 terabytes of data a week, just loading the previous day's logs into the system can be a challenge. It used to take a full day, Foust said.

"With MapReduce, HIVE, and Hadoop, we're doing it in near-real-time fashion," he said. "We're pulling in data every five minutes, hourly, every two minutes -- it just depends on the frequency of how fresh our data needs to be."

And actual searches can be even more dramatically fast. Searching among a month's load of logs could take anywhere between 20 minutes to an hour depending on how busy the server was, he said.

"In our environment within HIVE, it has been more like a minute to get the same deal," Fowkes said.

Aside from a boost in data-mining firepower, Hadoop's HDFS file system brings a robust level of availability to the data warehouse environment, too.

"If you're running a job and something fails on a system, it will dynamically readjust," said Fowkes, explaining that a failure of a node or a hard drive isn't the show-stopper it used to be. Instead, the system is able to reapportion the data based on the number of remaining nodes.

With a fast and effective infrastructure set up and running, Zions uses the data for dozens of purposes. Database logs, firewall, antivirus, IDS logs, plus industry-specific logs like wire ACS deposit applications and credit data are all pulled together into a centralized syslog server.

While queries are written in Java, it takes more than an off-the-shelf Java programmer to put together meaningful queries and make sense of what they return. That's where Aaron Caldiero comes in. As senior data scientist at Zions, he plays the part of "part computer scientist, part statistician, and part graphic designer," he explains.

Caldiero's job is to collect and centralize the data, design methods of synthesizing it (ranging from basic logic to machine-learning algorithms), and then present it in a coherent way.

His approach has achieved incredible results for his organizations, but it may be foreign for security professionals.

"It's a bottom-up process where you're putting the data first," Caldiero said.

Compiling huge amounts of data allows analysts to draw trends, patterns, or correlations that they might never have found had they put the questions first and sorted through terabytes of data for the answers.

It's an approach that has worked well for Zion and Wood, and his team believes it could be well-applied elsewhere. Wood stressed that the power of big data analytics isn't just for big companies, either.

"You can start with a single box in your environment," he said, stressing that it is a technology well-suited for security, but the expectation needs to be set that "big data strategy is a journey, not a destination. It's not a product you're going to buy; it's not something you're going to stand up there and be done with."

3. NATIONAL SECURITY ENVIRONMENT: THREATS OF BIG DATA

With the increased availability of data with the criminals the number and scope of attacks have also increased. Attacks are typically performed for getting access to sensitive data or to steal funds, or to damage reputation. Identity theft for instance becomes simpler with the availability of information from multiple resource. After getting hold of sufficient information, criminals use social engineering to gather the rest of the data even like logon credentials. Availability of Big Data makes detection of identity theft a harder task to accomplish.

In the next section we will discuss the challenges involved in exploiting Big Data for National security.

4. EXPLOITING BIG DATA FOR NATIONAL SECURITY - CHALLENGES

The Cloud Security Alliance in their report has highlighted top ten big data specific security and privacy challenges (CSA, 2012) as follows:

1. Secure computations in distributed programming frameworks;
2. Security best practices for non-relational data stores;
3. Secure data storage and transactions logs;
4. End-point input validation/filtering;
5. Real-time security/compliance monitoring;
6. Scalable and composable privacy-preserving data mining and analytics;
7. Cryptographically enforced access control and secure communication;
8. Granular access control;
9. Granular audits;
10. Data provenance.

In order to realize the true potential of Big Data for national security there exist numerous other challenges which are specific to the national security context. These include the challenges involved in gathering and aggregating data from multiple sources, storing managing the data thus collected for easy access and analysis, making sense of the raw data thus obtained and utilizing it for avoiding or mitigating the impact of a potential crime. Now we will briefly discuss some of the major challenges involved in the present system.

4.1. Siloed Data

Traditional Government IT systems are stand alone and Proprietary and there is lack of integrated information store. Collecting and analyzing this massive data from the application siloes in the public sector in real time is beyond the existing information handling techniques.

4.2. Rigidity of Conventional Systems

The conventional systems are rigid and are not designed to deal with the unstructured nature of Big Data. These systems normally are constrained to predefined schemes and changing them to make suitable for Big Data applications will be difficult.

4.3. Noisy and Incomplete Data Sets

Existing databases could contains lot of missing data points and noisy features making them infeasible for complex analytic applications. Proper pre-processing will be required prior to using these datasets in applications and that itself is a rigorous task. Security related applications demand real time or near real time processing and hence cannot afford longer time requirements for pre-processing.

4.4. Authenticity and Integrity of Data

Since the quality of results will depend on the data used, it is important that the sources from which data sets are obtained are reliable. The authenticity and integrity of data should be verified before using it for security related applications.

4.5. Privacy Issues

Advances in Big data analytics make privacy violations easier and issue is more complex when dealing with sensitive government data and data of individuals. The collected data could be of interest to many. These could include people from industries who can use it for marketing purposes or criminals who can use it for some fraudulent activities. Hence creating safeguards like data masking should be done to prevent abuse of big data. By this way we can make sure that the data is used only for the purpose it was collected and privacy can be ensured.

4.6. Security of Big Data

We will need new systems and tools to deal with the unique security problems presented by big data environment. Most of the traditional security solutions are not designed to take care of the cluster environment and hence new approaches keeping in mind the distributed architecture should be developed to meet the security requirements. The massive amounts of unstructured data that is being created daily such as customer transaction details including credit card numbers, data on purchasing habits, mobile communication data from cell towers etc. opens new doors for cyber criminals and hence Big Data requires a different approach to security.

4.7. Budgetary Restrictions

There is a need for robust IT infrastructure for efficient capturing and analyzing of large volumes of unstructured data. There is always a tradeoff between processing speed and accuracy. For national security applications, we need fast yet accurate analytics deployments and this demands more provisioning in the budget.

4.8. Workforce

Availability of talented workforce who can develop and use Big Data technologies is another challenge faced in the national security context.

5. BIG DATA ANALYTICS FOR CRITICAL INFRASTRUCTURE PROTECTION (CIP)

Critical Infrastructures are vital assets like public health systems, financial networks, air-traffic control systems etc. These are essential for the functioning of the society and economy. The volume of information related to critical infrastructures is increasing day by day and most of the time it crosses the peta byte threshold. Big Data analytics can play an instrumental role in protecting the critical infrastructure of a nation. Classifying critical assets and streamlined deployment of security solutions capable of taking care of distributed nature of Big Data is needed for ensuring the protection of critical infrastructures. By leveraging machine learning in the Big Data platform can help in the early detection and prevention of attacks to the critical infrastructure.

Now we will discuss two use cases of security analytics in the big data context:

Use Cases 1 - Intrusion Detection Using Big Data: Intrusion detection is a crucial part of Cyber security in a society which is increasingly dependent of computerized systems. Traditional supervised learning methods using relational databases are not suitable for highly scalable big data analysis environments and improvements to intrusion detection could be achieved by using big data technologies. Big Data models to deal with Intrusion Detection. (Suthaharan, 2014) identifies 3 big data classification problems as: (1) An ML technique that is trained on a particular labeled datasets or data domain may not be suitable for another dataset or data domain that the classification may not be robust over different datasets or data domains; (2) An ML technique is in general trained using a certain number of class types and hence a large varieties of class types found in a dynamically growing dataset will lead to inaccurate classification results; and (3) An ML technique is developed based on a single learning task, and thus they are not suitable for today's multiple learning tasks and knowledge transfer requirements of Big Data analytics. The author suggests an integration of modern technologies, Hadoop Distributed File Systems and Cloud Technologies, with the latest representation-learning technique and support vector machine to predict network intrusions through Big Data classification strategy. Similarly, the authors in (Lee Y, 2013) have proposed Hadoop technologies to measure and analyze Internet traffic for a DDOS Detector. A distributed IDS architecture based on Snort and Hadoop technologies is proposed in (Cheon J, 2013). Heterogeneity among the actual Sensors, IDSs, Analyzers, or even SIEMs can be beneficial for Intrusion Detection and greater geographical and organizational heterogeneity should be employed for Intrusion Detection (Richard Zuech, Intrusion detection and Big Heterogeneous Data: a Survey, 2015). Situational awareness could further be improved by alert and event correlation beyond geographical and organizational boundaries.

Use Cases 2 - Social Network Analysis to Detect Crime: Today Social media has become a main communication medium and it is becoming one of the biggest source of social data. Billions of people are connected thru smartphones and tablets and computers and processing these vast quantities of data demands big data technologies. Social Network Analysis (SNA) is a set of powerful techniques that can be used to identify clusters, patterns and hidden structures within social networks. SNA can be used to detect criminal activities. For example, this could be used for detecting suspicious online financial activities or for predicting crime pattern. In this relation extraction can be used to identify persons, and relationship between them. Regression based algorithms could be used to associate different objects in a social network.

Use Cases 3 - Law Enforcement Analytics: Law enforcement agencies deal with tremendous amount of data on a day to day basis. These data include call records, video surveillance data and thousands of police reports. The Internet of Things (IoT), sensors and devices produce large volume of data. By analyzing such data, long term trends and hidden patterns could be revealed which could help in predictive policing. A white paper by CTOlabs.com describes that big data analysis has been highly effective in law enforcement and can make police departments more effective, accountable, efficient, and proactive (CTOlabs.com, 2012). The author explains this using the following example: "Take, for example, dividing a city into policing districts and beats, a process every department has to conduct regularly due to crime trends and changing demographics. Patrol is the backbone of policing, and these divisions determine where patrol officers are allocated, with officers typically patrolling, answering calls for, and staying within their beat throughout their shift. Departments that do not use data analysis at all divide their city into equal portions, which is problematic as it assigns the same manpower to high crime and quiet areas. Others use crime statistics to draw up boundaries, but given the many factors involved, patrol areas are rarely a great fit. For example, distribution of officers can have an effect on crime, so a new beat map may change the very data a department is analyzing. Also, if size is predicated only on crime, quiet beats may grow too large to effectively patrol. An officer's ability to receive backup should also be considered, as well as contingencies for reshuffling beats when officers have days off and get sick or injured. In a relatively large department, analysts may look at millions of calls for service over several years to best plan patrols, but type of crime is also a factor. Fairly distributing resources also means screening for biases and confounding variables, such as wealthier or more politically connected neighborhoods having a louder voice and getting more attention than those really in need.

Hadoop provides a platform to solve all of those problems. It makes storing historical records, even phone calls and videos, cheap, as they can be kept on commodity hardware. It lets you analyze them after the fact in any way you want, as Hadoop works with raw data and implements a schema-on-read, adding whatever structure you need whenever you need it. It can also run similar analysis for other resources to allow an agency to run more smoothly at a lower price, for example tracking gas consumption by cruisers, rates of ammunition used at the firing range, serial numbers on stolen goods, and paper and form usage at stations."

6. TOOLS AND TECHNOLOGIES

Although traditional systems have been developed for analyzing event logs and network flows and for detecting intrusions and malicious activities, they are not always adequate to handle large scale heterogeneous data. New techniques such as databases related to the Hadoop ecosystem are emerging to analyze security data and improve security defenses. The various tools which can help in analyzing big data include Hive (a query language), Pig (a platform for analyzing large datasets) and Mahout (for building data mining algorithms). Hive facilitates querying and managing large datasets residing in distributed storage (Apache, Apache Hive TM, 2015). Pig consists of a high-level language for expressing data analysis programs, coupled with infrastructure for evaluating these programs. Its structure is amenable to substantial parallelization, which in turns enables them to handle very large data sets (Apache, Welcome to Apache Pig!, 2015). Mahout provides free implementations of distributed or otherwise scalable machine learning algorithms focused primarily in the areas of collaborative filtering, clustering and classification. It also provides Java libraries for common mathematical operations (Sean Owen, 2011). Relatively new frameworks like Spark are being developed to improve the efficiency of machine learning algorithms. Many of the implementations use the Apache Hadoop platform.

There are also several databases designed specifically for efficient storage and query of Big Data. These include Cassandra, CouchDB, Greenplum Database, HBase, MongoDB, and Vertica. Apache

Cassandra is an open source distributed database management system designed to handle large amounts of data across many commodity servers, providing high availability with no single point of failure. Cassandra has support for clusters spanning multiple data centers, with asynchronous masterless replication allowing low latency operations for all clients (planetcassandra, 2015). CouchDB is a database for the web which stores data as JSON documents and it supports master-master setups with automatic conflict detection. (J. Chris Anderson, 2010). In this data access and query could be done with the web browser and index, combine, and transform of documents could be done using JavaScript. Greenplum Database utilizes a shared-nothing, massively parallel processing (MPP) architecture with the ability to utilize the full local disk I/O bandwidth of each system (EMC, 2010). HBase is a non-relational database that runs on top of HDFS. Its tight integration with Hadoop makes scalability with HBase easier (George, 2011). MongoDB is a document database that provides high performance, high availability, and easy scalability. It stores data in JSON documents with lot of features of a traditional RDBMS such as secondary indexes, dynamic queries, sorting, rich updates, upserts and easy aggregation (Chodorow, 2013). HP Vertica provides advanced SQL analytics as a standards-based relational database with full support for SQL, JDBC, and ODBC. It also has numerous built-in analytical functions, including geospatial, time series and pattern matching (Agrawal, 2014). Apart from these there are scalable stream processing tools such as IBM InfoSphere which are designed for designed for stream computing. InfoSphere Streams is an advanced analytic platform that allows user-developed applications to quickly ingest, analyze and correlate information as it arrives from thousands of real-time sources with the capacity to handle very high data throughput rates, up to millions of events or messages per second (IBM, 2015). TIBCO StreamBase is a high-performance system for rapidly building applications that analyze and act on real-time streaming data. The goal of StreamBase is to offer a product that supports developers in rapidly building real-time systems and deploying them easily (TIBCO, 2015).

Case Study 1 - BotCloud Research Project (Jerome Francois, 2011): A botnet is a network of compromised hosts (bots) which are controlled by an attacker also called the botmaster and are a major threat of the current Internet. BotCloud leverages the MapReduce paradigm for analyzing enormous quantities of Netflow data to identify infected hosts participating in a botnet. 720 million netflow records (77GB) covering only 23 hours were collected from a major Internet operator was used in this project for analysis which is done by a small Hadoop cluster of 12 commodity nodes. BotCloud relies on BotTrack, which examines host relationships using a combination of PageRank and clustering algorithms. The time for analyzing the complete dataset was shown as reduced by a factor of seven by this small Hadoop cluster.

Case Study 2 Airavat - Security and Privacy for MapReduce (Roy, 2010): Airavat is an integration of mandatory access control and differential privacy. It is a MapReduce-based system which provides strong security and privacy guarantees for distributed computations on sensitive data. Mandatory access control (MAC) cannot be overridden by users, prevents information leakage via storage channels such as files, sockets, and program names. Differential privacy is a methodology for ensuring that the output of aggregate computations does not violate the privacy of individual inputs (Dwork, 2006). Airavat enables the execution of potentially untrusted data-mining and data-analysis code on sensitive data. Its objective is to accurately compute general or aggregate features of the input dataset without leaking information about specific data items. Data providers put access control labels on their data and upload them to Airavat. Airavat ensures that the result of a computation is labeled with the union of all input labels. Data providers must also create a privacy policy by setting the value of several privacy parameters. Airavat uses SELinux to execute untrusted code in a sandbox-like environment and to ensure that local and HDFS files are safeguarded from malicious users. Airavat reducers enforce differential privacy by adding exponentially distributed noise to the output of the computation.

7. EXISTING BIG DATA APPROACHES FOR NATIONAL SECURITY

Now we will discuss about some of the Big Data initiatives made by leading countries for national security. [Source: (Gang-Hoon Kim, 2014)]

U.S.: The U.S. government and IBM in 2002 collaborated to develop a massively scalable, clustered infrastructure resulting in IBM InfoSphere Stream and IBM Big Data to achieve real-time analysis of high volume streaming data,. They are platforms for discovery and visualization of information from thousands of real-time sources, encompassing application development and systems management built on Hadoop, stream computing, and data warehousing. Both are widely used by government agencies and business organizations. The U.S. government has launched Data.gov as a step toward government transparency and accountability. It is a warehouse of datasets covering transportation, economy, health care, education, and human services and a data source for multiple applications (U.S. Government. Data.gov). The Internal Revenue Service has been integrating big data-analytic capabilities into its Return Review Program (RRP), which by analyzing massive amounts of data allows it to detect, prevent, and resolve tax-evasion and fraud cases (National Information Society Agency, 2012).

U.K.: The U.K. government has implemented the U.K. Horizon Scanning Centre (HSC) in 2004 to improve the government's ability to deal with cross-departmental and multi-disciplinary challenges.

Asia: South Korea's Big Data Initiative aims to establish pan-government big-data-network-and-analysis systems; promote data convergence between the government and the private sectors; build a public data-diagnosis system; produce and train talented professionals; guarantee privacy and security of personal information and improve relevant laws; develop big-data infrastructure technologies; and develop big-data management and analytical technologies. To address national security, infectious diseases, and other national concerns, the Singapore government launched the Risk Assessment and Horizon Scanning (RAHS) program. By Collecting and analyzing large-scale datasets, it proactively manages national threats, including terrorist attacks, infectious diseases, and financial crises. (Habegger, 2010).The Japanese government has initiated several programs to address the consequences of the Fukushima earthquake, tsunami, and nuclear-power-plant disaster and the reconstruction and rehabilitation of affected areas, as well as relief of related social and economic consequences with the help of Big Data.

7.1. Case Study: NSA PRISM and MUSCULAR

National Security Agency PRISM (Planning Tool for Resource Integration, Synchronization, and Management) is a top-secret data-mining program aimed at terrorism detection and other pattern extraction authorized by federal judges working under the Foreign Intelligence Surveillance Act (FISA). This project uses big data technologies and allows the U.S. intelligence community to gain access from nine Internet companies to a wide range of digital information, including e-mails and stored data, on foreign targets operating outside the United States. As per the Guardian, the National Security Agency has obtained direct access to the systems of Google, Facebook, Apple and other US internet giants. The program facilitates extensive, in-depth surveillance on live communications and stored information. The law allows for the targeting of any customers of participating firms who live outside the US, or those Americans whose communications include people outside the US. The breadth of the data it is able to obtain include: email, video and voice chat, videos, photos, voice-over-IP (Skype, for example) chats, file transfers, social networking details, and more. The court-approved program is focused on foreign communications traffic, which often flows through U.S. servers even when sent from one overseas location to another. As per director of National Intelligence James R. Clapper: "information collected under this program is among the most important and valuable foreign intelligence information we collect, and is used to protect our nation from a wide variety of threats. The unauthorized disclosure of information about this important and entirely legal program is reprehensible and risks important protections for the security of Americans."

PRISM is an heir, in one sense, to a history of intelligence alliances with as many as 100 trusted U.S. companies since the 1970s. The NSA calls these Special Source Operations, and PRISM falls under that rubric. Even when the system works just as advertised, with no American singled out for targeting, the NSA routinely collects a great deal of American content. That is described as "incidental," and it is inherent in contact chaining, one of the basic tools of the trade. To collect on a suspected spy or foreign terrorist means, at minimum, that everyone in the suspect's inbox or outbox is swept in. Intelligence analysts are typically taught to chain through contacts two "hops" out from their target, which increases "incidental collection" exponentially. (Sources: (theguardian, 2013), (washingtonpost, 2013), (baselinemag, 2013), (informationweek, 2013)).

As per the Washington Post revelation NSA has tapped into overseas links that Google and Yahoo use to communicate between their data centers. This program, codenamed MUSCULAR, harvests vast amounts of data. A top-secret memo dated January 9, 2013 says that the NSA gathered 181,280,466 new records in the previous 30 days. Those records include both metadata and the actual content of communications: text, audio, and video. Operating overseas gives the NSA more lax rules to follow than what governs its behavior stateside.

As per baseline PRISM is using something similar to Apache Hadoop: a massively distributed file system that can hold large volumes of unstructured data and process it in a fast and parallel way. This platform must be self-healing, horizontally scalable and built with off-the-shelf components. Like Hadoop, it most likely works by sending the program to the data rather than the more traditional approach of ingesting the data into the program. According to InformationWeek, the centerpiece of the NSA's data-processing capability is Accumulo, a highly distributed, massively parallel processing key/value store capable of analyzing structured and unstructured data. Accumulo is based on Google's BigTable data model, but NSA came up with a cell-level security feature that makes it possible to set access controls on individual bits of data. Without that capability, valuable information might remain out of reach to intelligence analysts who would otherwise have to wait for sanitized data sets scrubbed of personally identifiable information. One of Accumulo's strengths is finding connections among seemingly unrelated information and as per Dave Hurry, head of NSA's computer science research section: "By bringing data sets together, Accumulo allowed us to see things in the data that we didn't necessarily see from looking at the data from one point or another," Accumulo gives NSA the ability "to take data and to stretch it in new ways so that you can find out how to associate it with another piece of data and find those threats."The power of this capability is finding patterns in seemingly innocuous public network data -- which is how one might describe the data accessed through the Prism program -- yet those patterns might somehow correlate with, say, a database of known terrorists or data on known cyber warfare initiatives. Where prior intelligence techniques have largely been based on knowing patterns and then alerting authorities when those patterns are detected, security and intelligence analysts now rely on big data to provide more powerful capabilities than analytics alone.

8. CONCLUSION AND SUMMARY

Big data technologies have a big role to play in the fight against terrorism and crime and in various other situations related to law enforcement and national security. By analyzing the data like the data from social media, emails, telecommunication systems, web logs etc security insight can be improved considerably. In this chapter we have discussed the scope of Big Data in extending cyber intelligence and enhancing national security. We have presented the case study of Zions Bancorporation in which they could increase processing efficiency using Hadoop technologies. We have also discussed the threats posed by Big Data to public safety and the challenges faced in implementing Big Data security solutions. Then we have discussed Big Data Analytics for Critical Infrastructure Protection. Three use cases, first one related to intrusion detection, the second one related to social network crime analytics and the third one related to law enforcement analytics has also been discussed. The tools and technologies for big data has been discussed along with the case studies BotCloud research project and Airavat. We have also discussed some of the existing initiatives by national governments (US UK and Asis) using Big Data technologies to address major national challenges involving terrorism, natural disasters, healthcare etc. and finally a case study of NSA PRISM aimed at terrorism detection has been presented.

REFERENCES

Agrawal, R. (2014). *HP Vertica Essentials*. Amazon & Packt Publishing.

Apache. (2015). *Apache Hive TM*. Retrieved from apache.org: https://hive.apache.org/

Apache. (2015). *Welcome to Apache Pig!* Retrieved from pig.apache.org: https://pig.apache.org/

Ardenas, A. A. (2013). Big data analytics for security. *IEEE Security and Privacy, 11*(6), 74–76. doi:10.1109/MSP.2013.138

Baselinemag. (2013). *How PRISM Validates Big Data*. Retrieved from baselinemag.com: http://www.baselinemag.com/analytics-big-data/how-prism-validates-big-data

Cheon, J. C. T.-Y. (2013). Distributed processing of snort alert log using hadoop. *Int J Eng Technol*, 2685-2690.

Chodorow, K. (2013). *MongoDB: The Definitive Guide*. O'Reilly Media.

Chris Anderson, J. J. L. (2010). CouchDB: The Definitive Guide. O'Reilly Media, Inc.

CSA. (2012). *Top ten big data security and privacy challenges.* Retrieved from Cloud Security Alliance: www.isaca.org/groups/professional.../big-data/.../big_data_top_ten_v1.pdf

CTOlabs.com. (2012). *White Paper:B ig Data Solutions For Law Enforcement.* Author.

Dwork, C. (2006). *Differential privacy.* ICALP. doi:10.1007/11787006_1

EMC. (2010). Retrieved from http://www.emc.com/collateral/hardware/white-papers/h8072-greenplum-database-wp.pdf

Gang-Hoon Kim, S. T.-H. (2014). Big-Data Applications in the Government Sector. *Communications of the ACM*, 78–85.

George, L. (2011). *HBase: The Definitive Guide Random Access to Your Planet-Size Data.* O'Reilly Media.

Habegger, B. (2010). Strategic foresight in public policy: Reviewing the experiences of the U.K., Singapore, and the Netherlands. *Futures*, *42*(1), 49–58. doi:10.1016/j.futures.2009.08.002

IBM. (2015). *IBM InfoSphere Streams.* Retrieved from ibm.com: http://www-03.ibm.com/software/products/en/infosphere-streams

Informationweek. (2013). *Defending NSA Prism's Big Data Tools.* Retrieved from informationweek.com: http://www.informationweek.com/big-data/big-data-analytics/defending-nsa-prisms-big-data-tools/d/d-id/1110318?

Jerome Francois, S. W. (2011). BotCloud: Detecting Botnets Using MapReduce. *IEEE International Workshop on Information Forensics.*

Lee, Y. L. Y. (2013). Toward scalable internet traffic measurement and analysis with hadoop. *ACM SIGCOMM Comput Commun Rev*, 5-13.

National Information Society Agency. (2012). Retrieved from http://www.koreainformationsociety.com/2013/11/koreas-national-information-society.html

Planetcassandra. (2015). *What is Apache Cassandra?* Retrieved from http://planetcassandra.org: http://planetcassandra.org/what-is-apache-cassandra/

Richard Zuech, T. M. (2015). Intrusion detection and Big Heterogeneous Data: a Survey. *Journal of Big Data.*

Richard Zuech, T. M. (2015). Intrusion detection and Big Heterogeneous Data: A Survey. *Journal of Big Dat*, *2*(1), 3. doi:10.1186/s40537-015-0013-4

Roy, I. S. (2010). Airavat: Security and Privacy for MapReduce. *NSDI*, 297-312.

Sean Owen, R. A. (2011). *Mahout in Action.* Manning Publications.

Suthaharan, S. (2014). Big data classification: Problems and challenges in network intrusion prediction with machine learning. *Performance Evaluation Review*, *41*(4), 70–73. doi:10.1145/2627534.2627557

Tene, O., & Polonetsky, J. (2012). *Privacy in the age of big data: A time for big decisions.* Stanford Law Review Online.

Theguardian. (2013, June 6). *NSA Prism program taps in to user data of Apple, Google and others*. Retrieved from theguardian.com: http://www.theguardian.com/world/2013/jun/06/us-tech-giants-nsa-data

TIBCO. (2015). *TIBCO StreamBase Named Leader in Forrester Wave for Big Data Streaming Analytics Platforms 2014*. Retrieved from tibco.com: http://www.tibco.com/products/event-processing/complex-event-processing/streambase-complex-event-processing

Tudor Dumitras, D. S. (2011). *Toward a standard benchmark for computer security research: The Worldwide Intelligence Network Environment (WINE)*. Building Analysis Datasets and Gathering Experience Returns for Security. doi:10.1145/1978672.1978683

U.S. Government. Data.gov. (n.d.). Retrieved from http://www.data.gov

Washingtonpost. (2013, June 7). *U.S., British intelligence mining data from nine U.S. Internet companies in broad secret program*. Retrieved from washingtonpost.com: http://www.washingtonpost.com/investigations/us-intelligence-mining-data-from-nine-us-internet-companies-in-broad-secret-program/2013/06/06/3a0c0da8-cebf-11e2-8845-d970ccb04497_story.html

Zions, B. (2015). *A Case Study In Security Big Data Analysis*. Retrieved from darkreading.com: http://www.darkreading.com/analytics/security-monitoring/a-case-study-in-security-big-data-analysis/d/d-id/1137299?

Chapter 14
Big Data Models and the Public Sector

N. Nawin Sona
Government of India, India

ABSTRACT

This chapter aims to give an overview of the wide range of Big Data approaches and technologies today. The data features of Volume, Velocity, and Variety are examined against new database technologies. It explores the complexity of data types, methodologies of storage, access and computation, current and emerging trends of data analysis, and methods of extracting value from data. It aims to address the need for clarity regarding the future of RDBMS and the newer systems. And it highlights the methods in which Actionable Insights can be built into public sector domains, such as Machine Learning, Data Mining, Predictive Analytics and others.

INTRODUCTION

Big Data with its Volume, Variety and Velocity is an emerging area in the public sector. The public sector is a depository of enormous citizen related, infrastructure, economic, operational, statistical and archival data. Rapid growth in data with the 3Vs is matched by proliferation of new technological options to store, process and analyze them. However, despite the widespread use in the web based private enterprises, public sector adoption of Big Data technologies is limited. On a global scale, The United Nations E-Government Survey (2014) does not indicate extensive usage of Big Data technologies.

The use of Big Data has been pioneered in the USA, but is uneven across the public sector (Desouza, 2014). In the Executive of Office of the President of United States' factsheet, Big Data Across the Federal Government (2009), various uses are quoted from Departments of Defense, Homeland Security, Energy, Veterans Administration, Health and Human service among others. In USA, the TechAmerica Foundation-SAP Public Sector Survey (2012) is very indicative: although 63% of Federal and 76% of State IT officials say it is very important and extremely beneficial, the largest implementation barriers mentioned include a) privacy and policy concerns b) demonstrating the level of Return on Investment and c) lack of clear ownership of Big Data within the organization.

DOI: 10.4018/978-1-4666-9649-5.ch014

This gap needs to be filled by better understanding within the public sector about the technology and its methods and approaches. Palmer (2006) estimates that only half percent of all data is being analyzed for insight. Enormous data stand un-analyzed due to the limitations of traditional Business Intelligence tools, lack of flexibility of data integration and paucity of suitable algorithms to deliver analytics.

BACKGROUND

The newer Big Data technologies now enable the public sector to understand the patterns, and the ecosystem generating it, model the data, enable analytics, and in effect, extract actionable insights and eventually achieve prescriptive models. Various surveys, such as the World Economic Forum's "Global Information Technology Report 2014", have shown that there are effective and potential use cases of Big Data in public sector in improving Citizen Services, Medicine, Public Health, Education, Crime Mapping and prediction, emergencies such as epidemics, natural calamities and terrorist attacks, Urban Planning, Utilities planning, Power grid load balancing, Smart Cities, Smart Buildings, Predictive Modeling in fraud detection. Big Data also, has the potential for data driven policy making.

BIG DATA MODELS

Understanding the Data

Types of Data

Data is acknowledged as the "new oil" (Palmer, 2006). Today there is emergence of newer data formats and evolution of older ones. The RDBMS, SQL based systems relied on structured schema into which the highly cleaned and precisely formatted data was stored and processed. Structured data is a sine qua non in the transactional RDBMSs and for financial data where consistency and security reign supreme. Whereas, Semi-structured data (XML, JSON, RDF, YAML) are usually tagged and are Machine Readable and the aim is to make it Human Readable. And Unstructured data such as books, video, images, audio files, web pages, social media content, blog posts, comments on forums, streaming multimedia, are Human Readable data, and the aim is to make it Machine Readable. Other important data-types are Geospatial, Machine-to-machine (M2M) transmitted from mobile devices and sensors.

In formulating a Big Data deployment plan, it is necessary to understand the domain and its peculiar problems. The existing core transactional, operational data available for Business Intelligence (hereinafter BI), MIS, other ERP or CRM should be estimated. The frequency of data collection, the sources, whether streaming or static, freshness or staleness of data, frequency of updating and analysis are all factors that must be considered.

Big Data is useful where RDBMSs are limited by schema, query boundaries, cost of cleaning data and their lack of feasibility in processing unstructured and semi structured data. The question is not whether the choice is between Big Data and RDBMSs; but whether to use both Big Data *and* RDBMSs, or not. Hence, understanding available data relevant to the domain, which can be combined and mined for insight, would be crucial in designing a Big Data deployment model.

Bad and Unused Data

With Big Data's 3Vs, bad data is a given. The data within the data-warehousing environment, in various silos and data marts are highly cleaned, high cost data. With multiple streaming data sources, external sources, such as social media, and diversity in formats, quality standards are wildly variable. With sparse data, empty fields in tables, old data mixed with new, conflicting dependencies may occur. With issues of duplication, false records, invalid records, multi table queries (especially with joins) or nested queries, existing data warehousing tools get limited in time, feasibility and/or in cost.

Unstructured data was once also bad data and was never seen as sources of value. With Hadoop, for instance, through Hive and Sqoop, it is possible technically, within reasonable cost, using commodity hardware with cloud-based granularity to combine RDBMS data with completely schema free and unstructured data.

Public sector and inter agency and government-citizen sharing of data under the Open Government initiatives (USA, OECD, UN, EU) has brought large reusable, machine readable datasets available for users. Given the objective, approach, choice of algorithm, and method (pattern recognition, data mining or predictive analytics) even unstructured information could give insight (OECD, 2013).

Use Case - Crime Analysis and Predictive Models in various cities such as Chicago, Los Angeles have demonstrated live cases of Big Data being put to use in Real Time or Near Real Time (LAPD, 2014; Predpol, 2014).

Extraction of Insight

The public sector by extracting insight, and by translating that insight into action, will gain in operational as well as cost efficiencies, better response time and greater citizen benefit. Big Data is a potential way to see "the Big Picture": one starts by breaking out data from the silos and data marts, and combines it with contextual data. Resulting in a continuously validated model of understanding and response, prediction and prevention in the domain space.

In health services Big Data's impact may be far reaching as initial successes have demonstrated. For instance, disease typology and specialized care, such as Cancer tumor repository, patient hospital interactions such re-hospitalization studies and hospital borne infections are analyzed for insight from the Electronic Health Records (EHR). By real time analysis and modeling of vital signs and various streamed data from neo natal care units, Canadian health care has shown Big Data use in immediate lifesaving scenarios (Brooks, 2013).

In epidemics and emergency management, such as the Ebola outbreak, Big Data can be used to model and respond to geographic spread, genetic modifications of the virus, and of course by using twitter data, social media, web trawling, web scraping, Natural Language Processing algorithms and data mining, combined with geo-tagging, one can pin point the epidemic's extent and spread. Google flu trends is another excellent example of analytics in the web, using search queries.

Insight through Data Analysis would sometime throw up some surprising results. Apparently unrelated factors may be correlated; irrespective of the Bonferroni principle, they have lead to valid predictive models.

Big Data Models: A Transition

The database landscape has changed a lot since the RDBMS and Data Warehousing evolutions; many factors have contributed to the changes:

- IP based connectivity over traditional or proprietary connectivity standards;
- Cloud based data centers for PaaS, SaaS, and IaaS;
- Distributed storage systems, HDFS, Google;
- Distributed computing ecosystems, Hadoop;
- Cluster computing algorithms;
- Unstructured and streaming data;
- Open source distributions of various platforms, software available for large and small corporations;
- Crowdsourced and community led innovations through meet ups, hackathons and shared resources.

In this context, the transitions occurring in the non-SQL, namely NoSQL, and NewSQL ecosystem and it's interaction with the Apache Hadoop ecosystem of distributed file system and cluster computing will be explored.

Traditional RDBMS and Data Warehousing and Big Data

A brief overview of RDBMS (Relational Database Management Systems) environment would be necessary to appreciate the scope, scale and innovation (also the limitations) of Big Data systems. RDBMSs primarily store data in tables or tuples, linked with keys (primary and foreign), with indexing, and are the mainstay of transactional and operational data, in enterprise-scale Data Warehouses and in established Business Intelligence systems.

A Relational database, despite its name, does not establish relationships per se between the real world entities being reflected in the data model. The "relation" refers to the row of the table, which contains a series of values, mathematically represented by tuples. The relation is also between the tables. And the fact that the rows are the "relations" itself, has led to better models, such as the Columnar databases; the lack of weights, directionality, clear linkages or true "relationships" between values or entities has lead to Graph based databases.

OLTP, OLAP and Beyond

RDBMS is extremely robust, secure and fast in transactional scenarios. On Line Transaction Processing (OLTP) and On Line Analytical Processing (OLAP) including its basic Business Intelligence tools of slice and dice, roll up, drill down are still good for thousands and a few millions of fields of data. But with Big Data the scale is upwards from where the RDBMS trails off; Big Data and NoSQL databases and data stores tackle hundreds of millions or billions of fields of data. OLAP and its in-memory, multi-dimensional variation MOLAP, and relational variation ROLAP are still widely used; in simpler uses it could be just multidimensional pivot tables and 'online' here means a reasonable latency for the user and not essentially internet based.

Limitations of RDBMS systems come in with sophisticated queries, where entire database is involved – increasing cost in time, computation cycles and disk access. For some queries the time delay would be not desirable or results actionable, especially in today's "web-scale" interfaces. For instance, for on line marketing firm, RDBMS would be ideal to summarize all the orders of a single customer. But to find out all those who bought a particular product or to find out what other products were bought along with a particular product, where the entire database needs to be parsed to generate the reply, RDBMS systems have complications. These levels of large-scale queries would be done in Big Data technologies without complications, and at extremely high speeds.

Before Moving away from Relational Databases

- **ACID vs. BASE:** Before talking about abandoning RDBMS, its primary strength needs to be understood. One would invariably come across ACID (Atomicity, Consistency, Isolation and Durability) as one of its great advantages; coined by Andreas Reuter and Theo Härder (1983):
  - **Atomicity:** The transaction should execute fully or not at all. If any element of a transaction or operation fails the entire transaction is nullified;
  - **Consistency:** The database constraints are not violated by the transactions, and the rules of the transactions are followed, and effect of the completed valid transactions are reflected in the system;
  - **Isolation:** One transaction does not have access to other transactions;
  - **Durability:** The effects of a validly completed transaction cannot be undone and should persist in the database even in the event of system failure.

ACID is the fundamental guarantee any transaction based RDBMS should give. Isolation is taken care by the DBMS through various concurrency controls and locking. These features are good for horizontally scalable, tabular databases. Public sector data, like citizen information, social security, taxation, licenses, and utility billing data are primarily ACID compliant relational data, usually in Data Warehouses.

- **CAP Theorem:** Eric Brewer (2000) through the ACM Symposium on the Principles of Distributed Computing proposed the CAP Theorem, enlisting Consistency Availability and Partition tolerance as three tenets of Distributed Computing; since then explored in depth by Seth Gilbert and Nancy Lynch of MIT in 2002:
  - **Consistency:** Same data is accessed by entire distributed computing nodes at any given time;
  - **Availability:** System availability to requests and response at all time (irrespective of success or failure of the request);
  - **Partition Tolerance:** Tolerance of the system to partial loss of the system or to data.

It is notable that this version of consistency is often seen at transaction level in ACID, at system state level in distributed computing platforms. When many nodes exist in distributed systems (even in shared memory, shared disk or shared nothing configuration) loss of resources or data should not affect the rest of the system. This theorem and the discussion around it has driven database architecture and design to take note of data as the primary focus and the interpretation that at any given instance only two of the three of the CAP factors would be compliant has again led to a deviation from the relational data models. In fact this evolved into what is called the BASE conditions of current day databases.

BASE stands for:

- **Basically Available:** The availability of the system to the various nodes is guaranteed but, it is "basic" in the sense that some kind of response would be there;
- **Soft state:** Where the data is available even if it cached;
- **Eventual Consistency:** The system eventually "converges" to a consistent state, only to be dynamically altered again, however no transaction or operation is halted while verification for consistency, soft state is used and later reconciled.

The tongue in cheek ACID vs. BASE debate is very relevant to the Big Data technologies. For pattern recognition, social media data, sentiment analysis, twitter based geo tagged analytics, for recommendation systems, for collaborative filtering ACID requirements do not make a strong case. However, when rapid response, low latency, high tolerance, very large volumes are the priority then BASE would be sufficient. And when ACID properties are required as in financial transactions, banking systems, high security systems, then RDBMS are still the choice. And for BASE, newer Big Data technologies have paved the way combined with distributed ecosystems such as Apache Hadoop and the NoSQL databases.

NoSQL and NewSQL Databases

NoSQL databases and Hadoop ecosystem, first sidesteps ACID in favor of BASE conditions and finds various other features follow suit. Not Only SQL databases are:

- Highly horizontally scalable;
- Very fast;
- Flexible in structure and often schema-less (i.e. non tabular).

Types of NoSQL Databases

- **Columnar:** These use the column as the store of the data vis-a-vis the row, which is seen as the record and a relation in a tabular database. They have rapid record scanning, easier record addition, very high scalability and flexibility. E.g. BigTable, Hadoop, HBase, Cassandra, Cloudera.
- **Document Oriented:** These use both human readable and machine-readable semi structured formats. The original document, where applicable, is stored originally like an XML, PDF, binary or plain text formats and the human read meta data is stored together (as in XML or PDF), or in attached JSON or BSON document. Document oriented databases are quite popular in the NoSQL world.
- **Graph Databases:** These are based on the Graph Theory mathematics initially developed by Euler in the eighteenth century. Recognizing Nodes, Connections called Vertices and Edges, the graph is a actually a store of "relations" between the entities, complete with directionality, weight (properties of relations), and names (types of relations). For example, names of vertices could be persons A, B and C, relation names being friend, enemy with different combinations of mutual or single directional friendships or enmity of different intensities. Also notable is that the nodes or vertices are modeled on key value pairs, giving great analytical, and limitless scalability. Graph databases are very good for OLTP systems. They are either Native Graph Storage, which store the data itself as graphs or not. Also, they are classified as whether using Native Graph Processing or

not. Examples include a wide range from Neo4j (both Native Store and Processing), to FlockDB (both non-native).They are also in memory or single machine graph databases like Cassovary or distributed graph compute engines like Pegasus or Giraph. Advantages are they use graph algorithms and are technically more efficient and proponents see Hadoop as a brute force method of parallel processing poorer algorithms.

- **Key Value Stores:** Key value stores work by allocation of value against keys (attributes) in a format called an "associate array" or "map". They are advantageous for flexibility, speed and easy integration with other formats. MongoDB, DynamoDB, FoundationDB and Riak are popular key value based databases.

NewSQL Databases

NewSQL databases are mainly modified relational data models with SQL query interfaces. Prominent examples include H-Store. Notable is that SQL RDBMS were traditionally and largely not designed for distributed computing and storage platforms, wherein the overheads and the limitations would surface. Whereas, NewSQL systems are often parallel and distributed database systems, and hence become feasible for Big Data integration. NewSQL reduces the scale of operations onto manageable subsets of data, while retaining the interface and limit the concurrency control of RDBMS. Examples are H-Store, VoltDB, MemSQL, SAP HANA, Foundation DB and many others.

Scalability Factors in Public Sector

Public sector deals with large amounts of data, involving the entire country, state, county or city and relating to millions or sometimes billions of individuals. The data collected is also in many dimensions. With factors of hundreds of dimensions, each with many fields, and thousands of connections (in a graphical sense) in certain domains it amounts to billions of columns of data to analyze. This brings us to the scalability of databases: traditionally scalability is considered addition of records in the schema already defined and addition of memory, disk space, nodes or connections (Horizontal scalability) or additions of more processes and applications (Vertical scalability). In the context of Big Data, we are looking at many versions of Scalability:

- Scale of data addition (Streaming data, NoSQL columnar databases like HBase);
- Scale in variety of data increasing (Schema agnostic data processing, with eventual consistency);
- Scale of data access (HDFS, Hadoop Distributed File System);
- Scale of processing (Multicore processing, Multithread algorithms, Distributed, Parallel and Cluster computing platforms, for e.g. MapReduce);
- Scale of analysis (Visualization, simulation, deep analytics, wide analytics, multimodal analytics).

All these features are combined in Big Data ecosystems such as a Hadoop with MapReduce running on a Distributed cluster of "commodity computers", achieving "web-scale" operations, of course it has it's own limitations, namely ACID. But for flexibility in other operations Big Data has a distinct advantage.

Schema and Big Data

Schema is usually associated with the tabular RDBMS databases. Big Data has ushered in a complete range of data into itself purview: from schema free unstructured data and databases of NoSQL, to semi-structured flexible schema data, to schema bound databases with relaxed concurrency control, the range is quite wide.

Schema Types of RDBMS, NoSQL and NewSQL

The RDBMS' tabular nature, necessitates linkages between the tables, and thereby linkages between the "relations" by way of schema. Well-known schema of linkages are Star schema and Snowflake schema. These schemas are also used by the NewSQL databases, but with relaxed concurrency control, while maintaining ACID, as mentioned before.

Similarly NewSQL tries to merge the best of RDBMS world, with the advantages of distributed and parallel systems. They are highly scalable, maintain ACID compliance and give more efficient per node performance and are seen as suitable for OLTP environments to replace scale limited SQL RDBMS.

Fixed Schema vs. Schema-Less Databases

Schema in databases would not disappear, nor would RDBMS; as long as ACID and transactional fidelity are needed, schema bound systems and data warehouses will exist. As opposed to initial expectations, as it stands now, there is a strong indication that Hadoop and Hadoop like technologies are not going to completely replace the RDBMS environment. Hence, there is a great range of use cases from integration of schema bound and schema agnostic data to be analyzed on a single platform. As will be detailed later, Hadoop, with Hive query interface and Sqoop data imports from RDBMS, it is best of both worlds, which Big Data is allowing.

Hence, it is not a question of fixed schema vs. schema less. It is both together, which would give larger insight. Amazon or other web-based marketplaces use structured data for consistency and transactions and NoSQL or HDFS and other data mining tools for recommendations, clustering etc.

Flexibility: Schema on Read vs. Schema on Write

Traditional schema based systems would involve "Schema on write", the data is fitted into the modeled schema while it is written, or it is not written into it, at all. In the Data Warehousing milieu this means an ETL (Extract Transform Load) operation where the differing data is transformed to fit the schema and is loaded into the database, making it available for OLAP tools.

Big Data technologies veer towards the "Schema on Read" model, where the data is stored without typifying the schema or the data model. The common pool of data is read by the user, depending on the application, thereby, albeit, a virtual schema is created in the process of reading. The interesting offshoot of this approach is a subtle change from "Database" to "Distributed Datastore" such as Apache Cassandra, Google's BigTable, Druid used by Netflix, Amazon's Dynamo, HBase used by Facebook, Riak and Voldemort used by Linkedin. These distributed datastores are designed to be billions of rows and millions of columns, storing petabytes of data, across thousand nodes (Chang et al., 2006).

The distributed datastore is a lightweight but highly scalable datastore, spread over clusters. Hence the concomitant usage of Cloud services for hosting data, flexibility in deploying the cluster, managing the processors, all at fine granularity. This means that as the demand changes, the cloud service can be called to increase/decrease storage, processing capacity, memory, applications. Cloud deployment of distributed data store enables scaling on demand and would enable rapid modifications to the database with very low latency and rapid re-scaling.

Fixed, Flexible or Evolving Systems

The challenge is actually the change, especially the rate of change which public sector will have to deal with. With upcoming "Internet of Everything", "Internet of Things", "Industrial Internet", Deep data, High Power Computing (HPC), Big Data itself would rapidly evolve. The reading of the current scenario gives a "Primordial Soup" of Big Data technologies, how they would combine, mutate and eventually evolve is to be seen. Fundamentally the greatest advantages of the Big Data systems are the flexibility and scalability.

Big Data technologies today are mostly open source with various distributions. There are competing combinations of Hadoop with other databases such as MapR. Hadoop ecosystem itself is flexible to interact with the orthodox as well as the path breakers. Hence, in the future, flexibility would be the key to keep systems alive and responsive.

Public sector deals with Policies, Programs and Projects, as well as Infrastructure, Services, Utilities, Security and as well as Socio-Economic welfare activities. However, the data is vertical and often in agency specific data warehouses, data marts, and silos. Limiting data to silos and the restricted Business Intelligence tools would rob both the agencies for deeper insight into their own operations, by seeing it in context of data from other agencies, departments. Hence the choice between a schema agnostic or flexible schema and a bound schema ought to be taken based on ACID and transactional fidelity concerns.

Hence, Big Data's schema flexibility, cloud deployment, NoSQL and NewSQL, goes well with rapid changes that occur in needs of Governance. The recent economic crisis, various economic shocks to the oil industry, housing sector, banking, privacy concerns itself needs flexibility and rapid change in assessing the emergent situation and to respond with confidence. Policies change, so do programs and its approaches – flexibility and responsiveness is the need of public sector today. The aim ought to be rapid, yet deep assessment of domain problem and effective responses based on sound data.

Data Integration Challenges

The gap between the SQL/RDBMS systems and the NoSQL worlds are closing in. One approach is that of SQL like query languages like that of Hive within the Hadoop ecosystem, which is the user facing layer, or Pig within the same system which is more developer facing layer (Stonebraker, M., 2014).

Data Integration and NoSQL and NewSQL Systems

The main advantages of NoSQL are the schema flexibility, which make it evolvable seamlessly, scalability, which means ability to handle millions of users, large number of devices, respond to elastic loads, making it suitable for agile development and deployment in cloud architectures. Development times are less, and primarily making it easy to integrate with other database types because of its open structure.

Novel methods of data integration would be a little out of the box, with Data Visualization being a key aspect in which lots of visual analysis would help in identifying patterns and to select the data or to identify the bad from the good while integrating data. Schema mapping, entity clustering are other approaches which are being partially automated, with human expert interventions, through various new applications such as Data Wrangler, Data Tamer etc.

The Evolutions of New Data Models in Big Data: Hadoop and MapReduce, NoSQL and RDBMS

With many emergent technologies, the Big Data universe is in a state of constant flux. The technical options are quite vast and often confusion or misconceptions reign regarding capabilities of individual approaches, advantages of combinations technologies, limitations of such combinations, and of course technical feasibilities as well as cost and other efficiencies. This section aims to introduce the approaches of data handling and their interactions through the Hadoop and MapReduce Ecosystem.

Hadoop a Brief Introduction

Origins of Hadoop lie in the *Google GFS*, a distributed file system and *Google MapReduce* initiatives; later in 2006, Doug Cutting fleshed out the Hadoop system, and it has come to mean a complete eco-system. Hadoop is a distributed, cluster and parallel computing platform, which operates on a cluster of "commodity" hardware with high-speed interconnectivity. Earlier, only the supercomputers with MPP (Massive Parallel Processing) capabilities could achieve such tasks, now, with Cloud based deployment, the Hadoop ecosystem is able scale seamlessly and rapidly.

This is achieved by *HDFS*, the *Hadoop Distributed File System*, in which a single file is broken up into blocks, which are at least 64MB or above, as against a typical 4 to 32 KB block in other file systems. These blocks are distributed across nodes for storage across the cluster. The cluster itself is a stack or many stacks of processors and storages, and may run into many thousands, under a single roof. The HDFS itself has a single NameNode (a master node), which coordinates the cluster. It "names" other nodes, the Data Nodes, in which the broken up data is sent for storage. The storage is on a hard disk attached to the node. It is noted that this is a "shared nothing" architecture, where the resources of the cluster nodes are completely independent, thereby saving time in read/write, disk access time, memory bus bottlenecks, or in processor capacities. This is essence the cluster computing, parallel processing paradigm on which Hadoop operated. The HDFS manages in distributing the files, along with replication of a whole or part of the file between the nodes; this is critical and in a way the success of the HDFS rests on automating this capability very effectively. That the nodes, especially "commodity" hardware ones, are going to fail is a given; in the event of failures of connection, storage, processor, memory and/or connectivity, the distributed data should not be lost. This is where the BASE conditions, discussed earlier kick in: stepping aside the ACID conditions, HDFS manages the loss by replication and careful recovery of lost data by the NameNode. The user can set the levels of replication, and redundancy and recovery are taken care of by the HDFS system. In event of node failure, the NameNode calls the aborted data or process from the replicated node and completed the task.

MapReduce and Hadoop

Before going more into Hadoop it is necessary to appreciate MapReduce. MapReduce is a programming model, which operates over distributed platforms, of clusters or grids (across geographies or heterogeneous configurations). In MapReduce the program tasks are allocated to different nodes, based on a Key Value pair model. Each "Job" is split into "Tasks" by a master node called the JobTracker and assigned to various nodes in a cluster. The slave nodes called the TaskTracker acts on the task, and complete the task, returns the result based on the Key Value pair and moves onto the next task. The TaskTracker does this by setting up a virtual machine, in this case a Java VM to execute the task. The program itself is split into a MapFunction and a ReduceFunction. The Map function splits the job to various parts and "maps" it to the nodes in the cluster, the Shuffle step reorganizes the output of the MapFunction, such that all those with the same key are reassigned and collected to a single node. Then the ReduceFunction, collates the different parts of the results, from various keys, and combines them to form the final result.

It is notable that distributed storage and computation interact across the nodes depending on the configuration. The master node, for storage, the NameNode, and the master for MapReduce, the JobTracker are usually preferred to be separate. However, the slave node, for storage, the DataNode is the same as the TaskTracker. Given the cloud based deployment, the cluster configuration is easily customized as per the aim of the computation itself. This is in essence the Hadoop and MapReduce interaction.

The hardware involved is also critical, the master node, is recommended to have not less than 4 independent RAID 1TB disk drives and at least 64GB of RAM. Multicore processors is the norm, with 16 CPUs being recommended, with up to 10GB bandwidth connectivity. The cluster nodes are in the range of at least 8 x 2TB SATA drives each, with at least 24GB of RAM, and quad core processors for large applications. This is of course dependent on the application (http://www.hortonworks.com). Multithreading is another factor which is debated in the Big Data technologies; to take full advantage of the distributed and parallel processing systems, multithread programming and processing is recommended.

HDFS and the Hadoop Ecosystem

It is important to know that HDFS is not the only file system from which the data can be accessed – by way of various interfaces; the Hadoop system can get data into it:

- HDFS and NoSQL datastores, databases (Graphs, Columnar);
- HDFS and distributed column based databases (HBase);
- HDFS and NewSQL databases such as the OLTP VoltDB, which also uses distributed shared nothing architecture, through Sqoop, a proprietary interface for data exchange within the Hadoop ecosystem;
- HDFS and SQL like technologies like SAP HANA, with distributed cluster and shared nothing architecture suitable for Hadoop;
- HDFS can input formats such as flat files, text files, and binary files;
- HDFS can interact with RDBMS through Sqoop.

As can be seen, Hadoop's strengths are HDFS, flexibility, scalability, fault tolerance and replicability. If the entirety of the Hadoop ecosystem is considered, the advantages would be clearer. The Hadoop ecosystem comprises of:

- **HDFS:** Is a distributed file system on a cluster of nodes;
- **Pig:** Is a high-level data flow language, more developer oriented;
- **Hive:** Is a SQL like querying interface for users to be deployed in data warehouse environments;
- **Spark:** Is a compute engine on which various applications can be run including ETL, machine learning, stream processing, and graph computation;
- **Mahout:** Is a scalable machine learning and data mining library;
- **HBase:** Is a scalable distributed database;
- **Sqoop:** Is an important tool to import data into HDFS either directly or through Hive, from RDBMS and also other NoSQL formats.

The traditional data modeling role, which was a key factor in the RDBMS environment, is set to change. Of course it would be relevant in that system, but Big Data has different approaches to data modeling:

- **Store First and Ask Questions Later:** This is when the massive amount of data is not filtered out, and the questions are framed later – may be applied to Pattern Recognition, text analytics, sentiment analytics, predictive models;
- **Load First and Model Later:** This is when the unstructured or semi structured data is collected, and a "schema on read" approach is taken, by selectively analyzing the data that is relevant.

Both these approaches are offset by the opinions of those data scientists who firmly believe that good data science starts with questions and not with data. These divergent views exist, and the former needs to be evaluated carefully. The notion that data storage is almost free is gaining ground and that may not bode well at the scale of Big Data, which would deal with petabytes of data. Especially, the public sector could fall prey to both the approaches that all data is good, or potentially good. Hence, caution is advised.

Move the Code not the Data

This approach is the tenet of distributed computing and distributed storage. The cluster or grid computing platforms, as well as mobile computing platforms with better computational and memory capacity have encouraged this approach. For example, MapReduce programming model takes full advantage of the distributed storage of HDFS and literally sends the code to the node in the form of the map function and executed the tasks in a distributed manner. HDFS in tandem operates to replicate the data. Of course, if the data set is not big enough, the HDFS system or the MapReduce framework would waste the resources, when the data or the computation would be restricted to a smaller number of nodes in the cluster, while the rest of the nodes are idle. Hence, the volume, and the computational complexity are both factors. However, since Hadoop is seen as a more "brute force" compute, with relatively simpler algorithms, it is more a factor of volume.

NoSQL Data Modeling Techniques

Data mining with large data sets involve creating aggregates and dimensionality reduction. As briefly described by Lescovec, Rajaram and Ullman (2014) in terms of matrix algebra, it involves a smaller product of matrices which approximates the original matrix, where the matrix itself is a representation of the attributes and values, say a graph database.

Processing Power

With distributed store, and cluster or grid computing the processing power is much cheaper than what it used to be. Many factors are influential in this regard:

- Cluster computing requires commodity hardware and not supercomputers;
- Connectivity within the cluster is as much critical as the processors; because the speed of the connection would be the weakest link in the chain of a cluster computing;
- Computing power is now multicore, usually quadcore or sometimes hexa-core or more;
- Multithread programming would be required to take full advantage;
- In-memory computing would also mean better computations performance;
- Better algorithmic integration with actual applications would mean better utilization of processing power;
- Concurrency control, locking and other processes often consume lot of computation power;
- Failure tolerance must be built in the cluster;
- MTBF in a cluster is rather high, hence replication and redundancy is critical;
- Cloud Computing is an effective model for deploying varying configurations of computational powers;
- Fine grain, pay as you go billing for computation in Cloud is very cost effective;
- Rapid scaling of computation power is now possible by Cloud.

Right now the need of the hour is to have dedicated public sector cloud services. Many governments have launched Cloud Services in various configurations as Infrastructure, Platform or Software as services. Hybrid clouds have private and public Clouds merged for services and hosting.

Big Data: The Specters of Volume and Variety

Having such powerful tools in the arsenal of Big Data, it would be pertinent to gain traction with relevant amount and variety of data. Public sector is such that both are not only plenty, but it is bound to grow as more and more services go online and paper archiving (especially in less developed nations) increase the newer, but historical data. This would lead to both increase in both directions of time, with more and more archival data becoming available, combined with newer sources of data generated in the future. The historical, current and projected data would be critical to achieve predictive power and effective analysis.

Hence it is essential to grasp the volume and variety aspects in particular. Growth of data is something one has to plan for. Public sector and Governments have a large responsibility to itself and to the public to come up with viable and sound strategies to tackle the upcoming boom of data that the current century would see. Of course, storage is getting cheaper, so is the data generation point – every mobile device, phone, tablet, sensor is a generator of data.

Volume of Big Data

In the World Economic Forum GITR 2014, it is noted that an Exabyte (10^{18}) of data is created every day. Largely stored in data warehouses, where OLTP or OLAP activities are done mostly for Business Intelligence processes. IDC projects that the digital universe will reach 40 zettabytes (ZB) by 2020, an amount that exceeds previous forecasts by 5 ZBs, resulting in a 50-fold growth from the beginning of 2010, (IDC, 2012).

There may be scenarios where Volume is not yet there. What may not be "web-scale" would still be large amount of data in public sector. It is worthy to emphasize that Volume, if not readily available, can and should be created especially in the public sector. Federal or central agencies, State level agencies and Governments, as well as County/District level governments, City Governments, various agencies collect data. Also utility companies, and regulatory agencies, commissions, committees actively collect data. There are also data from Government or public sector funded Research institutions, grants, and surveys done by academic and policy institutions, which can be collated. Of course public sector data would also include data openly available, though not of government origin; private consulting companies, advocacy groups, various economic forums and councils, industrial associations, user groups also generate data – these are also potential sources to obtain a more holistic view at the domain in question.

Across domains also, diverse data sets could also be combined, these are sometimes the sources of surprising insight and have thrown open new ways of looking at the same old issues completely in a new light. For instance in the health sector, data of hospitalizations, patient visit frequency, spending on HNIs, health insurance data, corporate or educational data on absenteeism based on health, food spending and lifestyle diseases, pollution datasets and transportation aspects of health, emergency response data, housing information, vaccination data, health sample surveys could create a massive data set if combined.

Certain services are fundamental to public sector data, namely GPS tags, GIS data, which nowadays could be culled off Twitter or Social Media and secondly sensor information which public utilities have planted would be invaluable sources for infrastructure planning, utility optimization and in general, resource planning, urban planning, and area development.

Big Data Variety

Of the greatest challenges, yet to gain focus, is that of Variety. There staggering variety of data which public sector would be in possession of would have to be assessed. This is more due to other reasons such as:

- Data standards in public sector agencies would vary;
- Frequent or not so frequent changes in standards;
- Mismatched data standard migration of different agencies;
- Fast movers versus laggards in technology adoption;

- Sudden shifts in policy focus;
- Quality differences such as missing data, discontinuity, bias in selection, and scale of data collection.

Hence the variety is not just technical variety but variety in approaches, purposes, outcomes, quality, fidelity and other values of data. Bad data would be accompanying good. Qualitative variety is something of a reality that the emerging field of Data Science and the Data Scientist and Analyst would have to do in the public sector in a big way.

Technical variety in the data is something for which various approaches do exist in the form of ETL and other Data Cleaning, Schema Mapping techniques. In creating meaning out of existing silos of structured data, in combination with new sources, structures, types, qualities of data is a true challenge for Big Data. Hence, Data Integration and Data Transformation itself is a big task before Big Data processes. This is where more attention needs to be paid to create real value. Data integration itself is a large field with human readable, and M2M data, which could be integrated.

Large scale, Data Wrangling or Data Munging is going to be a major role for days to come when, agencies in search of insight would require diverse datasets to be integrated. Data Wrangling is a field in which large amount of automation is possible and newer products and platforms such as Data Wrangler, Data Tamer are showing the way. (Stonebraker, 2013).

Big Data Tool Box: What to do with Big Data?

With all the Big Data's volume and variety, it is pertinent to know what tools one could use. As seen earlier, storage is increasing at lower cost, so is the rate of generation of data especially unstructured data at very low cost. Processing power, memory, connectivity are all increasing; so what methods could be used to extract value from data is a very pertinent question. One would come across Data Mining, Machine Learning a lot in the analytics discussions. These sections aims to give a broad overview of these fields and compare it with the oldest data based field, namely, that of statistics.

Introduction to Machine Learning, Data Mining and Statistics

Statistics differs in a fundamental way in that it searches for certain answers, collects data with a purpose, designs methods of collection, decides the target, and analyses data by dealing with standardized tools and techniques.

Machine Learning can be described as follows: in a normal computation process, we have an input, a function which operates on the input, say data, and outputs a modified or processed data, in the form of desired result. It could be transformation, summarization, aggregation, classification, or any other manipulation of the data set. This is done by means of an algorithm operating on the input data to achieve the desired output.

In many cases, the data of input is known, and by other practical means, the output is also known, say a particular form of pattern of data with specific characteristics, but the algorithm is not known. This is where Machine Learning comes in. Machine Learning can be described as the process of using desired data, and with reference to input data available, and getting as output the algorithm. In essence it is an algorithm discovering process. And this algorithm is used on new data similar to the ones used to discover the algorithm, and the same result is achieved.

The process involves discovering recognizable certain regularities to the data. As Ethem Alpaydin (2010) describes in "Introduction to Machine Learning" that, if not the exact process, a good and useful approximation can be discovered and used via Machine Learning (hereinafter ML) techniques. He also clarifies the relation between ML and Data Mining, by describing that the application of machine learning methods to large databases is called Data Mining.

In other words, ML need not always operate on large data sets. A simpler example is the identification of spam by a mail user, to teach the mail service, the algorithm of classifying mail into spam and not spam, with respect to personal definition of spam. Famous data sets used in ML are rather small. Witten, Frank and Hall (2011) use, for example, for training and creating various algorithms, the famous Iris Flower data set. This data set was created by R.A.Fisher in 1936, which tries to define the 3 types of Iris flowers by 4 attributes in 150 instances, the 4 attributes (measurements) being sepal length, sepal width, petal length and petal width, and 3 types being Iris setosa, Iris versicolor and Iris virginica, with 50 instances each. By 'training' the algorithm different types of methods are discovered through Machine Learning better methods of a 'true' type identification can be done. All results are referenced against an ideal, and a percentage of accuracy of the algorithm is tested.

Ian Witten and others go ahead to differentiate ML and Statistics by stating that statistics has been more concerned with testing hypotheses, whereas machine learning has been more concerned with formulating the process of generalization as a search through possible hypotheses. In fact, many statistical processes generate the data by survey, sampling, designs questions to answer specific queries and with regard to the hypotheses at hand.

Having seen the difference between Machine Learning, Data Mining and Statistics, it is pertinent to see what is difference is between Data Mining and Exploratory Data Analysis. Hand, Mannila and Smyth (2001) ask the question whether Data Mining is merely Exploratory Data Analysis and answer that as follows. To summarize their explanation, statistics deals with smaller data sets compared to Data Mining, which may deal with millions of instances; Data Mining deals with high dimensional data, famously called the 'curse of dimensionality', which makes it difficult for traditional statistics to handle; statistics traditionally deals with tabular data sets, and not with unconventional data sets; quality of the data sets are higher in statistics, whereas the data sets of Data Mining are often with missing values, contaminated or corrupted, i.e. bad data. In short, they say, Data Mining subsumes Exploratory Data Analysis and goes beyond that due to large scale, and non-traditional data sets.

This difference is highly appreciable in the current context of Big Data. Big Data precisely deals with very large data sets, unstructured or semi-structured data sets and also is of uncertain source. Data Mining is a crucial process, using Machine Learning techniques to understand, and identify similar data and to extract meaning and value from it. Another important factor is that Data Mining does not aim to understand the true and actual relations between the variables (as in real life). It aims at generalizations which can be replicated and manipulated.

Hence, Machine Learning in itself is a vast field, and a complete survey of the field is beyond the scope and aim of this section. Of course, in general Machine Learning is broadly split into "Supervised Learning" and "Unsupervised Learning". The next section delves more into that.

Pattern Recognition: Neural Networks

Another few terms which one would come across are Pattern Recognition, Neural Networks and Text Mining. As seen earlier, where the class of data under analysis may be known qualitatively to different extents. Michie D., Spegelhalter D., and Taylor C (2009) who worked on the Statlog project describe that, if the 'true' class is known and the Machine Learning algorithm tries to identify this known class (say, human face from a large set of random image data points), it is called Pattern Recognition, it falls under the category of Supervised Learning. And when the class of data is to be inferred, but the 'true' class is not defined, then it is called Clustering or Unsupervised learning.

Neural networks are an established form of computational models by way of constructing mathematical "neurons" which are capable of "learning" patterns by "doing", that is, learning patterns which are difficult if not impossible to be manually or consciously described by humans. With Big Data computing power and scale, Neural Networks which were less preferred to many other Machine Learning techniques, may see resurgence.

Once used in industrial and scientific fields, now Neural Networks are more reachable, being popularly used in Speech Recognition, Handwriting Recognition, Face recognition, Computer Vision, for instance.

From Exploratory/Descriptive to Predictive Analytics and Prescriptive Analytics

With Big Data, the focus is shifting from understand or summarizing what is known (statistics and Business Intelligence), to what is unknown. Predictive Analytics is a large area where based on current and historical data, Models are built, scored against actual, assessed and deployed to predict the future. Public sector uses could be in environmental aspects, financial crises, health emergencies, infrastructure bottlenecks, traffic congestion etc.

The next stage would be Prescriptive Analytics where not only prediction is made, but with enough possibility and confidence, that actions are suggested akin to prescription of medicines based on established symptoms. A simple example would be a traffic diversion system, which automatically diverts traffic by predicting congestion, rerouting by understanding and while evaluating options of routes and destinations. Already Prescriptive Models are possible in Oil and Natural Gas where large amount of data are used to suggest drills and methods of drilling.

Neural Networks or Artificial Neural Networks (ANN) are *computational models* in which continuous approximate functions are modeled and predicted through large number of input variables and a desired output variable, which is usually linear. ANN involves designing "neurons" of code, both for input and for functional process. Often once designed it is "black box", where the efficacy of the output decides the approximations designed into the function.

Machine Readable Data and Natural Language Processing

With Open Data initiatives of various governments, more and more reusable Machine Readable (Machine to Machine M2M) data is being generated. Especially in the era of device to computer connections, and sophisticated modeling, machine readability will be on the rise. Also increasing is the Natural Language

Processing, of text information, social media comments and other web content. This is valuable data for public sector in the form of Text Mining, Sentiment Analysis to assess emergencies, trends or even public policy response.

The Deluge: Velocity Issues in Big Data

Velocity is one aspect of Big Data which is overwhelming. The rate at which data is generate with the volume, is what throws a large challenge to the computation power, choice of algorithms and the inventiveness of newer technologies. In this section the implications of tackling velocity, certain approaches and their future prospects would be seen.

High velocity data examples are click-stream data, GPS data from mobile devices which track real-time locations, social media, and various devices with sensors, and of course financial, say stock trading data. High velocity and volume together, momentum of data if you will, is a considerable factor in many a situation:

- Data is streaming;
- High velocity data has to be captured and analyzed;
- Real Time or Near Real Time analysis is required;
- Situations which are highly sensitive to response time would require continuous analysis;
- Delayed processing in many cases would make the data stale and therefore useless in terms of value.

Use cases include Disaster Management, Terrorist Attacks, Sentiment Analysis, Transient Trends & Streaming Analytics.

Near Real Time Analytics and Real Time Analytics

The Ability to process rapidly the incoming data, combined with ML and other techniques would enable to identify rapid trends or patterns emerging. Combined with Predictive and Prescriptive Analytics, public sector would see a growth in Real Time Decision Making or Near Real Time Decision Making and actions to follow suit. Use cases include natural or security emergencies, where Twitter data, or GPS locations, combined with sensor data could lead to lives being saved.

Internet of Everything (IoE), Internet of Things (IoT), Industrial Internet and Machine Intelligence

With the coming age of "Internet of Everything (IoE)" it is projected that previously unconnected places, devises, people, things and processes are going to be connected and transmitting data over Internet Protocol (IPv6). The World Economic Forum in 'The Global Information Technology Report 2014' states various estimates ranging from 13 to 50 billion devices being connected by 2020. And by 2017 half of the world's population (3.5 billion) would be connected to other devices (M2M) or to people (M2P).

Internet of Things (IoT) a subset of the IoE, sees not only devices, but subcomponents generating data. Including RFID tags, sensors and other automated devices, thereby producing context aware machines which continuously adapt and become "intelligent machines". "Industrial Internet" is the same system with end to end connectivity in manufacturing, inventory and logistics.

The current trend of deploying large number of sensors in various machines and "things", starting form static manufacturing machinery, to logistic containers, various vehicles, and including the components of machines has led to the so called "Internet of Things". There are huge amount of information generated and often streamed by these devices. A single Boeing flight generates about 1 TB of data. Big data technology is primarily used to improve system efficiency, monitor component performance, model and predict failure, and in preventive maintenance and continuity planning and in inventory planning, and emergency responses.

Use cases in public sector include Infrastructure planning, Smart Grids, Smart Environmental monitoring and assessments, smart cities, traffic control, failure predictions and asset maintenance to name a few.

Who's Afraid of the Big Bad Truth? Veracity, Privacy and Security

Although privacy concerns in Big Data deserve to be explored in depth, public sector as a collector, repository and user of very critical citizen centric data has a large responsibility in this issue. Public sector Big Data analytics even when using so called anonymized data has been shown to be identifiable. Standards have to be set and followed to save personal information from being misused. Big Data is in threat of turning Governments into the Big Brother with unbridled access to CCTV footage, biometrics, CDR, search records, banking transaction logs, social media and GPS locations. Civil society and well thought out, technically sound public policy is needed at this stage.

FUTURE RESEARCH DIRECTIONS

New Frontiers: Data Topology, Complexity Science and Big Data

Topological Analytics of Big Data

Gunnar Carlsson (2009) in his influential work "Topology and Data" published in the Bulletin of American Mathematical Society, outlines how large data sets could be understood by its pure geometrical and topological characteristics, which are essentially scale and metric free and are invariant in multidimensional space (multidimensional persistence). It is notable that the research was funded by DARPA. Topology makes a very promising trend for Big Data analytics and some pioneering start-ups such as Ayasdi have used it for large and complex data sets. Use cases arise in Environmental Sciences, Financial Data, Text analysis and other very high dimensional data spaces.

Modeling Complexity and Decision Sciences in Public Sector

Most existing models are relatively simple but effective, linear and logical regression models, and other ML techniques trade approximations for true understanding. Complexity science is a field which will gain traction with Big Data. Deeper insight through Complexity modeling such as applied Network Science and Graph theory, Scale free networks, Self-Organizing systems and Agent Based Models are emerging within the Big Data systems, and can harness complexity into Decision Sciences and lead to better Data Driven public Policy and action. Approaches such as the Data for Development (D4D), data commons and Open Data movement would also add to this needed direction.

CONCLUSION

Engineering Insight into Public Systems with Big Data Models

Big Data Models bring through various new technologies the confluence of Machine Learning, Data Mining, Pattern Recognitions and Predictive Modeling and set a new benchmark creating a merger of Data Science and Decision Science leading to extraction of value from data, especially with the 3Vs of data. Hence the appreciation of the technology behind the Big Data label would be a necessary condition to make full use of all options. These extracted values from data in public sector would lay a foundation for actionable insights, leading to robust data based policy and more effective and responsive governments and public agencies.

REFERENCES

Brewer, E. A. (2000). *Keynote address: Towards robust distributed systems*. Presented in Principles of Distributed Computing (PODC 2000), Portland, OR. Retrieved on 30th October 2014 from http://www.cs.berkeley.edu/%7Ebrewer/cs262b-2004/PODC-keynote.pdf

Brooks, A. (2013). *Perspective: Big data and Canadian healthcare — where are we now and what's the potential? International data corporation Health insights.* [Abstract]. Retrieved on 30th October 2014 from http://www.idc.com/getdoc.jsp?containerId=HI3CEH13

Carlsson, G. (2009). Topology and data. *Bulletin of the American Mathematical Society, 46*(2), 255–308. doi:10.1090/S0273-0979-09-01249-X

Chang, F., Dean, J., Ghemawat, S., Hsieh, W. C., Wallach, W. A., Burrows, M., & Gruber, R. E. et al. (2008). Bigtable: A distributed storage system for structured data. *ACM Transactions on Computer Systems, 26*(2), 4. doi:10.1145/1365815.1365816

Desouza, K. C. (2014). *Realizing the promise of big data: Implementing big data projects*. Retrieved on 30th October 2014 from http://www.businessofgovernment.org/sites/default/files/Realizing%20the%20Promise%20of%20Big%20Data.pdf

Gantz, J., & Reinsel, D. (2012). *The digital universe in 2020: Big data, bigger digital shadows, and biggest growth in the far east-United States*. Retrieved on 30th October 2014 from http://www.emc.com/collateral/analyst-reports/idc-digital-universe-united-states.pdf

Gilbert, S., & Lynch, N. (2002). Brewer's conjecture and the feasibility of consistent, available, partition-tolerant web services. *ACM SIGACT News, 33*(2), 51-59. Retrieved on 30th October 2014 from http://webpages.cs.luc.edu/~pld/353/gilbert_lynch_brewer_proof.pdf

Hand, D. J., Mannila, H., & Smyth, P. (2001). *Principles of Data Mining: Adaptive Computation and Machine Learning*. Cambridge, MA: MIT Press.

International Data Corporation. (2012). *The digital universe in 2020*. Retrieved on 30th October 2014 from http://www.emc.com/collateral/analyst-reports/idc-the-digital-universe-in-2020.pdf

Los Angeles Police Department. (2014). Recovered on 30th October 2014 from http://www.lapdonline.org/crime_mapping_and_compstat

McKinsey Global Institute. (2011). *Big data: the next frontier for innovation, competition and productivity*. Retrieved on 30th October 2014 from http://www.mckinsey.com/insights/business_technology/big_data_the_next_frontier_for_innovation

Olsson, J. (2013, October 15). *Load first, model later - What data warehouses can learn from big data* (Weblog post). Retrieved on 30th October 2014 from http://tdwi.org/Articles/2013/10/15/Load-First-Model-Later.aspx?Page=1

Organization for Economic Cooperation and Development. (2013). *Open government data: Towards empirical analysis of open government data initiatives*. Retrieved on 30th October 2014 from http://www.oecd.org/officialdocuments/publicdisplaydocumentpdf/?cote=GOV/PGC/EGOV(2012)7/REV1&docLanguage=En

Palmer, M. (2006, November 3). *Data is the new oil* (Weblog post). Retrieved on 30th October 2014 from Http://:ana.blogs.com/maestros/2006/11/data_is_the_new.html

Predpol. (2014). Recovered from http://www.predpol.com/about/

Stonebraker, M. (2013). *Data tamer: A scalable data curation system*. Retrieved from http://ilp.mit.edu/images/conferences/2013/ict/presentation/stonebraker.pdf

The Apache Software Foundation. (2014). *What is Hadoop?* Retrieved on 14/9/2014 http://hadoop.apache.org/#What+Is+Apache+Hadoop%3F

The Apache Software Foundation. (2014). *The Sqoop User Guide (v1.4.5)*. Retrieved from http://sqoop.apache.org/docs/1.4.5/SqoopUserGuide.html

The TechAmerica Foundation. (2013). *Big data and the public sector: A survey of IT decision makers in federal and state public sector organizations*. Retrieved on 30th October 2014 from http://www.techamerica-foundation.org/content/wp-content/uploads/2013/02/SAP-Public-Sector-Big-Data-Report_FINAL-2.pdf

Ullman, J. D., Leskovec, J., & Rajaraman, A. (2011). *Mining of Massive Datasets*. Cambridge University Press.

United Nations. (2014). *The United Nations E-Government Survey 2014: E-governance for the future we want*. Retrieved on 30th October 2014 from http://unpan3.un.org/egovkb/Portals/egovkb/Documents/un/2014-Survey/E-Gov_Complete_Survey-2014.pdf

Vogels, W. (2009). Eventually consistent. *Communications of the ACM, 52*(1), 40. doi:10.1145/1435417.1435432

Witten, I. H., & Frank, E. (2005). *Data Mining: Practical machine learning tools and techniques*. Morgan Kaufmann.

World Economic Forum. (2014). *Global information technology report 2014: Rewards and risks of big data*. Retrieved on 30th October 2014 from http://www3.weforum.org/docs/WEF_GlobalInformation-Technology_Report_2014.pdf

KEY TERMS AND DEFINITIONS

Anonymized Data: The data containing individual information, removed of traceable personal information so as to make it anonymous but still useful.

Graph Theory: The field of mathematics of mathematical objects with vertices, edges and their properties.

Internet of Things: Where various devices, machines, subcomponents, static and mobile are connected and continuously transmit data generated in real time on Internet protocol.

Predictive Analytics: Creating data models of expected behavior, scoring it against actual behavior, and deployed to predict approximated future behavior of a system.

Prescriptive Analytics: After predictive modeling, suggesting the alternatives to suitable action, based on actual conditions and the predicted behavior of the system.

RDBMS: Relational Database Management Systems are SQL based tabular, databases.

Topology: The field of mathematics dealing with properties of connected objects (called topological spaces) which are invariant over changes (homeomorphism).

Section 5

Big Data:
Emerging Issues

Chapter 15
Emerging Role of Big Data in Public Sector

Amir Manzoor
Bahria University, Pakistan

ABSTRACT

Technological advancements have made it easier to collect and store data. We are generating and storing data on a nearly pervasive basis and across multiple environments including work and home. Big data, a general term for the massive amount of digital data being collected from all sorts of sources, is too large, raw, or unstructured for analysis through conventional relational database techniques. For public managers, big data represents an opportunity to infuse information and technology into the design and management of organizations, personnel, and resources. Although the business sector is leading big-data-application development, the public sector has begun to derive insight to help support decision making in real time from fast-growing in-motion data from multiple sources. This chapter explores the big-data applications associated with the public sector and provide suggestions for follower governments.

1. INTRODUCTION

Collection and storage of data has now become easier with recent technological advancements. We generate and store vast amounts of data on daily basis. With dropping costs of storage devices, the costs of data storage have gone down. Today's organizations need to come up with strategies to leverage this data for developing insights that could help in evidence-based decision making.

Big data is general term that refers to the massive amounts of data collected from many sources including the web and the cloud. However, in its raw form, big data is not suitable for analysis using conventional relational database-based techniques of data analysis. It is estimated that around 2.5 quintillion bytes of data is added each day to the current amounts of data and approximately 90% of this new data is unstructured (Kim, Trimi, & Chung, 2014). This overwhelming amounts of big data offers new opportunities for discovery, value creation, and rich business intelligence for decision support in any organization. At the same, its use presents a new set of challenges involving complexity, security, risks to privacy, and need of new skills and technology. Big data has redefined the landscape of data manage-

DOI: 10.4018/978-1-4666-9649-5.ch015

ment. From the processes of extraction, transformation, and loading of data to cleaning and organizing this unstructured data we need new technologies (such as Hadoop) and skills.

Much of big data's growth has come from necessity. Data has been stored in various forms throughout history. One example is US consensus that was conducted in 1880. The US Census Bureau collected demographic information of 50 million people. The demographic information was collected about more than ten aspects. The data collected was logged by hand, microfilmed, and took approximately eight years for proper tabulation. Machine-readable punch cards were introduced in 1890 to streamline census data collection. With these punch cards, proper tabulation of census data took approximately one year. In the most recent census conducted in 2010, US Census Bureau employed a wide range of technologies to collect census data. These technologies include geographic information systems, social media, videos, intelligent character recognition systems, and sophisticated data-processing software. These technologies were instrumental in establishing a communication mechanism that reached every citizen.

There exist many big data success stories in private sector. In 2012, Merck, one of the largest pharmaceutical companies in the world, used specialized weather forecasts to anticipate hay fever in the year to come. These specialized weather forecasts provided both historical and current weather reports. Based on the analysis of this weather data, Merck concluded that the average pollen counts would be higher in upcoming warm weather in May. As such they anticipated an increased demand for allergy medication. This information was used in developing Merck's business strategies. Merck also used this information to prepare promotional material and establish a partnership with Wal-Mart. In this partnership, Merck developed personalized promotions based on zip codes. As a result of these personalized promotions, Merck's quarterly sales increased.

General motors used telematics for its OnStar technology. Telematics is the blending of computers and wireless telecommunications technologies, ostensibly with the goal of efficiently conveying information over vast networks to improve a host of business functions or government-related public services. OnStar is the leading provider of in-vehicle safety, security and connectivity services, and is now offered on nearly every GM vehicle sold in the U.S., Canada and China. OnStar technology provided various services (such as vehicle security) to assist drivers. OnStar technology also provided vast amounts of telemetry data gathered from the users. OnStar and GMAC insurance developed a joint program that utilized this telemetry data and offered low insurance premium to those users who travelled less. This program resulted in increased customer satisfaction. Top performing private companies use analytics five times more than the poorly performing companies. These firms are also able to make decisions based on rigorous analysis twice as fast as the poorly performing companies (Desouza, 2014). For public sector, big data is an emerging opportunity to streamline business processes, increased citizen engagement, innovate, and embrace evidence driven decision-making.

For public sector, big data is an opportunity to infuse technology into various aspects of organization including organizational design and management. The advancements in the fields data mining and information visualization has provided many resources to parse and traverse the vast amount of data available today that is spread across many networks and come from many resources (Stowers, 2013). It is expected that more than 1.5 million trained big data managers would be needed to leverage all the data generated globally on daily basis (Manyika et al., 2011). Data scientist is a new term that is now recognized as a key future skill organizations will seek (Desouza, 2014).

It can be said that big data in the public sector got the attention in the aftermath of the terrorist attacks on September 11, 2001. The 9/11 commission report identified many deficiencies in US ability to analyze the vast amount of data available. Such deficiencies were one significant cause that these terrorist attacks couldn't be prevented. Following the recommendations of 9/11 commission report, a directorate of National Intelligence was setup that was tasked with collection, analysis, interpretation, and implementation of various strategic plans of US government. Subsequently, the national security agency (NSA) started implementing various big data programs to beef up their global intelligence network.

Business sector is the leader in big-data-application development while the public sector has begun to explore the possibilities of using big data to help support real-time decision making (Kim, Trimi, & Chung, 2014). There exist many areas where big data can help governments serve their nations and overcome challenges. Some of these areas include reducing health care, creating job opportunities, and handling natural disasters and terrorism. However, it is still uncertain whether use of big data can actually result in the improvement of government operations. This is because in order leverage big data, it must first transformed into information through data organization and analytics. Doing so would require governments to develop new capabilities and adopt new technologies (such as Hadoop) (Kim, Trimi, & Chung, 2014). This chapter explores the big-data applications associated with the public sector and their possible impact on citizens' lives. Recommendations for follower countries are also provided.

2. BIG DATA APPLICATIONS: COMPARISON OF BUSINESSES AND GOVERNMENTS

The primary missions of businesses and governments do not conflict. However, they have different goals and values with businesses focused on profit generation and governments focusing on maintaining domestic tranquility, achieving sustainable development, securing citizens' basic rights, and promoting the general welfare and economic growth. In a competitive market environment, most businesses make short-term decisions with as few people as people. The process of decision making in public sector is longer and requires long consultations with a large number of diverse actors, including officials, interest groups, and ordinary citizens. To reduce risk and increase efficiency and effectiveness, public sector decision making requires many well-defined steps. As such, big data applications in public sector will likely differ between public and private sector. Businesses use big data to address customer needs and behavior, develop unique core competencies, and create innovative products and services. Governments use it to enhance transparency, increase citizen engagement, prevent fraud and crime, improve national security, and support the well-being of people (Kim, Trimi, & Chung, 2014).

The field of big data is still at its nascent stages. Most of the big data technologies and tools were introduced few years ago. The attributes and challenges of big data have been described in terms of "three Vs": volume, velocity, and variety. Volume refers to management of data storage, velocity refers to the speed of data processing, and variety refers to grouping data of different, seemingly unrelated data sets (i.e. structured, semi-structured, and non-structured data). In the course of doing business, organizations generate terabytes or even petabytes of data. Due to its vast amount and high speed of generation, it is very difficult and in-effective to manage and extract value from big data using conventional information technologies.

Variety is the most challenging attribute of big data. Information systems of today's organizations'' deals with heterogeneous datasets. For example HR information system deals with data of employees. Customer relationship management (CRM) system deals with data of customers only. Organization need economical ways of integrating heterogeneous datasets while allowing for newer sources of data.

These new sources of data can be new types of data or new sources of data. For example, an organization may need to integrate data from social media platforms with data extracted from its CRM system. Data generated from social media platforms need thorough analysis. This is because while this data can be of tremendous help for decision making it can also be manipulated.

Big data represents a big challenge for organizations today. With big data, data is spread across networks and no single organization own all the data it needs or can solely rely on only data it has. These networks on which the data reside are unique in a sense that they span organizations, systems, and individuals and bridge the public, private, and nonprofit entities. Big data represents an additional challenge for the organizations. It is very difficult for a single organization to gather all the skills/expertise needed to analyze and visualize big data. As such one critical requirement for organizations to leverage from use of big data is to develop viable collaborative partnerships.

The concept of big data has two components: a vast amount of data and a process through which some value can be derived from this data. Big data has changed the meaning of business intelligence. Now business intelligence means prediction and next-move decision making. We see new data management systems emerging to deal with big data. Hadoop is one good example. Hadoop is an open-source platform that supports the processing of large data sets in a distributed computing environment. Hadoop is a significant challenge for today's organizations especially small and medium enterprises. Hadoop requires hard to find expertise and experience. Many a times, organizations need to outsource such expertise and experience since it could be very difficult and expensive for them to search and find such expertise and skills. Since the skills required to analyze big data are complex and not solely technology-oriented, the greatest challenge for organizations is to find the right talent for big data analysis. For organizations, selecting a big data technology presents another significant challenge. They need to carefully evaluate the commercial (such as Casandra, Cloudera, Hortonworks, and MapR) and open source technologies (such as Hadoop).

2.1. Big Data Implementation: Public vs. Private Sector

Public and private sectors differ in their approaches of implementing big data projects. Different sets of guiding rules and organizational goals difficult if not impossible to easily transfer tried-and-true practices from one sector to another. Following are some of the major factors that differentiate big data implementation at public and private sector (Desouza, 2014).

2.1.1. Access, Control, and Data

Private sector organizations are skilled in immense amounts of information on individuals with limited pushback and this data collection is so ubiquitous that customers have come to expect it. Mobile apps developed by private sector organizations offer new innovative ways of data collection. When customers of a mobile app accept the app's terms and conditions, they actually allow the organization to collect information on them in real time. Some examples of personal information collected through such apps include user location, gender, unique identifier of the mobile device, contact list information, and pictures from photo libraries. In contrast, such data collection practices are neither common nor expected by the customers of the public sector organizations. However, these data collection practices are considered by many as violation of consumer privacy.

2.1.2. Consumer Perception

Private sector organizations collect and purchase consumer data from various sources. One good example is Amazon. Amazon uses the data about buying patterns of its over 152 million registered customers to generate targeted advertisement. Amazon doesn't sell this customer data to other companies rather they provide aggregated customer data to retailers and offer them targeted ads space. Facebook provides advertisers an opportunity to target potential customers by matching customers with their interests. For example, Facebook provides real-time, cookie-based customer targeting. If a customer visits a clothing retailer site that uses cookies and then customer visits Facebook then Facebook show ads of cloths. For public sector organizations, data collection outside the organizational boundaries is very challenging. Public sector organizations face increased difficulty obtaining data if the needed information is only available through a partnership with a private-sector firm. One most significant challenge is consumer perception of an organization's motivations. Data collection efforts by private organizations are generally perceived by consumers as non-invasive because the data is used to increase the firm's competitiveness. This is an acceptable motivation and may appreciate such data collection because it often results in intuitive applications that are easier to use. On the other hand, data collection efforts by public sector organizations are considered invasive because of their perceived little utility and possible ill use against consumers. One such example is US National Security Agency (NSA) data collection effort in which NSA collected large number of email address books from mail providers. NSA received heavy criticism for this activity. Little to none available evidence show that the data collected results in any improvements. As such, public sector organization need to come up with different strategies of data collection that address consumers' concern for privacy and ethical data collection and usage.

2.1.3. Investments in Information Technology

The private sector recognizes information technology (IT) as a critical element of being competitive and relevant in the marketplace and as such makes heavy investments in their IT infrastructures. Across a wide spectrum of industries, organization continue to infuse IT in their business processes and use IT to reach new customers. For public sector organizations, it is crucial to have IT project management abilities to ensure survival in the big data era.

2.1.4. Ethical and Privacy Concerns

For public sector organization ethical and privacy concerns of big data are more important. Public sector shouldn't ignore the negative aspects of big data capabilities. Big data significantly enhances organization's ability to know more about citizens and the potential to use such information in a harmful or discriminatory way. Cross-referencing of information can provide detailed analysis of groups of people. Such insight can be used in cases such as loan approval or hiring. This analysis can be purchased and most importantly people get affected don't know what is happening with their information. Many public sector managers remain unaware of a large element of potential harm in big data use. Take the example of the Sandy Hook Elementary School shooting in Connecticut. Using the Freedom of Information Act, a group of researchers obtained information regarding gun owners living in the suburbs of some counties in New York State and published an article that provided visual map of name and addresses of gun owners. Although the article was published with an intent to provide open knowledge, it was also a source of information for criminals that could use it to target people having no gun. Privacy is another significant ethical concern associated with big data analytics. As such, public sector organizations need to be very careful with respect to stewardship of big data they collect and analyze. They should consider various de-identification measures (anonymization, pseudonymization, encryption, key-coding etc.) to protect their customers. Even anonymized data can often be re-identified and attributed to specific individuals. Therefore, public sector organizations shouldn't depend solely on de-identification measures in their efforts to protect their customers' privacy.

2.2. Big Data Challenges in Public Sector

Besides general issues of big-data integration from multiple sources, public sector organizations also face some special challenges in their big data implementation plans. The most important is data collection. The data is collected from multiple channels (e.g. social networks and the Web) and from different sources (e.g. institutions, agencies, and departments). Data and information sharing among countries is a significant challenge and in this regard willingness of national governments is needed to share data and build systems for crime prevention. Another issue for cross-border information sharing is the language translation and interpretation of text semantics. This is important for preserving the true meaning of the content. However, doing so requires expensive and sophisticated tools. Data sharing within a country among different government departments and agencies is another challenge. The scale and scope of government data is growing over the years. The data collected by national and local governments is enormous with many attributes and values. The challenges of managing and analyzing this data is different from data collected by private sector organizations.

Silo, security, and variety are other big data issues for governments. Each government entity has its own silo of confidential public information and is often reluctant to share this information with other government entities. These isolated systems makes it difficult to integrate data among government entities. Communication failures can also affect these data integration efforts. For example, UK police and hospitals initiated a joint effort to share data on violent crimes. This initiative was a failure reportedly because of lack of communication among participating organizations. While most government data is structured, its collection from various sources and channels is a significant challenge. Different government entities use different software and solutions to extract information from datasets of different government entities. To use big data analytics on data available from legacy systems of different government entities a cohesive format is also needed.

Government entities must ensure citizens' rights of privacy while collecting and using big data for predictive analysis. Government entities need to address various legal, security, and compliance requirements related to data collection and use. In the U.S., the USA PATRIOT (Uniting and Strengthening America by Providing Appropriate Tools Required to Intercept and Obstruct Terrorism) Act allows legal monitoring and sometimes spying on citizens. The Electronic Communication Privacy Act allows email access without warrant. The proposed Cyber Intelligence Sharing and Protection Act (CISPA) would allow for the sharing of Internet traffic information between the U.S. government and technology and manufacturing companies. CISPA has raised serious concerns. By having access to all data for all entities in the U.S, US government will be in an ultimate position in big data game. There are also concerns that CISPA can be used for misconstrued profiling and/or inappropriate use of information. Collection, storage, and use of government big data requires special care. As such, data security is the primary attribute of government big data. Lack of sufficient security tools in most big data technologies of today has made big data security another challenge for public sector.

Regulatory compliance is another challenge for public sector big data implementation. This compliance is a more significant issue in highly regulated industries (such as financial services and health care). In United States, health-care regulations must be addressed when extracting knowledge from health-related big data. The Health Insurance Portability and Accountability Act (HIPAA) and the Health Information Technology for Economic and Clinical Health Act (HITECH) are two most important laws to be considered in public sector big data project in healthcare. HIPAA protects the privacy of individually identifiable health information, provides national standards for securing electronic data and patient records, and sets rules for protecting patient identity and information in analyzing patient safety events. HITECH was created in 2009 to stimulate the adoption of electronic health records (EHR) and supporting technology in the United States. The objective of HITECH was to protect the health records and electronic use of health information by various institutions. Big data by definition is massive amount of data. Since these two laws limit the collection of health-related data, the collection and analysis of vast amounts of data becomes complicated. As of February 2014, health-care information in the U.S. intended for big-data analytics is collected only from volunteers willing to share their own (Kim, Trimi, & Chung, 2014). Selection and implementation of big data technology to be used and finding appropriate skilled workforce for big data initiatives are two big data challenges that are shared by both public and private sector. However, big data challenges for public sector are more sever. Public sector organization need to break the silos among various government entities for data integration, comply with security and regulatory requirements, and establish sufficient control structures.

3. BIG DATA APPLICATION AREAS IN PUBLIC SECTOR

Public sector holds a lot of data to analyze. In the old way of analyzing data, we built buckets of data in the right tools that worked over that data. However, this approach and the ability to analyze across data is not scaling. Data in separate buckets can neither be correlated nor be used to extract more knowledge. By building larger enterprise data hubs, we can bring more of the data together faster and bring more workloads onto that data at work at it at the same time. Without having to replicate that data all over the place, we can produce new results because we can correlate more kinds of information.

There exist various big data application areas in public sector.

3.1. Bioinformatics

Exponential growth in the volume of data can used to drive improvements in health care and efficiencies within the sector. Using big data, information can be analyzed over patients and then offer the best treatments for those patients based on historical information research. The Medical Research Council (MRC), UK allocated £90 million investment to initiate various big data projects in the medical research field. The UK Government also announced a raft of funding for other big data projects, including £14 of investment to help make data being collected at four research centers available for research purposes (Out-Law.com, 2014). The National Institutes of Health (NIH), USA called the world's wealth of health data a formidable engine of discovery. NIH awarded $32 million in grants in a bid to make huge biomedical data sets accessible to researchers the world over (Out-law.com, 2014).The Big Data to Knowledge, or BD2K, initiative expected to invest $656 million over the next seven years to collect, analyze, catalog and disseminate research findings, genomic analyses, imaging scans and electronic health records. Made available broadly, that mass of data would allow researchers to glean new insights to improve health (Healy, 2014).

3.2. Fraud Detection

Fraud detection has traditionally focused on looking for factors such as known bad IP addresses or unusual login times. The powerful, fast, and advance big data analytics can detect fraud in real time and proactively identify risks. In USA, Centers for Medicare & Medicaid (CMS) implemented Virtual Research Data Center (VRDC) to extract knowledge and insights from large and complex collections of digital data. With the help of big data, Medicaid aims to detect and prevent fraud in a number of ways e.g. by analyzing unstructured data to reveal fraudulent activities and by profiling & segmenting claimants to identify those who are likely to commit fraud. Bureau of counselor affairs of State Department uses big data to look for fraud in the visa application process and in the process for all new immigration request for visas. In many ways, this big data application is the first line of defense for the nation and the ability to rapidly look over all of this information and detect anomalies is extremely important.

3.3. Geospatial Information

A significant proportion of the exabyte of newly georeferenced data per day is generated by sensor platforms. Sensors are driving advances in a variety of fields. Utilities are using smart meters and intelligent devices to measure the state of their networks in real-time. Traffic sensors measure traffic flow patterns and rates. Billions of cellphones have cameras and GPS embedded, both serving as new sources of sensor data – driving the explosion in Location Based Services that we are witnessing today. Department of Defense and the intelligence community is also using big data to help provide the right information to people over the battlefield. Research is being done by department of homeland security and others to provide information to first responders as they're en route to the scene (Shepard, 2012).

During the search for missing Malaysian Airlines flight 370, Dr. Shay Har-Noy's Geospatial Big Data division and Tomond (a project owned by Colorado-based satellite company DigitalGlobe that uses crowdsourcing to identify objects and places in satellite images) played a critical role in supporting US Department of Defense and the Australia Maritime Safety Authority and helping them more effectively deploy resources for such a difficult search. Using the power of crowdsourcing, Tomnod was able to get 8,000,000 people analyze millions of square kilometers of satellite imagery collected over the West coast of the continent. The two Malaysian Airlines tragedies have brought a heightened public awareness to the expectations and important role of the spatial industry in times of crisis. Through tools such as Tomnod, the public can become active participants in outcomes of global significance. Sometimes the actions of an individual with access to these crowd sourcing tools may save lives (Siba.com, 2014).

3.4. Cyber Security

Today's cyber security landscape presents a large number and variety of threats and risks. Big data analytics has significant applications in detecting crime and security breaches. According to Kar (2014), big data is expected to become a tool of security and fraud detection used by more than 25% gkobal firms. Using big data analytics, organizations can not only obtain faster access to their own data but also analyze the information from both internal and external sources to get a bigger picture of various threats.

Timely information is crucial to uncover security events. Big data is expected to change most computer security solutions including network monitoring, authentication and authorization of users, identity management, fraud detection, risk, and compliance. The future big data tools are expected to provide a number of advanced predictive capabilities and automated controls in real time (Kar, 2015).

3.5. Search Optimization

DigitalGov Search, formerly USASearch, offered a free, hosted-search service for federal, state and local government sites. The General Services Administration's Office of Citizen Services and Innovative Technologies provided the capability as part of its DigitalGov platform, which aimed to help agencies offer digital services to the public. The GSA's search technology was a big data initiative that aimed to make government data sets more accessible to the public. The effort to bolster search supported the agency's goal of "continually improving the interaction and experience" when citizens connect to the government.

4. UNIQUE COMPUTING REQUIREMENTS OF PUBLIC SECTOR

4.1. Data Provenance

As the government agencies started experimenting with the information technology, building prototypes and fielding solutions, they realized they needed more features, for example data provenance. We use the term data provenance broadly to refer to a description of the origins of a piece of data and the process by which it arrived in a database. Users need to understand where this this data come from, who has looked at it and who has modified that.

4.2. Enhanced Data Security

Users also need enhanced data security. User want to make sure that only the right people looking at this data and want to audit who is looking at this data.

4.3. Better, Faster Search

Users also need better faster ways to search over that data.

These three requirements, data provenance, enhanced security, and better search are key requirements in almost every government agency today. These three requirement can possibly only be provided by big data.

5. BIG-DATA APPLICATIONS IN LEADING E-GOVERNMENTS

Comparison of the big-data applications of leading e-government countries can reveal the focus of the current and future applications and serve as a guide for follower countries looking to initiate their own big-data applications.

5.1. United States of America

IBM and US government initiated a collaboration to develop a highly scalable, clustered infrastructure capable of analyzing in real-time high-volumes of streaming data. The outcome of this collaboration was two products: InfoSphere Stream and IBM Big Data. Both are widely used in both public and private sector for discovery and visualization of information from a wide array of resources.

Data produced by government agencies are often hard to find or are published in proprietary formats of limited utility. As a result, a wealth of information remains untapped by the ingenuity and creativity of the American people. In 2009, the U.S. government launched Data.gov. The purpose of data.gov is to increase public access to high value, machine readable datasets generated by the Executive Branch of the Federal Government. Data.gov is a citizen-friendly platform that provides access to Federal datasets. With a searchable data catalog, Data.gov helps the public find, access, and download non-sensitive Government data and tools in a variety of formats. By 6th of July, 2015, total 108,266 datasets were provided by data.gov covering transportation, economy, health care, education, and human services and the data source for multiple applications.

Aiming to make the most of the fast-growing volume of digital data, in March 2012, the Obama Administration announced a $200 million "Big Data Research and Development Initiative". This initiative involved involving multiple federal departments and agencies. The core objectives of this initiative were to advance state-of-the-art core technologies needed to collect, store, preserve, manage, analyze, and share huge quantities of data, to harness these technologies to accelerate the pace of discovery in science and engineering, strengthen our national security, and transform teaching and learning, and to expand the workforce needed to develop and use Big Data technologies (The Networking and Information Technology Research and Development (NITRD), 2015).

In November of 2014, the National Science Foundation published a Request for Input (RFI) about the establishment of a national network of Regional Innovation Hubs that would foster cross-sector collaborations and partnerships around Big Data. To establish this national network, the National Science Foundation announced a funding opportunity: the Big Data Regional Innovation Hubs (BD Hubs) program (The Networking and Information Technology Research and Development (NITRD), 2015).

In 2014, National Institute of Health (NIH) accumulated hundreds terabytes of data for human genetic variations on Amazon Web Services. In 2012, National Science Foundation (NSF) and NIIH started a joint program called The Core Techniques and Technologies for Advancing Big Data Science & Engineering program. This program aims to advance the core scientific and technological means of managing, analyzing, visualizing, and extracting useful information from large, diverse, distributed and heterogeneous data sets. The objectives of the program were to accelerate the progress of scientific discovery and innovation, to lead to new fields of inquiry that would not otherwise be possible, to encourage the development of new data analytic tools and algorithms, to facilitate scalable, accessible, and sustainable data infrastructure, to increase understanding of human and social processes and interactions, and to promote economic growth and improved health and quality of life (NSF, 2012). Facing an estimated $5 billion a year in tax revenue lost to identity theft refund fraud, the IRS is upgrading its software to make it harder for criminals to cash in bogus tax refunds (Reuters.com, 2013). The IRS is also developing a new system with big data-analytics capabilities, the Return Review Program, to replace the EFDS, which was implemented in 1994. The Return Review Program is expected to enhance the agency's ability to detect, resolve, and prevent criminal and civil tax noncompliance by analyzing massive amounts of data. US Department of Defense is also spending millions of dollars on big-data-related projects; one goal is developing autonomous robotic systems (learning machines) by harnessing big data. Many of the Defense Department's big data projects aim to make the best use of unmanned aerial vehicles (UAV). Some are designed to help analyze files, while others aim to use UAVs more efficiently for intelligence, surveillance and reconnaissance (ISR) work, which at times can come down to something as simple—though potentially huge—as storage (Costallow, 2014).

Local governments have also initiated big-data projects. The city of Syracuse launched a smart city project in collaboration with IBM. Launched in 2011, this project used big data to help predict and prevent vacant residential properties. At the state level, getting a unified view of the citizen is challenging due to the disparate nature of the data, the structure of the databases, and the restrictions imposed by privacy and security policies. IT department of Michigan State constructed a data warehouse of citizen information. This data warehouse was used by multiple government agencies and organizations to help provide better services. The State of Massachusetts started Big Data Initiative, which combines business and academic resources to accelerate big data usage and research in Massachusetts through a number of projects. This initiative consisted of a few main components. First component was the formation of a consortium of more than 100 local companies, research groups, and other organizations working on big data and analytics. Second was an internship program intended to place more than 2,000 international students into Massachusetts's data-analytics companies. Third was a grant program whereby the state provided matching funds for research projects at universities around the state. Intel committed $13 million to support research projects on big data and analytics at MIT, specifically. The state also planned to contribute $50,000 over two years for HackReduce, an incubator-style hacker space that would provide large-scale computing resources and mentorship for big data projects (Huang, 2012). US cities are also harnessing the power of big data by analyzing the data trends. City of New York analyzed the historical data to discover an important finding: in properties with tax liens the chance of a catastrophic fire was nine times more than the properties with no tax lien. The city of Chicago discovered through data analysis that complaint calls about trash bins in certain areas was likely followed by a call next week reporting rat infestation (Bonneville Research, 2014). The city of Seattle partnered with Microsoft and Accenture on a pilot project to reduce the area's energy usage. Using Microsoft's Azure cloud, the project will collect and analyze hundreds of data sets collected from four downtown buildings' management systems. With predictive analytics, then, the system will work to find out what's working and what's not — i.e. where energy can be used less, or not at all. The goal is to reduce power usage by 25%.

Volume and velocity are significant challenges for the United States Postal Service (USPS). USPS needs to sort approximately 160 billion pieces of mail in its 275 routing centers around the country. USPS also needs to perform sophisticated fraud detection scanning at rates up to 4 billion items per day. In 2013, USPS awarded a $16.7 million contract of a new big data system to FedCentric Technologies. With the new system, USPS were able to are able to get about 3.5 million scans per second (compared to 2,500 scans per second earlier). USPS is also operating one of the most powerful non-classified supercomputing databases on the planet to process and detect fraud on over 528 million mail pieces every day. The core of the USPS' supercomputing operations takes place at the Eagan IT and Accounting Service Center in Eagan, Minn. The supercomputing facility simultaneously processes data from 6,100 mail pieces per second from all over the country (Konkel, 2013).

The IRS collects over $2.4 trillion in taxes from nearly 250 million tax returns each year. Taxation is a heavily discussed topic in politics, and leaders face great pressure to find innovative ways to reduce revenue losses. The IRS reportedly loses an estimated $300 billion each year in taxpayer error or cheating tactics. To combat such loss, the IRS decided to use big data-analytics. Robo-audits is the new IRS program where IRS process tax returns by checking them against data from third-party records of all credit-card and electronic-payment data providers. It also use data from social media, email and other online activities. Collection and analysis of such data will allow the IRS to generate and track unique attributes regarding financial behaviors and aid in tax enforcement and combat noncompliance (Satran, 2013).

Big data is important to U.S. foreign policy. The Bureau of Conflict and Stabilization Operations (CSO) was established in the US Department of State. This bureau specialized in transitional societies (which are in need of direct intervention) and its objectives was to provide effective and coherent crisis response overseas. CSO analyzes large data sets that are essentially the sum of patterns, human behaviors, electronic signals, social media elements and everything tangible that creates masses of technological and non-technological data. CSO uses these big data sets to have fairly accurate information about many potential dangers, like timing of defections and growing factions. Using these insights, military can preemptively quash potential violence saving lives and money.

5.2. European Union

In 2010, The European Commission initiated its "Digital Agenda for Europe". The Digital Agenda forms one of the seven pillars of the Europe 2020 Strategy which sets objectives for the growth of the European Union (EU) by 2020. The Digital Agenda proposes to better exploit the potential of Information and Communication Technologies (ICTs) in order to foster innovation, economic growth and progress. The European Commission's Digital Agenda champions the Internet as a means to achieve economic and social progress. In 2012, the Commission initiated "Digital Agenda for Europe and Challenges for 2012". In this, European Commission focused on the potential of 'Big Data' to emphasize the economic potential of public data, the increasingly large and complex datasets that permeate the information economy.

5.3. United Kingdom

The U.K. government was one of the earliest implementer EU countries of big-data programs. The UK Foresight Horizon Scanning Centre (HSC) was set up in 2005 to explore future issues and trends over the next 50 years that may have an impact on public policy (Gov.uk, 2015). To help people understand how government works and how policies are made, UK government established data.gov.uk, a portal that brings all public data together in one searchable website. On this portal, datasets are available from all central government departments and a number of other public sector bodies and local authorities. This data can be used by technical people to build useful applications that help society, or investigate how effective policy changes have been over time. General public can use this data to analyze trends over time from one policy area, or to compare how different parts of government go about their work (data.gov.uk, 2015). DOME is a collaborative big data project of 20 countries, including Netherlands, Switzerland, and the U.K, with IBM. DOME is a supercomputing system able to handle a dataset in excess of one exabyte per day (more than double the daily traffic of the internet worldwide). This dataset would be derived from the Square Kilometer Array (SKA) radio telescope (the world's largest planned radio telescope). The aim of the DOME project is to address various scientific questions related to observable universe.

IBM worked with City of Dublin on using Big Data to identify and solve the root causes of traffic congestion in Dublin public transport network. The objective of big data use was to improve traffic flow and provide better mobility for commuters. By integrating data from a citywide network of sensors with geospatial data, city officials were able to better monitor and manage traffic in real time. In a collaboration with IBM researchers, City of Dublin's road and traffic department was able to combine Big Data streaming in from an array of sources (such as bus timetables, closed-circuit television cameras, GPS updates that each of the city's 1,000 buses transmits every 20 seconds) to build a digital map of the city overlaid with the real-time positions of Dublin's buses using stream computing and geospatial data (Hansen, 2013). Many cities across the world are working on the concept of "smart city". A smart city is the one capable of integrating datasets across heterogeneous systems, departments, and processes. This integrated is then analyzed in real-time to promote situational awareness and evidence-driven decision-making.

5.4. Asia

The United Nations' 2012 E-Government Survey gave high marks to several Asian countries, notably South Korea, Singapore, Japan, and Australia. These leaders have launched diverse initiatives on big data and deployed numerous projects.

5.4.1. South Korea

In South Korea, a big data task-force was created to play the leading role in utilizing big data and building the necessary infrastructures (Jee & Kim, 2013). The goals of this organization are to establish a pan-governmental big data network and analysis systems, promote data convergence between the government and the private sector, build a public data diagnosis system, improve the laws for the system, produce talented professionals and retrain them, guarantee the privacy and security of personal information, develop big data infrastructure technologies, and develop big data management and analytical technologies. The Big Data Initiative in Korea was launched in 2011 by the President's Council on National ICT Strategies (the highest-level coordinating body for government ICT policy). Some broad objectives of this initiative were to establish big data infrastructures and technologies, develop a data diagnostic system, produce trained big data professionals, and ensure privacy and security of personal information. The government established the Social Welfare Integrated Management Network System to improve the efficiency and quality of information and services, integrating 16 social welfare service institutions and 17 other public agencies. The system manages eligibility and personal information regarding residency, land, finance, taxes, and welfare. Notably it prevents duplicate benefit payments and fraud (Asian Development Bank, 2013). The Ministry of Science, ICT and Future Planning and the National Information Society Agency were planning to launch a service that will utilize big data and provide patients easy access to information about hospitals and estimated medical expenses related to their diseases. The service was expected to promote public health and streamline the management of medical facilities. The initiative is possible by connecting medical data and statistics of the Health Insurance Review & Assessment Service (HIRA).

The service would support the medical industry by providing information about the nationwide distribution of medicines, prescription tendencies, and medical equipment distribution, based on information from about 700,000 cases of pharmaceutical production (6.4 TB), 1.2 billion cases of pharmaceutical supply (6 TB), and medical devices (Businesskorea, 2014). The Korean Bio-Information Center plans to operate the National DNA Management System which, by integrating massive DNA and various types of medical patient information, will provide customized diagnosis and medical treatment to patients (Jee & Kim, 2013). Two Korean ministries, the Ministry of Food, Agriculture, Forestry and Fisheries and the Ministry of Public Administration and Security, plan to launch the Preventing Foot and Mouth Disease Syndrome system. This system will use big data related to animal disease overseas.

5.4.2. Singapore

Singapore government launched Risk Assessment and Horizon Scanning (RAHS) program in 2004. RAHS is a part of the National Security Coordination Secretariat (NSCS). The RAHS program explores methods and tools that complement scenario planning in anticipating strategic issues with significant possible impact on Singapore. With the help of its many international partners, RAHS develops an extensive range of processes to enable government agencies to collect, analyze, inform, model and monitor emerging strategic issues. These processes are supported by a wide range of products that enable analysts to better perform their roles. This includes the RAHS software platform which is specifically designed and developed with capabilities to support research and analysis using information extraction and visualization, modelling and survey tools. The RAHS Think Centre performs horizon scanning to identify emerging risks and opportunities and conduct research and analysis on emerging and cross-cutting issues. The RAHS Solutions Centre task is capacity building and engagement with agencies on policy projects. The Solution Centre explore new concepts that enhances policy making and to develop associated processes and tools. The RAHS Experimentation Centre experiments with new technological tools to enhance policy making and enhances and maintains RAHS system through systematic upgrade of the big-data infrastructure (rahs.gov.sg, 2015). The data.gov.sg portal is a project by the Ministry of Finance and the Infocomm Development Authority of Singapore. Data.gov.sg is the primary portal for users to discover data published by the Singapore Government and its agencies. Launched in June 2011, the portal brings together over 11,000 datasets from 70 government ministries and agencies. It also offers a listing of applications developed using government data and resources for developers (data.gov.sg, 2015).

5.4.3. Japan

In Japan, government initiated various big data projects such as Info-plosion by MEXT (Ministry of Education, Sports, Culture, Science and Technology), Grand Infomation Voyage by METI (Ministry of Economy, Trade and Industry) and the FIRST project. To assist in future disasters, the U.S. National Science Foundation (NSF) and the Japan Science and Technology Agency (JST) have embarked upon a joint funding program to support research that leverages Big Data and data analytics to transform disaster management for individuals and for society at-large (NSF, 2015). The Intelligent Traffic System (ITS) in Japan was designed to integrate people, roads and vehicles in order to resolve road traffic problems such as traffic congestion, traffic accidents and environmental degradation. Vehicle Information and Communication System (VICS), Electronic Toll Collection (ETC), and other ITS services were achieved by providing digital road maps(DRM), promoting development and introduction of road side devices, and forming a promotion organization linking concerned ministries and agencies and linking the government and the private sector.

5.4.4. Australia

The public sector organizations in Australia are using new techniques in big data to find useful patterns in the vast volumes of data they collect. In one initiative, the Australian Taxation Office was probing records to find evidence of the use of tax havens, and data-matching to identify small online retailers that are not meeting their compliance obligations. Australian Department of Human Resources use big data techniques to improve service delivery, including creating more personalized services and detecting fraud and compliance issues. Australian public sector holds enormous amounts of data available for analysis. Department of Human resources alone 23.4 million active Medicare records. A Centre of excellence in data analytics was launched in 2013 by the Australian Government Information Management Office. Numerous state-based big data initiatives are also in development. In one such initiative, Department of Justice in Victoria was analyzing data from the contact Centre and dispatch systems for the Victorian 000 emergency for forecasting purposes. The Australian Government Information Management Office (AGIMO) provides public access to government data through the Government 2.0 program, which runs the http://data.gov.au/ website to support repository and search tools for government big data. The government expects to save time and resources by using automated tools that let users search, analyze, and reuse enormous amounts of data (Howarth, 2014).

5.4.5. China

Chinese governments at both federal and provincial level are making concentrated efforts to leverage opportunities offered by big data. The Beijing municipal government reached a deal with IBM to use the tech company's advanced weather forecast and cloud computing technologies to solve the stubborn smog problem in the city. . A new social credit system aims to use big data to hold all citizens accountable for financial decisions as well as moral choices (ChinaTechNews, 2014). To establish reputation of a citizen, China implemented a numerical rating system based on citizens' financial standing, criminal record and social media behavior. While using financial, Internet and other data to evaluate individuals is not a new phenomenon, China will likely be the first nation to do it publicly and have the systematization and rationalization for doing so down to a numerical index. One of Chinese e-commerce giant Alibaba's subsidiaries, recently began its own rating system based on the spending habits of users of the popular Alipay service, which rates a person's credit on a scale of 350 to 950. Scores are based not only on a user's lending and spending numbers but also on what the money is going toward (FlorCruz, 2015).

6. PRACTICAL/MANAGERIAL IMPLICATIONS AND RECOMMENDATIONS

A review of big-data projects and initiatives in leading countries reveals few notable trends. First, most big-data projects appear to be using structured data. These projects do not use real-time and unstructured or semi-structured data. As such, these big data projects can be marginally classified as big-data projects. Second, public sector databases are becoming increasingly large and more complex and governments at different levels expects that the use of big data can enhance their ability to serve their citizens better. Governments also expect that the use of big data can help them address various major challenges associated with national economies, healthcare, unemployment, disaster management etc. However, most of today's big data applications of public sector are being used in citizens' affairs and not in the government sector. Third, most big data applications in government sector are in their early stages. Most applications are either being implemented or planned for future. Only a small number of big data applications are currently operational.

These trends provide several insights for follower countries regarding big data implementation in their public sector. First, each country has its own priorities with respect to the big data implementation in the public sector. These priorities are based on opportunities and threats based on the unique environment of a country. Some examples of threats and opportunities offer by environments are terrorism and health care in the U.S., terrorism in Pakistan, poverty in India, natural disasters in Japan, and national defense in South Korea. Based on these unique threats and opportunities, governments develop certain goals that are shared across various big data implementations in the public sector. Some examples of such shared goals are easy and equal access to public services and better citizen participation in public affairs. Second, there could be many big data implementations in the public sector that are dependent on data distributed across silos of various government entities. In such cases, the success of big data implementation would depend on how successfully this data can be managed and integrated. Governments would need a top-down approach and need big data control structures to successfully manage and integrated this data. On top of it, governments would need a separate entity tasked with developing strategies of effective big data management through modern emerging technologies. This entity would also be responsible for securing and/or developing the skilled human resources to manage the big data. Third, today's big data contains vast of amount of data-in-motion (such as data from social networks). Such data require real-time analysis using new technologies such as cloud computing and advanced analytics. At the same time governments need to use appropriate security technologies and legislation to protect individual citizens' privacy and security. Fourth, much government data is global in nature and can be used by a wide range of global users and decision makers to solve various global issues. One example is Global Earth Observation System of Systems (GEOSS) developed by the Group on Earth Observations (GEO). GEO is a collaborative international intergovernmental project. GEOSS is a global public infrastructure that provides comprehensive environmental data for information and analysis by a wide range of global audience. Governments also need to share data related to security threats, fraud, and illegal activities. One example is taxpayers' data sharing among different countries. Enacted by the United States Congress in 2010, Foreign Account Tax Compliance Act (FATCA) targets tax evasion by U.S. taxpayers who use foreign financial accounts by encouraging transparency and obtaining information on accounts held by them in other countries. The U.S. has signed, or is in negotiations to sign, FATCA agreements with more than 100 countries and jurisdictions worldwide (U. S. Embassy Minsk, 2015). To share and integrate such data, governments need an international collaborative effort that leverage appropriate technologies. Fifth, big technologies companies, such as IBM and Amazon, hosts various public datasets. Governments need to collaborate with such technology companies to share and integrate data hosted by them. Sixth, big data requires the collection of information from various sources and in different formats. Governments need to ensure that each public sector entity implementing big data projects develop a holistic cyber security strategy. This strategy should tailored to the threats and the risks specific to the demands of the particular public sector entity. A natural choice would be a single architecture that provide collection, indexing, normalization, analysis, and sharing of all the information. Ongoing investment in security products should be made and special attention should be placed on preparing the big data security teams. Public sector organizations may not have appropriate human resources skilled in data analysis. While the supply of such specialized data analysts is limited, public sector organizations may need to get external help to compensate for this critical lack of skill in their human resource pool.

7. CONCLUSION

Big data comes from in many forms (structured/stored, semi-structured/tagged, and unstructured/in-motion) and is becoming important for public sector organizations. Most public sector organizations today either lack or starting to develop the critical skills required to manage and analyze this big data. Big data programs are beginning to emerge and are expected to increase in prominence in the near future. Big data can provide significant benefits to public sector organizations in terms of increasing the efficiency of operations, mitigating risks, and increasing citizen engagement and value. To leverage big data, public sector organizations need a measured and calculated approach. Various stakeholders in public sector organizations recognize that a competitive advantage can be gained by managing and creating value from big data. Governments need a step-by-step approach towards big data projects. Governments also need to set right goals and realistic expectations for these big data projects. Success of these big data projects would depend on how successfully government organizations can integrate and analyze information, develop big data control structure, and support decision making through analytics.

This chapter has explored the challenges governments face and the opportunities they find in big data. Such insights can also help follower countries in trying to deploy their own big-data systems. Through a thorough analysis of big data implementations, follower countries may advance their big data implantation projects avoiding costly mistakes.

REFERENCES

Accenture. (2012). *Build It and They Will Come?* Retrieved from http://www.accenture.com/SiteCollectionDocuments/PDF/Accenture-Digital-Citizen-FullSurvey.pdf

Asian Development Bank. (2013). *Asian Development Outlook 2013 Update*. Asian Development Bank.

Bonneville Research. (2014, November 24). *Monday_Report_11-21-14*. Retrieved from http://www.bonnevilleresearch.com/~bonnevi0/images/stories/Monday%20Report/Monday_Report_11-21-14.html

Braham Group Inc. (2012). *Maximizing the Value Provided By a Big Data Platform*. Retrieved from http://public.dhe.ibm.com/common/ssi/ecm/en/iml14324usen/IML14324USEN.PDF

Broekema, C. P. (2012). DOME: Towards the ASTRON and IBM Center for Exascale Technology. In *Proceedings of the 2012 Workshop on High-Performance Computing for Astronomy Data*. doi:10.1145/2286976.2286978

Businesskorea. (2014, January 22). *Korea Develops Big Data-based Medical Information System* [Text]. Retrieved July 7, 2015, from http://www.businesskorea.co.kr/article/3029/medical-big-data-korea-develops-big-data-based-medical-information-system

Chen, H., Chiang, R. H. L., & Storey, V. C. (2012). Business Intelligence and Analytics: From Big Data to Big Impact. *Management Information Systems Quarterly*, *36*(4), 1165–1188.

ChinaTechNews. (2014, July 15). *Big Data Used By Beijing Government To Alleviate Pollution - ChinaTechNews.com - The Technology Source for the Latest Chinese News on Internet, Computers, Digital, Science, Electronics, Law, Security, Software, Web 2.0, Telecom, and Wireless Industries*. Retrieved from http://www.chinatechnews.com/2014/07/15/20725-big-data-used-by-beijing-government-to-alleviate-pollution

Costallow, T. (2014, October 24). *How big data is paying off for DOD -- Defense Systems*. Retrieved from http://defensesystems.com/articles/2014/10/24/feature-big-data-for-defense.aspx

data.gov.sg. (2015). Retrieved from http://data.gov.sg/common/about.aspx

data.gov.uk. (2015). *About | data.gov.uk*. Retrieved from http://data.gov.uk/about

Desouza, K. C. (2014). *Realizing the Promise of Big Data | IBM Center for the Business of Government*. Retrieved from http://www.businessofgovernment.org/report/realizing-promise-big-data

European Commission. (2010). *A Digital Agenda for Europe*. Retrieved from http://ec.europa.eu/digital-agenda/

FlorCruz, M. (2015, April 28). *China To Use Big Data To Rate Citizens In New "Social Credit System"*. Retrieved from http://www.ibtimes.com/china-use-big-data-rate-citizens-new-social-credit-system-1898711

Gov.uk. (2015). *Horizon Scanning Programme Team - Groups - GOV.UK*. Retrieved from https://www.gov.uk/government/groups/horizon-scanning-programme-team

Habegger, B. (2010, February). Strategic foresight in public policy: Reviewing the experiences of the U.K., Singapore, and the Netherlands. *Futures*, *42*(1), 49–58. doi:10.1016/j.futures.2009.08.002

Hansen, C. (2013). *IBM CSI Newsblog*. Retrieved from https://www-304.ibm.com/connections/blogs/CSI/entry/big_data_helps_city_of_dublin_improve_its_public_bus_transportation_network_and_reduce_congestion?lang=it_it

Healy, M. (2014, October 9). Big data, meet big money: NIH funds centers to crunch health data. *Los Angeles Times*. Retrieved from http://www.latimes.com/science/sciencenow/la-sci-sn-big-data-money-20141009-story.html

Howarth, B. (2014, June 13). *Big data: how predictive analytics is taking over the public sector*. Retrieved from http://www.theguardian.com/technology/2014/jun/13/big-data-how-predictive-analytics-is-taking-over-the-public-sector

Huang, G. T. (2012, May 29). *Massachusetts' New Big-Data Initiative to Include MIT, Intel, and HackReduce*. Retrieved from http://www.xconomy.com/boston/2012/05/29/massachusetts-new-big-data-initiative-to-include-mit-intel-and-hackreduce/

IBM. (2011). *IBM's Smarter Cities Challenge: Syracuse*. Retrieved from http://smartercitieschallenge.org/city_syracuse_ny.html

Jee, K., & Kim, G.-H. (2013). Potentiality of big data in the medical sector: Focus on how to reshape the healthcare system. *Healthcare Informatics Research*, *19*(2), 79–85. doi:10.4258/hir.2013.19.2.79 PMID:23882412

Kar, S. (2014, February 12). *Gartner Report: Big Data will Revolutionize the Cybersecurity in Next Two Year | CloudTimes*. Retrieved from http://cloudtimes.org/2014/02/12/gartner-report-big-data-will-revolutionize-the-cybersecurity-in-next-two-year/

Kar, S. (2015, January 2). *Looking Back at Top Big Data Stories and Trends of 2014 | CloudTimes*. Retrieved from http://cloudtimes.org/2015/01/02/looking-back-at-top-big-data-stories-and-trends-of-2014/

Kim, G.-H., Trimi, S., & Chung, J.-H. (2014). Big-data applications in the government sector. *Communications of the ACM*, *57*(3), 78–85. doi:10.1145/2500873

Konkel, F. (2013, March 15). *Supercomputing, big data: The postal service's hidden cool factor -- FCW*. Retrieved from http://fcw.com/articles/2013/03/25/postal-service-big-data.aspx

Labrinidis, A., & Jagadish, H. V. (2012). Challenges and Opportunities with Big Data. *Proc. VLDB Endow.*, *5*(12), 2032–2033. doi:10.14778/2367502.2367572

Lohr, S. (2012, February 11). Big Data's Impact in the World. *The New York Times*. Retrieved from http://www.nytimes.com/2012/02/12/sunday-review/big-datas-impact-in-the-world.html

Manyika, J., Chui, M., Brown, B., Bughin, J., Dobbs, R., Roxburgh, C., & Byers, A. H. (2011, May). *Big data: The next frontier for innovation, competition, and productivity | McKinsey & Company*. Retrieved from http://www.mckinsey.com/insights/business_technology/big_data_the_next_frontier_for_innovation

Mayer-Schönberger, V., & Cukier, K. (2013). *Big Data: A Revolution that Will Transform how We Live, Work, and Think*. Houghton Mifflin Harcourt.

McAfee, A., & Brynjolfsson, E. (2012, October). Big data: The management revolution. *Harvard Business Review*, 61–68. PMID:23074865

McKinsey Global Institute. (2011). *Big Data: The Next Frontier for Innovation, Competition, and Productivity*. Retrieved from http://www.mckinsey.com/insights/business_technology/big_data_the_next_frontier_for_innovation

Murdoch, T. B., & Detsky, A. S. (2013). THe inevitable application of big data to health care. *Journal of the American Medical Association*, *309*(13), 1351–1352. doi:10.1001/jama.2013.393 PMID:23549579

National Information Society Agency. (2012). *Evolving World on Big Data: Global Practices*. Retrieved from http://www.koreainformationsociety.com/2013/11/koreas-national-information-society.html

NSF. (2012). *Core Techniques and Technologies for Advancing Big Data Science & Engineering (BIG-DATA)(nsf12499)*. Retrieved July 7, 2015, from http://www.nsf.gov/pubs/2012/nsf12499/nsf12499.htm

NSF. (2015, March 30). *National Science Foundation (NSF) News - New U.S.-Japan collaborations bring Big Data approaches to disaster response | NSF - National Science Foundation*. Retrieved from http://www.nsf.gov/news/news_summ.jsp?cntn_id=134609

Office of Science and Technology Policy, Executive Office of the President. (2012). *Fact Sheet: Big Data Across the Federal Government*. Retrieved from http://www.whitehouse.gov/administration/eop/ostp

Office of Science and Technology Policy, Executive Office of the President. (2012). *Obama Administration Unveils 'Big Data' Initiative: Announces $200 Million in New R&D Investments*. Retrieved from http://www.whitehouse.gov/administration/eop/ostp

Ohlhorst, F. J. (2013). *Big Data Analytics: Turning Big Data Into Big Money*. Hoboken, NJ: John Wiley & Sons.

Out-law.com. (2014). *Big data can improve health outcomes, say experts*. Retrieved from http://www.out-law.com/en/articles/2013/november/big-data-can-improve-health-outcomes-say-experts/

Out-Law.com. (2014, February 7). *£50m funding for "medical bioinformatics" projects*. Retrieved November 1, 2014, from http://www.out-law.com/articles/2014/february/50m-funding-for-medical-bioinformatics-projects/

Plant, R. (2013). CISPA: Information without representation? *Big Data Republic*. Retrieved from http://www.bigdatarepublic.com/author.asp?section_id=2635&doc_id=262480

President's Council of Advisors on Science and Technology. (2010). *Designing a Digital Future: Federally Funded Research and Development in Networking and Information Technology*. Retrieved from http://www.whitehouse.gov/sites/default/files/microsites/ostp/pcast-nitrd-report-2010.pdf

President's Council on National ICT Strategies. (2011). *Establishing a Smart Government by Using Big Data*. Washington, DC: Author.

rahs.gov.sg. (2015). *RAHS - RAHS Programme: Origin and Progress*. Retrieved from http://www.rahs.gov.sg/public/www/content.aspx?sid=2952

Reuters.com. (2013, August 26). IRS lags in program to spot tax refund fraud: watchdog. *Reuters*. Retrieved from http://www.reuters.com/article/2013/08/26/us-usa-tax-refund-fraud-idUSBRE97P0WQ20130826

Satran, R. (2013, May 9). *Next Target of IRS Robo-Audits: Small Business*. Retrieved from http://money.usnews.com/money/personal-finance/articles/2013/05/09/next-target-of-irs-robo-audits-small-business

Shepard, E. (2012, July 2). *Geospatial Advances Drive Big Data Problem, Solution*. Retrieved from https://sensorsandsystems.com/article/features/27558-geospatial-advances-drive-big-data-problem,-solution.html

Sherry, S. (2012). 33B pounds drive U.K. government big data agenda. *Big Data Republic*. Retrieved from http://www.bigdatarepublic.com/author.asp?section_id=2642&doc_id=254471

Siba.com. (2014, August 17). *Siba - Newsfeed - Spatial Industries Business Association - SIBA*. Retrieved from http://www.siba.com.au/News/News-Articles/Big-Spatial-Data-in-Emergency-Management.aspx

Stone, D. A. (2002). *Policy Paradox: The Art of Political Decision Making*. New York: W.W. Norton & Company, Inc.

Stonebraker, M. (2012). What does 'big data' mean? *Blog@CACM*. Retrieved from http://cacm.acm.org/blogs/blog-cacm/155468-what-does-big-data-mean/fulltext

Stowers, G. (2013). *The Use of Data Visualization in Government | IBM Center for the Business of Government.* Retrieved July 6, 2015, from http://www.businessofgovernment.org/report/use-data-visualization-government

The Networking and Information Technology Research and Development (NITRD). (2015). *Big Data (BD SSG) - NITRDGROUPS Portal.* Retrieved July 7, 2015, from https://www.nitrd.gov/nitrdgroups/index.php?title=Big_Data_(BD_SSG)

U. S. Embassy Minsk. (2015, March 18). *2015 Programs and Events.* Retrieved from http://minsk.usembassy.gov/fatca031815.html

U. S. Government. (n.d.). Retrieved from http://www.data.gov

United Nations. (2012). *E-government Survey 2012: E-government for the People.* Retrieved from http://www.un.org/en/development/desa/publications/connecting-governments-to-citizens.html

Zikopoulos, P.C., Eaton, C., DeRoos, D., Deutsch, T., & Lapis, G. (n.d.). *Understanding Big Data: Analytics for Enterprise-Class Hadoop and Streaming Data.* McGraw-Hill.

Chapter 16
Opportunities and Challenges of Big Data in Public Sector

Anil Aggarwal
University of Baltimore, USA

ABSTRACT

Data has always been the backbone of modern society. It is generated by individuals, businesses and governments. It is used in many citizen-centric applications, including weather forecasts, controlling diseases, monitoring undesirables etc. What is changing is the source of data. Advances in technology are allowing data to be generated from any devise at any place in any form. The challenge is to "understand", "manage" and make use of this data. It is well known that government generates unprecedented amount of data (ex: US census), the question remains: can this data be combined with technology generated data to make it useful for societal benefit. Governments and non-profits, however, work across borders making data access and integration challenging. Rules, customs and politics must be followed while sharing data across borders. Despite these challenges, big data application in public sector are beginning to emerge. This chapter discusses areas of government applications and also discusses challenges of developing such systems.

BIG DATA

Data is everywhere. Data collection starts as soon as an individual steps out into the public domain. In many cases, data collection may even start within the private domain (when an individual is under surveillance). The data is a gold mine with hidden value. The challenge is to find the gold. Traditionally, data was collected and used to generate reports (ex: census reports) and maybe some intelligence (ex: homeland database). Data was well-behaved and could be represented in traditional relational or object-oriented form. This is changing as new data is generated from very different sources like social networking, weblogs, sensors and "smart" devices, to name a few. This data contains a "double gold" mine, which includes the gold value of the structured data and the additional gold value of unstructured data. The challenge is to find this "double gold". This data is being generated at an unprecedented rate. According to a recent IDC (2015) forecast "...the Big Data technology and services market will grow at a 26.4% compound annual growth rate to $41.5 billion through 2018, or about six times the growth rate

DOI: 10.4018/978-1-4666-9649-5.ch016

of the overall information technology market. Additionally, by 2020, IDC believes that line of business buyers will help drive analytics beyond its historical sweet spot of relational (performance management) to the double-digit growth rates of real-time intelligence and exploration/discovery of the unstructured worlds". Given the abundance of data it is not surprising there is a race to find "the double gold" in the data. Before we discuss application and challenges, a brief description of big data is presented.

According to Gartner.com, "Big data is high-volume, high-velocity and high-variety information assets that demand cost-effective, innovative forms of information processing for enhanced insight and decision making". Big data is also defined as data which cannot be processed by conventional means. The 4 Vs (velocity, variety, veracity and volume) have become the standard characteristics of big data.

Big data is typically unstructured and cannot be processed by conventional relational, structured query language (SQL), implying new techniques and new systems need to be developed, mastered and used. The next section briefly describes the big data system development process followed by opportunities and challenges.

BIG DATA DEVELOPMENT PROCESS

Big data system development process is similar to other systems, with the difference being the scale and nature of computing. The following steps are necessary for a project of this magnitude to succeed:

- Collect
- Manage/architecture
- Process
- Act

Each of these steps has its challenges. By some estimates, 90% of the data generated by devices is not useful. Therefore, the first step is to identify relevant data which requires functional expertise. Managing data would require data integration of structured and unstructured data. Several non-relational databases (key-value, key-document, graph) are emerging that can be used. However, the processing of this structure can be quite challenging. Typical processing is based on massive parallel processing that typically uses a HADOOP like structure. This requires creating clusters and replicating them. The task is to create the appropriate cluster to balance load. Once data is stored and defined it needs to be processed. Traditional languages like SQL are not appropriate. The challenge is to develop new languages that can help in processing. Once data is processed, the next step is to understand the output and apply it.

The next section describes opportunities in the public sector.

Opportunities of Big Data

Not all public sector applications are suitable for big data applications. Big data applications are suitable for the types of analysis that includes "discovery", "interrogation", "insights', etc. For example, they are suitable to study sentiment analysis (ex: citizen's reaction to a new highway), study terrorists cells (network analysis), and tracking diseases (ex: Ebola using network analysis). They are not suitable for traditional processing like tax record processing, creating budget analysis, census directory, etc. Figure

Figure 1. Big data applications

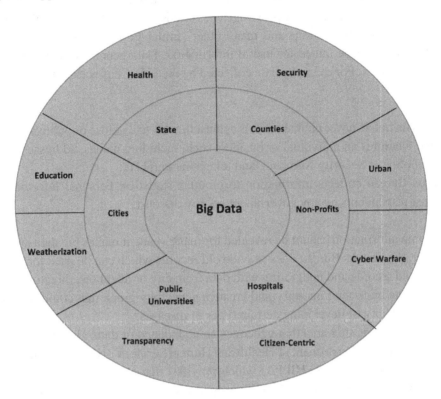

1 summarizes various applications of big data. The list is by no means complete since any public sector can find suitable big data applications.

Figure 1 describes two levels. The first level describes various non-profit entities (state, federal, parliament, regions, organizations, etc.) that can use big data to improve services to their customers. The second level describes the areas where big data applications can be useful (security, transparency, tracking, etc.). The list is endless and it is not feasible to describe all possible applications. This chapter focuses on government and some non-profits' application of big data.

Since governments generate an abundance of data, it can used for many different applications to:

- Improve security of citizens;
- Improve traffic congestion;
- Control spread of diseases;
- Reduce corruption by providing more transparency;
- Improve weatherization;
- Urban planning.

In addition to government, non-profits can use big data to understand their subscriber base, sentiment of their viewers, quality of their programming, etc. Kim et al (2014) also discuss various big data initiatives taken by many different countries to improve the government's ability to deal with cross-departmental and multi-disciplinary challenges.

The public sector is huge consisting of governments at different levels (county, city, state, federal, Congress, senate, parliaments, etc.), non-profit agencies (ex: Red Cross, Doctors Without Borders, etc.), public hospitals, academic institutions and many other similar groups. These groups generate large volumes of data which can be mined for useful information. Data generated by the U.S. government agencies must follow rules. For example, data collected by the U.S. Census Bureau must adhere to Title -13, which states:

- Private information is never published. It is against the law to disclose or publish any private information that identifies an individual or business such, including names, addresses (including GPS coordinates), Social Security Numbers, and telephone numbers;
- The Census Bureau collects information to produce statistics. Personal information cannot be used against respondents by any government agency or court.

Given that some information cannot be revealed for many years, it makes big data applications challenging. However, the Census Bureau does provide old records which can be used for genealogical applications. Using old records and integrating with data from city or telephone directories, churches and clubs, individuals can track their ancestry and create a genealogy graph that could help in identifying their DNA and probability of developing certain types of diseases.

The Health Sector is another area that generates an abundance of data. However, data generated is bound by the policies of the Department of Health and Human Services' (HHS) and the Health Insurance Portability and Accountability Act (HIPPA) which provides that all *"individually identifiable health information"* held or transmitted by a covered entity or its business associate, in any form or media, whether electronic, chapter, or oral remains protected. The Privacy Rule calls this information "protected health information (PHI). "Individually identifiable health information" is information, including demographic data, that relates to:

- The individual's past, present or future physical or mental health or condition;
- The provision of health care to the individual; or
- The past, present, or future payment for the provision of health care to the individual, and that identifies the individual or for which there is a reasonable basis to believe it can be used to identify the individual. Individually identifiable health information includes many common identifiers (e.g., name, address, birth date, Social Security Number)."

Given that none of the raw data can be used, it creates a challenge for HHS to use this data effectively. However, the agency allows usage of data if it is de-identified, which HHS defines as "health information neither identifies nor provides a reasonable basis to identify an individual." This should allow better exploration of big data.

An important application related to health data is identifying pandemics and controlling it as much as possible. In these situations, it is important to identify spatial areas where disease could spread. If spatial information (latitude and longitude) about an infected individual is available, visualization techniques can be used to study hot areas over time. The rate of change in a hot area would indicate vulnerable areas. Figure 2 contains fictitious new deadly disease data for regions in Africa. Data is mocked after World Health Organization (WHO) data. Data consists of 5,500 records that were filtered to records containing number of "new" cases over two consecutive reported periods. From Figure 2, it appears that

Figure 2.

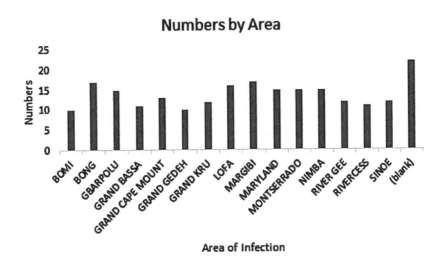

new disease cases are spreading mostly in the Moga, Margibi and Lofa areas of Liberia for the period studied. These areas are in the north central region of Liberia. This would imply these areas need closer scrutiny to control the spread of this new disease.

If researchers need to control the spread among people, they can study the contact of infected patients using graphical analysis and infer which links of people are likely to feel the impact of this disease.

There are many other areas where opportunities exist for big data application. Some are summarized below:

- **Dark Side of Big Data:** Since no person or entity is responsible for monitoring the Internet, it gives a feeling of anonymity to its users. This often results in fake sites and fake accounts, generating an abundance of hate, threats, lies, unlawful recruiting and conducts. Big data can help in detecting, monitoring and tracking such activities. For example, home grown terrorism is also becoming a threat to the society. Local/state/federal authorities can use social media, friend network and sentiment analysis to monitor suspects. Sentiment analysis can analyze the mind and state of the suspected terrorist and any inflammatory posting can start a trigger and alert authorities. Terrorist groups are recruiting the millennium generation with false promises. Authorities can monitor web sites, videos, and message patterns of these recruiting sites and keep track of visitors to those sites. Visitor information could be integrated with their travel patterns and social demographics to develop a visitor's profile. Looking at profiles of previous recruits, authorities can assess the likelihood of specific millennials joining the terrorist group;

- **Human Right Campaign:** The United Nations Charter sets forth the "inherent dignity" and the "equal and inalienable rights of all members of the human family." Upholding these human rights principles as "the foundation of freedom, justice, and peace in the world" is fundamental to every undertaking of the United Nations. Social media has not only helped change governments (Egypt, Libya, etc.) but has also help change geography (new country Liberland - Liberland is using crowdfunding for its operations). Citizen's blogging, posting and videos can be integrated to identify human right abuses and violators;

- **Smart Cities:** Another area where big data is making a big impact is cities. Smart city uses technology to enhance the quality of life of its people. Cities are collecting lots of data from both traditional sources like tax records, property records, courts, traffic accidents, etc., and also from non-traditional sources like police body cameras, street cameras, apps and social media. Data from different sources need to be integrated and analyzed for smart urban planning, smart transportation, smart sanitation, smart crime prevention, etc. Concepts of smart city are moving to emerging and even third world countries. According to the Washington Post (June 26, 2015), India recently announced a $7.5 billion initiative to develop 100 smart cities, not a small undertaking given the urban population of almost 350 million in crowded cities. The Post article continues, "...the smart-cities rubric has become fashionable among global urban planners who want to use digital technology and big data to create surveillance-heavy intelligent systems that control how people live, consume energy, go to work, and stay healthy and safe". It is encouraging that big data applications are becoming global.

In addition, we describe two successful big data applications.

First, Patterson (2009) describes an application of big data in the Tennessee Valley project. "The Tennessee Valley Authority has built a data collection and analysis system called the Open Phasor Data Collector, or OpenPDC, on Hadoop. OpenPDC monitors data streaming at volume from sensors attached to power generation systems. These sensors, deployed around the power grid, report the health and status of each generation facility, and its response to loads on the power grid. Close monitoring and rapid response to changes in the state of the grid allow utilities to minimize or prevent blackouts, and to manage capacity better. This reduces operating costs and better controls greenhouse gas emissions and other environmental risks".

Second, in discussing improving transparency of government with big data analytics, United Nations reported that "Pulse Lab Jakarta worked with the Nusa Tenggara Barat (NTB) provincial government to explore the contribution of advanced data analytics to local government decision-making by generating insights from a combination of existing formal complaint systems (LIPOR) and passive feedback from citizens on social media like Twitter. " The results demonstrate the potential utility of (a) near real-time information on public policy issues and their corresponding locations within defined constituencies, (b) enhanced data analysis for prioritization and rapid response, and (c) deriving insights on different aspects of citizen feedback. The publication of citizen feedback on public-facing dashboards can enhance transparency and help constituents understand how their feedback is processed".

The above applications are a few examples of opportunities of how big data can be used by the public sector to minimize risks for its citizens and to make government more responsive to them. The next section describes the challenges of big data.

Challenges of Big Data

Big data systems creates challenges at many levels from data integration to data analysis to availability of qualified personnel. Specific big data challenges are discussed below:

- **Data Integration:** As mentioned, data is captured at source and generated in a variety of formats. Social networking sites like Twitter, Instagram and Facebook generate data that may contain picture, texts, videos, temporal and spatial information. Data collected from sensors may contain

Figure 3. Smart devices

temporal, spatial and video data, data collected from company document will have textual data. Smart phone and smart watch (see Figure 3) contains hundreds of apps for phone, web, pictures (camera), text, e-mail etc. These are built into these small smart device generating multi structured data.

The challenge is to integrate this data with structured data and analyze it effectively. Currently, HADOOP, an open system architecture, allows for some integration with massive parallel processing mostly in batch mode (Olson, 2009; Dean et al, 2004). However, there are no plug-in applications to integrate this variety of data. Several vendors are working in this direction:

- **Lack of Standardization:** Since big data is still emerging, technology architecture like platforms /hardware/software are evolving. Currently, these are demand driven, creating heterogeneous products. Different environments do not fit with each other creating interoperability and integration issues. For example, HADOOP platform, used by most big data system developers is open source system. This provides flexibility for expert users but problems for naïve users. Though open source allows users to customize their applications, it also creates problem for naïve users and developers and restricts its usage to only the few who are competent in specific technology. What is needed is a proprietary system built on HADOOP that can standardize most applications. Many vendors are moving in this direction;
- **Data Quality, Incomplete Data:** One of the biggest challenge in analyzing data is the quality of data. Since most data is collected from social sites, it can be biased and fraudulent. With no Internet controls, it is easy to target people, governments and create fake identities. Commenting on military fraud, Foster (2015) noted, Hackers launched "romance scams," in which fake profiles of servicemen abroad connect with loved ones at home, or even initiate online relationships. Once the targeted party believes they are communicating with a real person, the hacker will request money. One unnamed military official in particular has some 30 imposter Facebook accounts. More troubling is the nearly 100 fake Skype accounts – the most popular means of communication between military personnel and loved ones at home, and thus the easiest target for "romance

scams." In a Gartner (2012) study, they cautioned that 10 to 12% of postings are fake. This raises the question of data quality of social sites. There are attempts by both social networking site providers, government and researchers to monitor and filter such activities. Several researchers (Castillo, 2011; Gupta et al., 2013; Gupta et al., 2015; Friggeri et al., 2014, etc.) have discussed models and techniques to filter such postings. Universities are offering courses in digital forensics to assist in detecting such fraud. Governments are taking an active role in prosecuting people that write fake reviews, create fake sites and engage in otherwise illegal activities. Many governments (Australia, U.K. and many others) and states like New York are actively pursuing people or businesses that post fake reviews. Clark (2013) noted that New York Attorney General penalized businesses that were involved in writing fake reviews. Unfortunately this problem is bound to get worse as more people use the Internet and social sites. What is needed is a joint effort by content providers, government and cyber detectives to stop this abuse.

Another problem is incomplete data. In many cases data is unavailable or incomplete. Missing data treatment may be acceptable in some applications like sentiment analysis where there is an abundance of data and law of averages can account for missing data. In addition, researchers (King et al., 2001; Gelman et al., 2004, etc.) have proposed techniques like Bayesian, that can assist in handling missing data. Missing data, however, can be catastrophic for some applications where approximation will not work. For example, in Figure 2, most disease detected cases were in unknown areas. This can be challenging for government officials who are trying to control the disease. Incomplete data is usually a problem with third world countries where population may not want to discuss or divulge information due to taboos, fear or unknown consequences. For example, with the Ebola outbreak in Africa, patients were scared to go for treatment for fear of abandonment by family or society. It would be impossible to collect data in such cases. Researchers will have to convince patients and the government to provide data, or simply work with the available data:

- **Privacy:** One of the biggest challenges of government generated data is privacy. The Privacy Act of 1974, as amended at 5 U.S.C. 552a, protects records that can be retrieved by personal identifiers such as a name, social security number, or other identifying number or symbol. There are many government regulations like the HIPPA, SORNs, etc. that protect data from unauthorized access. This can create roadblocks to getting the full benefit of big data. For example, in Figure 2, data only provided the number of people confirmed with new diseases in Liberia. However, other demographic information like gender, age, education were masked or not available. This of course does not allow further analysis in terms of gender, age, income etc. impact on the new disease. Is it more prominent in males than females? Or certain age groups? Or certain income levels? Is there any cause-effect relationship? Researchers are working on algorithms that would allow coding data without identifying individuals. This would provide for better big data analysis;

- **Lack of Qualified People:** Government can have all the data and hardware/software it wants but nothing can be achieved if data cannot be processed by qualified personnel. As mentioned, big data combines many different data types and analytics, it also requires personnel with different backgrounds. Data base managers are needed to collect, filter and manage data; data scientists are need to create models, analyze them and business managers are needed to act on the findings. For example, structured Query language (SQL) is a matured language that is taught everywhere and is useful for processing structured data and there are enough competent people to develop systems based on structured data and SQL language. As big data started to emerge, NOSQL evolved, which requires knowledge in "R", "python" or a similar language to develop query. This implies users developing a system using NOSQL must learn programming language first. This slows the process down due to lack of qualified data scientists. The problem is not only design and analysis but interpretation of results. One famous example is the Google dengue experiment. Ginsberg et al (2009) describes a "method of analyzing large numbers of Google search queries to track influenza-like illness in a population. Because the relative frequency of certain queries is highly correlated with the percentage of physician visits in which a patient presents with influenza-like symptoms, we can accurately estimate the current level of weekly influenza activity in each region of the United States, with a reporting lag of about one day. This approach may make it possible to utilize search queries to detect influenza epidemics in areas with a large population of web search users." However, it turned out that it did not predict flu very well. This is due to influenza-like symptoms are not always associated with influenza. This case shows the importance of the business manager who must understand the model, the logic and the assumptions and interpret the results cautiously.

Given that big data application requires a multitude of skills, no one person can have knowledge in all these areas. Big data applications are almost always group driven. This may create application problems since people with these qualifications may be at different locations, speak different dialects and live in different time zones. On the bright side, however, universities have started offering courses in data analytics, business intelligence and big data. It is expected that in a few years there will be an adequate supply of such personnel:

- **Data in Silos:** One of the biggest problem in government is that data is in individual silos. Each department/unit has its own data, rules and standards. This is partly due to size of each unit. Data sharing is not the norm. Agencies are often reluctant to share data with other agencies. Lack of coordination among government agencies has resulted in losses. For example, unauthorized social security payments to dead people, subsidies to rich people, release of convicts, and terrorists getting by the no-fly list, to name a few. In the digital age, it is important to coordinate and share data. In turn, this generates a volume of data. In the early 1990's, it would be impossible to integrate data from different units due to their volume. Advances in storage technology and cloud storage is making it easier and feasible to integrate data from multiple government units. For example, when the Department of Homeland Security developed the database, it had to coordinate, merge and integrate data from multiple agencies. The challenge, of course, was data integration since data comes in many forms, texts, biometrics and pictures. Once the system became operational there were many false positives and false negatives which allowed innocent people to be flagged and terrorists to slip by. (Laudon and Laudon, 2015). The system is evolving and becoming more user-friendly. Integrated systems, like the terrorist tracking system, are generating an abundance of data which needs to be integrated with unstructured data generated by social media. This would assist in flagging a suspect as positive, negative or a maybe. Unfortunately, seamless integration is currently not available. What is needed is interoperable systems that can integrate a variety of data seamlessly;

Figure 4. Standardized Big Data platform

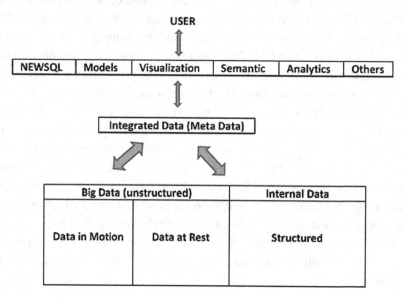

- **Lack of "Plug-in" Software/Hardware:** For big data to be successful, government and organizations will need "plug-in" applications. This would require a user-friendly layer of applications over heterogeneous products. A software system like Microsoft office suite would be needed for a naïve person to take advantage of big data application. The evolution of SQL to NOSQL to NEWSQL is an example of where there is an attempt to develop a new user-friendly query language (NEWSQL) that parallels an old query language (SQL). Since many more users are familiar with SQL than NOSQL, it increases big data applicability by naïve users.

In summary, what is needed is an integrated big data platform which can overcome many of the current challenges. Figure 4 describes a big data platform which integrates data, user-friendly and easy to use.

For big data to be widely accepted and used, end-users need a user-friendly plug-in off-the-shelf system that can:

- Integrate structured and unstructured data;
- Filter data at the source in real time;
- Be queried in simple SQL type language;
- Analyze data at the source in real time;
- Analyze both data at rest and data in motion in real time.

Many organizations have started their efforts in this direction, including IBM's Big Insights platform. It contains many user-friendly functionalities to store and analyze both data at rest and data in motion. The system is evolving and in the future, it may provide plug-in applications. Many vendors are also developing integrated platforms and hopefully there will be a plug-in platform for big data architecture in the near future.

CONCLUSION

Governments, non-profits and other public agencies are recognizing the importance of big data. The new form of data requires new ways of modeling and querying. We have explored the opportunities and challenges that must be overcome to make big data a success. Many isolated applications based on structured data have been reported but "true" big data applications are still missing. This is due to the lack of an integrated system that can incorporate multi structured data, explore it in real time, understand outcomes and apply it for public good. Big data cannot be done in isolation; it should be the joint effort of a public-private-academic partnership since no one entity can have all the necessary skill.

The challenges are numerous as are the opportunities. We have not even scratched the surface of big data applications. Ultimately, with the use of big data, governments will be able to better understand each and every person and customize their services accordingly. Services will become citizen-centric, government-centric and global-centric. We illustrate some areas where big data opportunities exist.

Citizen-Centric Applications

These applications are individual oriented and should benefit individuals. Some examples include:

- Job creation
- Health care costs
- Weatherization
- Security
- Genealogy
- Police-citizen relations
- Salary parity

Government-Centric Applications

These are inter-governmental applications that will benefit the general population. Some examples include:

- Controlling human trafficking
- Money laundering
- Forecasting natural disasters
- Urban planning
- Detecting and controlling pandemics
- Detect government waste
- Monitor transparency
- Control political corruption
- Detecting anomalies in government programs
- Detecting misuse/stealing of government data

Global-Centric Applications

These are intra-nations applications that would benefit countries in maintaining security, peace and harmony across the globe. Some examples include:

- Monitoring terrorists
- Monitoring rogue governments
- Cyber warfare
- Controlling pandemics
- Cyber security
- Track spies/double agents

These applications are not mutually exclusive but are categorized for illustration purposes only. For example, a global centric pandemics application will help individuals, governments and nations in controlling the spread of disease, and eventually controlling health care costs.

Most current big data applications, as already mentioned, are based on structured data due to the challenges discussed above. Big data, however, is here to stay. More and more social sites are emerging and their usage is exploding. The amount of data generated is increasing exponentially. Much of this data needs to be tapped. What is lacking is the platform that can provide integrated off-the-shelf solutions. Vendors are working in that direction.

This chapter has discussed some current and future applications of big data in the public sector, as well as the challenges facing big data applications. The list is by no means complete. As new information and techniques develop, old challenges will disappear and new ones will emerge. This chapter is the beginning and not an end of big data application and challenges.

REFERENCES

Castillo, C., Mendoza, M., & Poblete, B. (2011, March). Information credibility on twitter. In *Proceedings of the 20th international conference on World Wide Web* (pp. 675-684). ACM. doi:10.1145/1963405.1963500

Clark, P. (2013). New York State Cracks Down on Fake Online Reviews. *Bloomberg News*. Available at: http://www.bloomberg.com/bw/articles/2013-09-23/new-york-state-cracks-down-on-fake-online-reviews

Dean, J., & Ghemawat, S. (2004). MapReduce: Simplified Data Processing on Large Clusters. In *Proceedings of the Sixth Symposium on Operating System Design and Implementation*. San Francisco, CA: Academic Press.

Foster, J. (2015). *A Match Made in Heaven: Fraud and Social Media*. Available at: http://www.securityweek.com/match-made-heaven-fraud-and-social-media

Friggeri, A., Adamic, L. A., Eckles, D., & Cheng, J. (2014, May). Rumor cascades. In *Proceedings of the Eighth International AAAI Conference on Weblogs and Social Media*. AAAI.

Gartner Press Release, (2012). *Gartner Says By 2014, 10-15 Percent of Social Media Reviews to Be Fake, Paid for By Companies*. Available at: http://www.gartner.com/newsroom/id/2161315

Gartner.com. (n.d.). *Answering Big Data's 10 Biggest Vision and Strategy Questions*. Author.

Gelman, A., & Meng, X. L. (Eds.). (2004). *Applied Bayesian modeling and causal inference from incomplete-data perspectives*. John Wiley & Sons. doi:10.1002/0470090456

Ginsberg, J., Mohebbi, M. H., Patel, R. S., Brammer, L., Smolinski, M. S., & Brilliant, L. (2009). Detecting influenza epidemics using search engine query data. *Nature*, *457*(7232), 1012–1014. doi:10.1038/nature07634 PMID:19020500

UN Global Pulse. (2015). *Mining Citizen Feedback Data for Enhanced Local Government Decision-Making*. Global Pulse Project Series no.16.

Gupta, A., Kumaraguru, P., Castillo, C., & Meier, P. (2014, May). Tweetcred: A real-time Web-based system for assessing credibility of content on Twitter. In *Proc. 6th International Conference on Social Informatics (SocInfo)*. HHS. Retrieved from http://www.hhs.gov/ocr/privacy/hipaa/understanding/summary/index.html

Gupta, A., Lamba, H., Kumaraguru, P., & Joshi, A. (2013, May). Faking Sandy: characterizing and identifying fake images on Twitter during Hurricane Sandy. In *Proceedings of the 22nd international conference on World Wide Web companion* (pp. 729-736). International World Wide Web Conferences Steering Committee.

IDC. (n.d.). *Big data and Analytics*. Available at: https://www.idc.com/prodserv/4Pillars/bigdata

Kim, G., Trimi, S., & Chung, J. (2014). Big-Data Applications in the Government Sector. *Communications of the ACM*, *57*(3), 78–85. doi:10.1145/2500873

King, G., Honaker, J., Joseph, A., & Scheve, K. (2001, March). Analyzing incomplete political science data: An alternative algorithm for multiple imputation. In American Political Science Association (Vol. 95, No. 01, pp. 49-69). Cambridge University Press.

Laudon, K., & Laudon, J. (2015). *Management Information Systems: Managing the Digital Firm, 14/E*. Pearson Pub.

Olson, M. (2010). Hadoop: Scalable, flexible data storage and analysis. *IQT Quarterly*, *1*(3), 14–18.

Patterson, J. (2009). The Smart Grid: Hadoop at the Tennessee Valley Authority (TVA). *Cloudera Blog*. Retrieved from http://www.cloudera.com/blog/2009/06/smart-grid-Hadoop-Tennessee-valley-authority-tea/

U.S. Census Bureau. (n.d.). Retrieved from https://www.census.gov/history/www/reference/privacy_confidentiality/title_13_us_code.html

Compilation of References

Abdullah, N.A., Nishioka, D., Tanaka, Y., & Murayama, Y. (2015). User`s Action and Decision Making of Retweet Messages towards Reducing Misinformation Spread during Disaster. *Journal of Information Processing, 23*(1), 31-40.

Abdullah, N. A., Nishioka, D., Tanaka, Y., & Murayama, Y. (2014). A Preliminary Study on User's Decision Making towards Retweet Messages.*Proceedings of 29th International Conference on ICT Systems Security and Privacy Protection (SEC2014)* (pp. 359-365). doi:10.1007/978-3-642-55415-5_30

Acar, A., & Muraki, Y. (2011). Twitter for crisis communication: Lessons learned from Japan's tsunami disaster. *International Journal of Web Based Communities, 7*(3), 392–402. doi:10.1504/IJWBC.2011.041206

Accenture. (2012). *Build It and They Will Come?* Retrieved from http://www.accenture.com/SiteCollectionDocuments/PDF/Accenture-Digital-Citizen-FullSurvey.pdf

Addis, B., Ardagna, D., Capone, A., & Carello, G. (2014). Energy-aware joint management of networks and Cloud infrastructures. *Computer Networks, 70*, 75–95. doi:10.1016/j.comnet.2014.04.011

Agarwal, R., & Dhar, V. (2014). Editorial—Big Data, Data Science, and Analytics: The Opportunity and Challenge for IS Research. *Information Systems Research, 25*(3), 443–448. doi:10.1287/isre.2014.0546

Agichtein, E., Castillo, C., Donato, D., Gionis, A., & Mishne, G. (2008). Finding high-quality content in social media. In *Proceedings of the 2008 International Conference on Web Search and Data Mining* (pp. 183-194). ACM.

Agrawal, D., Bernstein, P., Bertino, E., Davidson, S., Dayal, U., Franklin, M., ... Widom, J. (2011). *Challenges and Opportunities with Big Data 2011-1*. Academic Press.

Agrawal, R. (2014). *HP Vertica Essentials*. Amazon & Packt Publishing.

Agrawal, R., & Srikant, R. (2000). Privacy-preserving data mining. *SIGMOD Record, 29*(2), 439–450. doi:10.1145/335191.335438

Akerkar, R. (2013a). *Big Data Computing*. Chapman and Hall/CRC. doi:10.1201/b16014

Ala-Kurikka, S. (2010). *Enel: Italy reaping first-mover benefits of smart meters*. Retrieved May 30, 2015, from http://www.euractiv.com/italy-reaping-first-mover-benefits-smart-meters-enel

Aminzadeh, N., Sanaei, Z., & Ab Hamid, S. H. (2014). Mobile storage augmentation in mobile cloud computing: Taxonomy, approaches, and open issues. *Simulation Modelling Practice and Theory*. doi:10.1016/j.simpat.2014.05.009

Anderson, J. D. (1985). Indexing systems: Extensions of the mind's organizing power. In B. D. Ruben (Ed.), *Information and behavior* (pp. 287–323). New Brunswick, NJ: Transaction Books.

Ang-Hoon Kim, S. T.-H. (2013). Big-Data Applications in the Government Sector. *Communications of the ACM, 57*, 78–85.

Apache. (2015). *Apache Hive TM*. Retrieved from apache.org: https://hive.apache.org/

Apache. (2015). *Welcome to Apache Pig!* Retrieved from pig.apache.org: https://pig.apache.org/

Ardenas, A. A. (2013). Big data analytics for security. *IEEE Security and Privacy, 11*(6), 74–76. doi:10.1109/MSP.2013.138

Arnold-Moore, T. J., Anderson, P., & Sacks-Davis, R. (1997). Managing a digital library of legislation. In *ACM/IEEE-CS Joint Conference on Digital Libraries* (pp. 175–183). ACM/IEEE.

Arthur, L. (2013). *Big Data Marketing: Engage Your Customers More Effectively and Drive Value*. Wiley.

Ash, J. S., & Bates, D. W. (2005). Factors and forces affecting EHR system adoption: Report of a 2004 ACMI discussion. *Journal of the American Medical Informatics Association, 12*(1), 8–12. doi:10.1197/jamia.M1684 PMID:15492027

Asian Development Bank. (2013). *Asian Development Outlook 2013 Update*. Asian Development Bank.

Aslam, J., Lim, S., Pan, X., & Rus, D. (2012). City-scale traffic estimation from a roving sensor network. In *Proceedings of the 10th ACM Conference on Embedded Network Sensor Systems* (pp. 141-154). ACM. doi:10.1145/2426656.2426671

Australian Government. (2013, March). *Big Data Strategy*. Author.

Awaluddin, M. (2014). The Partnership Between Business and Government towards Sustainable City Development. In ICT For Smart Society (ICISS), (pp. 131-138). IEEE. doi:10.1109/ICTSS.2014.7013162

Baele, E., & Devreux, H. (2014, December). MOBIB: the card of the future. *Eurotransport*. Retrieved May 30, 2015, from http://www.eurotransportmagazine.com/

Baker, K. S., & Bowker, G. C. (2007). Information ecology: Open system environment for data, memories, and knowing. *JIIS Journal of Intelligent Information Systems, 29*(1), 127–144. doi:10.1007/s10844-006-0035-7

Baltimore Sun. (2015). Man Charged with Damaging hoses at CVS fire. *Baltimore Sun*.

Baraniuk, R. G. (2007). Compressive sensing. *IEEE Signal Processing Magazine, 24*(4), 118–121. doi:10.1109/MSP.2007.4286571

Barrett, M. A., Humblet, O., Hiatt, R. A., & Adler, N. E. (2013). Big Data and disease prevention: From quantified self to quantified communities. *Big Data, 1*(3), 168–175. doi:10.1089/big.2013.0027

Baselinemag. (2013). *How PRISM Validates Big Data*. Retrieved from baselinemag.com: http://www.baselinemag.com/analytics-big-data/how-prism-validates-big-data

Basu, A. (2014). *Real-Time Healthcare Analytics on Apache Hadoop using Spark and Shark*. White Paper Intel Distribution for Apache Hadoop Software, Big Data Analytics Healthcare.

Bates, M. J. (1989). The design of browsing and berrypicking techniques for the online search interface. *Online Review, 13*(5), 407–424. doi:10.1108/eb024320

Batty, M. (2013). Big data, smart cities and city planning. *Dialogues in Human Geography, 3*(3), 274–279. doi:10.1177/2043820613513390

Belaud, J.-P., Negny, S., Dupros, F., Michéa, D., & Vautrin, B. (2014). Collaborative simulation and scientific big data analysis: Illustration for sustainability in natural hazards management and chemical process engineering. *Computers in Industry, 65*(3), 521–535. doi:10.1016/j.compind.2014.01.009

Bettencourt, L. M. (2013). *The Uses of Big Data in Cities*. Santa Fe Institute Working Paper.

Bian, J., Topaloglu, U., & Yu, F. (2012, October). Towards large-scale twitter mining for drug-related adverse events. In *Proceedings of the 2012 international workshop on Smart health and wellbeing* (pp. 25-32). ACM. doi:10.1145/2389707.2389713

Big Data. (n.d.a). In *Merriam-Webster dictionary*. Retrieved October 27, 2014, from http://www.merriam-webster.com/dictionary/big_data

Big Data. (n.d.b). In *Oxford dictionaries*. Retrieved October 27, 2014, from http://www.oxforddictionaries.com/definition/english/big-data

Big Data. (n.d.c). In *Gartner IT Glossary*. Retrieved October 27, 2014, from http://www.gartner.com/it-glossary/big-data

Bizer, C., Heath, T., & Berners-Lee, T. (2009). Linked data - the story so far. Int J Semantic Web Inf Syst. *Special Issue on Linked Data, 53*(3), 1–22.

Blair, D. C., & Kimbrough, S. O. (2002). Exemplary documents: A foundation for information retrieval design. *Information Processing & Management, 38*(3), 363–379. doi:10.1016/S0306-4573(01)00027-9

Blei, D. M. (2012). Probabilistic Topic Models. *Communications of the ACM, 55*(4), 77–84. doi:10.1145/2133806.2133826

Bollier, D., & Firestone, C. M. (2010). *The promise and peril of big data*. Washington, DC: Aspen Institute, Communications and Society Program.

Bonneville Research. (2014, November 24). *Monday_Report_11-21-14*. Retrieved from http://www.bonnevilleresearch.com/~bonnevi0/images/stories/Monday%20Report/Monday_Report_11-21-14.html

Booker, E. (2014). Ebola Fight Hampered By Poor Analytics. *Information Week*. Available at: http://www.informationweek.com/government/big-data-analytics/ebola-fight-hampered-by-poor-analytics/d/d-id/1306998

Bookstein, A., & Swanson, D. R. (1976). Probalistic models for automatic indexing. JASIS. *Journal of the American Society for Information Science, 25*(5), 312–318. doi:10.1002/asi.4630250505

Boone, R. (2013). Er is geen blauwdruk voor de informatisering van Justitie. *Legal World*. Retrieved July 7, 2014, from http://www.legalworld.be/

Borgman, C. L., Bowker, G. C., Finholt, T. A., & Wallis, J. C. (2009). Towards a virtual organization for data cyberinfrastructure. In *Proceedings of the 9th ACM/IEEE-CS Joint Conference on Digital Libraries* (pp. 353–356). New York: ACM Press. doi:10.1145/1555400.1555459

Borkar, V. R., Carey, M. J., & Li, C. (2012). Big data platforms: What's next? *XRDS: Crossroads. The ACM Magazine for Students, 19*(1), 44–49. doi:10.1145/2331042.2331057

Borthakur, D. (2007). *The Hadoop Distributed File System: Architecture and Design*. Academic Press.

Bové, L. (2012, February 24). Justitie prutst met miljoenenclaim over computers. *De Tijd*. Retrieved Aug 19, 2014, from http://www.tijd.be/

Bové, L. (2013, August 29). België scoort slecht in informatisering justitie. *De Tijd*. Retrieved July 7, 2014, from http://www.tijd.be/

Bowker, G. C. (1996). The history of information infrastructures: The case of the international classification of diseases. *Information Processing & Management, 32*(1), 49–61. doi:10.1016/0306-4573(95)00049-M

Boyd, C. M., Darer, J., Boult, C., Fried, L. P., Boult, L., & Wu, A. W. (2005). Clinical practice guidelines and quality of care for older patients with multiple comorbid diseases: Implications for pay for performance. *Journal of the American Medical Association, 294*(6), 716–724. doi:10.1001/jama.294.6.716 PMID:16091574

Braham Group Inc. (2012). *Maximizing the Value Provided By a Big Data Platform.* Retrieved from http://public.dhe.ibm.com/common/ssi/ecm/en/iml14324usen/IML14324USEN.PDF

Braman, S. (2011). Defining information policy. *Journal of Information Policy, 1.*

Brand, A. (2010). *Storage device and method thereof for integrating network attached storage with cloud storage services.* Israel: United States Patent and Trademark Office.

Brand, A. (2011). *Cloud connector for interfacing between a network attached storage device and a cloud storage system.* Israel: United States Patent and Trademark Office.

Brand, A. (2013). *Remote access service for cloud-enabled network devices.* Israel: United States Patent and Trademark Office.

Breugelmans, J. (2014). *Big Data vs Business Intelligence.* Retrieved May 24, 2014, from http://visual-intelligence.nu/

Brewer, E. (2000). *Towards robust distributed systems.* Paper presented at Principles of Distributed Computing, Portland, OR. Available at: https://www.youtube.com/watch?v=H_nz936whfE

Brewer, E. A. (2000). *Keynote address: Towards robust distributed systems.* Presented in Principles of Distributed Computing (PODC 2000), Portland, OR. Retrieved on 30th October 2014 from http://www.cs.berkeley.edu/%7Ebrewer/cs262b-2004/PODC-keynote.pdf

Broekema, C. P. (2012). DOME: Towards the ASTRON and IBM Center for Exascale Technology. In *Proceedings of the 2012 Workshop on High-Performance Computing for Astronomy Data.* doi:10.1145/2286976.2286978

Brooks, A. (2013). *Perspective: Big data and Canadian healthcare — where are we now and what's the potential? International data corporation Health insights.* [Abstract]. Retrieved on 30th October 2014 from http://www.idc.com/getdoc.jsp?containerId=HI3CEH13

Brown, B., Chui, M., & Manyika, J. (2011). Are you ready for the era of 'big data'? *The McKinsey Quarterly, 4,* 24–35.

Brown, J. S., & Duguid, P. (2002). *The social life of information.* Boston: Harvard Business School Press.

Buckley Owen, B., Cooke, L., & Matthews, G. (2012). Information Policymaking in the United Kingdom: The Role of the Information Professional. *Journal of Information Policy, 2*(0).

Bughin, J., Chui, M., & Manyika, J. (2010). Clouds, Big Data, and smart assets: Ten tech-enabled business trends to watch. *The McKinsey Quarterly, 56*(1), 75–86.

Burghard, C. (2012). *Big Data and Analytics Key to Accountable Care Success.* IDC Health Insights.

Burnside, E. S., Rubin, D. L., Fine, J. P., Shachter, R. D., Sisney, G. A., & Leung, W. K. (2006). Bayesian network to predict breast cancer risk of mammographic microcalcifications and reduce number of benign biopsy results: Initial experience. *Radiology, 240*(3), 666–673. doi:10.1148/radiol.2403051096 PMID:16926323

Businesskorea. (2014, January 22). *Korea Develops Big Data-based Medical Information System* [Text]. Retrieved July 7, 2015, from http://www.businesskorea.co.kr/article/3029/medical-big-data-korea-develops-big-data-based-medical-information-system

Cambria, E., Rajagopal, D., Olsher, D., & Das, D. (2013). Big social data analysis. *Big Data Computing,* 401-414.

Candès, E. J., Romberg, J. K., & Tao, T. (2006a). Robust uncertainty principles: Exact signal reconstruction from highly incomplete frequency information. *IEEE Transactions on Information Theory*, *52*(2), 489–509. doi:10.1109/TIT.2005.862083

Candès, E. J., Romberg, J. K., & Tao, T. (2006b). Stable signal recovery from incomplete and inaccurate measurements. *Communications on Pure and Applied Mathematics*, *59*(8), 1207–1223. doi:10.1002/cpa.20124

Candès, E. J., & Wakin, M. B. (2008). An introduction to compressive sampling. *IEEE Signal Processing Magazine*, *24*(2), 21–30. doi:10.1109/MSP.2007.914731

Carlsson, G. (2009). Topology and data. *Bulletin of the American Mathematical Society*, *46*(2), 255–308. doi:10.1090/S0273-0979-09-01249-X

Caroleo, B., Tosatto, A., & Osella, M. (2015). Making Sense of Governmental Activities Over Social Media: A Data-Driven Approach. In Decision Support Systems V–Big Data Analytics for Decision Making (pp. 34-45). Springer International Publishing. doi:10.1007/978-3-319-18533-0_4

Carr, D. F. (2006). *How Google Works*. Retrieved from http://www.baselinemag.com/c/a/Infrastructure/How-Google-Works-1/

Casas, J., Ferrer, J. L., & Garcia, D. (2010). Traffic simulation with aimsun. *Fundamentals of Traffic Simulation*, *1*, 173–232.

Castaneda, C., Nalley, K., Mannion, C., Bhattacharyya, P., Blake, P., Pecora, A., & Suh, K. S. et al. (2015). Clinical decision support systems for improving diagnostic accuracy and achieving precision medicine. *Journal of Clinical Bioinformatics*, *5*(1), 4. doi:10.1186/s13336-015-0019-3 PMID:25834725

Castiglione, A., Pizzolante, R., De Santis, A., Carpentieri, B., Castiglione, A., & Palmieri, F. (2014). Cloud-based adaptive compression and secure management services for 3D healthcare data. *Future Generation Computer Systems*. doi:10.1016/j.future.2014.07.001

Castillo, C., Mendoza, M., & Poblete, B. (2011, March). Information credibility on twitter. In *Proceedings of the 20th International Conference on World Wide Web* (pp. 675-684). ACM. doi:10.1145/1963405.1963500

Cerra, A., Easterwood, K., & Power, J. (2012). *Transforming Business: Big Data, Mobility, and Globalization*. John Wiley & Sons.

Chandran, R., Sridhar, K. T., & Sakkeer, M. A. (2014). *MPP SQL Engines: Architectural Choices and Their Implications on Benchmarking. In Advancing Big Data Benchmarks* (pp. 179–192). Switzerland: Springer International Publishing.

Chang, F., Dean, J., Ghemawat, S., Hsieh, W. C., Wallach, D. A., Burrows, M., ... Gruber, R. E. (2006). *Bigtable: A Distributed Storage System for Structured Data*. Google.

Chang, F., Dean, J., Ghemawat, S., Hsieh, W. C., Wallach, D. A., Burrows, M., & Gruber, R. E. et al. (2008). Bigtable: A Distributed Storage System for Structured Data. *ACM Transactions on Computer Systems*, *26*(2), 1–26. doi:10.1145/1365815.1365816

Chang, R. M., Kauffman, R. J., & Kwon, Y. (2013). (in press). Understanding the paradigm shift to computational social science in the presence of big data. *Decision Support Systems*.

Charalabidis, Y., & Askounis, D. (2008). Interoperability registries in eGovernment. In *Hawaii International Conference on System Sciences, Proceedings of the 41st Annual* (pp. 195–195). IEEE.

Charalabidis, Y., Lampathaki, F., & Psarras, J. (2009). Combination of interoperability registries with process and data management tools for governmental services transformation. In *System Sciences, 2009. HICSS'09. 42nd Hawaii International Conference on* (pp. 1–10). IEEE.

Charles, D., Furukawa, M., & Hufstader, M. (2012). Electronic Health Record Systems and Intent to Attest to Meaningful Use Among Non-federal Acute Care Hospitals in the United States: 2008-2011. *ONC Data Brief, 1*, 1–7.

Chatfield, A. T., Scholl, H. J., & Brajawidagda, U. (2014). #Sandy Tweets: Citizens' Co-Production of Time-Critical Information during an Unfolding Catastrophe. *Proceedings of the 47th Hawaii Int. Conference on System Sciences (HICCS-47)*, (pp. 1947-1957). doi:10.1109/HICSS.2014.247

Chauhan, R., & Kumar, A. (2013, November). Cloud computing for improved healthcare: Techniques, potential and challenges. In E-Health and Bioengineering Conference (EHB), 2013 (pp. 1-4). IEEE.

Chawla, N. V., & Davis, D. A. (2013). Bringing Big Data to personalized healthcare: A patient-centered framework. *Journal of General Internal Medicine, 28*(3), 660–665. doi:10.1007/s11606-013-2455-8 PMID:23797912

Chelimsky, E. (1991). On the Social Science Contribution to Governmental Decision-Making. *Science, 254*(5029), 226–231. doi:10.1126/science.254.5029.226 PMID:17787972

Chen, F., & Neill, D. B. (2015). Human Rights Event Detection from Heterogeneous Social Media Graphs. *Big Data, 3*(1), 34–40. doi:10.1089/big.2014.0072

Cheng, V. S., & Hung, P. C. (2006). Health Insurance Portability and Accountability Act (HIPPA) Compliant Access Control Model for Web Services. *International Journal of Healthcare Information Systems and Informatics, 1*(1), 22–39. doi:10.4018/jhisi.2006010102

Chen, H. (2011). Design Science, Grand Challenges, and Societal Impacts. *ACM Transactions on Management Information Systems, 2*(1), 1–10. doi:10.1145/1929916.1929917

Chen, H., Chiang, R. H. L., & Storey, V. C. (2012). Business intelligence and analytics: From big data to big impact. *Management Information Systems Quarterly, 36*(4), 1165–1188.

Chen, H., Chiang, R., & Storey, V. (2012). Business Intelligence and Analytics: From Big Data to Big Impact. *Management Information Systems Quarterly, 36*(4), 1165–1188.

Chen, R., & Sakamoto, Y. (2014). Feelings and Perspective matter: Sharing of Crisis Information in Social Media. *Proceedings of the 47th Hawaii Int. Conference on System Sciences (HICCS-47)*, (pp. 1958-1967). doi:10.1109/HICSS.2014.248

Cheon, J. C. T.-Y. (2013). Distributed processing of snort alert log using hadoop. *Int J Eng Technol*, 2685-2690.

ChinaTechNews. (2014, July 15). *Big Data Used By Beijing Government To Alleviate Pollution - ChinaTechNews.com - The Technology Source for the Latest Chinese News on Internet, Computers, Digital, Science, Electronics, Law, Security, Software, Web 2.0, Telecom, and Wireless Industries*. Retrieved from http://www.chinatechnews.com/2014/07/15/20725-big-data-used-by-beijing-government-to-alleviate-pollution

Chodorow, K. (2013). *MongoDB: The Definitive Guide*. O'Reilly Media.

Chong, B., Yang, Z., & Wong, M. (2003). Asymmetrical impact of trustworthiness attributes on trust, perceived value and purchase intention: a conceptual framework for cross-cultural study on consumer perception of online auction. *Proceedings of the 5th international conference on Electronic Commerce(ICEC2003)*, (pp. 213-219). doi:10.1145/948005.948033

Chowell, G., Viboud, C., Hyman, J. M., & Simonsen, L. (2014). *The Western Africa Ebola virus disease epidemic exhibits both global exponential and local polynomial growth rates*. arXiv preprint arXiv:1411.7364

Chris Anderson, J. J. L. (2010). CouchDB: The Definitive Guide. O'Reilly Media, Inc.

Chris, P. (2012). *Centralizing healthcare Big Data in the cloud.* Retrieved from http://blogs.computerworld.com/cloud-computing/20488/centralizinghealthcare-big-data-cloud

Clark, P. (2013). New York State Cracks Down on Fake Online Reviews. *Bloomberg News.* Available at: http://www.bloomberg.com/bw/articles/2013-09-23/new-york-state-cracks-down-on-fake-online-reviews

Clarke, R. Y. (2013). *Smart Cities and the Internet of Everything: The Foundation for Delivering Next-Generation Citizen Services.* Alexandria, VA: Tech. Rep.

Committee on the Analysis of Massive Data et al. (2103). *Frontiers in Massive Data Analysis.* The National Academies Press.

Cormode, G., Garofalakis, M., Haas, P., & Jermaine, C. (2012). *Synopses for Massive Data: Samples, Histograms, Wavelets and Sketches.* doi:10.1561/1900000004

Cormode, G., & Muthukrishnan, S. (2005). Improved data stream summaries: The count-min sketch and its applications. *Journal of Algorithms, 55*(1), 58–75. doi:10.1016/j.jalgor.2003.12.001

Costa, F. F. (2014). Big data in biomedicine. *Drug Discovery Today, 19*(4), 433–440. doi:10.1016/j.drudis.2013.10.012 PMID:24183925

Costallow, T. (2014, October 24). *How big data is paying off for DOD -- Defense Systems.* Retrieved from http://defensesystems.com/articles/2014/10/24/feature-big-data-for-defense.aspx

Court, D. (2015). Getting big impact from big data. *The McKinsey Quarterly.*

Cox, M., & Ellsworth, D. (1997). Application-controlled demand paging for out-of-core visualization. *IEEE 8th conference on Visualization* (pp. 235-244). Phoenix: IEEE.

Cox, A. (1997). *Business Success. In Midsomer Norton.* Bath: Earlsgate Press.

Crawford, T. (2014). *Are Enterprises Prepared for the Data Tsunami?* Available at: http://avoa.com/2014/01/20/are-enterprises-prepared-for-the-data-tsunami/

CSA. (2012). *Top ten big data security and privacy challenges.* Retrieved from Cloud Security Alliance: www.isaca.org/groups/professional.../big-data/.../big_data_top_ten_v1.pdf

CTOlabs.com. (2012). *White Paper:B ig Data Solutions For Law Enforcement.* Author.

Cukier, K., & Mayer-Schoenberger, V. (2013). *The Rise of Big Data: How It's Changing the Way We Think About the World.* Retrieved from http://www.foreignaffairs.com/articles/139104/kenneth-neil-cukier-and-viktor-mayer-schoenberger/the-rise-of-big-data

Cumbley, R., & Church, P. (2013). Is "Big Data" creepy? *Computer Law & Security Report, 29*(5), 601–609. doi:10.1016/j.clsr.2013.07.007

Currion, P., Silva, C., & Van de Walle, B. (2007). Open source software for disaster management. *Communications of the ACM, 50*(3), 61–65. doi:10.1145/1226736.1226768

Czajkowski, G. (2014). *Sorting Petabytes with MapReduce - The Next Episode.* Google.

d *ata.gov.sg* . (2015). Retrieved from http://data.gov.sg/common/about.aspx

data.gov.uk . (2015). *About | data.gov.uk.* Retrieved from http://data.gov.uk/about

Davenport, T. H., & Dyché, J. (2013). *Big Data in Big Companies*. International Institute for Analytics.

Dawes, S. S. (1996). Interagency Information Sharing: Expected Benefits, Manageable Risks. *Journal of Policy Analysis and Management, 15*(3), 377–394. doi:10.1002/(SICI)1520-6688(199622)15:3<377::AID-PAM3>3.0.CO;2-F

Dean, J., & Ghemawat, S. (2004). MapReduce: Simplified Data Processing on Large Clusters. In *Proceedings of the Sixth Symposium on Operating System Design and Implementation*. San Francisco, CA: Academic Press.

Dean, J., & Sanjay Ghemawat, S. (2008). MapReduce: Simplified data processing on large clusters. *Communications of the ACM, 51*(1), 107–113. doi:10.1145/1327452.1327492

DeNardis, L. (2010). E-Governance Policies for Interoperability and Open Standards. *Policy & Internet, 2*(3), 129–164. doi:10.2202/1944-2866.1060

Desouza, K. C. (2014). *Realizing the Promise of Big Data | IBM Center for the Business of Government*. Retrieved from http://www.businessofgovernment.org/report/realizing-promise-big-data

Desouza, K. C. (2014). Realizing the Promise of Big Data: Implementing Big Data Projects. IBM center for The Business of Government. India.

Desouza, K. C. (2014). *Realizing the promise of big data: Implementing big data projects*. Retrieved on 30th October 2014 from http://www.businessofgovernment.org/sites/default/files/Realizing%20the%20Promise%20of%20Big%20Data.pdf

Deutsh, M. (1960). The effect of motivational orientation upon trust and suspition. *Human Relations, 13*(2), 123–139. doi:10.1177/001872676001300202

Dhar, V. (2013). Data Science and Prediction. *Communications of the ACM, 56*(12), 64–73. doi:10.1145/2500499

Diakopoulos, N. (2014). Algorithmic Accountability. *Digital Journalism, 0*(0), 1–18.

Diaz, M., Juan, G., & Oikawa Lucas, A. R. (2012). *Big Data on the Internet of Things.Sixth International Conference on Innovative Mobile and Internet Services in Ubiquitous Computing*. doi:10.1109/IMIS.2012.198

Domingos, P. (2012). A Few Useful Things to Know About Machine Learning. *Communications of the ACM, 55*(10), 78–87. doi:10.1145/2347736.2347755

Donoho, D. L. (2006). Compressed sensing. *IEEE Transactions on Information Theory, 52*(4), 1289–1306. doi:10.1109/TIT.2006.871582

Duan, L., Street, W. N., & Xu, E. (2011). Healthcare information systems: Data mining methods in the creation of a clinical recommender system. *Enterprise Information Systems, 5*(2), 169–181. doi:10.1080/17517575.2010.541287

Duarte, M., & Eldar, Y. (2011). Structured Compressed Sensing: From Theory to Applications. *IEEE Transactions on Signal Processing, 59*(9), 4053–4085. doi:10.1109/TSP.2011.2161982

Dugdale, J., Van de Walle, B., & Koeppinghoff, C. (2012). Social media and SMS in the haiti earthquake.*Proceedings of the 21st Int. Conference on World Wide Web (WWW '12 Companion)*. ACM. doi:10.1145/2187980.2188189

Dutcher, J. (2014). *John Wilbanks: Let's Pool Our Medical Data*. Retrieved August 21, 2014, from http://datascience.berkeley.edu/john-wilbanks-lets-pool-medical-data/

Dutcher, J. (2014, September 3). What is Big Data. *Data Science at Berkeley Blog*. Retrieved from http://datascience.berkeley.edu/what-is-big-data/

Dwork, C. (2006). *Differential privacy*. ICALP. doi:10.1007/11787006_1

Earle, T. C., & Cvetkovich, G. (1995). *Social trust: Toward a cosmopolitan society.* Westport, CT: Praeger Press.

Ebadollahi, S., Coden, A. R., Tanenblatt, M. A., Chang, S. F., Syeda-Mahmood, T., & Amir, A. (2006, October). Concept-based electronic health records: opportunities and challenges. In *Proceedings of the 14th annual ACM international conference on Multimedia* (pp. 997-1006). ACM. doi:10.1145/1180639.1180859

Ebejer, J.-P., Fulle, S., Morris, G. M., & Finn, P. W. (2013). The emerging role of cloud computing in molecular modelling. *Journal of Molecular Graphics & Modelling, 44,* 177–187. doi:10.1016/j.jmgm.2013.06.002 PMID:23835611

Eddy, N. (2013). *Big Data Adoption, Investment Plans Grow.* Gartner, Inc. Retrieved from http://www.eweek.com/small-business/big-data-adoption-investment-plans-growgartner.html#sthash.ypLZZpMk.dpuf

Elbashir, M. Z., Collier, P. A., Sutton, S. G., Davern, M. J., & Leech, S. A. (2013). Enhancing the Business Value of Business Intelligence: The Role of Shared Knowledge and Assimilation. *Journal of Information Systems, 27*(2), 87–105. doi:10.2308/isys-50563

Elevant, K. (2014). Who wants to "share weather"? The impacts of off-line interactions on online behavior. In *Proceedings of the 47th Hawaii Int. Conference on System Sciences (HICCS-47),* (pp. 1884- 1893).

EMC. (2010). Retrieved from http://www.emc.com/collateral/hardware/white-papers/h8072-greenplum-database-wp.pdf

E-parts. (n.d.). Retrieved from http://www.eparts-jp.org/

e-skill, UK. (2013). *Big Data Analytics: Adoption and Employment Trends.* Retrieved from http://www.sas.com/offices/europe/uk/downloads/bigdata/eskills/eskills.pdf

European Commission. (2009). *European Interoperability Framework (EIF) for pan-European eGovernment Services.* Interoperable Delivery of European eGovernment Services to public Administrations. Retrieved from http://ec.europa.eu/idabc/en/document/2319/5644.html

European Commission. (2010). *A Digital Agenda for Europe.* Retrieved from http://ec.europa.eu/digital-agenda/

Ezaki Glico Co. Ltd. (n.d.). *Office Glico.* Available: http://www.glico.co.jp/en/corp/officeglico.html

Faghmous, J. H., & Kumar, V. (2014). A Big Data Guide to Understanding Climate Change: The Case for Theory-Guided Data Science. *Big Data, 2*(3), 155-163.

Feldman, B., Martin, E. M., & Skotnes, T. (2012). Big Data in Healthcare Hype and Hope. *October 2012. Dr. Bonnie, 360.*

Feldman, E. (2010, December22). A piece of my mind. The day the computer tried to eat my alligator. *Journal of the American Medical Association, 304*(24), 2679. doi:10.1001/jama.2010.1805 PMID:21177498

Fisher, D. (2005). Using egocentric networks to understand communication. *IEEE Internet Computing, 9*(5), 20–28. doi:10.1109/MIC.2005.114

FlorCruz, M. (2015, April 28). *China To Use Big Data To Rate Citizens In New "Social Credit System".* Retrieved from http://www.ibtimes.com/china-use-big-data-rate-citizens-new-social-credit-system-1898711

Fortune. (2012). *What Data Says About Us.* New York: Time Inc.

Foster, J. (2015). *A Match Made in Heaven: Fraud and Social Media.* Available at: http://www.securityweek.com/match-made-heaven-fraud-and-social-media

Foucart, S. & Rauhut, H. (2013). *A Mathematical Introduction to Compressive Sensing, Applied and Numerical Harmonic Analysis.* Springer Science + Business Media.

Fourneau, J.-M., & Pekergin, N. (2002). Benchmark. In M. C. Calzarossa & S. Tucci (Eds.), *Performance 2002* (Vol. 2459). Heidelberg, Germany: Springer.

Friedman, N., Linial, M., Nachman, I., & Pe'er, D. (2000). Using Bayesian Networks to Analyze Expression Data. *Journal of Computational Biology*, 7(3/4), 601–620. doi:10.1089/106652700750050961 PMID:11108481

Friggeri, A., Adamic, L. A., Eckles, D., & Cheng, J. (2014, May). Rumor cascades. In *Proceedings of the Eighth International AAAI Conference on Weblogs and Social Media*. AAAI.

Galliers, R. (2003). Change as crisis or growth? Toward a trans-disciplinary view of information systems as a field of study: A response to Benbasat and Zmud's call for returning to the IT. *Journal of the Association for Information Systems*, 4(6), 337–351.

Gama, J. (2010). *Knowledge Discovery from Data Streams*. Chapman & Hall/CRC. doi:10.1201/EBK1439826119

Gambetta, D. (1988). Can we trust trust? In D. Gambetta (Ed.), *Trust: Making and breaking cooperative relations* (pp. 213-237). Department of Sociology, University of Oxford. Available online from the following site: http://www.sociology.ox.ac.uk/papers/gambetta213-237.pdf

Gantz, J., & Reinsel, D. (2012). *The digital universe in 2020: Big data, bigger digital shadows, and biggest growth in the far east-United States*. Retrieved on 30th October 2014 from http://www.emc.com/collateral/analyst-reports/idc-digital-universe-united-states.pdf

Gao, S., Li, L., Li, W., Janowicz, K., & Zhang, Y. (2014). Constructing gazetteers from volunteered Big Geo-Data based on Hadoop. *Computers, Environment and Urban Systems*. doi:10.1016/j.compenvurbsys.2014.02.004

Gartner Press Release, (2012). *Gartner Says By 2014, 10-15 Percent of Social Media Reviews to Be Fake, Paid for By Companies*. Available at: http://www.gartner.com/newsroom/id/2161315

Gartner, Inc. (2012a). *Gartner Says Big Data Will Drive $28 Billion of IT Spending in 2012*. Retrieved October 27, 2014, from http://www.gartner.com/newsroom/id/2200815

Gartner, Inc. (2012b). *Gartner Says Big Data Creates Big Jobs: 4.4 Million IT Jobs Globally to Support Big Data By 2015*. Retrieved October 27, 2014, from http://www.gartner.com/newsroom/id/2207915

Gartner. (2010). *Big data and its impact*. Garner Report.

Gartner. (2013). *Gartner IT Glossary Big Data*. Retrieved from http://www.gartner.com/it-glossary/big-data

Gartner. (2014). *IT Glossary*. Retrieved June 12, 2014, from http://www.gartner.com/it-glossary/?s=big+data

Gartner.com. (n.d.). *Answering Big Data's 10 Biggest Vision and Strategy Questions*. Author.

Gartner.com. (n.d.). *Answering Big Data's 10 Biggest Vision and Strategy Questions*. Retrieved from http://www.gartner.com

Gelman, A., & Meng, X. L. (Eds.). (2004). *Applied Bayesian modeling and causal inference from incomplete-data perspectives*. John Wiley & Sons. doi:10.1002/0470090456

George, L. (2011). *HBase: The Definitive Guide Random Access to Your Planet-Size Data*. O'Reilly Media.

George, L. (2011). *HBase: The Definitive Guide*. O'Reilly Media.

Ghemawat, S., Gobioff, H., & Leung, S. T. (2003). The Google file system. In *Proceedings of the Nineteenth ACM Symposium on Operating Systems Principles - SOSP '03*. ACM.

Gil Press. (2013). *$16.1 Billion Big Data market: 2014 Predictions From IDS And IIA*. Retrieved from http://www.forbes.com/sites/gilpress/2013/12/12/16-1-billion-big-data-market-2014-predictions-from-idc-and-iia

Gilbert, A., Indyk, P., Iwen, M., & Schmidt, L. (2014). A compressed Fourier transform for big data. IEEE Signal Processing Magazine, 31(5), 91 - 100

Gilbert, S., & Lynch, N. (2002). Brewer's conjecture and the feasibility of consistent, available, partition-tolerant web services. *ACM SIGACT News, 33*(2), 51-59. Retrieved on 30th October 2014 from http://webpages.cs.luc.edu/~pld/353/gilbert_lynch_brewer_proof.pdf

Gilbert, S., & Lynch, N. (2012). Brewer's conjecture and the feasibility of consistent, available, partition-tolerant web services. *ACM SIGACT News, 33*(2).

Ginsberg, J., Mohebbi, M. H., Patel, R. S., Brammer, L., Smolinski, M. S., & Brilliant, L. (2009). Detecting influenza epidemics using search engine query data. *Nature, 457*(7232), 1012–1014. doi:10.1038/nature07634 PMID:19020500

Github. (2013). *Storm Codebase*. Github.

Gloor, P. (2000). *Making the e-Business Transformation*. London: Springer-Verlag. doi:10.1007/978-1-4471-0757-6

Goes, P. (2014). Editor's Comments: Big Data and IS Research. *Management Information Systems Quarterly, 38*(3), iii–viii.

Gov.uk. (2015). *Horizon Scanning Programme Team - Groups - GOV.UK*. Retrieved from https://www.gov.uk/government/groups/horizon-scanning-programme-team

Government of Japan. (2015a). *Disaster Management in Japan*. Cabinet Office. Available: http://www.bousai.go.jp/1info/pdf/saigaipamphlet_je.pdf

Government of Japan. (2015b). *White Paper 2014*. Ministry of Internal Affairs and Communications. Available: http://www.soumu.go.jp/johotsusintokei/whitepaper/ja/h24/pdf/n2020000.pdf

Green, E. D., Guyer, M. S., Green, E. D., Guyer, M. S., Manolio, T. A., & Peterson, J. L. (2011, February10). Charting a course for genomic medicine from base pairs to bedside. *Nature, 470*(7333), 204–213. doi:10.1038/nature09764 PMID:21307933

Grimes, S. (2012). *Unstructured data and the 80 percent rule*. Retrieved from http://clarabridge.com/default.aspx?tabid=137&ModuleID=635&ArticleID=551

Groves, P., Kayyali, B., Knott, D., & Van Kuiken, S. (2013). The 'big data 'revolution in healthcare. *McKinsey Quarterly*. Retrieved from http://www-01.ibm.com/software/data/bigdata/industry-healthcare.html

Groves, P., Kayyali, B., Knott, D., & Van Kuiken, S. (2013). The 'Big Data' revolution in healthcare. *The McKinsey Quarterly*.

Gulla, J. (2012, February). Sevens Reasons IT Projects Fail. *IBM Systems Magazine*. Retrieved May 13, 2014, from http://www.ibmsystemsmag.com/

Gupta, A., Kumaraguru, P., Castillo, C., & Meier, P. (2014, May). Tweetcred: A real-time Web-based system for assessing credibility of content on Twitter. In *Proc. 6th International Conference on Social Informatics (SocInfo)*. HHS. Retrieved from http://www.hhs.gov/ocr/privacy/hipaa/understanding/summary/index.html

Gupta, A., Lamba, H., Kumaraguru, P., & Joshi, A. (2013). Faking Sandy: Characterizing and identifying fake images on Twitter during Hurricane Sandy. *Proceedings of the 22nd International Conference on World Wide Web (WWW 2013 Companion)*, (pp. 729–736). Academic Press.

Gupta, A., Lamba, H., Kumaraguru, P., & Joshi, A. (2013, May). Faking Sandy: characterizing and identifying fake images on Twitter during Hurricane Sandy. In *Proceedings of the 22nd international conference on World Wide Web companion* (pp. 729-736). International World Wide Web Conferences Steering Committee.

Habegger, B. (2010). Strategic foresight in public policy: Reviewing the experiences of the U.K., Singapore, and the Netherlands. *Futures*, *42*(1), 49–58. doi:10.1016/j.futures.2009.08.002

Hagar, C. (2012). Crisis informatics: Perspectives of trust–Is social media a mixed blessing? *Student Research Journal*, *2*(2). Available: http://scholarworks.sjsu.edu/slissrj/vol2/iss2/2/

Halevi, G., & Moed, H. F. (2012). The evolution of big data as a research and scientific topic: Overview of the literature. *Research Trends, 30.*

Halevy, A., Norvig, P., & Pereira, F. (2009). The Unreasonable Effectiveness of Data. *IEEE Intelligent Systems*, *24*(2), 8–12. doi:10.1109/MIS.2009.36

Hand, D. J., Mannila, H., & Smyth, P. (2001). *Principles of data mining*. Cambridge, MA: MIT Press.

Hand, D. J., Mannila, H., & Smyth, P. (2001). *Principles of Data Mining: Adaptive Computation and Machine Learning*. Cambridge, MA: MIT Press.

Han, J., Wang, C., & El-Kishky, A. (2104). Bringing structure to text: mining phrases, entities, topics, and hierarchies. *Proceedings of the 20th ACM SIGKDD international conference on Knowledge discovery and data mining*. ACM.

Hansen, C. (2013). *IBM CSI Newsblog*. Retrieved from https://www-304.ibm.com/connections/blogs/CSI/entry/big_data_helps_city_of_dublin_improve_its_public_bus_transportation_network_and_reduce_congestion?lang=it_it

Hartas, D. (2015). *Educational research and inquiry: Qualitative and quantitative approaches*. Bloomsbury Publishing.

Hartzband, D. D. (2011). *Using Ultra-Large Data Sets in Health Care*. e-healthpolicy.org.

Hassanieh, H., Indyk, P., Katabi, & Price, E. (2012). Nearly Optimal Sparse Fourier Transform. *ACM-SIAM Symposium on Discrete Algorithms*. ACM.

Healy, D. D., & Brady, D. J. (2008). Compression at the Physical Interface. IEEE Signal Processing Magazine, 25(2)

Healy, M. (2014, October 9). Big data, meet big money: NIH funds centers to crunch health data. *Los Angeles Times*. Retrieved from http://www.latimes.com/science/sciencenow/la-sci-sn-big-data-money-20141009-story.html

Hearst, M. A. (2009). *Search user interfaces*. New York: Cambridge University Press. doi:10.1017/CBO9781139644082

Helms, J. (n.d.). *Five Examples of How Federal Agencies Use Big Data*. Retrieved from http://www.businessofgovernment.org/BigData3Blog.html

Hernandez, D. (2014). *Activity trackers like Fitbit bring big data to US healthcare*. Available at: http://www.wired.co.uk/news/archive/2014-03/07/internet-things-health

Herzberg, B. (2014). *The Next Frontier for Open Data: An Open Private Sector*. Retrieved June 21, 2014, from http://blogs.worldbank.org/voices/next-frontier-open-data-open-private-sector

Hilz, S. R., Van de Walle, B., & Turoff, M. (2009). The domain of emergency management information. In Information systems for emergency management (pp.3-20). M.E. Sharp.

HONDA. (2011). *News Release*. Available: http://www.honda.co.jp/news/2011/4110428.html

Hoover, W. (2013). *Transforming Health Care through Big Data Strategies for leveraging Big Data in the health care industry*. Institute for Health Technology Transformation.

Howarth, B. (2014, June 13). *Big data: how predictive analytics is taking over the public sector*. Retrieved from http://www.theguardian.com/technology/2014/jun/13/big-data-how-predictive-analytics-is-taking-over-the-public-sector

HP. (2012). *Big security for Big Data*. Retrieved from http://www.hpenterprisesecurity.com/collateral/ whitepaper/ BigSecurityforBigData0213.pdf

Huai, Y., Lee, R., Zhang, S., Xia, C. H., & Zhang, X. (2011, October). DOT: a matrix model for analyzing, optimizing and deploying software for Big Data analytics in distributed systems. In *Proceedings of the 2nd ACM Symposium on Cloud Computing* (p. 4). ACM. doi:10.1145/2038916.2038920

Huang, G. T. (2012, May 29). *Massachusetts' New Big-Data Initiative to Include MIT, Intel, and HackReduce*. Retrieved from http://www.xconomy.com/boston/2012/05/29/massachusetts-new-big-data-initiative-to-include-mit-intel-and-hackreduce/

Hu, H., Wen, Y., Chua, T. S., & Li, X. (2014). Toward scalable systems for big data analytics: A technology tutorial. *Access, IEEE, 2*, 652–687. doi:10.1109/ACCESS.2014.2332453

Hurwitz, J., Nugent, A., Halper, F., & Kaufman, M. (2013). *Big Data For Dummies*. Hoboken, NJ: John Wiley & Sons, Inc.

IBM Redbook. (2014). Information *Governance Principles and Practices for a Big Data Landscape*. Retrieved from http://www.redbooks.ibm.com/redbooks/pdfs/sg248165.pdf

IBM Website. (2014). Retrieved from http://www.ibm.com/big-data/us/en/

IBM. (2011). *IBM's Smarter Cities Challenge: Syracuse*. Retrieved from http://smartercitieschallenge.org/city_syracuse_ny.html

IBM. (2013). *IBM's smarter cities challenge: Syracuse*. Armonk, NY: IBM Corporate. Available from: http://smartercitieschallenge.org/ executive_reports/SmarterCities-Syracuse.pdf

IBM. (2014). *What is the Hadoop Distributed File System (HDFS)?*. IBM.

IBM. (2015). *IBM InfoSphere Streams*. Retrieved from ibm.com: http://www-03.ibm.com/software/products/en/infosphere-streams

IBM. (n.d.). *Analytics: The real-world use of big data in financial services*. IBM Institute for Business.

ibm.com. (n.d.). *Achieving Small Miracles from Big Data*. Available at: https://www.ibm.com/smarterplanet/global/files/ca__en_us__healthcare__smarter_healthcare_data_baby.pdf

IDC. (2010). *Big Data technologies*. IDC Report.

IDC. (2012). *Worldwide Big Data Technology and Services 2012-2015 Forecast*. International Data Corporation. Retrieved from http://www.idc.com

IDC. (2015). *Report*. Available at: https://www.idc.com/prodserv/4Pillars/bigdata

IDC. (n.d.). *Big data and Analytics*. Available at: https://www.idc.com/prodserv/4Pillars/bigdata

Indyk, P., & Kapralov, M., (2014, October). Sample-Optimal Sparse Fourier Transform in Any Constant Dimension. *FOCS*.

Informationweek. (2013). *Defending NSA Prism's Big Data Tools*. Retrieved from informationweek.com: http://www.informationweek.com/big-data/big-data-analytics/defending-nsa-prisms-big-data-tools/d/d-id/1110318?

Intel. (2015). *Big Data Visualization: Turning Big Data Into Big Insights*. Retrieved from http://www.intel.com/content/dam/www/public/us/en/documents/white-papers/big-data-visualization-turning-big-data-into-big-insights.pdf

International Data Corporation. (2012). *The digital universe in 2020*. Retrieved on 30th October 2014 from http://www.emc.com/collateral/analyst-reports/idc-the-digital-universe-in-2020.pdf

Iwate Disaster IT Support. (2011). Available: www.go-iwate.org

James Manyika, M. C. (2011). *Big data:nThe next frontier for innovation,competition and productivity*. India: McKinsey & Company.

Janssen, M., Chun, S. A., & Gil-Garcia, J. R. (2009). Building the next generation of digital government infrastructures. *Government Information Quarterly*, *26*(2), 233–237. doi:10.1016/j.giq.2008.12.006

Jee, K., & Kim, G. H. (2013). Potentiality of Big Data in the medical sector: focus on how to reshape the healthcare system. *Healthcare Informatics Research, 19*(2), 79-85.

Jee, K., & Kim, G.-H. (2013). Potentiality of big data in the medical sector: Focus on how to reshape the healthcare system. *Healthcare Informatics Research*, *19*(2), 79–85. doi:10.4258/hir.2013.19.2.79 PMID:23882412

JEITA. (2011). *Information and Communication Supporter*. Available: http://www.jeita.or.jp/ictot/

Jensen, F. V., & Nielsen, T. D. (2007). *Bayesian Networks and Decision Graphs. Information Science and Statistics series* (2nd ed.). Springer. doi:10.1007/978-0-387-68282-2

Jensen, P. B., Jensen, L. J., & Brunak, S. (2012). Mining electronic health records: Towards better research applications and clinical care. *Nature Reviews. Genetics*, *13*(6), 395–405. doi:10.1038/nrg3208 PMID:22549152

Jerome Francois, S. W. (2011). BotCloud: Detecting Botnets Using MapReduce. *IEEEInternational Workshop on Information Forensics*.

Jing, L., & Yingqun, C. (2014, April 21). When Big Data can lead to big profit. *The China Daily*. Retrieved from http://www.chinadailyasia.com/business/2014-04/21/content_15131425.html

Johnstone, J. C. (2004). Earnings Manipulation Risk, Corporate Governance Risk, and Auditors'. *Planning and Pricing Decisions*, *79*, 277–304.

Joseph, R. C., & Johnson, N. A. (2013). Big Data and Transformational Government. *IT Professional*, *15*(6), 43–48. doi:10.1109/MITP.2013.61

Jung, J. (2012). Social Media Use & Goals after the Great East Japan Earthquake. *First Monday*, *17*(8), 8–6. doi:10.5210/fm.v17i8.4071

Kaidi, Z. (2000). *Data visualization*. National University of Singapore.

Kaisler, S., Armour, F., Espinosa, J. A., & Money, W. (2013, January). Big Data: Issues and challenges moving forward. In *System Sciences (HICSS), 2013 46th Hawaii International Conference on* (pp. 995-1004). IEEE.

Kambatla, K., Kollias, G., Kumar, V., & Grama, A. (2014). Trends in Big Data Analytics. *Journal of Parallel and Distributed Computing*, *74*(7), 2561–2573. doi:10.1016/j.jpdc.2014.01.003

Kantardzic, M. (2011). *Data mining: concepts, models, methods, and algorithms*. John Wiley & Sons. doi:10.1002/9781118029145

Kar, S. (2014, February 12). *Gartner Report: Big Data will Revolutionize the Cybersecurity in Next Two Year | Cloud-Times*. Retrieved from http://cloudtimes.org/2014/02/12/gartner-report-big-data-will-revolutionize-the-cybersecurity-in-next-two-year/

Kar, S. (2015, January 2). *Looking Back at Top Big Data Stories and Trends of 2014 | CloudTimes*. Retrieved from http://cloudtimes.org/2015/01/02/looking-back-at-top-big-data-stories-and-trends-of-2014/

Karau, H., Konwinski, A., Wendell, P., & Zaharia, M. (2014). *Learning Spark: Lightning Fast Big Data Analytics* (1st ed.). O'Reilly Media.

Kayyali, B., Knott, D., & Van Kuiken, S. (2013). *The big-data revolution in US health care: Accelerating value and innovation*. Mc Kinsey & Company.

Khorey, L. (2012). Big Data, Bigger Outcomes. *Journal of American Health Information Management Association*, *83*(10), 38–43. PMID:23061351

Kim, G.-H., Trimi, S., & Chung, J.-H. (2014). Big-data Applications in the Government Sector. *Communications of the ACM*, *57*(3), 78–85. doi:10.1145/2500873

King, G., Honaker, J., Joseph, A., & Scheve, K. (2001, March). Analyzing incomplete political science data: An alternative algorithm for multiple imputation. In American Political Science Association (Vol. 95, No. 01, pp. 49-69). Cambridge University Press.

Kobielus, J. (2013). *Measuring the Business Value of Big Data*. Retrieved July 11, 2014, from http://www.ibmbigdatahub.com/blog/measuring-business-value-big-data

Koh, H. C., & Tan, G. (2011). Data mining applications in healthcare. *Journal of Healthcare Information Management*, *19*(2), 65. PMID:15869215

Konkel, F. (2013, March 15). *Supercomputing, big data: The postal service's hidden cool factor -- FCW*. Retrieved from http://fcw.com/articles/2013/03/25/postal-service-big-data.aspx

Konrad, R. (2013). *The three big data pillars: Hadoop, SAP HANA and business intelligence*. Retrieved from http://www.t-systems.com/news-media/the-three-big-data-pillars-hadoop-sap-hana-and-business-intelligence-bi-/1149004

Kourtesis, D., Alvarez-Rodríguez, J. M., & Paraskakis, I. (2014). Semantic-based QoS management in cloud systems: Current status and future challenges. *Future Generation Computer Systems*, *32*, 307–323. doi:10.1016/j.future.2013.10.015

Krehbiel, K. (1991). *Information and legislative organization*. Ann Arbor, MI: University of Michigan Press.

Kroenke and Auer. (2015). Database Concepts (7th ed.). Pren_hall Pub.

Kubicek, H., Cimander, R., & Scholl, H. J. (2011). *Organizational Interoperability in E-Government: Lessons from 77 European Good-Practice Cases*. Springer. doi:10.1007/978-3-642-22502-4

Labrinidis, A., & Jagadish, H. V. (2012). Challenges and Opportunities with Big Data.*Proc. VLDB Endow.*, *5*(12), 2032–2033. doi:10.14778/2367502.2367572

Lam, C. (2010). *Hadoop in Action*. Manning Publications.

Lämmel, R. (2008). Google's Map Reduce programming model — Revisited. *Science of Computer Programming*, *70*(1), 1–30. doi:10.1016/j.scico.2007.07.001

Laney, D. (2001). *3D Data Management: Controlling Data Volume, Velocity and Variety*. Retrieved from http://blogs.gartner.com/doug-laney/files/2012/01/ad949-3D-Data-Management-Controlling-Data-Volume-Velocity-and-Variety.pdf

Laudon, K., & Laudon, J. (2015). *Management Information Systems: Managing the Digital Firm, 14/E*. Pearson Pub.

LaValle, S., Lesser, E., Shockley, R., Hopkins, M. S., & Kruschwitz, N. (2013). Big Data, analytics and the path from insights to value. *MIT Sloan Management Review, 21*.

Lazer, D., Kennedy, R., & Vespignani, A. (2014). The Parable of Google Flu: Traps in Big Data Analysis. *Science, 343*(6176), 1203–1205. doi:10.1126/science.1248506 PMID:24626916

Lee, C. O., Lee, M., Han, D., Jung, S., & Cho, J. (2008, July). A framework for personalized Healthcare Service Recommendation. In *e-health Networking, Applications and Services, 2008. HealthCom 2008. 10th International Conference on* (pp. 90-95). IEEE.

Lee, Y. L. Y. (2013). Toward scalable internet traffic measurement and analysis with hadoop. *ACM SIGCOMM Comput Commun Rev*, 5-13.

Lee, K. K. Y., Tang, W. C., & Choi, K. S. (2013). Alternatives to relational database: Comparison of NoSQL and XML approaches for clinical data storage. *Computer Methods and Programs in Biomedicine, 110*(1), 99–109. doi:10.1016/j.cmpb.2012.10.018 PMID:23177219

Letouzé, E. (2012, May). Big Data for Development:Challenges & Opportunities. *UN Global Pulse*.

Lewis, D. J., & Weigert, A. (1985). Trust as a social reality. *Social Forces, 63*(4), 967–985. doi:10.1093/sf/63.4.967

Lewis, J. R. T. (1995). Reinventing (open) government: State and federal trends. *Government Information Quarterly, 12*(4), 427–455. doi:10.1016/0740-624X(95)90078-0

Liebwald, D. (2013). Vagueness in law: a stimulus for'artificial intelligence & law'. In *Proceedings of the Fourteenth International Conference on Artificial Intelligence and Law* (pp. 207–211). doi:10.1145/2514601.2514628

Lin, H., & Chou, L. Cheng, & Chiang. (2014). Temporal Event Tracing on Big Healthcare Data Analytics. In *Proceedings of Big Data (BigData Congress), 2014 IEEE International Congress on*. IEEE.

Linden, G., Smith, B., & York, J. (2003). Amazon.com recommendations: Item-to-item collaborative filtering. *Internet Computing, 7*(1), 76–80. doi:10.1109/MIC.2003.1167344

Li, R., Xu, Z., Kang, W., Yow, K. C., & Xu, C.-Z. (2014). Efficient multi-keyword ranked query over encrypted data in cloud computing. *Future Generation Computer Systems, 30*, 179–190. doi:10.1016/j.future.2013.06.029

Liu, W., & Park, E. K. (2014, February). Big Data as an e-Health Service. In *Computing, Networking and Communications (ICNC), 2014 International Conference on* (pp. 982-988). IEEE. doi:10.1109/ICCNC.2014.6785471

Liu, W., Park, E. K., & Krieger, U. (2012, October). eHealth interconnection infrastructure challenges and solutions overview. In *e-Health Networking, Applications and Services (Healthcom), 2012 IEEE 14th International Conference on* (pp. 255-260). IEEE.

Lodha, R., Jain, H., & Kurup, L. (2014). Big Data Challenges: Data Analysis Perspective. *International Journal of Current Engineering and Technology*.

Lohr, S. (2012, February 11). Big Data's Impact in the World. *The New York Times*. Retrieved from http://www.nytimes.com/2012/02/12/sunday-review/big-datas-impact-in-the-world.html

Lomotey, R. K., & Deters, R. (2013, June). Terms extraction from unstructured data silos. In *System of Systems Engineering (SoSE), 2013 8th International Conference on* (pp. 19-24). IEEE. doi:10.1109/SYSoSE.2013.6575236

Los Angeles Police Department. (2014). Recovered on 30ᵗʰ October 2014 from http://www.lapdonline.org/crime_mapping_and_compstat

Loshin, D. (2013). *Big Data Analytics: From Strategic Planning to Enterprise Integration with Tools, Techniques, NoSQL, and Graph.* Waltham: Elsevier Inc.

Lu, X. & Han, R. (n.d.). *On Big Data Benchmarking.* Ohio State University.

Luo, W., & Najdawi, M. (2004). Trust-building measures: A review of consumer health portals. *Communications of the ACM, 47*(1), 108–113. doi:10.1145/962081.962089

Lu, Y. Q. (2014). Research on E-Government Model Based on Big Data. In *Advanced. Materials Research, 989*(994), 4905–4908. doi:10.4028/www.scientific.net/AMR.989-994.4905

Mackenzie, D. (2009). *Compressed Sensing Makes Every Pixel Count.* Retrieved from http://www.ams.org/samplings/math-history/hap7-pixel.pdf

Mancini, M. (2014). Exploiting Big Data for Improving Healthcare Services. *Journal of e-Learning and Knowledge Society, 10*(2).

Manyika, J., Chui, M., Brown, B., Bughin, J., Dobbs, R., Roxburgh, C., & Byers, A. H. (2011). *Big data: The next frontier for innovation, competition, and productivity.* Retrieved October 27, 2014, from http://www.mckinsey.com/insights/business_technology/big_data_the_next_frontier_for_innovation

Manyika, J., Chui, M., Brown, B., Bughin, J., Dobbs, R., Roxburgh, C., & Byers, A. H. (2011, May). *Big data: The next frontier for innovation, competition, and productivity | McKinsey & Company.* Retrieved from http://www.mckinsey.com/insights/business_technology/big_data_the_next_frontier_for_innovation

Manyika, J., Chui, M., Brown, B., Bughin, J., Dobbs, R., Roxburgh, C., & Byers, A. H. (n.d.). *Big data: The next frontier for innovation, competition, and productivity.* Retrieved from http://www.mckinsey.com/Insights/MGI/Research/Technology_and_Innovation/Big_data_The_next_frontier_for_innovation

Marchionini, G., Haas, S., Plaisant, C., & Shneiderman, B. (2006). Integrating data and interfaces to enhance understanding of government statistics: Toward the national statistical knowledge network project briefing. In *International Conference on Digital Government Research Dg.o* (pp. 334–335). Academic Press.

Mardis, E. R. (2010, November 26). The $1,000 genome, the $100,000 analysis? *Genome Medicine, 2*(11), 84. doi:10.1186/gm205 PMID:21114804

Markonis, D., Schaer, R., Eggel, I., Muller, H., & Depeursinge, A. (2012). Using MapReduce for large-scale medical image analysis. In *2012 IEEE Second International Conference on Healthcare Informatics, Imaging and Systems Biology* (p. 1). IEEE. doi:10.1109/HISB.2012.8

Mateo, R. M. A. (2013). Scalable Adaptive Group Communication for Collaboration Framework of Cloud-enabled Robots. *Procedia Computer Science, 22*, 1239–1248. doi:10.1016/j.procs.2013.09.211

Matthijssen, L. (1998). A task-based interface to legal databases. *Artificial Intelligence and Law, 6*(1), 81–103. doi:10.1023/A:1008291611892

Mayer-Schönberger, V., & Cukier, K. (2013). *Big Data: A revolution that will transform how we live, work, and think.* Houghton Mifflin Harcourt.

Mayer-Schönberger, V., & Cukier, K. (2013). *Big Data: A Revolution that Will Transform how We Live, Work, and Think.* Houghton Mifflin Harcourt.

May, W. F. (1983). *The Physician's Covenant*. Philadelphia: Westminster Press.

McAfee, A., & Brynjolfsson, E. (2012, October). Big data: The management revolution. *Harvard Business Review*, 61–68. PMID:23074865

McAfee, A., Brynjolfsson, E., Davenport, T. H., Patil, D. J., & Barton, D. (2012). Big Data. The management revolution. *Harvard Business Review*, *90*(10), 61–67. PMID:23074865

McKinsey Global Institute. (2011). *Big data: the next frontier for innovation, competition and productivity*. Retrieved on 30th October 2014 from http://www.mckinsey.com/insights/business_technology/big_data_the_next_frontier_for_innovation

McKinsey Global Institute. (2011). *Big data: The next frontier for innovation, competition, and productivity*. Retrieved from http://www.mckinsey.com/~/media/McKinsey/dotcom/Insights%20and%20pubs/MGI/Research/Technology%20and%20Innovation/Big%20Data/MGI_big_data_full_report.ashx

McKinsey Global Institute. (2011). *Big Data: The Next Frontier for Innovation, Competition, and Productivity*. Retrieved from http://www.mckinsey.com/insights/business_technology/big_data_the_next_frontier_for_innovation

McKinsey Global Institute. (2011). *Big Data: The next frontier for innovation, competition, and productivity*. Retrieved from http://www.mckinsey.com/mgi/publications/big_data/pdfs/MGI_big_data_full_report.pdf

McKinsey Report. (2011). *Big data: The next frontier for innovation, competition, and productivity*. McKinsey Global Institute Report. Available at: http://www.mckinsey.com/insights/business_technology/big_data_the_next_frontier_for_innovation

Michele, O. C. (2012, October). Big Data, Bigger Outcomes Enterprise Systems and Data Management. *Journal of American Health Information Management Association*, *83*(10), 38–43.

Miller, H. E. (2013). Big-data in cloud computing: A taxonomy of risks. *Information Research*, *18*(1), 571.

Ming, Z., Luo, C., Gao, W., Han, R., Yang, Q., Wang, L., & Zhan, J. (2014). *BDGS: A Scalable Big Data Generator Suite in Big Data Benchmarking. In Advancing Big Data Benchmarks* (pp. 138–154). Switzerland: Springer International Publishing.

Mobile Marketing Data (MMD) Labo. (2011) Survey on social media use after the Great East Japan Earthquake. *MMD SurveySummary*. Available: http://mmd.up-date.ne.jp/news/detail.php?news_id=799.html (in Japanese)

Mohanty, S., Jagadeesh, M., & Srivatsa, H. (2013). *Big Data Imperatives: Enterprise Big Data Warehouse, BI Implementations and Analytics*. Apress. doi:10.1007/978-1-4302-4873-6

Molesworth, A. M., Cuevas, L. E., Connor, S. J., Morse, A. P., & Thomson, M. C. (2003). Environmental risk and meningitis epidemics in Africa. *Emerging Infectious Diseases*, *9*(10), 1287–1293. doi:10.3201/eid0910.030182 PMID:14609465

Moore, G. E. (1965). Cramming More Components onto Integrated Circuits. *Electronics Magazine*, 4.

Mount Sinai Hospital. (2014). *Fast Company names Icahn School of Medicine as one of world's top ten most innovative companies in big data*. Press Release. Retrieved September 21, 2014, from http://www.mountsinai.org/about-us/newsroom/press-releases/fast-company-names-icahn-school-of-medicine-as-one-of-worlds-top-ten-most-innovative-companies-in-big-data

Mountain, I. (2012, October). The Impact of Big Data on Government. *IDC Government Insights*.

Mukai, M. (2012). *Research on a Model for Decision Making in Retweet which caused Spreading of False Rumor in Emergencies*. (Master Dissertation). Iwate Prefectural University. (in Japanese)

Murayama, Y.(2014). Issues in Disaster Communications. *Journal of Information Processing, 22*(4). doi:10.2197/ipsjjip.22.558

Murayama, Y., Saito, Y., & Nishioka, D. (2013). Trust Issues in Disaster Communication. *Proceedings of HICSS-46,* 335–342.

Murdoch, T. B., & Detsky, A. S. (2013). The inevitable application of Big Data to health care. *Journal of the American Medical Association, 309*(13), 1351–1352. doi:10.1001/jama.2013.393 PMID:23549579

Nambiar, R., Bhardwaj, R., Sethi, A., & Vargheese, R. (2013, October). A look at challenges and opportunities of Big Data analytics in healthcare. In *Big Data, 2013 IEEE International Conference on* (pp. 17-22). IEEE. doi:10.1109/BigData.2013.6691753

Nash, D. B. (2014). Harnessing the power of big data in healthcare. *American Health & Drug Benefits, 7*(2), 69.

National Information Society Agency. (2012). *Evolving World on Big Data: Global Practices.* Retrieved from http://www.koreainformationsociety.com/2013/11/koreas-national-information-society.html

National Information Society Agency. (2012). Retrieved from http://www.koreainformationsociety.com/2013/11/koreas-national-information-society.html

National Police Agency of Japan. (2015). *Damage Situation and Police Countermeasures associated with 2011 Tohoku district - off the Pacific Ocean Earthquake.* Emergency Disaster Countermeasures Headquarters. Available: http://www.npa.go.jp/archive/keibi/biki/higaijokyo_e.pdf

National Research Council. (1989). *Improving risk communication.* National Academy Press.

Nelson, F. (2014). *Coca-Cola Drinks In New Social Data.* Retrieved September 3, 2014, from http://www.networkcomputing.com/networking/coca-cola-drinks-in-new-social-data/d/d-id/1100837

NESSI. (2012, December). *Big Data A New World of Opportunities.* NESSI White Paper.

NICT. (2011). *President's Council on National ICT Strategies. Establishing a smart government by using Big Data.* Seoul, Korea: President's Council on National ICT Strategies.

Nirmala, M. B. (2014). A Survey of Big Data Analytics Systems: Appliances, Platforms, and Frameworks. Handbook of Research on Cloud Infrastructures for Big Data Analytics, 392.

NIST Special Publication 1500-1. (2015). *DRAFT NIST Big Data Interoperability Framework: Volume 1, Definitions.* Author.

NSF. (2012). *Core Techniques and Technologies for Advancing Big Data Science & Engineering (BIGDATA)(nsf12499).* Retrieved July 7, 2015, from http://www.nsf.gov/pubs/2012/nsf12499/nsf12499.htm

NSF. (2015, March 30). *National Science Foundation (NSF) News - New U.S.-Japan collaborations bring Big Data approaches to disaster response | NSF - National Science Foundation.* Retrieved from http://www.nsf.gov/news/news_summ.jsp?cntn_id=134609

Odlum, M., & Yoon, S. (2015). What can we learn about the Ebola outbreak from tweets? *American Journal of Infection Control, 43*(1), 563–571. doi:10.1016/j.ajic.2015.02.023 PMID:26042846

Office of Science and Technology Policy, Executive Office of the President. (2012). *Fact Sheet: Big Data Across the Federal Government.* Retrieved from http://www.whitehouse.gov/administration/eop/ostp

Office of Science and Technology Policy, Executive Office of the President. (2012). *Obama Administration Unveils 'Big Data' Initiative: Announces $200 Million in New R&D Investments*. Retrieved from http://www.whitehouse.gov/administration/eop/ostp

Ohlhorst, F. J. (2012). *Big Data analytics: turning Big Data into big money*. Hoboken, NY: John Wiley & Sons. doi:10.1002/9781119205005

Ohlhorst, F. J. (2013). *Big Data Analytics: Turning Big Data Into Big Money*. Hoboken, NJ: John Wiley & Sons.

Oleszek, W. J. (2001). *Congressional procedures and the policy process (vol. 5)*. CQ Press.

Olofson, C. W., & Vesset, D. (2012). *Big Data: Trends, Strategies and SAP Technology*. Report ICD #236135.

Olson, M. (2010). Hadoop: Scalable, flexible data storage and analysis. *IQT Quarterly, 1*(3), 14–18.

Olsson, J. (2013, October 15). *Load first, model later - What data warehouses can learn from big data* (Weblog post). Retrieved on 30th October 2014 from http://tdwi.org/Articles/2013/10/15/Load-First-Model-Later.aspx?Page=1

Open Government Data Platform India. (2015). *Information about Open Government Data (OGD) Platform India*. Retrieved from https://data.gov.in/about-us

Orcutt, M. (2014). Hackers Are Homing in on Hospitals. *Technology Review*. Retrieved September 15, 2014, from http://www.technologyreview.com/news/530411/hackers-are-homing-in-on-hospitals/

Organization for Economic Cooperation and Development. (2013). *Open government data: Towards empirical analysis of open government data initiatives*. Retrieved on 30th October 2014 from http://www.oecd.org/officialdocuments/publicdisplaydocumentpdf/?cote=GOV/PGC/EGOV(2012)7/REV1&docLanguage=En

Out-law.com. (2014). *Big data can improve health outcomes, say experts*. Retrieved from http://www.out-law.com/en/articles/2013/november/big-data-can-improve-health-outcomes-say-experts/

Out-Law.com. (2014, February 7). *£50m funding for "medical bioinformatics" projects*. Retrieved November 1, 2014, from http://www.out-law.com/articles/2014/february/50m-funding-for-medical-bioinformatics-projects/

Pagallo, U. (2013). Robots in the cloud with privacy: A new threat to data protection? *Computer Law & Security Report, 29*(5), 501–508. doi:10.1016/j.clsr.2013.07.012

Palmer, M. (2006, November 3). *Data is the new oil* (Weblog post). Retrieved on 30th October 2014 from Http://:ana.blogs.com/maestros/2006/11/data_is_the_new.html

Panicker, R. (2013). Adoption of Big Data Technology for the Development of Developing Countries. In *Proceedings of National Conference on New Horizons in IT*.

Pardo, T. A., Nam, T., & Burke, G. B. (2012). E-Government Interoperability Interaction of Policy, Management, and Technology Dimensions. *Social Science Computer Review, 30*(1), 7–23. doi:10.1177/0894439310392184

Parka, H. W., & Leydesdorffb, L. (2013). Decomposing social and semantic networks in emerging "big data" research. *Journal of Informetrics, 7*(3), 756–765. doi:10.1016/j.joi.2013.05.004

Paskin, J. (2014). Sha Hwang, the Designer Hired to Make Obamacare a Beautiful Thing. *Business Week*. Retrieved May 14, 2014, from http://www.businessweek.com/

Patra, D., Ray, S., Mukhopadhyay, J., Majumdar, B., & Majumdar, A. K. (2009, December). Achieving e-health care in a distributed EHR system. In *e-Health Networking, Applications and Services, 2009. Healthcom 2009. 11th International Conference on* (pp. 101-107). IEEE. doi:10.1109/HEALTH.2009.5406205

Patterson, J. (2009). The Smart Grid: Hadoop at the Tennessee Valley Authority (TVA). *Cloudera Blog*. Retrieved from http://www.cloudera.com/blog/2009/06/smart-grid-Hadoop-Tennessee-valley-authority-tea/

Peary, B. D. M., Shaw, R., & Takeuchi, Y. (2012). Utilization of Social Media in the East Japan Earthquake and Tsunami and its Effectiveness. *Journal of Natural Disaster Science*, *34*(1), 3–18. doi:10.2328/jnds.34.3

Pentland, A., Lazer, D., Brewer, D., & Heibeck, T. (2009). Using reality mining to improve public health and medicine. *Studies in Health Technology and Informatics*, *149*, 93–102. PMID:19745474

Petty, R. E., & Cacioppo, J. T. (1981). *Attitudes and persuasion: Classic and contemporary approaches*. Dubuque, IA: William C. Brown.

Peumans, K. (2014). *Informatisation de la Justice: de l'âge de la pierre au 21e siècle*. Press Release. Retrieved July 7, 2014, from http://justice.belgium.be/fr/ordre_judiciaire/reforme_justice/nouvelles/news_pers_2014-03-14.jsp

Ping, L., & Zhang, C. (2011). *A new algorithm for compressed counting with applications in Shannon entropy estimation in dynamic data*. COLT.

Pita, R., Pinto, C., Melo, P., Silva, M., Barreto, M., & Rasella, D. (2015). A Spark-based workflow for probabilistic record linkage of healthcare data. In *the Workshop Proceedings of the EDBT/ICDT 2015 Joint Conference (March 27, 2015, Brussels, Belgium) on CEUR- WS.org*.

Planetcassandra. (2015). *What is Apache Cassandra?* Retrieved from http://planetcassandra.org: http://planetcassandra.org/what-is-apache-cassandra/

Plant, R. (2013). CISPA: Information without representation? *Big Data Republic*. Retrieved from http://www.bigdatarepublic.com/author.asp?section_id=2635&doc_id=262480

Polsby, N. W. (1968). The Institutionalization of the U.S. House of Representatives. *The American Political Science Review*, *62*(1), 144–168. doi:10.2307/1953331

Power, D. J. (2014). Using 'Big Data' for analytics and decision support. *Journal of Decision Systems*, *23*(2), 222–228. doi:10.1080/12460125.2014.888848

Prajapati, V. (2013). *Big Data Analytics with R and Hadoop*. Mumbai: Packt Publishing.

Predpol. (2014). Recovered from http://www.predpol.com/about/

President's Council of Advisors on Science and Technology. (2010). *Designing a Digital Future: Federally Funded Research and Development in Networking and Information Technology*. Retrieved from http://www.whitehouse.gov/sites/default/files/microsites/ostp/pcast-nitrd-report-2010.pdf

President's Council on National ICT Strategies. (2011). *Establishing a Smart Government by Using Big Data*. Washington, DC: Author.

Priyanka, K., & Kulennavar, N. (n.d.). *A Survey On Big Data Analytics In Health Care*. Academic Press.

Quaadgras, A., Ross, J. W., & Beath, C. M. (2013). You May Not Need Big Data After All. *Harvard Business Review*.

Qureshi, B., & Koubâa, A. (2014). Five Traits of Performance Enhancement Using Cloud Robotics: A Survey. *Procedia Computer Science*, *37*, 220–227. doi:10.1016/j.procs.2014.08.033

Raghupathi, W. (2010). Data Mining in Health Care. In S. Kudyba (Ed.), *Healthcare Informatics: Improving Efficiency and Productivity* (pp. 211–223). Taylor & Francis. doi:10.1201/9781439809792-c11

Raghupathi, W., & Raghupathi, V. (2013). An Overview of Health Analytics. *J Health Med Informat*, *4*(132), 2.

Raghupathi, W., & Raghupathi, V. (2014). Big Data analytics in healthcare: Promise and potential. *Health Information Science and Systems*, 2(1), 3. doi:10.1186/2047-2501-2-3 PMID:25825667

rahs.gov.sg . (2015). *RAHS - RAHS Programme: Origin and Progress*. Retrieved from http://www.rahs.gov.sg/public/www/content.aspx?sid=2952

Rajaraman, A., & Ullman, J. D. (2011). *Mining of massive datasets*. Cambridge University Press. doi:10.1017/CBO9781139058452

Rajendra Akerkar (2013b). Improving Data Quality on Big and High-Dimensional Data. *Journal of Bioinformatics and Intelligent Control, 2*(1), 155-162.

Rajendra Akerkar. (2010). *Priti Sajja*. Knowledge Based Systems, Jones & Bartlett Pub.

Ramakrishnan, N., Hanauer, D., & Keller, B. (2010). Mining electronic health records. *Computer*, *43*(10), 77–81. doi:10.1109/MC.2010.292

Ranganathan, S., Nicolis, S. C., Spaiser, V., & Sumpter, D. J. (2015). Understanding Democracy and Development Traps Using a Data-Driven Approach. *Big Data*, *3*(1), 22–33. doi:10.1089/big.2014.0066

Raue, S., Azzopardi, L., & Johnson, C. W. (2013). #trapped!: Social media search system require-ments for emergency management professionals.*Proceedings of the 36th International ACM SIGIR Conference on Research and Development in Information Retrieval*, (pp. 1073–1076). doi:10.1145/2484028.2484184

Relyea, H. C. (1989). Historical Development of Federal Information Policy. In C. R. Mcclure & P. Hernon (Eds.), *United States Government Information Policies* (pp. 25–48). ABLEX publishing.

Reuters.com. (2013, August 26). IRS lags in program to spot tax refund fraud: watchdog. *Reuters*. Retrieved from http://www.reuters.com/article/2013/08/26/us-usa-tax-refund-fraud-idUSBRE97P0WQ20130826

Reynolds, B., & Seeger, M. (2005). Crisis and Emergency Risk Communication as an Integrative Model. *Journal of Health Communication*, *10*, 43–55. doi:10.1080/10810730590904571 PMID:15764443

Richard Zuech, T. M. (2015). Intrusion detection and Big Heterogeneous Data: a Survey. *Journal of Big Data*.

Richard Zuech, T. M. (2015). Intrusion detection and Big Heterogeneous Data: A Survey. *Journal of Big Dat, 2*(1), 3. doi:10.1186/s40537-015-0013-4

Riegelsberger, J., Sasse, M. A., & McCarthy, J. D. (2003). Privacy and trust: Shiny happy people building trust? Photos on e-commerce websites and consumer trust.*Proceedings of CHI2003*, *5*(1), 121-128.

Riegelsberger, J., Sasse, M. A., & McCarthy, J. D. (2005). The mechanics of trust: A framework for research and design. *International Journal of Human-Computer Studies*, *62*(3), 381–422. doi:10.1016/j.ijhcs.2005.01.001

Rijmenam, V. (n.d.). *4 Benefits for the Public Sector When Governments Start Using Big Data*. Retrieved from https://datafloq.com/read/4-benefits-public-sector-governments-start-big-dat/171

Robinson, N. (2005). IT excellence starts with governance. *Journal of Investment Compliance*, *6*(3), 45–49. doi:10.1108/15285810510659310

Rousseau, R. (2012). A view on big data and its relation Informetrics. *Chinese Journal of Library and Information Science*, *5*(3), 12–26.

Roy, I. S. (2010). Airavat: Security and Privacy for MapReduce. *NSDI*, 297-312.

Rudder, C. (2014). *Dataclysm, Who we Are*. Crown Publishers.

Russom, P. (2011). *Big data analytics.* TDWI Best Practices Report, Fourth Quarter.

Sahana Japan. (2011). Available: http://www.sahana.jp/

Saito, Y., Fujihara, Y., & Murayama, Y. (2012). A Study of Reconstruction Watcher in Disaster Area. *Proceedings of CHI2012*, 811–814.

Salminen, A., Tague-Sutcliffe, J., & McClellan, C. (1995). From text to hypertext by indexing. *ACM Transactions on Information Systems, 13*(1), 69–99. doi:10.1145/195705.195717

Sanal Nair, D. J. (2014). Corporate governance and firm performances -An empirical evidence from the leading Indian Corporates. India.

Saraiya, P., North, C., Vy Lam, , & Duca, K. A. (2006). An Insight-Based Longitudinal Study of Visual Analytics. *IEEE Transactions on Visualization and Computer Graphics, 12*(6), 1. doi:10.1109/TVCG.2006.85 PMID:17073373

Saran, C. (2014). *HMRC uses Hadoop to tackle corporate tax avoidance.* Retrieved from http://www.computerweekly.com/news/2240217592/HMRC-uses-Hadoop-to-tackle-corporate-tax-avoidance>

SAS White Paper. (2013). *How Governments are Using the Power of High-Performance Analytics.* Retrieved from http://www.sas.com/resources/whitepaper/wp_61955.pdf

Sathi, A. (2012). *Big Data Analytics: Disruptive Technologies for Changing the Game.* Boise: Mc Press.

Satran, R. (2013, May 9). *Next Target of IRS Robo-Audits: Small Business.* Retrieved from http://money.usnews.com/money/personal-finance/articles/2013/05/09/next-target-of-irs-robo-audits-small-business

Sawant, N., & Shah, H. (2013). *Big Data Application Architecture Q&A: A Problem - Solution Approach.* New York: Apress. doi:10.1007/978-1-4302-6293-0

Schafer, J. (2009). The Application of Data-Mining to Recommender Systems. Encyclopedia of Data Warehousing and Mining, 1, 44-48.

Scheuner, M. T., de Vries, H., Kim, B., Meili, R. C., Olmstead, S. H., & Teleki, S. (2009, July). Are electronic health records ready for genomic medicine? *Genetics in Medicine: Official Journal of the American College of Medical Genetics, 11*(7), 510–517. doi:10.1097/GIM.0b013e3181a53331 PMID:19478682

Schoenherr, T., & Speier-Pero, C. (2015). Data Science, Predictive Analytics, and Big Data in Supply Chain Management: Current State and Future Potential. *Journal of Business Logistics, 36*(1), 120–132. doi:10.1111/jbl.12082

Schouten, P. (2013). Big Data in health care. *Healthcare Financial Management: Journal of the Healthcare Financial Management Association, 67*(2), 40-42.

Scola, N., & Peterson, A. (2014). *Data is Uber's business. But protecting it may be its biggest weakness.* Retrieved from https://www.washingtonpost.com/blogs/the-switch/wp/2014/11/18/data-is-ubers-business-but-protecting-it-may-be-its-largest-weakness/

Sean Owen, R. A. (2011). *Mahout in Action.* Manning Publications.

Shaman, J., Yang, W., & Kandula, S. (2014). Inference and forecast of the current West African Ebola outbreak in Guinea, Sierra Leone and Liberia. *PLoS Currents, 6.* PMID:25642378

Shannon, C. E. (1949). Communication Theory of Secrecy Systems. *The Bell System Technical Journal, 28*(4), 656–715. doi:10.1002/j.1538-7305.1949.tb00928.x

Sharma, V., Guttoo, D., & Ogra, A. (2014, May). Next generation citizen centric e-services. In *IST-Africa Conference Proceedings, 2014* (pp. 1-15). IEEE. doi:10.1109/ISTAFRICA.2014.6880672

Shepard, E. (2012, July 2). *Geospatial Advances Drive Big Data Problem, Solution.* Retrieved from https://sensorsand-systems.com/article/features/27558-geospatial-advances-drive-big-data-problem,-solution.html

Sherry, S. (2012). 33B pounds drive U.K. government big data agenda. *Big Data Republic.* Retrieved from http://www.bigdatarepublic.com/author.asp?section_id=2642&doc_id=254471

Shin, J., Kayser, S. R., & Langaee, T. Y. (2009). Pharmacogenetics: From discovery to patient care. *American Journal of Health-System Pharmacy, 66*(7), 625–637. doi:10.2146/ajhp080170 PMID:19299369

Shmueli, G., & Koppius, O. R. (2011). Predictive Analytics in Information Systems Research. *Management Information Systems Quarterly, 35*(3), 553–572.

Siba.com. (2014, August 17). *Siba - News feed - Spatial Industries Business Association - SIBA.* Retrieved from http://www.siba.com.au/News/News-Articles/Big-Spatial-Data-in-Emergency-Management.aspx

Simon, P. (2013). *Too Big to Ignore: The Business Case for Big Data.* Hoboken, NJ: Wiley.

Sittig, D. F., Wright, A., Osheroff, J. A., Middleton, B., Teich, J. M., Ash, J. S., & Bates, D. W. et al. (2008, April). Grand challenges in clinical decision support. *Journal of Biomedical Informatics, 41*(2), 387–392. doi:10.1016/j.jbi.2007.09.003 PMID:18029232

Slovic, P. (1993). Perceived risk, trust, and democracy. *Risk Analysis, 13*(6), 675–682. doi:10.1111/j.1539-6924.1993.tb01329.x

SlugPost. (2014). *Jan Dhan Yojna –Problems and Flaws in implementation.* Retrieved on October 24, 2014 from http://indianexpress.com/article/india/india-others/jan-dhan-yojana-concern-over-scope-for-misuse-slow-roll-out-of-debit-cards/

SmartAmerica. (2014). Retrieved from http://nist.gov/el/smartamerica.cfm

Soares, S. (2012, April 2). Big Data: A Boon For Governance Professionals. *IBM Data Magazine.*

Sondergaard, P. (2013). *Gartner Analyst Opening Keynote Gartner. Symposium/ITxpo 2013.* Retrieved October 27, 2014, from http://www.gartnereventsondemand.com/index.php?t=trailer&e=SYM23&i=K2

Speier, C., & Morris, M. G. (2003). The influence of query interface design on decision-making performance. *Management Information Systems Quarterly, 27*(3), 397.

Srinivasan, U., & Arunasalam, B. (2013). Leveraging Big Data Analytics to Reduce Healthcare Costs. *IT Professional, 15*(6), 21–28. doi:10.1109/MITP.2013.55

Star, S. L. (1999). The Ethnography of Infrastructure. *The American Behavioral Scientist, 43*(3), 377–391. doi:10.1177/00027649921955326

Star, S. L., & Griesemer, J. R. (1989). Institutional Ecology, "Translations" and Boundary Objects. *Social Studies of Science, 19*(3), 387–420. doi:10.1177/030631289019003001

Stebbins, R. A. (2001). Exploratory Research in the Social Sciences. *Sage (Atlanta, Ga.).*

Stephens, R. T. (2004). A framework for the identification of electronic commerce design elements that enable trust within the small hotel industry.*Proceedings of ACMSE*, (pp. 309-314). doi:10.1145/986537.986613

Stewart, R. J., Trinder, P. W., & Loidl, H. W. (2011). Comparing high level mapreduce query languages. In *Advanced Parallel Processing Technologies* (pp. 58–72). Springer Berlin Heidelberg. doi:10.1007/978-3-642-24151-2_5

Stonebraker, M. (2012). What does 'big data' mean? *Blog@CACM*. Retrieved from http://cacm.acm.org/blogs/blog-cacm/155468-what-does-big-data-mean/fulltext

Stonebraker, M. (2013). *Data tamer: A scalable data curation system*. Retrieved from http://ilp.mit.edu/images/conferences/2013/ict/presentation/stonebraker.pdf

Stone, D. A. (2002). *Policy Paradox: The Art of Political Decision Making*. New York: W.W. Norton & Company, Inc.

Storageserver.com. (2014). *How Big Data analytics is helping in searching for missing Malaysian Airlines Flight MH370*. Author.

Stowers, G. (2013). *The Use of Data Visualization in Government | IBM Center for the Business of Government*. Retrieved July 6, 2015, from http://www.businessofgovernment.org/report/use-data-visualization-government

STP. (2012). *Office of Science and Technology Policy, Executive Office of the President of the United States. The Obama administration unveils the "Big Data" initiative: announces $200 million in new R&D investments*. Washington, DC: Executive Office of the President.

Strauch, C., Sites, U. L. S., & Kriha, W. (2011). *NoSQL databases. Lecture Notes*. Stuttgart Media University.

Streichenberger, I. (2014). *Press release (par. 3, par. 5)*. Retrieved August 7, 2014, from https://www.inbloom.org/

Strong, M., & Oakley, J. (2011). Bayesian Inference for Comorbid Disease Risks Using Marginal Disease Risks and Correlation Information From a Separate Source. *Medical Decision Making*, *31*(4), 571–581. doi:10.1177/0272989X10391269 PMID:21212441

Sultan, N. (2013). Cloud computing: A democratizing force? *International Journal of Information Management*, *33*(5), 810–815. doi:10.1016/j.ijinfomgt.2013.05.010

Sun, X., & Jiao, Y. (2009). *pGrid: Parallel Grid-Based Data Stream Clustering with MapReduce*. Report. Oak Ridge National Laboratory.

Sundararajan, A., Provost, F., Oestreicher-Singer, G., & Aral, S. (2013). Information in Digital, Economic, and Social Networks. *Information Systems Research*, *24*(4), 883–905. doi:10.1287/isre.1120.0472

Sunil Soares, T. D. (2012, April 7). Big Data Governance: A Framework to Assess Maturity. *IBM Data Magazine*.

Sun, J., & Reddy, C. K. (2013, August). Big Data analytics for healthcare. In *Proceedings of the 19th ACM SIGKDD international conference on Knowledge discovery and data mining* (pp. 1525-1525). ACM. doi:10.1145/2487575.2506178

Suthaharan, S. (2014). Big data classification: Problems and challenges in network intrusion prediction with machine learning. *Performance Evaluation Review*, *41*(4), 70–73. doi:10.1145/2627534.2627557

Tallon, P. (2013). Corporate Governance of Big Data: Perspectives on Value, Risk, and Cost. *IEEE Computer Society*, *46*(6), 32–38. doi:10.1109/MC.2013.155

Tanaka, Y., Sakamoto, Y., & Matsuka, T. (2012). Transmission of Rumor and Criticism in Twitter after the Great Japan Earthquake. *Proceedings of the 34th Annual Conference of the Cognitive Science Society*, (pp. 2387-2392).

Tan, C. H., Agichtein, E., Ipeirotis, P., & Gabrilovich, E. (2014, February). Trust, but verify: Predicting contribution quality for knowledge base construction and curation. In *Proceedings of the 7th ACM international conference on Web search and data mining* (pp. 553-562). ACM.

Taylor Shelton, A. P. (2014). Mapping the data shadows of Hurricane Sandy: Uncovering the sociospatial dimensions of 'big data'. *Geoforum*, *52*, 167–179. doi:10.1016/j.geoforum.2014.01.006

Tene, O., & Polonetsky, J. (2012). *Privacy in the age of big data: A time for big decisions.* Stanford Law Review Online.

Tewari, R. (2014). *Jan Dhan Yojna: Concern over scope for misuse, slow roll-out of debit cards.* Retrieved on October 23, 2014 Retrieved from http://slugpost.com/2014/09/04/jan-dhan-yojana-problems-flaws-implementation/

The Apache Software Foundation. (2014). *The Sqoop User Guide (v1.4.5).* Retrieved from http://sqoop.apache.org/docs/1.4.5/SqoopUserGuide.html

The Apache Software Foundation. (2014). *What is Hadoop?* Retrieved on 14/9/2014 http://hadoop.apache.org/#What+Is+Apache+Hadoop%3F

The Health Foundation. (2012). *Birmingham Children's Hospital NHS Trust: Continuous remote monitoring of ill children.* Retrieved May 30, 2015, from: http://www.health.org.uk/areas-of-work/programmes/shine-eleven/related-projects/birmingham-children-s-hospital-nhs-foundation-trust/

The Networking and Information Technology Research and Development (NITRD). (2015). *Big Data (BD SSG) - NITRDGROUPS Portal.* Retrieved July 7, 2015, from https://www.nitrd.gov/nitrdgroups/index.php?title=Big_Data_(BD_SSG)

The TechAmerica Foundation. (2013). *Big data and the public sector: A survey of IT decision makers in federal and state public sector organizations.* Retrieved on 30th October 2014 from http://www.techamericafoundation.org/content/wp-content/uploads/2013/02/SAP-Public-Sector-Big-Data-Report_FINAL-2.pdf

The White House Office of Science and Technology Policy. (n.d.). Big Data is a Big Deal. *OSTP Blog.* Accessed February 21, 2014, http://www.whitehouse.gov/blog/2012/03/29/big-data-big-deal

Theguardian. (2013, June 6). *NSA Prism program taps in to user data of Apple, Google and others.* Retrieved from theguardian.com: http://www.theguardian.com/world/2013/jun/06/us-tech-giants-nsa-data

Thomas, J. J., & Cook, K. A. (2005). *Illuminating the Path: The Research and Development Agenda for Visual Analytics.* IEEE Computer Society.

Thorpe, J., MacRaAmirali, B. & Salehi-Abari, A. (2013). Usability and Security Evaluation of GeoPass: a Geographic Location-Password Scheme. In *Proceedings of the Ninth Symposium on Usable Privacy and Security (SOUPS '13)*, (pp. 1-14). doi:10.1145/2501604.2501618

TIBCO. (2015). *TIBCO StreamBase Named Leader in Forrester Wave for Big Data Streaming Analytics Platforms 2014.* Retrieved from tibco.com: http://www.tibco.com/products/event-processing/complex-event-processing/streambase-complex-event-processing

Tudor Dumitras, D. S. (2011). *Toward a standard benchmark for computer security research: The Worldwide Intelligence Network Environment (WINE).* Building Analysis Datasets and Gathering Experience Returns for Security. doi:10.1145/1978672.1978683

Turner, V., Reinsel, D., & Gantz, J. F. (2014). *The Digital Universe of Opportunities: Rich Data and the Increasing Value of the Internet of Things.* Retrieved September 3, 2014, from http://www.emc.com/leadership/digital-universe/index.htm

Turoff, M. (2002). Past and future emergency response information systems. *Comm. of the ACM, 45*(4).

Tyagi, P. K. (2015). *Using Cross-Lagged Correlation Analysis to Derive Causal Inferences in Quasi-Experimental Marketing Research.* Springer International Publishing. doi:10.1007/978-3-319-10966-4_71

U. S. Embassy Minsk. (2015, March 18). *2015Programs and Events.* Retrieved from http://minsk.usembassy.gov/fatca031815.html

U. S. Government. (n.d.). Retrieved from http://www.data.gov

U.S. Census Bureau. (n.d.). Retrieved from https://www.census.gov/history/www/reference/privacy_confidentiality/title_13_us_code.html

U.S. Government. Data.gov . (n.d.). Retrieved from http://www.data.gov

Uber. (2014). Retrieved from https://www.uber.com/about

Udi Hoitash, R. H. (2009). *Corporate Governance and Internal Control over Financial Reporting: A Comparison of Regulatory Regimes.* Academic Press.

Ullman, J. D., Leskovec, J., & Rajaraman, A. (2011). *Mining of Massive Datasets.* Cambridge University Press.

UN Global Pulse. (2015). *Mining Citizen Feedback Data for Enhanced Local Government Decision-Making.* Global Pulse Project Series no.16.

UNESCO. (1975). *Intergovernmental Conference on the Planning of National Documentation, NATIS, national information systems: COM- 74/NATIS/3 Rev.* Paris: UNESCO.

United Nations. (2012). *E-government Survey 2012: E-government for the People.* Retrieved from http://www.un.org/en/development/desa/publications/connecting-governments-to-citizens.html

United Nations. (2014). *The United Nations E-Government Survey 2014: E-governance for the future we want.* Retrieved on 30th October 2014 from http://unpan3.un.org/egovkb/Portals/egovkb/Documents/un/2014-Survey/E-Gov_Complete_Survey-2014.pdf

United States National Commission on Libraries and Information Science. (1982). *Public sector/private sector interaction in providing information services: Report to the NCLIS from the Public Sector/Private Sector Task Force.* Washington, DC: US National Commission on Libraries and Information Science, Government Printing Office.

United States. (2014). *United States Code Classification Tables.* Retrieved July 2, 2014, from http://uscode.house.gov/classification/tbl110pl_2nd.htm

United States Emergency Economic Stabilization Act of 2008, 122 Stat. 3765. 110 HR 1424. (2008). Retrieved from https://www.congress.gov/bill/110th-congress/house-bill/1424

UPMC. (2013). Retrieved from http://www.upmc.com/media/newsreleases/2013/pages/upmc-big-data-tech-breast-cancer-research.aspx

Usha. (2013). *Data Governance for Big Data Systems.* L&T Infotech.

Van der Aalst, W. M. P., & Kumar, A. (2003). XML-Based Schema Definition for Support of Interorganizational Workflow. *Information Systems Research, 14*(1), 23–46. doi:10.1287/isre.14.1.23.14768

Van der Meulen, R., & Rivera, J. (2013). *Gartner Predicts Business Intelligence and Analytics Will Remain Top Focus for CIOs Through 2017.* Press Release. Retrieved September 3, 2014, from http://www.gartner.com/newsroom/id/2637615

Van Noortwijk, K., Visser, J., & Mulder, R. V. D. (2006). Ranking and Classifying Legal Documents using Conceptual Information. *The Journal of Information Law and Technology, 2006*(1).

Vanleemputten, P. (2013, August 29). Informatisation de la Justice: la Belgique parmi les plus mauvais élèves. *Datanews.* Retrieved May 20, 2015, from http://www.datanews.be/

Varonen, Kortteisto, & Kaila. (2008). What may help or hinder the implementation of computerized decision support systems (CDSSs): a focus group study with physicians. *Family Practice, 25*(3), 162-167. doi:10.1093/fampra/cmn020

Varshney, K. R., Chen, G. H., Abelson, B., Nowocin, K., Sakhrani, V., Xu, L., & Spatocco, B. L. (2015). *Targeting Villages for Rural Development Using Satellite Image Analysis.* Big Data.

Venner, J. (2009). *Pro Hadoop.* Apress. doi:10.1007/978-1-4302-1943-9

Viaene, S. (2014). Zorg ervoor dat je technologie mee kan. *Business Bytes.* Retrieved May 15, 2015, from http://business. telenet.be/nl/artikel/zorg-ervoor-dat-je-technologie-mee-kan

Villars, R. L., Olofson, C. W., & Eastwood, M. (2011). *Big Data: What it is and why you should care.* White Paper, IDC.

Vogels, W. (2009). Eventually consistent. *Communications of the ACM, 52*(1), 40. doi:10.1145/1435417.1435432

Wachowicz, G. O., & Portugali, Y. (2012). Smart cities of the future. *The European Physical Journal. Special Topics, 214*(1), 481–518. doi:10.1140/epjst/e2012-01703-3

Wall Street Journal. (2014, June 3). Can Data From Your Fitbit Transform Medicine?. *Wall Street Journal.*

Wallis, N. (2012). *Big Data in Canada: Challenging Complacency for Competitive Advantage.* IDC.

Wang, F., Ercegovac, V., Syeda-Mahmood, T., Holder, A., Shekita, E., Beymer, D., & Xu, L. H. (2010, November). Large-scale multimodal mining for healthcare with mapreduce. In *Proceedings of the 1st ACM International Health Informatics Symposium* (pp. 479-483). ACM. doi:10.1145/1882992.1883067

Ward, J. S., & Barker, A. (2013). *Undefined By Data: A Survey of Big Data Definitions.* arXiv preprint arXiv:1309.5821

Warden, P. (2011). *Big Data Glossary.* Sebastopol, CA: O'Reilly Media.

Wasan, S. K., Bhatnagar, V., & Kaur, H. (2006). The impact of data mining techniques on medical diagnostics. *Data Science Journal, 5*, 119–126. doi:10.2481/dsj.5.119

Washington, A. L., & Griffith, J. C. (2007). Legislative Information Websites: Designing Beyond Transparency. In A. R. Lodder & L. Mommers (Eds.), *Legal Knowledge and Information Systems JURIX 2007 The Twentieth Annual Conference* (p. 192). JURIX.

Washington, A. L. (2014). Government Information Policy in the Era of Big Data. *Review of Policy Research, 31*(4), 319–325. doi:10.1111/ropr.12081

Washingtonpost. (2013, June 7). *U.S., British intelligence mining data from nine U.S. Internet companies in broad secret program.* Retrieved from washingtonpost.com: http://www.washingtonpost.com/investigations/us-intelligence-mining-data-from-nine-us-internet-companies-in-broad-secret-program/2013/06/06/3a0c0da8-cebf-11e2-8845-d970ccb04497_story. html

Wegner, P. (1996). Interoperability. *ACM Computing Surveys, 28*(1), 285–287. doi:10.1145/234313.234424

White, C., Plotnick, L., Kushma, J., Hiltz, S. R., & Turoff, M. (2009). An online social network for emergency management. *International Journal of Emergency Management, 6*(3-4), 369–382. doi:10.1504/IJEM.2009.031572

White, T. (2009). *Hadoop: The Definitive Guide.* O'Reilly Media.

WIDE. (n.d.). *Post-disaster Recovery Internet Project.* Available: http://msg.wide.ad.jp/pdrnet/

Wilkerson, J. D., & Washington, A. L. (2012). *PI-Net Poli-Informatics NSF 1243917.* Retrieved from http://poliinformatics.org

Willis, C., & Losee, R. M. (2013). A random walk on an ontology: Using thesaurus structure for automatic subject indexing. *Journal of the American Society for Information Science and Technology, 64*(7), 1330–1344. doi:10.1002/asi.22853

Wilson, E. (1988). Integrated information retrieval for law in a hypertext environment. In *Annual International ACM SIGIR Conference On Research And Development In Information Retrieval* (pp. 663–677). doi:10.1145/62437.62505

Witten, I. H., & Frank, E. (2005). *Data Mining: Practical machine learning tools and techniques.* Morgan Kaufmann.

Wixom, B., Thlini, A., Douglas, D., Goul, M., Gupta, B., Iyer, L., & Turetken, O. et al. (2014). The Current State of Business Intelligence in Academia: The Arrival of Big Data. *Communications of the Association for Information Systems, 34*(1).

World Economic Forum. (2014). *Global information technology report 2014: Rewards and risks of big data.* Retrieved on 30th October 2014 from http://www3.weforum.org/docs/WEF_GlobalInformationTechnology_Report_2014.pdf

Xue, X., & Croft, W. B. (2012). Automatic query generation for patent search. In *Proceedings of the 18th ACM conference on Information and knowledge management* (CIKM '09). Academic Press.

Yahoo. (2014). *Continuuity Raises $10 Million Series A Round to Ignite Big Data Application Development Within the Hadoop Ecosystem.* Retrieved from finance.yahoo.com

Yamagishi, T. (1998). *The structure of trust: The evolutionary games of mind and society.* Tokyo: University of Tokyo Press. Retrieved from http://toshio-yamagishi.net/english/books/index.cgi

Yamagishi, T. (2008). *Why Isn't Japan a Safe Place Anymore?* Tokyo: Shueisha International. (In Japanese)

Yina, W. (2010, April). Application of EHR in health care. In *Multimedia and Information Technology (MMIT), 2010 Second International Conference on* (Vol. 1, pp. 60-63). IEEE. doi:10.1109/MMIT.2010.32

Yong, Y. (2005, December). Unexpected Increased Mortality After Implementation of a Commercially Sold Computerized Physician Order Entry System. *Pediatrics, 116*(6), 1506–1512. doi:10.1542/peds.2005-1287 PMID:16322178

Yoo, I., Alafaireet, P., Marinov, M., Pena-Hernandez, K., Gopidi, R., Chang, J. F., & Hua, L. (2012). Data mining in healthcare and biomedicine: A survey of the literature. *Journal of Medical Systems, 36*(4), 2431–2448. doi:10.1007/s10916-011-9710-5 PMID:21537851

Yoshimura, A. (2004). *Sanriku Kaigan Otsunami (Sanriku Offshore Great Tsunami).* Tokyo: Bungei Shunju. (in Japanese)

Young, C. M. (2003). *Driving Organizational Change: Key Issues.* Retrieved July 19, 2014, from https://www.gartner.com/doc/383466

Zhang, F. Fiaidhi, & Mohammed. (2012). Real-Time Clinical Decision Support System with Data Stream Mining. *Journal of Biomedicine and Biotechnology.* doi:10.1145/1645953.1646295

Zhang, Q., Pang, C., Mcbride, S., Hansen, D., Cheung, C., & Steyn, M. (2010, July). Towards health data stream analytics. In *Complex Medical Engineering (CME), 2010 IEEE/ICME International Conference on* (pp. 282-287). IEEE. doi:10.1109/ICCME.2010.5558827

Zhong, T., Doshi, K., Tang, X., Lou, T., & Lu, Z. L. (2014). *Big Data Workloads Drawn from Real-Time Analytics Scenarios Across Three Deployed Solutions. In Advancing Big Data Benchmarks* (pp. 97–104). Switzerland: Springer International Publishing.

Zikopoulos, P.C., Eaton, C., DeRoos, D., Deutsch, T., & Lapis, G. (n.d.). *Understanding Big Data: Analytics for Enterprise-Class Hadoop and Streaming Data.* McGraw-Hill.

Zikopoulos, P. C., Eaton, C., deRoos, D., Deutsch, T., & Lapis, G. (2011). *Understanding Big Data - Analytics for Enterprise Class Hadoop and Streaming Data* (1st ed.). McGraw-Hill Osborne Media.

Zions, B. (2015). *A Case Study In Security Big Data Analysis.* Retrieved from darkreading.com: http://www.darkreading.com/analytics/security-monitoring/a-case-study-in-security-big-data-analysis/d/d-id/1137299?

About the Contributors

Anil K. Aggarwal is a Professor in the Merrick School of Business at the University of Baltimore. Dr. Aggarwal is Fulbright scholar and held Lockheed Martin Research and BGE Chair at the University of Baltimore. He has published in many journals, including Computers and Operations Research, Decision Sciences, Information and Management, Production and Operation Management, e-Service, Decision Sciences - Journal of Innovative Education, Journal of Information Technology Education: Innovations in Practice, Total Quality Management & Business Excellence, eService, International Journal of Web-Based Learning and Teaching Technologies and Journal of EUC and many national and international professional proceedings. He has published three edited books web-based education (2) and one on cloud computing. His current research interests include web-based education, business ethics, big data, virtual team collaboration and cloud computing.

* * *

Nor Athiyah Abdullah is currently a Ph.D. student in Graduate School of Software and Information Science, Iwate Prefectural University, Japan. She received the B.S. degree of I.T (Software Engineering) from University of Malaysia Terengganu (UMT) in 2009 and M.S. degree of Computer Science from University of Science Malaysia (USM) in 2011, both in Malaysia. Her research interests include online social media, human aspect of human computer interaction and disaster communication. She is a member of IPSJ.

Rajendra Akerkar is a professor at Western Norway Research Institute, Norway. He is also a chairman of Technomathematics Research Foundation, India. He has authored 13 books and more than 120 research articles. His current research focuses on intelligent information management, big data analytics, hybrid computing and web mining.

George Avirappattu earned his doctorate from University of Wisconsin-Milwaukee under Dr. Rainer Picard. He currently is an associate professor of Mathematics at Kean University, NJ. His interests include statistics, signal processing, and pattern recognition.

Yukun Bao is currently a Professor at school of management, Huazhong University of Science and Technology, and a deputy director of Center for Modern Information Management, Huazhong University of Science and Technology. His research interests are computational intelligence and its applications in business, finance and engineering, evolutionary computation and optimization, business intelligence, data mining and industrial engineering. He has published more than 50 scientific papers in national and international journals and conferences, and some of them appeared in IEEE Transactions on Cybernetics, Information Sciences, Energy, Applied Soft Computing, Energy Economics, Neurocomputing, Engineering Applications of Artificial Intelligence, Knowledge based Systems and so forth. He has been the PI for three projects funded by National Science Foundation of China and received Excellent Faculty Award from IBM in 2012. He is a councilor of the Chinese Association of Computer Simulation, senior member of IEEE and professional activity chair of IEEE Wuhan Section. He has served as Associate Editor of Neurocomputing (Elsevier), Program Committee Member for several international conferences and regular reviewer for journals such as IEEE Transactions on Neural Networks and Learning Systems, Applied Soft Computing, Knowledge based Systems, European Journal of Operational Research, Tourism Management, Electronic Commerce Research and Applications, Computers in Human Behavior and so on.

Alireza Bolhari got his bachelor of science in Industrial Engineering from Iran University of Science and Technology and masters' degree in Information Technology Management (Advanced Information Systems) from Shahid Beheshti University in 2011 and is a member of International Association of Computer Science & Information Technology. Now he is a PhD candidate in Information Technology Management (Business Intelligence) and a lecturer at Islamic Azad University. His research interests are information technology management (behavioral and organizational aspects of information technology), business intelligence, information systems, Big Data and ethical decision making.

Kevin Carillo is an assistant professor in Information Systems at Toulouse Business School France. His research interests include big data, free/open source software communities, and online communities. He owns a PhD in Information Systems from Victoria University of Wellington, New Zealand.

Ahmad Yusairi Bani Hashim is senior lecturer in the Department of Robotics and Automation, Faculty of Manufacturing Engineering, Universiti Teknikal Malaysia Melaka. His research interests are Bioengineering, Robotics and Scientific Computing.

Md. Rakibul Hoque is an Assistant Professor of Management Information Systems at University of Dhaka, Bangladesh. His research interests include technology adoption, e-Health and ICT4D. Mr. Hoque has published number of research articles in peer-reviewed academic journals, and has presented papers in international conferences. He had the opportunity to work in a number of research projects in Bangladesh, China, Australia and Saudi Arabia. Mr. Rakibul is the member of Association for Information Systems (AIS), UNESCO Open Educational Resources Community, IEEE, Internet Society and ISACA. He is currently pursuing his PhD at Huazhong University of Science and Technology, China. Contact: Department of Management Information Systems, Faculty of Business Studies, University of Dhaka, Bangladesh.

Dhiraj Jain is an Associate Professor of Finance at Symbiosis Centre for Management Studies- Symbiosis International University, Pune. He has qualified the UGC-NET, a Ph. D and a Fellow Member of the Insurance Institute of India. He has worked for the industry for13 years and has been into academics since the past 8 years. His areas of interest include Security Analysis & Portfolio Mgt., Financial Derivatives & Financial Planning. He has been a corporate trainer for Reliance Mutual Fund, Pru-ICICI and many other broking houses for the past 8 years and has conducted more than 100 training sessions for various corporate, bankers, brokers and investors. He has also been associated with BSE for content development. He has 85 papers published in various National and International Journals. He has presented papers in various conferences of National & International repute. Two students have already completed their PHD under his guidance.

Jürgen Janssens is Senior Consultant at TETRADE Consulting, with a focus on Project & Portfolio Management. His experience include projects in Energy & Utilities, Press & Publishing, and Glass Manufacturing; in diverse locations: Belgium, France, Italy, Spain, Czech Republic, Brazil. Jürgen has a Master in Architectural Engineering from the KU Leuven (Belgium) and an MBA in Finance from the International University of Monaco (Monaco); and pursued Executive Education programs in Strategy & Big Data at Columbia University (USA) and MIT (USA). He has collaborated on several cross-industry newsletters & forums. His professional interests include cross-functional collaborations, Entrepreneurship, Global dynamics, Big Data & Digitalization, Finance and Writing.

Amir Manzoor holds a bachelor's degree in engineering from NED University, Karachi, an MBA from Lahore University of Management Sciences (LUMS), and an MBA from Bangor University, United Kingdom. He has many years of diverse professional and teaching experience working at many renowned national and internal organizations and higher education institutions. His research interests include electronic commerce and technology applications in business.

Yuko Murayama is a Professor in the Department of Software and Information Science at Iwate Prefectural University, Japan. Her research interests include internet, network security, security, trust and anshin, and disaster information processing. She had a B.Sc. in Mathematics from Tsuda College, Japan in 1973 and had been in industry in Japan. She had M.Sc. and Ph.D. both from University of London (attended University College London) in 1984 and 1992 respectively. She had been a visiting lecturer from 1992 to 1994 at Keio University, and a lecturer at Hiroshima City University from 1994 to 1998. She has been with Iwate Prefectural University since April 1998. She is IFIP Vice President as well as TC-11 Chair. She serves as the Chair of the Security Committee for IPSJ (Information Processing Society of Japan) as well as a secretary for IPSJ Special Interest Group on security psychology and trust (SIG on SPT). She is a senior life member of IEEE, as well as a member of ACM, IPSJ, IEICE and ITE.

Dai Nishioka is a lecturer in the Department of Software and Information Science at Iwate Prefectural University, Japan. His research interests include human aspects of security, psychological influences on computer security and trust. He received a M.S. degree and Ph.D. in Software and Information Science from Iwate Prefectural University in 2008 and 2012. He had been a research assistant from 2012 to 2013 and a research associate from 2013 to 2014 at Iwate Prefectural University.

Yuvraj Sharma is working as a business Associate at Cognus Technology Ltd, Udaipur. He has been involving in preparing market research reports for the UK clients. He performed tasks related to retrieval and analysis of data to evaluate market perception of customers towards new and existing products as well as he also strategic recommendation to client towards adopting new IT technology. He has completed his MBA in IT from Pacific University in 2014, Udaipur and B-tech in computer science from Rajasthan Technical University, Kota in 2010. He has been worked as a software associate in Sarayu Issue Management Pvt. Ltd, Mumbai. His area of interest includes Big Data, ERP & Database management system and research projects related to IT & its implementation into various fields. He has cleared Microsoft Certification Professional Exam [70-536] Net Framework 2.0 Core Foundation.

N. Nawin Sona is an officer of the Indian Administrative Service (IAS) with 15 years of service in various key positions in Urban Administration, Local Governance and Policy Implementation in Government of India, Maharashtra State. He holds a Mechanical Engineering degree from Anna University, Chennai. Has done Public Policy courses from Duke University, USA and Professional Education course from MIT, Computer Science and Artificial Intelligence Lab, on Big Data. Has passionate interest in introducing technology in Public Sector has resulted in many National and State level awards, in UID project, Smart Cities, Financial Inclusion. Also has an avid interest in GIS.

Anne L. Washington, PhD is an Assistant Professor in the School of Policy, Government, and International Affairs at George Mason University in Arlington, Virginia. As a digital government scholar, her research focuses on the production, meaning and retrieval of public sector information. The project was developed with John D. Wilkerson, Professor of Political Science and Kevin Shotwell of the University of Washington as part of a 2012-2015 grant that introduced political informatics. PI-NET, the Poli-Informatics Collaborative Network grant leveraged open government data and computational analysis to bring big data principles to the study of governance.

Jyotsna Talreja Wassan is serving as an Assistant Professor in Dept. of Computer Science, Maitreyi College, University of Delhi, India. She is teaching and training students in Computer Science subjects like Programming Languages, Operating Systems, Data Structures, Networks, and Theory of Computers etc. for the past five years. Prior to that, she worked as Software Engineer in St. Microelectronics, Greater Noida, India. She is M.Sc. in Computer Science from University of Delhi. The author has contributions to Encyclopedia of Business Analytics and Optimization compiled by Dr. John Wang, 2014. She has couple of publications in the area of Big Data Modelling.

Index

Become an IRMA Member

Members of the **Information Resources Management Association (IRMA)** understand the importance of community within their field of study. The Information Resources Management Association is an ideal venue through which professionals, students, and academicians can convene and share the latest industry innovations and scholarly research that is changing the field of information science and technology. Become a member today and enjoy the benefits of membership as well as the opportunity to collaborate and network with fellow experts in the field.

IRMA Membership Benefits:

- **One FREE Journal Subscription**

- **30% Off Additional Journal Subscriptions**

- **20% Off Book Purchases**

- Updates on the latest events and research on Information Resources Management through the IRMA-L listserv.

- Updates on new open access and downloadable content added to Research IRM.

- A copy of the Information Technology Management Newsletter twice a year.

- A certificate of membership.

IRMA Membership $195

Scan code to visit irma-international.org and begin by selecting your free journal subscription.

Membership is good for one full year.

Printed in the United States
By Bookmasters